How the Dismal Science Got Its Name

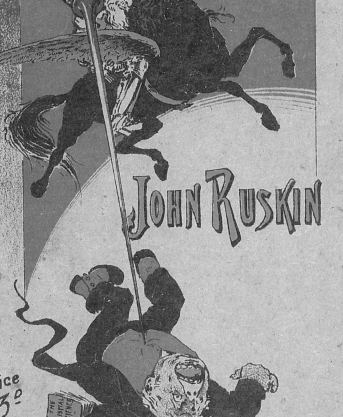

JOHN RUSKIN

Price 3d

Printed and Published
at the Office of
"COPE'S TOBACCO PLANT,"
Lord Nelson Street,
Liverpool.   1893.

How the
Dismal Science
GOT ITS NAME

Classical Economics and the
Ur-Text of Racial Politics

David M. Levy

Ann Arbor
THE UNIVERSITY OF MICHIGAN PRESS

2004   2003   2002   2001   4   3   2   1

A CIP catalog record for this book is available from the British Library.

Library of Congress Cataloging-in-Publication Data

Levy, David M.
    How the dismal science got its name : classical economics and the
ur-text of racial politics / David M. Levy.
        p.   cm.
    Includes bibliographical references and index.
    ISBN 0-472-11219-8 (Cloth : alk. paper)
    1. Economics.   2. Economics—Sociological aspects.   3. Racism.   I.
Title.
HB71 .L546   2001
330'.09—dc21   2001001402

Ur-Text

The hidden original from which all others descend in confused and imperfect fashion.

Contents

Acknowledgments

Unbeknownst to me, this book began in 1968 when, as a graduate student of economics at the University of Chicago, I learned from Earl Hamilton the racial context of the "dismal science" label. This simple fact has made it more costly for me than it seems to have been for others to accept that hoariest of copybook maxims that because the classical economists and their modern heirs hold kindred free market doctrines we occupy the same rightist political position. Episodically for the next thirty years I have struggled to understand this racial context. And I have puzzled over the fact that it is so little known.

Along the way, I have remembered what I learned first from George Stigler, that in the classical teaching of Adam Smith trade is based in language. When this doctrine is taken as seriously as it was by Smith's disciples, one can move seamlessly from an economic account of behavior to an understanding of what it means to be human.

I also learned from Stigler, although the lesson was oblique and did not sink in until many years later when I was working on statistical ethics with Susan Feigenbaum, that the "scholar as truth seeker" model is flatly inconsistent with the rational choice perspective. As a result of ongoing research with Sandra Peart, I have now come to hold not only this position but also the harder one that the scholar as truth seeker is the source of much wickedness. This assumption induces a heterogeneity of motivation in our models because now we hold that scholars who pursue truth are made out of different stuff than we ordinary people, who, after all, seek not truth but happiness.

This book could not have been even imagined, let alone completed, without the help provided to me by the Library of Congress. I am particularly grateful for help in understanding the Rare Book Room and for the loan of a research shelf. Without direct experience with the Library of Congress, one cannot possibly imagine how vast the resources are that were freely and graciously put at my disposal.

The George Mason University Department of Economics, chaired by Walter Williams, and the Public Choice Center, directed by James Buchanan, Tyler Cowen, and Roger Congleton, have been necessary conditions for the completion of this work. Few are the economics departments that take the history of our discipline seriously and as a consequence attract competent students in the area. I should like to single out three gifted students who have helped me in a vast number of ways: Nicola Tynan, Andrew Farrant, and Maria Pia Paganelli. I was delighted that they were able to present their own research at the Summer Institute for the Preservation of the Study of the History of Economics, which the Earhart Foundation supported in the summer of 2000. They and Brian O'Roark, Clair Smith, and Joseph Johnson have saved me much embarrassment.

Chapter 1 exists because Wendy Motooka pressed upon me the need to take Ruskin seriously. Denise Albanese helped me to read the frontispiece image and think less like a moralist and more like an economist. Maria Pia Paganelli saw wings that had flown by everyone else and caught many errors. David George saw the second face in the image. Royall Brandis, James Buchanan, Suzanne Carbonneau, Arthur Diamond Jr., Bryan Caplan, Sandy Darity, Christine Holden, Harro Maas, Sandra Peart, Salim Rashid, and A. M. C. Waterman have given me help and encouragement. Earlier versions were presented at meetings of the Eastern Economic Association in March 2000 and the History of Economics Society in Vancouver in June 2000. I acknowledge with thanks the research support of the Mercatus Center. The quotations from the trial *Ruskin v Cope Bros* and W. Lewin's letter are used by courtesy of the University of Liverpool Library.

Without the vigorous encouragement provided by Christine Holden, chapter 2 would not exist. Maria Pia Paganelli, who purports to be my student, helped me to read its images and persuaded this working econometrician that in art there are no error terms.

Chapter 5 appeared in volume 23 of the *Journal of the History of Economic Thought* in March 2001. Reprinted with permission. The suggestions and criticisms of the editor, Steven Medema, and his readers were of vast help. I am under obligation to the Huntington Library for gracious permission to quote from its collection of Kingsley letters. Thanks are due to Denise Albanese, Timothy Alborn, Martin Bernal, John C. Bradbury, James Buchanan, George Caffentzis, Bryan Caplan, David Collander, Tyler Cowen, Sandy Darity, Stephen Darwall, Cynthia Earman, Stanley Engerman, David Fand, Andrew Farrant, Craufurd Goodwin, Christine Holden, Samuel Hollander, Ali Khan, Hartmut Kliemt, Wendy Motooka, Jerry Muller, Sandra Peart, Thomas Johann Prasch, Robert Tollison, Nicola Tynan, and Walter Williams for extraordinarily helpful comments on and support of my previous work on the conflict between economists and racists. I have been fortunate to be able to present early states of this work at the Kress History of Economics Seminar in Cambridge, at the York University–University of Toronto History of Economics Workshop, the 1997 History of Economics Society Conference, and the Global Studies Institute at Johns Hopkins. The Economics Department at

George Mason helped finance a trip to attend the 1997 American Statistical Association meetings in Anaheim and to visit the Huntington Library.

Chapter 6 is reprinted with an improvement from *Reflections on the Classical Canon: Essays for Samuel Hollander,* edited by Sandra Peart and Evelyn Forget (New York: Routledge, 2000). I am grateful for Routledge for permission to reprint. Peart found the Whately review of *Uncle Tom's Cabin* for me. Thanks are due for comments on earlier drafts from James Buchanan and Larry Moss and thanks, too, to Wendy Motooka and Gordon Wood for clarifying conversations. Most of my reading was done at the Library of Congress. I am in the particular debt of Cynthia Earman of the Rare Book Room, who initiated me into the mysteries of the collection-specific shelf list. Andrew Farrant, Maria Pia Paganelli, and Nicola Tynan saved me many errors when they helped me check the quotations. I would also like to express my gratitude to the organizers of the Hollander conference, Evelyn Forget and Sandra Peart, for arranging such a wonderful party for Sam. I also thank the Center for Study of Public Choice for a research grant. All the errors are my responsibility.

For chapter 7, Wendy Motooka and Bryan Caplan each put a detailed list of pointed queries at my disposal. Andrew Farrant found many errors in previous versions. An earlier version was presented at Peter Boettke's Kaplan Seminar on Political Economy at George Mason University.

Chapter 9 was previously published as "A Partial Spectator in the Wealth of Nations: A Robust Utilitarianism," in the *European Journal of the History of Economic Thought* 2 (1995): 299–326. Reprinted with permission from Taylor & Francis Ltd. (<http://www.tandf.co.uk/journals/>). This gave me the opportunity to correct a mistake (the word *spectator* occurs twice in Adam Smith's *Wealth of Nations,* not once). I discussed various aspects of this chapter with Susan Feigenbaum for years. Lisa Oakley helped sharpen the argument. An earlier version was presented at the 1993 History of Economics Society meetings. I benefited from the lively discussion that followed. I particularly would like to thank Mary Ann Dimand for her formal comments and both Warren Samuels and Jeremy Shearmur for their informal comments.

Chapter 10 is reprinted from the *American Journal of Economics and Sociology* 58 (1999). I thank Tyler Cowen and G. George Hwang for their comments on a previous version.

Chapter 11 was previously published in *Economic Inquiry* 35 (1997): 672–78. Reprinted with permission of Oxford University Press. The earliest version was presented at the 1994 History of Economics Society meetings in Babson Park, where I benefited from the useful comments of Jerry Evensky. A later version received detailed comments from Wendy Motooka and Thomas Borcherding. Without a fellowship at the Research School of Sciences (Director's Section) at the Australian National University, obtained through the good offices of Geoffrey Brennan, I would not have thought seriously about Australian languages. Brian O'Roark saved me from many errors when the old computer file was lost.

Chapter 12 first appeared as "Bishop Berkeley Exorcises the Infinite: Fuzzy Consequences of Strict Finitism," in *Hume Studies* 18 (1992), from which it is reprinted with permission. I have changed some notation and dropped some technical digressions to help make the point which is important for my argument clearer. The original essay grew out of discussions with Jennifer Roback about fuzzy economic theory. Earlier versions were presented at the 1991 meetings of the History of Economics Society and the Western Economic Association. I have benefited from the comments of Tim Brennan, John Conlon, and James Buchanan. Clair Smith found many errors when this chapter was reconstructed. After the completed manuscript was sent to the Press, Bridget Butkevich has attempted the heroic task of verifying the quotations. The reader will soon appreciate how important this is.

Quotations from the following volumes of the *Glasgow Edition of the Works and Correspondence of Adam Smith* are reprinted with permission of Oxford University Press:

Essays on Philosophical Subjects, edited by W. P. D. Wightman and J. C. Bryce (London: Clarendon, 1980). © Oxford University Press 1980.
Lectures on Jurisprudence, edited by R. L. Meek, D. D. Raphael, and P. G. Stein (London: Clarendon, 1978). © Oxford University Press 1978.
Lectures on Rhetoric and Belles Lettres, edited by J. C. Bryce (London: Clarendon, 1983). © Oxford University Press 1983.
An Inquiry into the Nature and Causes of the Wealth of Nations, edited by W. B. Todd (London: Clarendon, 1976). © Oxford University Press 1976.
The Theory of Moral Sentiments, edited by D. D. Raphael and A. L. Macfie (London: Clarendon, 1976). © Oxford University Press 1976.

Just as this book is being bundled off to be set into type, I have had the vast pleasure of seeing an illustrated summary of it—as well as ongoing research with Sandra Peart—launched on Liberty Fund's web site, <www.econlib.org>. There the reader can find both texts and art which are germane for the argument.

Finally, I wish to thank Ellen McCarthy for her faith, Jennifer Wisinski for her meticulous intolerance of my infelicities, Jillian Downey for her design of the book's interior, Stephanie Milanowski for the design of the dust jacket, and Carol Roberts for the index.

Preface: Answering the Obvious Question

What is a vile, racist cartoon doing illustrating a book on classical economics? Are my politics that far right?

As the whole of the book concerns these racial questions, let me pass over them for a little while to consider other aspects of this image. The figure sitting on a winged horse—so the authorities inform us—represents that cultural critic of capitalism, John Ruskin. The horse (Pegasus) is an old trope about the power of poets, as servants of the inspiring Muses, to rise above the world and look down upon it. From this vantage, poets and humanists more generally are supposed to see things hidden from earthbound mortals. When in 1849 Thomas Carlyle, whom Ruskin called "master," coined the term *dismal science* to describe economics, he juxtaposed it against an older "gay science," the art of poetry. The image is thus (in part) that of a war between poetry and economics. I shall ask the reader, who reflexively roots for the poets: "Why?"

The war between the poets and the economists can be understood if we ask what the poet can see from a Pegasus-eye view. One thing he can see—or at least that which is reported—is a hierarchical order. The spontaneous order of markets seems to make no sense from this vantage.[1] "Anarchy plus the constable" is Carlyle's description of what he understands well enough to oppose. Another thing that can be seen from a Pegasus-eye view is the Great Man. Assuming that Great Men are the cause and not the result of history, Carlyle was systematic enough to propose that in a rightful hierarchy there is worship of Great Men. *Hero worship* is the term he employs.

Economists of the classical period proposed to explain the spontaneous order by developing an account from *inside* human nature.[2] We trade one thing for another because we believe that this act will be to our benefit. Access to this

---

1. "Spontaneous order" is F. A. Hayek's useful description of precisely what it is that economists have been trying to explain for two centuries (1976).

2. The difference between neoclassical and classical economic foundations will be important in the argument to come. Only classical foundations can be used to give a defining characteristic of human status. Humans are not the only race that satisfies neoclassical axioms of consumer choice.

belief state is what gives classical economics its power. Renouncing this interior access, the poet on a high horse sees only the dumb reordering of matter. What one gains another loses. This understanding of the inner workings of people is inaccessible when viewed from atop Pegasus. In the nineteenth-century classical period of economics, the economists made a strong commitment to human equality as an analytical device. With this device, the economists found themselves opposed to a hierarchical Great Man approach. Under the egalitarian assumption, there were no Great Men, at least not in any sense in which *great* does not mean only *lucky*.

Is that a black man being killed? The Pegasus-eye view of the social order tells us only about the really existing hierarchy. In the 1850s, that time in which the poetic opposition to economics was most savage and best informed, there was racial slavery in the American South. The kindred slavery in the British Empire had ended within living memory. Such a hierarchy those poets with whom we are concerned took to be part of the nature of things. As the contemporary economists with their analytical egalitarianism could not see the desirability of racial slavery, but only the white exploiting the black, a ferocious debate ensued.

In this book, the reader will find a discussion of the Ruskin image that begins everything, a few graphs of the type that conveys meaning to economists, some symbols, and several hundred thousand words. The relationship among these components is simple. I did not discover the Ruskin image until the words were almost all written, the graphs drawn, and the symbols pointed in the right direction. Having done all this, it seemed that the image provided a useful introduction to a cluster of texts. One text stands out as worthy of particular attention. It contains of the first usage of the term *dismal science,* those words that are so easy to read in the image. This is Thomas Carlyle's 1849 "Occasional Discourse on the Negro Question."[3] It is in the judgment of Stephen Darwall the "ur-text of racial politics."[4]

The purpose of the book is threefold, an intention reflected in a threefold introduction provided in chapters 1–4. Visually, how are we to understand the image of Ruskin? There are two pieces here, although I had only planned to use one. Chapter 1 offers a symbolic reading of the image. As *Cope's Tobacco Plant* was a public relations project of a Liverpool tobacco firm, I think we need not worry overly much about the subtle nuances of Victorian imagery. My reading received an incisive objection: the face in the image is that of a real man

---

3. Photographic images of Carlyle's article, John Stuart Mill's January 1850 response, and what I read as Carlyle's February 1850 retort are available on the Web as documentation for seemingly incredible assertions <www.econlib.org>.

4. This was described as "one of the most nakedly racist tracts to be laid before the English reading public" (Walvin 1973, 165–66).

who is not black. Who is he? Chapter 2 tells this story, as I propose to test my symbolic reading by finding the man who fits the symbols.

In these two chapters we find crude racist fury coming at classical economics from a poetical direction. This raises a theoretical question: what is this debate all about? Chapter 3 explains this phase of the argument to come. And, since my account will differ from the authoritative treatments in which there is no racial element, I shall ask a metatheoretical question: why is this war between the economists and the poets in the mid–nineteenth century so hard to get right? Chapter 4 speaks to this.

As this war of words between poets and economists continues, it will be interesting to ask modern scholars who claim to speak for the poets what they have to say about the older debates.

Part 1
Two Sciences in Collision: The Dismal and the Gay

ONE

Poets Come, Bringing Death to Friends of the Dismal Science

An Interpretative Image

In 1893, admirers of that immensely famous cultural critic of capitalism, John Ruskin, who were associated with a Liverpool industrial publication-cum-literary journal, *Cope's Tobacco Plant*, produced *Ruskin on Himself and Things in General*. This numbers thirteen in their attractive series, Smoke-Room Booklets, which was available through both bookstores and tobacconists. Although Ruskin himself had nothing to do with it, and it contains less than sixty pages of extracts from published material with an introduction by William Lewin, the *Cope* volume is interesting enough to have been noticed in the great, thirty-nine-volume, Library Edition of Ruskin's work. It was reprinted at least three times in the 1970s at the beginning of the great Ruskin revival.[1]

Perhaps as a visual aid to interpreting these extracts—for those who buy reading matter at tobacco stores may have less time on their hands than those who frequent only bookstores—an interpretative illustration in red, gold, and black is provided on the cover. In the top left-hand corner, we see a caricature of John Ruskin holding a medieval lance and mounted on a snorting horse, jet black with red wings. Ruskin has just killed a dark-skinned human figure—red mouth gaping, setting off the sharp white teeth, uncomprehending eyes wide open—sprawled with arms and head thrown back, face up toward the lower right-hand corner.[2] Although well dressed in spats and a gentlemen's formal attire, Ruskin's enemy seems to be imagined as of a kind other than Ruskin himself.[3] Finding an image of Otherness in this commercial context is perhaps

---

1. So says the Library of Congress catalog. The only reprint I have seen lacks the cover image.

2. Royall Brandis (personal communication) queries whether the figure is in fact dead or about to be killed. There is no blood visible. Is there visible blood on the customary dragon?

3. Dark skin seems to be a general purpose indicator of Otherness. For example, Frank Felsenstein describes the representation of a Jewish peddlar in Hogarth's *Canvassing for Votes* this way: "Although Hogarth does not dress him in the full-length coat or cloak of continental Jewry, his black beard, pronounced nose, and dark complexion leave us in no doubt of his ethnic origin" (1995, 55).

unsurprising. The Smoke-Room Booklets were a production of *Cope's Tobacco Plant;* the tobacco business in Britain and America had a long history of using racial and ethnic imagery to sell its products.[4]

Let us look carefully at the image. In it, the wild-haired Ruskin with a bearded, thin white face and aquiline nose contrasts vividly with the nearly hairless, dark, broad face and flat nose of the one he has slain. The dark-skinned figure's hands resemble claws, and the serpentlike arabesque of the formal dress tail curls as though to pun with a "tail" of another sort.[5] His teeth are strange and disturbing. In his left hand, he clutches a bag with two labels: the words *Wealth of Nations* appear beneath the symbols "L. S. D." Clearly, the artist, John Wallace (one of *Cope's* regular illustrators), is taking Adam Smith's more abstract title literally—"pounds, shillings and pence." Beside the sprawled figure is a volume, perhaps something he was reading as death overtook him, with the following words on the cover: "The Dismal Science." Armed only with sharp teeth and claws and such insight as might be found in the "Wealth of Nations" or the "Dismal Science," he died alone, with only these abstractions and the now useless L. S. D. as companions.

What might this interpretative image mean? If the dark-skinned human figure caricatures a black person—apelike face, sharp pointed teeth, and the tail of the dangerous subhuman—are we being invited to read a defense of genocide? How is this possible? This is from Liverpool of 1893, not Munich of 1933.[6] Surely that cannot be a right reading of the image if only because the figure's dress and the L. S. D. suggest wealth. How could black people, as slaves emancipated within living memory, be represented that way? Moreover, there are aspects of the figure that seem not right if we take Negro caricature in commercial advertisements as paradigmatic of the Other.[7] Not only is this figure dangerous, with nonhuman teeth, but neither the stereotypical curly hair nor the exaggerated lips are evident.[8] If, on the other hand, the figure repre-

---

4. There is a discussion in *Cope's* concerning the agreement of Boston tobacconists to abolish the use of the "Little Nigger" statue. See "Tobacconists' Signboards and Advertisements," *Cope's Tobacco Plant* 1 (June 1870): 27.

5. Denise Albanese contributed the reading of the "tail" as serpent and linked this with the St. George image.

6. "In the genealogical tree of the Nazi doctrines such Latins as Sismondi and Georges Sorel, and such Anglo-Saxons as Carlyle, Ruskin and Houston Stewart Chamberlain, were more conspicuous than any German" (Von Mises 1951, 578).

7. The nearest caricature suitable for comparison is only four pages away (Ruskin 1893, viii). This is an advertisement that reproduces in "FacSimile" the label of Cope's Bristol Bird's Eye brand tobacco. Here the head, shoulders, and chest of a dark-skinned, *placid, curly-haired,* broad-faced, flat-nosed figure puffing a pipe appears. The exaggerated lips prominent in many of the caricatures reprinted by James Walvin (1973) are not obvious on the label figure. James Buchanan helped here.

8. Aside from the dangerousness—an odd image with which to sell pipe tobacco—the hair and the teeth seem to be most dramatic difference between the image of Ruskin's enemy and the image on Cope's Bristol Bird's Eye brand.

sents only a personification of economics, Ruskin's ideological bête noire, which "The Dismal Science" and "Wealth of Nations" encourage us to believe, why is economics represented with a darker skin and broader face than Ruskin? The otherwise appealing answer—that the image represents a merger of a black person and the discipline of economics—requires that we solve both sets of puzzles at the same time and tell how these aspects unite. Evidence, perhaps, of such a merger can be seen if one covers the red mouth and the nose: another face appears, and the wavy lines on the forehead of the first face become the mouth of the second face.[9]

Freedom in the "Best Sense" in Death and Slavery

In search of what the image might mean, let us consider what the editor of this volume has to say on the matter of black and white people. In his introductory material, William Lewin quotes the lines about slavery from Ruskin's 1853 chapter in *Stones of Venice*, entitled "The Nature of Gothic," which may bear on our puzzle. Ruskin considers the products of market specialization, which can be seen anywhere in Britain:

> Look round this English room of yours, about which you have been proud so often, because the work of it was so good and strong, and the ornaments of it so finished. Examine again all those accurate mouldings, and perfect polishings, and unerring adjustments of the seasoned wood and tempered steel. Many a time you have exulted over them, and thought how great England was, because her slightest work was done so thoroughly. (1893, 4)[10]

For Ruskin, these products provide evidence of the worst form of slavery:

> Alas! if read rightly, these perfectnesses are signs of a slavery in our England a thousand times more bitter and more degrading than that of the scourged African, or helot Greek. (4)

There was a nonmetaphorical type of slavery in America as Ruskin wrote these words. Ruskin's words would not suggest to him, as they might to a modern

---

9. I owe this reading to David George (2000). He points out that it solves the problem of the missing curly hair. I pass along the question he raises: is the second face Jewish?

10. The text in the Everyman edition is Ruskin 1925, 2:148, and in the most recent Penguin edition Ruskin 1997, 85. Passages that Lewin does not quote make Ruskin's opposition to Adam Smith clear: "We have much studied and much perfected, of late, the great civilised invention of the division of labour; only we give it a false name. It is not, truly speaking, the labour that is divided; but the men:—Divided into mere segments of men—broken into small fragments and crumbs of life; so that all the little pieces of intelligence that is left in a man is not enough to make a pin, or a nail, but exhausts itself in making the point of a pin, or the head of a nail" (1921–27, 2:150–51).

reader, the implication that English "slaves" are fleeing to the New Orleans market for human flesh to sell themselves and improve *their* quality of life. Ruskin would not expect the British slaves to understand their plight. The minds of these slaves have been broken on the wheel of the division of labor, becoming no more than "an animated tool."[11]

At a technical level, Ruskin's crusade against economics might be profitably seen as a vast polemic against the economist's device of imputing value in exchange from the point of view of choosing agents. Value is determined by the outside choice of the Maker "of things and of men," that great Critic on high.[12] Ruskin asserts that the metric by means of which choosing agents evaluate the consequences of their own choices—by profit or material gain—sums to zero in exchange.[13] Consequently, there cannot be a science of exchange in which gain is involved.[14] It is the role of poet and critic to evaluate the order revealed by different social forms. Exchange occurs just when and only when the critic approves and agrees that there is an *advantage*.[15] And then Ruskin explains just why on his scale of value a black slave's life and death are of no concern. *These* slaves, safe within a hierarchy, already have freedom in their slavery and their death:

---

11. The phrase from *Nature of the Gothic* is quoted by Lewin (Ruskin 1893, 4).

12. "The value of a thing, therefore, is independent of opinion, and of quantity. Think what you will of it, gain how much you may of it, the value of the thing itself is neither greater nor less. For ever it avails, or avails not; no estimate can raise, no disdain repress, the power which it holds from the Maker of things and of men" (Ruskin 1903–12, 17:85).

13. "Profit, or material gain, is attainable only by construction or by discovery; not by exchange. Whenever material gain follows exchange, for every *plus* there is a precisely equal *minus*. (ibid., 91).

14. "The Science of Exchange, or, as I hear it has been proposed to call it, of 'Catallactics,' considered as one of gain, is, therefore, simply nugatory" (ibid., 92).

15. Ruskin asserts that while there is no profit in exchange there can be "advantage." "Thus, one man, by sowing and reaping, turns one measure of corn into two measures. That is Profit. Another, by digging and forging, turns one spade into two spades. That is Profit. But the man who has two measures of corn wants sometimes to dig; and the man who has two spades wants sometimes to eat:—They exchange the gained grain for the gained tool; and both are the better for the exchange; but though there is much advantage in the transaction, there is no profit. Nothing is constructed or produced" (ibid., 90–91). Just exchange requires mutual advantage: "The general law, then, respecting just or economical exchange, is simply this—There must be advantage on both sides (or if only advantage on one, at least no disadvantage on the other) to the persons exchanging" (93). As I read the argument, *advantage* is Ruskin's technical term, which includes the notion of "need," something that the choosing agent may not know. "I have hitherto carefully restricted myself, in speaking of exchange, to use the term 'advantage'; but that term includes two ideas: the advantage, namely, of getting what we *need,* and that of getting what we *wish for*" (94). J. T. Fain (1982, 210–12), who criticizes attacks on Ruskin's economics for paying insufficient attention to Ruskin on the mutual "advantage" of exchange, does not explain how "advantage" differs from "gain." This is my attempt to fill in this gap.

> Men may be beaten, chained, tormented, yoked like cattle, slaughtered like summer flies, and yet remain in one sense and the best sense, free. (Ruskin 1893, 4)

What is really important is how the poet on Pegasus views matters; only "slavery" to a machine is real:

> But to smother their souls within them, to blight and hew into rotting pollards the suckling branches of their human intelligence, to make the flesh and skin which, after the worms's work on it, is to see God, into leathern thongs to yoke machinery with,—this it is to be slavemasters indeed. (4)

Why would it matter to workers in a hierarchy if their death is ordered on a whim? They are free of the machine and the market,

> and there might be more freedom in England, though her feudal lords' lightest words were worth men's lives, and though the blood of the vexed husbandman dropped in the furrows of her fields, than there is while the animation of her multitudes is sent like fuel to feed the factory smoke, and the strength of them is given daily to be wasted into the fineness of a web, or racked into the exactness of a line! (4)[16]

Slavery as freedom in the "best sense" is Carlyle's doctrine. Here is one of many such declarations from his *Past and Present,* complete with "brass collars, whips and handcuffs":

> Liberty? The true liberty of man, you would say, consisted in his finding out, or being forced to find out the right path, and walk thereon. To learn, or to be taught, what work he actually was able for; and then, by permission, persuasion, and even compulsion, to set about doing of the same! . . . If thou do know better than I what is good and right, I conjure thee in the name of God, force me to do it, were it by never such brass collars, whips and handcuffs, leave me not to walk over precipices! (Carlyle 1965, 211–12)

In fact, black people really were "beaten, chained, tormented, yoked like cattle," as they really were "slaughtered like summer flies" on the Middle Pas-

---

16. "This characteristic passage is worth a digression, for it explains many passages in which Ruskin glorifies slavery and feudal conditions. Many of his contradictions and fantastic beliefs turn out to be merely rhetorical" (Fain 1956, 24). Fain somehow neglects to consider how the Eyre controversy sheds light on the "merely rhetorical" interpretation.

sage to service the demands of the American slave system. And this Ruskin's readers at the time would have known perfectly well. An article in Charles Dickens's magazine testifies that the "horrors of the middle passage" had entered common knowledge.[17] But, in comparison with the white "slaves" of modern Britain, for Ruskin these slaves under a social hierarchy—new-style American slavery or old feudalism or even older Spartan slavery—"remain in one sense and the best sense free."

Against Adam Smith's doctrine that to be human is to exchange freely, Ruskin juxtaposes a doctrine that to be human is to be improved by our betters, those who can make men the way a potter makes pottery. This remaking is where the true "advantage" lies.[18] If it were possible to bring about the liberation of British slaves—to replace slavery to the machine with slavery to their betters—with the deaths of black slaves, how would Ruskin on his high, winged horse value this? Would not their slaughter "like summer flies" be of no account? Their "freedom" in Ruskin's "best sense" would not be altered for the worse because they are already in the care of their betters, that is, us. Whatever we decide for them, however we decide to remake their human clay, even if it means throwing it back into the fire, must be right. In the warm embrace of a hierarchy, their well-being is fixed: there can be no change for the worse. But improving the well-being of whites is an advantage, a plus. A zero added to a plus makes a plus.

But perhaps this exercise is unfair to Ruskin, as it supposes he can make the leap from theoretical assertions to practical matters. The modern authorities have singled out Ruskin's series of letters—*Fors Clavigera*—for special attention as representing the center of his social concerns and literary devices.[19] This text seems appropriate, as the very title suggests violence against enemies. The difficulty of selecting a practical matter for analysis is which one. Let the contemporary discussion captured in the Making of Amer-

---

17. "There is probably scarcely a full-grown person in this kingdom, who, in connection with the slave trade, has not heard of the 'horrors of the middle passage'" (Hollingshead 1858, 84).

18. "This is Mr. Ruskin's condemnation of our modern social condition; that we manufacture every thing except men. 'We blanch cotton, strengthen steel, and refine sugar, and shape pottery; but to brighten, to strengthen, to refine, or to form a single living spirit, never enters into our estimate of advantages'" (Lewin in Ruskin 1893, 4).

19. What better evidence can there be than that provided by the first shot in what promises to be an entertaining priority fight? Here John Rosenberg (2000, 32), in his review of Tim Hilton's *Ruskin: The Later Years*: "*Fors Clavigera*, the most daringly original of all of Ruskin's writings, a judgement with which Tim Hilton concurs. I have written at length about *Fors Clavigera*, but Hilton writes as if he believes he has discovered it. I recognize many of my own perceptions in his characterization of the work, but only as an unhappy parent might recognize his own best features blotched in those of his ungainly child." This originality claim is a century off. The selection by Lewin (Ruskin 1893) is mainly from *Fors Clavigera*, as pointed out at Ruskin 1903–12, 38:115.

ica data base select one: Ruskin's analysis of the impact of railroad travel on the worker. Here from letter 44—as quoted in a nineteenth-century American periodical—is Ruskin's discussion of the impact of this agent of industrialization:

> In old times, if a Coniston peasant had any business at Ulverstone, he walked to Ulverstone; spent nothing but shoe-leather on the road, drank at the streams, and if he spent a couple of batz when he got to Ulverstone, "it was the end of the world." But now he would never think of doing such a thing! He first walks three miles in a contrary direction to a railroad-station, and then travels by railroad twenty-four miles to Ulverstone, paying two shillings fare. During the twenty-four miles transit, he is idle, dusty, stupid; and either more hot or cold than is pleasant to him. In either case he drinks beer at two or three of the stations, passes his time, between them, with anybody he can find, in talking without having anything to talk of; and such talk always becomes vicious. He arrives at Ulverstone, jaded, half-drunk, and otherwise demoralized, and three shillings, at least, poorer than in the morning. Of that sum a shilling has gone for beer, threepence to a railway shareholder, threepence in coals, and eighteen pence has been spent in employing strong men in the vile mechanical work of making and driving a machine, instead of his own legs, to carry the drunken lout. The results, absolute loss and demoralization to the poor on all sides, and iniquitous gain to the rich. Fancy, if you saw the railway officials actually employed in carrying the countryman bodily on their backs to Ulverstone, what you would think of the business! And because they waste ever so much iron and fuel besides to do it, you think it a profitable one.[20]

In the image of the drunken, demoralized, "idle, dusty, stupid" "drunken lout," the reader has just encountered the contemporary stereotype of the Irish.[21] The wickedness of industrialization comes because it induces racial degeneration: from English to Irish.

St. George and the What?

Can this reading be right? Although Lewin quotes Ruskin correctly and the racial degeneration induced by a railroad is plain enough, how can that be what he meant? As nothing escaped the editors of the Library Edition of *The Works*

---

20. "Ruskin's 'Fors Clavigera'" (1878, 61).

21. Sandra Peart and David Levy (2000) give the details in terms of the linked contemporary discussion in anthropology and eugenics.

of John Ruskin, let us appeal to them for help correcting our misunderstanding of the image's message. After a very thorough technical description of the volume in question, we read:

> Issued in brown paper wrappers, with a caricature portrait on the front of Ruskin as St. George. Price 3d.[22]

This is surely part of the puzzle. The sharp teeth, the claws, and the "tail" evoke the dragon, and perhaps the dragon had stolen the wealth of the English nation before he was overtaken by St. George on Pegasus? And if we turn the image upside down we behold human arms morphing into dragon's wings![23] With the help of the *Oxford English Dictionary* (OED) we can expand upon this reading to ask about the *winged* horse.[24] The OED entry for *Pegasus* clears up this matter:

> The winged horse fabled to have sprung from the blood of Medusa when slain by Perseus, and with a stroke of his hoof to have caused the fountain Hippocrene to well forth on Mount Helicon. Hence, by modern writers (first in Boiardo's *Orlando Innamorato* c. 1490), represented as the favourite steed of the Muses, and said allusively to bear poets in the "flights" of poetic genius.

Taking note of "The Dismal Science" in the image and looking up the origin of that phrase—the details in due course—we find Thomas Carlyle juxtaposing a "gay science" against the dismal. Appealing for help on the gay science in the OED, we find it to be poetry.[25] Thus we are to read the image: "John Ruskin, Poet, Slays the Dragon."

The trouble is of course that this is not the standard issue fairy tale dragon. This image, with dark skin juxtaposed against Ruskin's white skin, with broad face contrasting with Ruskin's narrow one, has apelike features. How does St. George's dragon take this form? The editors seem uninterested in helping us

---

22. E. T. Cook and Alexander Wedderburn (1912, 38:115). They add the following tantalizing information: "This publication was the subject of proceedings in the Chancery Division before Mr. Justice Stirling on November 24, 1893, Messrs. Cope submitting to an order for a perpetual injunction." This line is quoted by Richard Altick (1951, 344), who gives no further information.

23. Maria Pia Paganelli saw this first.

24. The image of St. George's horse drawn by a very young and very bloodthirsty Ruskin, reprinted in Spear 1984, 131, has no wings. Nor does the horse in the 1885 Charles Murray image, which is reprinted in Casteras 1993, 184–85.

25. "The gay science: a rendering of *gai saber*, the Provençal name for the art of poetry" (*Oxford English Dictionary* [hereafter OED], 1992). Denise Albanese helped me here.

with this puzzle.[26] Nor do they tell us what the bag with "L. S. D." and "Wealth of Nations" or the book with "The Dismal Science" on it might mean.

Richard Altick, who reports the visual images of other Smoke-Room Booklets carefully[27] and informs the reader that *Tobacco Plant* tolerated Ruskin's antitobacco views, when he discusses the Ruskin booklet and the Cook-Weddeburn commentary, is silent about the illustration.[28]

The Rational Silence of the Commentators

Rational choice theory, the standard authorities inform us, is a branch of the mathematics of constrained optimization. Given our desires, it asks: what is the best we can do subject to the constraints we face? That solution is the rational choice. But this rational choice model is not the account that rational choice theorists commonly employ when we need to explain how scholars behave. We are supposed to be truth seekers.[29] And failure to engage in truth seeking is the source of moral outrage (Feigenbaum and Levy 1993). When the economist becomes an expert witness, the truth-seeking model loses all plausibility.[30]

I propose that we leave the moralizing aside and begin to think like empirical economists about the choices of economists and other scholars.[31] Regard-

---

26. "Already, thanks to several recent publications from Ruskin manuscripts, the reading public has begun to realize that, as editors, E. T. Cook (later Sir E. T. Cook) and Alexander Wedderburn were highly selective and far from reasonably dispassionate. But no one has as yet suspected that through their imposing array of thirty-nine volumes, they prepared, in actuality, a gigantic trap which not one subsequent biographer of Ruskin has managed to escape" (Viljoen 1956, 3).

27. "The frontispiece of Number Nine (1893) showed a stained-glass triptych, in each of whose panels appeared the figure of the anti-nicotinist who had long since become familiar to the Cope audience through the exertions of the *Tobacco Plant* artist: a clergyman with umbrella, long ulster, gaiter, big feet, and pious mien—the direct forbear of the lugubrious prohibitionists drawn by Rollin Kirby twenty-five years ago" (Altick 1951, 341).

28. Ibid., 344. In footnote 8, Altick cites the Ruskin volume in the Smoke-Room Booklet series and the sentence following the "Ruskin as St. George" interpretation by Cook and Wedderburn.

29. Ruskin coherently supposes pastor-teachers to be truth seekers, who are distinguished from seekers after gain: "And the duty of all these men is, on due occasion, to *die* for it. . . . The Pastor, rather than teach Falsehood. . . . The Merchant—what is *his* "due occasion" of death?" (1903–12, 17:40).

30. Luke Froeb and Bruce Kobayashi (1996) and Richard Posner (1999) are developing an economics of expert witnessing. The American Statistical Association code of ethics (2000) is designed to constrain the testimony of statistical workers.

31. "[T]he doctrine of Right and Wrong, is perpetually disputed, both by the Pen and the Sword: Whereas the doctrine of Lines, and Figures, is not so; because men care not, in that subject what be truth, as a thing that crosses no mans ambition, profit, or lust. For I doubt not, but if it had been a thing contrary to any mans right of dominion, or to the interest of men that have dominion, *That the three Angles of a Triangle should be equall to two Angles of a Square;* that doctrine should have been, if not disputed, yet by the burning of all books of Geometry, suppressed, as farre as he whom it concerned was able" (Hobbes 1968, 166).

less of how we ought to behave, I propose that the model of the scholar as expert witness is *the* appropriate model to be used upon all occasions when we need to explain how we—we economists, we humanists—do in fact make choices. The problem with moral outrage as an analytical engine is that it gives no prediction as to how behavior changes as constraints change.

Consider the problem facing a scholar offering an interpretation of difficult texts. What might serve as motivation? One goal that seems unproblematic is a desire for completeness, to be able to tie the various aspects together in a manageable whole. But scholars have desires about the direction of the interpretation; they have preferences about outcomes that they affect subject to various constraints (Feigenbaum and Levy 1996).

For simplicity, I shall suppose that a maximally complete interpretation is an unbiased interpretation. That is to say, when all the pieces fit together there will be no disagreement about how the author stands on any issue. The interested scholar forces his author's work in the preferred direction by selectively omitting texts.[32] To model interpretation as a rational choice, we need only specify desires and constraints. This is accomplished in figure 1.

Indifference curves I and II characterize the goals of the scholar over these two goods: completeness and direction. In keeping with the statistical origin of this model of rational choice scholarship, the favored direction is labeled "bias." This is one scholar's desires; presumably, there will be scholars with opposing desires. Figure 1 also recognizes two constraints—the inner, shaded polygon and the outer, unshaded polygon. When the inner polygon serves as the constraint, the interested scholar offers interpretation i^*; when the outer polygon serves as the constraint, interpretation i^{**} is forthcoming. The constraint that we shall explore is the state of common knowledge held by the audience for whom the interpretation is offered. When memory is green, i^* results; when memory fades, i^{**} appears. If the image refers even tangentially to real people, the interpretation of a humane Ruskin is ill served by talking about this competing interpretation.[33]

---

32. Edward Leamer (1983) and Frank Denton (1985) provide classic discussions of specification search in an econometric context.

33. "In making their selections from the manuscripts, the editors seem to have been guided by two principles. First, nothing should be made public which might reflect adversely, from their point of view, either upon Ruskin or upon any member of his family, although (as a corollary to this first principle) if there was any conflict between the interests of Ruskin and of some member of his family, Ruskin should be favored" (Viljoen 1956, 16). "Cook, as part of his effort to refashion Ruskin as a man of more liberal outlook, stressed the personal relationship of Ruskin and Darwin" (O'Gorman 1999, 37).

As I may be the first to note Altick's silence, let me quote from the final paragraph of his study: "In sum, the publishing activities of the firm of Cope form an honorable little chapter in the history of Victorian journalism. At a time when, in the view of many observers, England was 'shooting Niagara' culturally as well as politically, with the proliferation of cheap newspapers and magazines frankly designed to strike the lowest common denominator of popular taste, the *Tobacco*

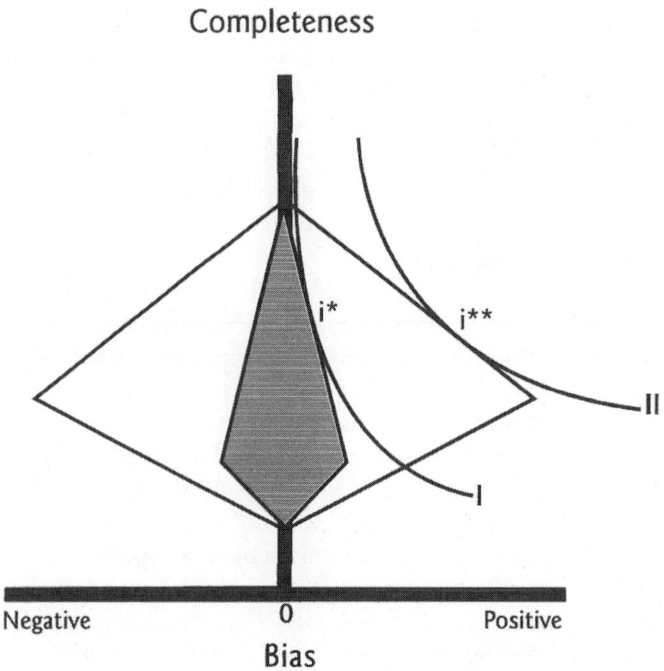

Fig. 1.   Optimal interpretation

The Death of Real People?

For a context that refers to the death of real people, let us read the first two sentences on the first page of the first issue of *Cope's Tobacco Plant* (March 1870) in a article entitled "Why Can't Great Britain Grow Tobacco?"

> Most readers will regard this question as though it were equivalent to the good old query—Why can't a man do as he likes? But even the law of perfect liberty, as laid down by the humanitarian jurist, John Stuart Mill . . .[34]

"Humanitarian jurist, John Stuart Mill" refers to what? Mill was, at the time *Cope's* lead type was still hot, the head of the Jamaica Committee, which was attempting to bring charges against John Eyre for his murderous policies in

---

Plant did its substantial bit to maintain a lively interest in literary topics among ordinary middle-class readers. Seldom, before or since, could an Englishman get as much good reading matter for his twopence" (1951, 350). We shall encounter the Carlyle text about which Altick winks, *Shooting Niagara*, when we come to the Eyre controversy.

34. *Cope's Tobacco Plant* 1 (March 30, 1870): 1.

Jamaica. Although Thomas Carlyle was greatly admired by those who wrote for *Cope's Tobacco Plant*—Smoke-Room Booklet number five is Carlyle's *Table Talk*—there was one aspect of his career that they wished otherwise:

> True, he scandalised a good many worthy people by his savage partisanship of Governor Eyre, who flogged the poor blacks of Jamaica—men and women—with piano-forte wire woven into the cats. There we think the old Titan was wrong.[35]

The wire whips used against women as an explicit policy of state terror seemed to most outrage public opinion.[36] A well-informed supporter of Eyre, the driving force behind the most racially charged form of British anthropology, James Hunt judged that Eyre's action was theoretically informed and that of course Carlyle was one of those theorists providing racial insight.[37] And of course Ruskin stood with Carlyle. This is the problem for the liberal interpretation of Ruskin.[38]

Let J. A. Hobson explain much of this in his 1898 *defense* of Ruskin:

---

35. "Famous Smokers I: Thomas Carlyle," *Cope's Tobacco Plant* 1 (April 1871): 152. *Cope's* seems more troubled by the controversy than the violence: "Governor Eyre was not worthy of such an illustrious champion, for had he been a governor of the Carlyle stamp, he would have ruled Jamaica with the intrepid and active intelligence which would have effectually prevented that tragical despair, which precipitated the insubordination, which he had to check at last with a bloody and vengeful hand. But even here, in what we must regard as Carlyle's vehement and brutal errors, his doctrine has an element of generous ferocity in it."

The original draft, taken from Carlyle's handwriting, of the statement for the defense of Governor Eyre was published when events in Germany revived discussions of race and state terror. "That after much investatn, it does not appear Govr. Eyre fell into any serious mistake, or committed unknowingly, much less knowingly, any noticeable fault, in dealing with this frightful and immeasurable kindlg of black unutterabilities but trod it out straightway with a clearness of exact discernmt, with a courage and skill and swiftness which seems to us to be of heroic quality" (Olivier 1933, 337).

36. "Holding his political enemy, Gordon, ultimately responsible for instigating the rebellion, Eyre had him arrested and taken to Morant Bay, where, on extraordinarily flimsy evidence, he was found guilty and hanged. When the final tallies of the government's repression were made, they revealed that a terrible vengeance had been unleashed: 439 dead, hundreds flogged, and 1,000 houses burned. . . . Despite orders for restraint, people were flogged with whips made of twisted, knotted wires, and scores were shot or hung after drumhead court-martials. Commanders were quite explicit about the objective of official violence: they intended to instill terror" (Holt 1992, 302).

37. "We were at first not a little astonished at the decisive measures taken by Governor Eyre: measures which could alone have resulted from a most thorough insight into the negro character" (Hunt 1866a, 16). In discussing Robert Knox's doctrine of racial war, Carlyle is brought in as economic prophet: "He [Knox] would have that latest of all ethnological puzzles to some—the present 'insurrection in Jamaica;' an insurrection, however, which he, as we have already seen, foretold on scientific principles, which Carlyle, in his tract on 'The Nigger Question,' hinted at as probable on grounds of social economy" (25–26). This is the R. Knox, the anatomist, whom Ruskin cites approvingly (1921–27, 3:44) in a technical, nonracial context.

38. "Despite widespread genuflexion, Ruskin's influence on the social policies of British socialism remains inadequately explored. Bernard Shaw in 1920 suggestively remarked that a main

Order, reverence, authority, obedience, these words are always on his lips, these ideas always present in his mind. Radical and revolutionary doctrines and movements, as he interprets them, imply the rejection and overthrow of these principles, and are denounced accordingly. Liberty and equality he scornfully repudiates as the negation of order and government. "No liberty, but instant obedience to known law and appointed persons; no equality, but recognition of every betterness and reprobation of every worseness."

His detestation of liberty and equality brought him into strange company and into strange historic judgements. With Carlyle and the autocratic Tory party of the day he stood for "order and a strong hand" in the Jamaica business, taking a leading part on the Eyre Defence Committee. (202)

Frederic Harrison in 1902 explicitly juxtaposes visions of Ruskin: Ruskin as Judge Lynch ill becomes a Ruskin with "beautiful thoughts":

In 1865–66 the sanguinary suppression of a negro riot in Jamaica, and the summary execution of Gordon by Governor Eyre, roused fierce indignation, and committees were formed to prosecute—and to defend Mr. Eyre. Carlyle, always on the side of martial law and against the slave, dragged Ruskin into the Eyre defence, which he warmly supported, and to which he subscribed £100. It was startling to some persons to find the author of *Unto this Last*, this "merciful, just and godly" person, on the side of lawless oppression of the weak. But his Tory instincts and the influence of Carlyle may account for this and much more. (119–20)

Nineteenth-century defenders of Ruskin were tightly constrained by common knowledge. One does not easily forget the first imperial administrative massacre. But time passes, and the technology of genocide improves. The state of this art moves from the killing of hundreds to the killing of millions. Early ventures are overshadowed and easily forgotten.[39] The set of feasible interpretations widens as the Eyre controversy falls out of common knowledge.

Let us consider what late-twentieth-century Ruskin commentators make of the Eyre episode. My impression is that they choose not to mention it.[40]

---

cause of the weakness of Marxism in Britain was that those within the socialist movement who were inclined to violence and state terror had no need of Marx; they already had their prophet in Ruskin" (Harris 1999, 27). George Orwell (1968, 1:119) describes Shaw's opinions as "Carlyle & water."

39. "What had seemed so extraordinary to John Stuart Mill and his comrades—administrative massacre, rule by terror—has become a commonplace in the imperial history of our century" (Semmel 1962, 178).

40. Consider the claim by Spear (1984, 150): "Ruskin's attack on the labor theory of value and the nature of his substitute for it is a signal instance of his uncanny ability to arrive at progressive conclusions by regressive methods." Justifying a racial massacre is "progressive" just how? I do not believe that I have seen a wonderful instance of optimal silence except that evidenced in Spear's reading Carlyle's exterminationism as just talk.

However, we can be more precise than that. In George Cate's 1988 *John Ruskin: A Reference Guide,* which contains annotations on well over three hundred scholarly works, Eyre is mentioned precisely *once.*[41] And this occurs in the comforting context of an article retelling the story that Carlyle dragged Ruskin into the controversy over Eyre's "vigorously suppressing" a riot.[42] The fact that the standard work on the British debates comprising the Governor Eyre controversy—Semmel (1962)—is not mentioned is deeply suggestive of how the relaxation of the constraint imposed by common knowledge can be exploited by those hawking pleasing interpretations.

Perhaps the new century will see a change. For, behold, the most recent full-length life of Ruskin (Hilton 2000, 105–7) discusses his "poor cause" in the Eyre case with a reasonable amount of care and usefully links Carlyle's *Shooting Niagara* to Ruskin's *Time and Tide.*[43] But even after reading Hilton one might come away thinking that Ruskin had no more to do with Eyre than the other Victorian sages.

Against all these assertions, it bears repeating what Semmel emphasizes: it was Ruskin himself who, first among the sages, alerted his peers to Eyre's importance to their common cause.[44] Ruskin's 1865 letter to the *Daily Telegraph* repays more careful reading than it generally receives.

In this letter, Ruskin opens with compliments to J. S. Mill and Thomas Hughes. He declares himself to be a "King's man" in opposition to the "Mob's men" and then gets down to the business at hand. That business is slavery in America and slavery in Europe. As we read what Ruskin wrote in the early 1850s about life and death for slaves real and metaphorical, let us consider what he says now when the death of black people is real:

---

41. George Cate's (1988, 138) index entry for "Eyre" refers to one 1948 article, although in Cate 1982 (120), Semmel (1962) is authoritative.

42. Cate (1988, 59) describes Eyre as "vigorously suppressing an uprising against his rule." "Vigorously"—wire whips and judicial lynch. A literature in which "St. George and the Negro" is an unproblematic image will find this a comfort. Cate continues: "Ruskin did much work as an especial favor to his mentor and close friend Thomas Carlyle, who chaired the committee. Tennyson and Dickens were also members of the committee" (59)

43. Here is my reservation. Hilton (2000, 106) describes the anti-Eyre and pro-Eyre groups. "It is significant that the main movers of these groups were largely outside Parliament." Then Hilton recites the names of the moving spirits of the Jamaica Committee, which include J. S. Mill and John Bright. Hilton does not recognize that they are members of Parliament. Semmel (1962) would have cleared this up.

44. "Ruskin had thus been the first of the literary men to come to the defence of Governor Eyre. It was even possible that the noted critic, very close to Carlyle at this period, had helped Jane to interest her husband in the Eyre affair" (Semmel 1962, 109). On April 10, 1866, Jane Carlyle (1883, 325) writes about a conversation that went like this. She responds to the challenge "But no *man* living could stand up for Eyre now!" with the "'I hope Mr. Carlyle does,' I said. 'I haven't had an opportunity of asking him; but I should be surprised and grieved if I found him sentimentalising over a pack of black brutes!'" The Carlyle-Ruskin letters about Eyre date from September 1866 (Cate 1982, 119–23).

Not that I like slavery, or object to the emancipation of any kind or number of blacks in due place and time. (1903–12, 18:551)[45]

The letter is dated December 20, 1865. An agreement of April 9, 1865, at the Appomattox Court House, settled one dispute about slavery, regardless of whether the time and place was right, a thought to which we shall return. Ruskin continues charging that those objecting to Eyre's actions are unaware of the full dimensions of "slavery." This gives some context to the "due place and time":

But I understand something more by "slavery" than either Mr. J. S. Mill or Mr. Hughes; and believe that white emancipation not only ought to precede, but must by law of all fate precede, black emancipation. (551)[46]

The "law of all fate" is of course the standard Carlylean appeal to as-if divine revelation. Then, perhaps conscious of the need to address the unbelievers in his audience, Ruskin launches an argument by means of parallel construction:

I much dislike the slavery, to man, of an African labourer, with a spade on his shoulder; but I more dislike the slavery, to the devil, of a Calabrian robber with a gun on his shoulder. (551)

African slaves have men with spades as masters, men no different than other men. There are other forms of slavery in which one serves the devil himself. Now we compare America and England:

I dislike the American serf-economy, which separates, occasionally, man and wife; but I more dislike the English serf-economy, which prevents men being able to have wives at all. (551)

What kind of an attack on British capitalism is the argument that "English serfs" do not have wives?[47] And in any event how are we to read "occasionally"?

---

45. This was reprinted earlier in Ruskin 1880, 2:31–32.

46. Ruskin racialized the history of architecture with kindred insight: "But it may be incidentally observed, that if the Greeks did indeed receive the Doric from Egypt, then the three families of the earth have each contributed their part of its noblest architecture; and Ham, the servant of the others, furnishes the sustaining or bearing member, the shaft; Japheth the arch; Shem the spiritualisation of both" (1921–27, 1:13).

47. To a sensible scholar like Bernard Semmel, this line must make no sense whatsoever. He does not quote it (1962, 108–9). Let me thank Wendy Motooka, who provided a bracing correction for my temptation to rely upon even this best of all secondary sources! The Malthusian controversy dealt with the necessity of delaying marriage (Levy 1999b). The neo-Malthusians—Francis Place through Mill himself—defended contraception as a way to allow poor people to afford early marriage.

Are an American husband and wife upon occasion temporarily separated or is it upon occasion that an American husband and wife are permanently separated by their master's interests. We continue, reading about Eliza pursued by dogs, carrying little Harry across the ice, in juxtaposition to something:[48]

> I dislike the slavery which obliges women (if it does) to carry their children over frozen rivers; but I more dislike the slavery which makes them throw their children into wells. (551)

Then Ruskin reveals his contempt for market exchange: the kidnapping and serial rape of black girls—prostitution compelled by the lash[49]—is less of a moral issue for him than white girls prostituting themselves for money.

> I would willingly hinder the selling of girls on the Gold Coast: but primarily, if I might, would the selling of them in Mayfair. (551)

Ruskin, it should be as clear as can be, views black slavery and "white slavery" this way: black slaves have men as masters to make them better; white slaves lack this boon, subject as they are to "devils" and the machine. And white English people are "fated" to be more important than black people. By defending Eyre's actions with these arguments, Ruskin reveals that for him the deaths of distant black people in the interests of nearby white people are advantageous. His political actions in the mid-1860s on behalf of Eyre are in accord with our reading of his words of 1853.

The Death of a Discipline?

As we have learned much from Cook and Wedderburn's commentary on *Cope's* image, we should attend to what else they have to teach. Here they

---

48. Cook and Wedderburn (in Ruskin 1903–12, 18: 551) and the editor of *Arrows of the Chace* (Ruskin 1880, 2:345) both give *Uncle Tom's Cabin* as references. Is there a novel, an *Uncle Tom's Cabin* of the "English serfs," to which Ruskin is referring? The line in Ruskin's letter that Semmel does not quote—English serfs without wives—seems to me to make sense in and only in the context provided by Charles Dickens's *Hard Times*, an argument to which I shall return. Stephen and Rachael are doomed by Dickens's plot to pass their lives in separate bedrooms. Ruskin's inability to distinguish the real world from characters in books has been pointed out: "[Patmore's poem] *The Angel in the House* would reappear in *Sesame and Lilies*, the book written expressly for Rose La Touche at the height of Ruskin's love for her. It is a poem that contributed to his disastrous assumptions about the girl he wished to wed" (Hilton 1985, 212).

49. A convenient example is found in the article by George Stephens that is included in Lord Denman's republished attack on Dickens's views on slavery: "The national conscience was awakened to inquiry, and inquiry soon produced conviction. Could it be otherwise than a sin to enslave the soul by enchaining the body? Could it be otherwise than sinful to compel prostitution by the lash?" (Denman 1853, 56).

describe the relationship between Carlyle and Ruskin and their battle with the common foe, giving useful information in their note, which I embed within their text:

> Ever since Ruskin had entered the field against "the dismal science," [Note: Carlyle's favourite phrase for Political Economy was first used by him in *The Nigger Question* (1853) . . .] his relations with Carlyle had grown more and more intimate and affectionate. As each new shaft was hurled by Ruskin, Carlyle applauded and exhorted the younger man to fresh onslaughts.[50]

There is an error in this text, although it is of little consequence. The term *dismal science* did not originate in Carlyle's 1853 booklet *Occasional Discourse on the Nigger Question*, it originated in an 1849 essay in *Fraser's* entitled "Occasional Discourse on the Negro Question."[51]

Before we read this article for ourselves, let James Froude, Carlyle's great and inexorably candid biographer, explain the importance of the article and booklet. They attack the role of economics in the emancipation of British slaves:

> A paper on the Negro or Nigger question, properly the first of the "Latter-day Pamphlets," was Carlyle's declaration of war against modern Radicalism. . . . His objection was to the cant of Radicalism; the philosophy of it, "bred of philanthropy and the Dismal Science," the purport of which was to cast the atoms of human society adrift, mocked with the name of liberty, to sink or swim as they could. Negro emancipation had been the special boast and glory of the new theory of universal happiness. The *twenty million of indemnity* and the free West Indies had been chanted and celebrated for a quarter of a century from press and platform. (1885, 2:14–15; emphasis added)

The "twenty million of indemnity," which I have emphasized, will turn out to be important for my reading of the puzzle posed by the image. But first we turn to the first appearance of the "dismal science" in the English language. We find an older "gay" science and a newer dismal science in contrast. We have learned the gay science is poetry. And how might we read the dismal science economics?

---

50. Cook and Wedderburn in Ruskin 1903–12, 18:xlvi.

51. The standard edition of the 1853 pamphlet, which is paired with Mill's response to the 1849 article, is by Eugene August (Carlyle 1971). The OED entry for *dismal* has the date right but the title wrong: "1849 Carlyle *Nigger Question, Misc. Ess.* (1872) VII. 84 'The Social Science—not a 'gay science', but a rueful,—which finds the secret of this Universe in 'supply and demand' what we might call, by way of eminence, the *dismal science.*'"

> Truly, my philanthropic friends, Exeter Hall Philanthropy is wonderful: and the Social Science—not a "gay science," but a rueful—which finds the secret of this universe in "supply-and-demand," and reduces the duty of human governors to that of letting men alone, is also wonderful. Not a "gay science," I should say, like some we have heard of; no, a dreary, desolate, and indeed quite abject and distressing one: what we might call, by way of eminence, the *dismal science*. These two, Exeter Hall Philanthropy and the Dismal Science, led by any sacred cause of Black Emancipation, or the like, to fall in love and make a wedding of it,—will give birth to progenies and prodigies; dark extensive moon-calves, unnameable abortions, wide-coiled monstrosities, such as the world has not seen hitherto! (Carlyle 1849, 672–73)

Can we read dismal science as the "Negro science?"[52] And perhaps we might pay attention to the possibility of "wide-coiled monstrosities" resulting from the marriage of economics and the cause of black emancipation.

Foreshadowing their roles two decades later, John Stuart Mill responded (Mill 1850). Then, in what I read as Carlyle's response to Mill, he adds to this, the familiar doctrine of emancipation through slavery, the consideration that when slavery fails, genocide is justified. The reader who has never thought of racial extermination as a policy option might wish to read carefully.[53] As the "Negro Question" is the report of a speech, here is another speech:

> —Work, was I saying? My indigent unguided friends, I should think some work might be discoverable for you. Enlist, stand drill; become, from a nomadic Banditti of Idleness, Soldiers of Industry! I will lead you to the Irish Bogs, to the vacant desolations of Connaught now falling into Cannibalism. . . .
>
> To each of you I will then say: Here is work for you; strike into it with manlike, soldierlike obedience and heartiness, according to the methods here prescribed,—wages follow for you without difficulty; all manner of just remuneration, and at length emancipation itself follows. Refuse to strike into it; shirk the heavy labour, disobey the rules,—I will admonish and endeavour to incite you; if in vain, I will flog you; if still in vain, I will at last shoot you,—and make God's Earth, and the forlorn-hope in God's Battle, free of you. (Carlyle 1850b, 54–55)

---

52. Stephen Darwall gave me this reading years before either of us had seen the *Cope's* image!

53. "Like the other calls to order in the *Latter-Day Pamphlets*, the violence of the prime minister's speech is an impotent violence. It is impotent not because of some psychological failing on Carlyle's part, but because, as the context of the speech makes clear, Carlyle has little hope that the speech will be given, let alone action taken" (Spear 1984, 111). Governor Eyre's actions must have been seen as heaven-sent confirmation of the policy, which, instructively enough, Spear never mentions.

Now we begin to make sense of *Cope's* image: the death of Negroes and the death of a science are linked because what we call classical economics is from Carlyle's point of view the "Negro science." And perhaps Carlyle is right here, just as he is right about many other things about the doctrines of those he opposed.

But *Cope's* image is of Ruskin not of Carlyle. Moreover, the Carlyle entry in the Smoke-Room Booklet series (Carlyle 1890), has a simple cameo on the cover. The division of labor in the death of classical economics between Carlyle and Ruskin is explained by Harrison:

> Such was the man who, in the pages of the *Cornhill Magazine,* then edited by his friend Thackeray, undertook, with all the sublime faith in himself of the Knight of La Mancha, to demolish the solid array of what had held the field for two generations as Political Economy, *i.e.* the consolidated and rigid doctrine of Ricardo, Malthus, and M'Culloch. Ruskin's assault was not quite strictly original. Carlyle, whom he called his master, had continually poured forth his epigrams, sarcasm, and nicknames about the "dismal science" and its professors. Dickens, Kingsley, and other romancers, had fiercely inveighed against the Gradgrind philosophy of labour and the moral and social curse it involved. . . . Ruskin was thus not by any means the first to throw doubts over the gospel of Ricardo and M'Culloch. But he was no doubt the first to open fire on the very creed and decalogue of that gospel, and he certainly was the first to put those doubts and criticisms into trenchant literary form such as long stirred the general public as with a trumpet note. (1902, 96–7)

But the reference in the *Cope's* image is "Wealth of Nations" not "Principles of Political Economy and Taxation" or "Population." The reference is to a work of an eighteenth-century economist, not a nineteenth-century one. How do we read this?

The Image of Wealth

The bag that the figure of the slain Other clasps has two lines written on it. The first is "L. S. D."; the second is "Wealth of Nations." Not only is the bag surely meant to represent monetary wealth (in addition to the book title) but the clothing represents considerable riches. How is this consistent with our supposed reading of the human figure with Negro characteristics?

Let us first consider the book that is so titled. The most outrageous claim in the *Wealth of Nations,* from the Carlyle-Ruskin point of view, is the hardest rational choice doctrine and the equivalent analytical egalitarianism. Why are these equivalent? In Smith's version of rational choice theory, the physical differences among people are trivial. Race does not matter; there are only incentives and history:

The difference of natural talents in different men is, in reality, much less than we are aware of; and the very different genius which appears to distinguish men of different professions, when grown up to maturity, is not upon many occasions so much the cause, as the effect of the division of labour. The difference between the most dissimilar characters, between a philosopher and a common street porter, for example, seems to arise not so much from nature as from habit, custom, and education. When they came into the world, and for the first six or eight years of their existence, they were, perhaps, very much alike, and neither their parents nor play-fellows could perceive any remarkable difference. About that age, or soon after, they come to be employed in very different occupations. The difference of talents comes then to be taken notice of, and widens by degrees, till at last the vanity of the philosopher is willing to acknowledge scarce any resemblance. But without the disposition to truck, barter, and exchange, every man must have procured to himself every necessary and conveniency of life which he wanted. All must have had the same duties to perform, and the same work to do, and there could have been no such difference of employment as could alone give occasion to any great difference of talents. (1976a, 28–29)

Here is Ruskin's hierarchical alternative wrapped up with portents of life and death:

[I]f there be any one point insisted on throughout my works more frequently than another, that one point is the impossibility of Equality. My continual aim has been to show the eternal superiority of some men to others, sometimes even of man to all others; and to show also the advisability of appointing such persons or person to guide, to lead, or on occasion even to compel and subdue, their inferiors according to their own better knowledge and wiser will. My principles of Political Economy were all involved in a single phrase spoken three years ago at Manchester: "Soldiers of the Ploughshare as well as Soldiers of the Sword": and they were all summed in a single sentence in the last volume of *Modern Painters*—"Government and co-operation are in all things the Laws of Life; Anarchy and competition the Laws of Death." (1903–12, 17:74–75)

Here is how Froude explains Carlyle's social policy as it was put forward in the "Negro Question." The trope that characterizes the Carlylean position is that racial slavery is an instance of Teutonic feudalism:

He did not mean that the "Niggers" should have been kept as cattle, and sold as cattle at their owners' pleasure. He did mean that they ought to have been treated as human beings, for whose souls and bodies the whites were responsible; that they should have been placed in a position suited to their capacity, like that of the English serfs under the Plantagenets. (1885, 2:15)

This should make clear both Ruskin's views of good slavery as they were expressed in his "Nature of the Gothic," which Lewin quoted, as well as the line in Ruskin's letter on Eyre about black emancipation in "due place and time." This presumably means when slavery turns Negroes white. Given sufficient time and sexual usage, this might not be an idle thought.

What about the "L. S. D." on the bag and the rich clothing? West Indian emancipation—as Froude noted—required a payment by the British taxpayer of 20 million pounds.[54] If the 20 million is the basis of this aspect of the image, then the spats and fancy dress surely signify that the Negro is an undeserving recipient. Safe within an understandable hierarchy, the black slave was better off than the "white slaves" from whom the 20 million was taken. Perhaps this parliamentary deal is viewed as robbery and so the homicide is justifiable?

That the transfer was undeserving is an assertion one finds in Carlyle's 1844 *Past and Present:*

O Anti-Slavery Convention, loud-sounding long-eared Exeter-Hall—But in thee too is a kind of instinct towards justice, and I will complain of nothing. Only, black Quashee over the seas being once sufficiently attended to, wilt thou not perhaps open thy dull sodden eyes to the "sixty-thousand valets in London itself who are yearly dismissed to the streets, to be what they can, when the season ends;"—or to the hungerstricken, pallid, *yellow-*coloured "Free Labourers" in Lancashire, Yorkshire, Buckinghamshire, and all other shires! These Yellow-coloured, for the present, absorb all my sympathies: if I had a Twenty Millions, with Model-Farms and Niger Expeditions, it is to these that I would give it! Quashee has already victuals, clothing; Quashee is not dying of such despair as the yellow-coloured pale man's. Quashee, it must be owned, is hitherto a kind of blockhead. The Haiti Duke of Marmalade, educated now for almost half a century, seems to have next to no sense in him. Why, in one of those Lancashire Weavers, dying of hunger, there is more thought and heart, a greater arithmetical

54. "In 1833 the great Act passed, emancipating all the negro slaves in British Colonies and decreeing payment of twenty million in compensation to the slave-owner" (Morley 1851, 402). The deal was very complicated. Even with the money and a tariff, the slaves needed to endure a seven-year period of transition, what was called an "apprenticeship." A very young T. B. Macaulay, then in Parliament, seems to have effected a reduction from the initial offer of twelve years to seven with one speech. The Jamaica crisis, which produced Carlyle's "Negro Question," was partly caused by the reneging on the tariff (Denman 1853). Macaulay in midcentury debates stands for more than a pungent stylist and the "Whig" historian: he was the last link connected by memory to Wilberforce himself. Macaulay's remarkable analysis of anti-Semitism juxtaposed against Robert Southey's position is studied in Felsenstein 1995, 250–52.

> amount of misery and desperation, than in whole gangs of Quashees. It must be owned, thy eyes are of the sodden sort; and with thy emancipations, and thy twenty-millionings and long-eared clamourings, thou, like Robespierre with his pasteboard *Être Suprême,* threatenest to become a bore to us. (1965, 275)

Here is a passage from Carlyle's 1849 "Negro Question," in which the 20 million pounds are also mentioned, with the unsubtle suggestion as to why they might have been better spent elsewhere:

> Exeter Hall, my philanthropic friends, has had its way in this matter. The Twenty Millions, a mere trifle despatched with a single dash of the pen, are paid; and far over the sea, we have a few black persons rendered extremely "free" indeed. Sitting yonder with their beautiful muzzles up to the ears in pumpkins, imbibing sweet pulps and juices; the grinder and incisor teeth ready for every new work, and the pumpkins cheap as grass in those rich climates: while the sugar-crops rot round them uncut, because labour cannot be hired, so cheap are the pumpkins;—and at home we are but required to rasp from the breakfast loaves of our own English labourers some slight "differential sugar-duties," and lend a poor half-million or a few poor millions now and then, to keep that beautiful state of matters going on. (671)

If we read the image through the Carlylean worldview, we can understand why newly emancipated slaves would be supposed to have stolen from white people. This would also explain the seeming anomaly in dress. We do not think of newly emancipated slaves this way, but the Carlyleans did.

Miscegenation and the "Nigger Philanthropist"

We began with a puzzle as how to read John Wallace's image. Clearly, it is an image of the war between economics and poetry. The juxtaposition of Ruskin on Pegasus with "The Dismal Science" suffices for this identification.

But still we have not confronted the problem of who Ruskin's enemy is. Is the enemy supposed to be a real person, someone of an apelike race? The best evidence for this reading is Ruskin's activity on behalf of Governor Eyre. This tells us that his 1853 words about the irrelevance of the death of black slaves is more than cheap talk. Is Ruskin's enemy supposed to be a personification of economic science? The best evidence for this reading is that the Carlyle-Ruskin emphasis on hierarchy in opposition to markets had a clear racial dimension. "The Dismal Science" can be read as the "Negro Science."

But there is another possible reading, which mixes both of these. Let us return to the text in which Carlyle coins the term *dismal science* and reread the next line:

> These two, Exeter Hall Philanthropy and the Dismal Science, led by any sacred cause of Black Emancipation, or the like, to fall in love and make a wedding of it,—will give birth to progenies and prodigies; dark extensive moon-calves, unnameable abortions, wide-coiled monstrosities, such as the world has not seen hitherto! (1849, 672–73)

Perhaps this gives us our third possibility. If the figure represents the union between "Black Emancipation" and "The Dismal Science," they have indeed had a wedding, and from this miscegenation a "dark extensive moon-calf," a "wide-coiled monstrosity," has been born. And it grew and grew until it was dispatched by Ruskin. This is the reading I should prefer.

This reading suggests that the Victorian "sages" read friends of the dismal science out of the white race. Is there any nonoblique textual evidence for this? From his most famous 1867 statement on the Eyre controversy, *Shooting Niagara*, here is Carlyle's description of the Jamaica Committee: "a small loud group, small as now appears, and nothing but a group or knot of rabid Nigger-Philanthropists, barking furiously in the gutter" (14).[55] Of course, this can be read as implying that the Jamaica Committee has left the white race, that it is simply crusading on behalf of nonwhites, or both. What forces the reading to be *both* of these possibilities is the word *knot*, which, when describing a group of people, has a special connotation in contemporary discussions. It has an Irish reference:

> The native Irish, who had been reduced to the condition of labourers, would club together and establish co-operative societies, or "Knots," of from ten to twenty families. (Sigerson 1870, 476)[56]

As we shall see, Carlyle proposes the common identity of black people and Irish. Thus, he has read the "Nigger-Philanthropists" out the white race.

But this in turn reveals a deeper puzzle. One does not need to have seen the image on the Smoke Room Booklet to know all about Carlyle's and Ruskin's

---

55. This paragraph is the result of Peart and Levy 2000, which argues for the importance of *Shooting Niagara*. Its link to *Time and Tide*, noted by Hilton (2000, 107), shows when Ruskin continues the mad dog image (1903–12, 17:437): "And it is a curious thing to me to see Mr. J. S. Mill foaming at the mouth . . ." See also page 445, where writing political economy is a far worse crime than "boldly to sign warrant for the sudden death of one man, known to be an agitator." Shaw (1921) gets the violence in Ruskin right.

56. The usage is not explicitly defined in the OED's definition of *knot*, even though one of the quotations illustrating *knot* as a group of people has an Irish context.

views on racial slavery. On the contrary, the image can be read because we know all too well what they thought about such matters.[57] What is so attractive about hierarchical order that modern scholars, who present the Victorian sages as guides for their time if not ours, "overlook" the facts that the theorized alternative to markets pressed by the nineteenth-century literary sages was racial slavery? And for these theorists the judicial murder of people of color was a policy option?[58]

Appendix: Ruskin v. Cope Bros.

As noticed previously, the highest authorities on matters concerning Ruskin, the editors of the great Library Edition, and on matters concerning *Cope's Tobacco Plant*, Richard Altick, have called attention to the case *Ruskin v. Cope Bros.* over the booklet which bears the image reproduced on the cover of this book.[59] What was the issue at the suit that led to the rapid withdrawal of the thirteenth of the Smoke Room Booklets? Perhaps those legally responsible for Ruskin, who was then incapacitated, were outraged by the cover image and appealed to the court to distance him from this sort of representation? Here these authorities do not speak.

In 1957 the University of Liverpool acquired the magnificent book collection and the papers of John Fraser who edited and printed both *Cope's Tobacco Plant* and the Smoke Room Booklets. In these papers there is a transcription of the court reporter's shorthand report of the trial held November 24, 1893 (Fraser 667).

In the transcript we can read the statement from Mr. Buckley who represents Ruskin's interests. After some pleasantries noting the fame of the contending parties, he describes the booklet to the Court:

> The subject of the application is an advertisement as I suppose I must call it which the Defendants have thought proper to put forward of their goods which is almost in its Entirety if not absolutely a bare faced & impudent reproduction of Mr. Ruskin's publication. A copy of the production should be handed to your Lordship and I will ask your Lordship to look at it. (Fraser 667, 1–2)

---

57. "You would imagine that no human being could ever have been under the slightest delusion as to what Ruskin meant and was driving at" (Shaw 1921, 8).

58. "After the events of 1865 English racial antagonisms crystallized more clearly than at any time since the collapse of the slave lobby. Eyre found enormous support for his legalized savagery, notably from Ruskin, Tennyson, Kingsley, Dickens and Carlyle. Their public utterances and those from sympathetic newspapers revived the very worst English attitudes towards the Negro" (Walvin 1973, 172).

59. This section, written after Chapter 2, owes its existence to Katy Hooper of the Library of the University of Liverpool who made the arrangements for my visit and who constructed the guide upon which I depended to the Cope material in the Fraser Collection.

He begins with the cover:

> It bears upon the face of it, outside, a representation of a horseman mounted on a horse, and from the features which it bears I suppose it is meant to represent Mr Ruskin, and he is impaling a figure at the bottom holding a bag which bears upon it the words "L.S.D. Wealth of Nations." (Fraser 667, 2)

And what do we make of this?

> I suppose that must be a representation of Mr. Ruskin's well known antipathy to political economy. (Fraser 667, 2)

It is interesting that the identification of anti-economics is made from the *Wealth of Nations* reference and not the "Dismal Science."

And the impaled figure? Nothing further is said. The silence seems to confirm Walter Bagehot's sneer that no one in his heart grieved for the death of a political economist.

After discussing various Cope's advertisements and Walter Lewin's preface, about which no objections were made, the body of the text is described:

> From page 7 to page 57—that is to say the whole of the body of the work—it is proved that those are simply verbatim reprints of passages from "Fors Clavigera" and they contain many of the most prominent and well known passages which are often referred to in that well known book. In fact it is about as gross an infringement of the authors rights as can be conceived. (Fraser 667, 3–4)

Then the argument sharpens:

> Then I will ask your Lordship to look at pages 58 & 59 because there is evidence of bad faith, in this sense. I shall tell your Lordship that Mr George Allen is Mr John Ruskin's publisher; and your Lordship will see upon page 58 a list of 6 books given and those are all books written by Mr Ruskin and which are published by Mr George Allen, Orpington Kent as his publisher; and your Lordship will find there is a note at the foot of page 58 which states that to be so, and upon the top of page 59 your Lordship will find "Ruskin on himself and things in general with an introductory notice by Walter Lewin Copes smokeroom booklets no 13 threepence." That is the booklet or pamphlet or whatever it is called the subject of the present application.

> Then follow two other works "Studies in Ruskin by Edward J. Cook" which is published by George Allen and another work "John Ruskin a Bibliographical biography by William E. A. Axon reprinted from Volume 5 of the papers of the Manchester Literary Club 1879." From the form in which that is put forward the unwary reader would be induced to think that this thing is a thing issued by Mr George Allen, because here is the publishers circular at the end of the book showing the things that he publishes. At the foot of page 58 you find "Mr George Allen publisher" placed before the interpolation of this little book and between them "Studies in Ruskin some aspects of the work and teaching of John Ruskin by E. J. Cook" intending I should have thought to have led to the conclusion that this is a book which had Mr Ruskin's authority. (Fraser 667, 4–5)

Thus we read Ruskin's attorney objecting to the authentic look of the booklet—beginning with the cover and ending with the bibliography. The case over the booklet was not because it was a misrepresentation of Ruskin's views; rather, it was too close a representation.

There are three factual matters which were claimed by the Cope attorney. First, in spite of the fact that there is a price marked on the cover, the booklets were given away so Cope's was not profiting from the sales. Second, *Cope's Tobacco Plant* had been assiduously calling attention to Ruskin's views since April 1875. Third, the booklet was if anything something which would increase the sales of Ruskin's own books, not take away sales. Ruskin's views (other than his views on tobacco!) and Cope's products were tied together. Cope's response raises a wonderful problem. Why was a commercial venture using antimarket ideology as a public relations device?

In a letter to Cope's attorney, the booklet's editor Walter Lewin seems to claim that if Ruskin had been in his right mind there would have been no suit, that this was a mutually beneficial form of advertising:

> Poor old Ruskin, I suppose, has nothing to do with it—only observe as dummy for a dull secretary or publisher, who had not the sense to leave a good advertisement alone. Not one person could have been prevented from buying Ruskin's books, by reading the Booklet, but I doubt not many were led on by it, to them. I suspect that suggestion that the sale had increased, went home. (Fraser 667 (Lewin letter) 1–2)[60]

---

60. The role of Cope's words and images in the attack on economics is something which Sandra Peart and I are considering.

TWO

Ecce Homo: Symbols Make the Man

A Topical Falsification of a Symbolic Reading?

There was a day when I believed that I would have to retract my reading of the John Wallace image on the cover of *John Ruskin on Himself and Things in General*. As I had presented this reading at one conference, had promised to present it at another, and was planning to use it to open a book, the reader can easily believe that I was not amused.

On May 23, 2000, I received an e-mail missive from Christine Holden. She asserted, emphatically, that the image must be read topically. The "dragon's" face was that of a real person who was not Negro. That is a fact. In the twenty-nine years I have known her, she has never been wrong on an important matter of fact.

So why had I single-mindedly a pursued a symbolic interpretation? There are two reasons: one good and one not so good. The good one is that I had spent the last five years immersed in the language community, in which the "dismal science" had meaning. The not so good reason is that as an American who specializes in the history of economic theory I have no idea what most of the debaters look like. Thomas Carlyle and J. S. Mill are familiar, of course, but I am not sure, for instance, that I would have recognized the image on the winged horse as Ruskin without the label. If I remember it correctly, when I first saw the image, I read the title of the cartoon book before looking elsewhere.

It would not be good to give up a theory without developing its implications, so what might be said in favor of a symbolic interpretation? In fact, there is something that I had not noticed before. The Cope's tobacco advertisements themselves contain symbolic opposition! On the rear cover of Smoke Room Booklet number 5 (Carlyle 1890), there appears an advertisement for Cope's Golden Cloud brand in which the oppositional figure that Richard Altick had noted appears.[1] The same figure of a wowser—to use that invaluable Aus-

---

1. "A clergyman with umbrella, long ulster, gaiter, big feet, and pious mien" complete with a leaflet in his pocket upon which one can read "Anti-Tobac" (Altick 1951, 341). The broad-brimmed hat suggests a Quaker.

tralian term, which entered the language two decades later[2]—appears on the rear of the James Thomson (1889) entry in the series. There he seems shocked by an advertisement for the Smoke Room Booklets series itself, as he gazes at a list that features a *Smoker's Text Book* as well as the Thomson, Charles Lamb, and Carlyle entries.

Moreover, the St. George image is neither the first nor the only instance in which Cope's features Ruskin himself doing violence to the symbolic enemies of the Carlyleans. One of Cope's major promotions was a colored sheet described with characteristic wit as the *Peerless Pilgrimage to Saint Nicotine of the Holy Herb*—sized 17.5 x 22 inches and priced at sixpence for 1878 subscribers to *Cope's Tobacco Plant* and one shilling for others (fig. 2).

It features what seem to be naturalistic caricatures of literary and political figures. Along with this massive color sheet, there is a booklet entitled *Cope's Key* and a sepia decoding card with numbers.[3] Here we easily find an image of the mounted Carlyle (numbered 7 in the figure) followed by Ruskin (9). Ruskin's horse is trampling a sorry sort of person who is labeled Cant. The easily identifiable broad-brimmed hat, which has been kicked off his head, and the tract in his hand, unreadable on the card but proclaiming "Anti-Tobac" in the original painting, identifies him as the dread wowser.[4] The suggestion of horns indicates perhaps the reason why he is being crushed. The "verse" I quote explains why Ruskin is doing violence to this demonic enemy. Ruskin is introduced with broad enough hints as tagging along behind Carlyle. Carlyle himself is simply identified:

> he is called Carlyle,
> That is, the doughtiest carle in all our isle.
> Him followeth his loyal Squire (9); and he
> Hath wrought brave things in Venice of the Sea,
>
> .   .   .   .
>
> He rideth ramping like a new St. George,
>
> .   .   .   .
>
> Beneath his horse a scurvy wretch is sprawling,

2. The OED entry for *wowser*, which describes a latter-day Puritan with an authoritarian ideology, does not allow for the existence of a free market wowser. The difference, as illustrated by a homey example, is important and might help explain certain gaps in this book. The OED wowser, who as a University of California at Berkeley student in the 1960s, when invited to a party promising drugs, sex and rock and roll, would have (1) declined or (2) informed the authorities. The free market variant would attend in search of an argument but, expecting to be episodically bored, would take a book along for amusement.

3. The watercolor original has neither numbers nor lettering other than that attached to the wowser (Wallace 1878).

4. A smaller version of the image is included in as a plate in Thomson 1889. The poster's tract is "Political Economy."

Fig. 2. Cope's modern pilgrims. (From *Cope's Key*.)

> With vast jaws open for a monstrous bawling;
> A lank and long-eared mar-joy, mainly bent
> On shuffling through the sloughs of discontent;
> Incapable of pleasure even in pelf,
>
> . . . .
>
> A blatant brawler, bilious and bad-blooded,
> With heart, mind, soul and sense all muddle-muddied;
> An Anti sour 'gainst all things sweet and good,
> Who'd make earth ante-hell an if he could,
> Whose head is wooden and himself stark wood;[5]
> A puny infidel to our sweet Saint;
> There let the horses kick him till he faint;
> Why should he come a-lying by the way
> In hopes to disarrange our fair array? (*Cope's Key* 1878, 18–19)

Thus, there is actually something to be said for a symbolic reading of the Ruskin image. The Cope's Smoke Room Booklets are full of symbolic opposition. And Ruskin himself as St. George is set against the common enemy, demonic forces that threaten Englishmen.

There are topical references in the *Pilgrimage* also that may provide a context for the racial violence in the Smoke Room Booklet image.[6] Consider the three diminished human figures—numbers 31, 32, and 33—sitting on a potato in the lower left corner and the two similarly sized figures—numbers 34 and 35—being held in a bottle. At this distance, who but a specialist might glance at the image and tell us who these figures represent and why they are so imagined?[7] No matter. This *Pilgrimage* is designed precisely to puzzle even its contemporaries; the *Key* is provided to open all these mysteries to anyone who wishes to read it:

> That insects who believe their country is well served when she is made contemptible should drop by the way and be transformed, as Parnell (33), Biggar (32), and O' Connor Power (31)—the Colorado Beetles who devour the metaphorical potato; or bottled for exhibition—as Nolan (34) and Gray (35), over whom the compatriot O'Sullivan (36) keeps watch—is not wonderful. The congratulation arises on the happy circumstance that no orisons of theirs can reach the shrine of Nicotinus.[8]

---

5. Here the "printer's devil" adds in a note: "*Wood* here means *mad*." This is certainly a novel way to meet the demands of the rhyme scheme!

6. This section owes its existence to a chance visit from Maria Pia Paganelli. She saw everything first, including the need to look up *Colorado beetle*.

7. In the color original (Wallace 1878), the sense is easier to spot.

8. The OED entry for *Colorado beetle* informs us that in the larval stage it is the dangerous potato bug and provides this quotation from 1877 (the year before the image was printed): "Act 40

The subhumanization of the Irish nationalists, putting humans-insects on a potato or in bottles for display, is pretty clear. The public's health demands their extermination. But it is not over yet. The nastiest part, the aspect that persuades me that this is no joke, requires that one know that an "orison" is a prayer and the "happy circumstance" is not simply the death that comes to all of us but, in this Christian language community, death without hope. Hamlet saw his chance to kill Claudius at prayer but passed it over, thinking that Claudius deserved death and Hell, not death and hope. More than 120 years have passed; still, read the words and the hate screams: life in a bottle for the subhuman and a death suitable only for beasts, one without Christian hope, for those who threaten the public health. Like *Hamlet* itself, we who have survived the twentieth century know how *this* story ends.[9]

Thus, Cope's practice has both topical and symbolic opposition. How interesting. The reader, who has surely figured out the next step, will perhaps wonder what has taken me so long to get around to it. Adam Smith's sympathetic principle, which explains this asymmetry, does not allow exchange of minds, only positions, and the reader has not been rattled.

Behold, the Man

Now, I've caught up with the reader. What if the Ruskin image is *both* topical and symbolic? That is surely what Holden meant: the symbols are instantiated in a real person. Can the symbols lead us to the man? If so, the symbolic reading is made more nearly complete along the lines required by Holden.

We can collect the important symbolic elements from above. (1) He must be known as an economist. (2) He must be involved in the general racial debates on Mill's side. (3) He must be on the Jamaica Committee and against Eyre. The topical requirements seem to me to add the following elements to the list. (4) His face must be recognizable in 1893 without a label. (5) He must be viewed by the Carlyleans as an oppositional figure perhaps as important as Mill himself. (6) From the violence in the picture, he must have been the subject of deep hatred. (7) He has a broad face, without much hair on the front of his head, with neither beard nor mustache. Together the first six elements of this list point to a very small number of public figures or they point to no one at all.

The first six elements of the list suggest one and only one person to me: John Bright.[10] Before we see what Bright actually looked like, I shall move through the list, checking those requirements that are satisfied.

& 41 Vict. c 68 Sect.1 The Privy Council may make such orders as they think expedient to prevent the introduction into Great Britain of the *Doryphora Decemlineata* or Colorado Beetle."

9. Zyklon-B, the agent of the final solution, is an insecticide. The OED gives the following edification: "1944 Chem. Abstr. XXXVIII. 3416 The application of Cyclon B (0.4 g./cc.) for 24 hrs. destroyed all insects but imparted a peculiar taste to the tobaccos."

10. I actually thought of John Bright for 1, 2, 4, and 5. Items 3 and 6 occurred to me as I was checking. The reader has to remember that I was rattled!

1. Economist? A leading member of the Anti–Corn Law League and the cohead of the "Manchester School of Economics" (Grampp 1960).

Check!

2 and 5. Antiracism? In the following paragraph, the cofounder of the British eugenics movement, W. R. Greg, attacks Mill and Bright for race-blind theorizing.

> "Purchase the estates of English and absentee landlords, and then re-sell them to Irish middle-class tenants in decent-sized farms," says Mr. Bright, who, again, like Mr. Mill, fancies that an Irishman is an English or a Scotch or a Swiss or Belgian cultivator. (1869, 79)[11]

Check!

3 and 5. Anti-Eyre? Bernard Semmel tells us this from the inside of Jamaica Committee debates:

> John Stuart Mill, strongly supported by John Bright, was the most forceful advocate of prosecution. This was a matter he was determined to see through to its end, he asserted. If Eyre were not prosecuted, Mill argued, every rascally colonial official would be given a free hand to perform mischief, and a horrible precedent affecting the liberties of Englishmen would be set. (1962, 69–70)

The 1866 *Fraser's* article by James Archer quoted next is so vile that the editor prefaces the piece with this information:

> The writer of this article has been personally connected with the scenes which he describes; a temperate expression of *white* opinion from Jamaica itself will not be unwelcome at the present crisis, although of *evidence* of the intended rebellion it will be seen that he contributes nothing, and appears to be unaware of the necessity for such a thing. (Archer 1866, 161)

Archer tells us what we need to know about Bright:

> The Governor, constantly on the move, had arrested Mr. G. W. Gordon, the supposed instigator of these disasters, and conveyed him on board H. M. S. *Wolverine,* whence he was removed to Morant Bay, tried by a court-martial, and executed within three days after its sentence. On the

---

11. Peart and Levy (2000) consider Greg's role in the Carlylean-eugenics enterprise and quote the paragraph attacking Mill. For Greg's role in the Anti-Corn Law campaign, see Grampp 1960, 107, 110–11.

legality or necessity of this "murder," as it is described by Mr. Bright, we offer no opinion pending the report of Sir Henry Storks. (176–77)

At this point, the editor interjects the following telling footnote:

After perusing the reports of the court-martial, the reader will probably be less forbearing. The evidence on which Mr. Gordon was convicted was not enough to hang a dog upon. (177)

Check!

4. Familiar face? For reasons that are beyond my competence, Bright's face seems to have been difficult to draw well.[12] No matter, there is a grand statute available for inspection at the Birmingham Art Gallery, Albert Square, in Manchester and the Houses of Parliament (Bright 1930, 538).

Check!

5. Opposition? Perhaps the best statement of the comparative public importance of Bright and J. S. Mill comes in the 1867 *Punch* cartoon used as the frontispiece in a collection of Bright cartoons (*Punch* 1878). In it, we see Mill himself as cupbearer to a brass-knuckled Bright, who is exercising on a crowned punching bag we are encouraged to read as "Aristocracy."

Let me provide two addition examples of Carlylean opposition in a literary context, which seem to me to illustrate the depth of the hostility. In 1855, a year after returning from his adventures in Mecca, Richard Burton published a pseudo-Arabic poem, *The Kasîdah* which contains the following stanza:

See not that something in Mankind
    That rouses hate or scorn or strife,
Better the worm of Izraîl
    Than Death that walks in the form of life.
(Burton 1926, bk. 9, stanza 29)

Burton glosses *Izraîl* as "The Angel of Death."[13] This is surely a reference to Bright's 1853 "Angel of Death" speech protesting the carnage of the Crimean War.[14]

---

12. Bright 1930, 433: "To Mr. Millais. Gave him an hour and a half. Progress; but he is not well satisfied. He finds the 'mouth' the difficult feature, as other artists have found it." This is, of course, "Mr J. E. Millais, the great painter" (Bright, 428).

13. At Yom Kippur, by tradition, two scapegoats are selected and lots are drawn, one for the Lord and one for Azazel, an angel of death.

14. "The Angel of Death has been abroad throughout the land; you may almost hear the beating of his wings. There is no one, as when the first-born were slain of old, to sprinkle with blood the lintel and the two side-posts of our doors, that he may spare and pass on; he takes his victims from the castle of the noble, the mansion of the wealthy and the cottage of the poor and lowly, and it is on behalf of all these classes that I make this solemn appeal" (Bright 1930, 190).

In Anthony Trollope's little-studied novel *The Fixed Period*, the colony's perfectly reasonable plan to exterminate the old people is thwarted by the untimely arrival of a gunboat sent by the British Minister of Benevolence.[15] The gunboat's name is the *H. M. S. John Bright* (Trollope 1993, 116).

Check!

6. Violence toward Bright? Bright's overarching political radicalism has been described in the standard account of the Manchester School as "subversive."[16] But was there violence in a racial context? Here we can appeal to Bright's diary from the time of Eyre:

> To *Star* office: talk about Jamaica prosecutions with Mr. Gorrie and Chesson. Received note warning me of plot to assassinate me on Tuesday next! My letters contain many that are curious, and some that are insulting and offensive." (1930, 295)

And from the other side let us read Carlyle's *Shooting Niagara* as he whoops up his fellow "progressives." The words I emphasize in the passage suggest that Eyre's opponents have taken leave of their human status. They have lost the ability to cry havoc and unleash the dogs of war; they are the disease-ridden dogs of war:

> [R]eal and fundamental, anterior to all written laws and first making written laws *possible*, there must have been, and is, and will be coeval, with Human Society, from its first beginnings to its ultimate end, an actual *Martial Law*, of more validity than any other law whatever. Lordship, if there is no written law that three and three shall be six, do you wonder at the Statute-Book for that omission? . . .
>
> Truly one knows not whether less to venerate the Majesty's Ministers, who, instead of rewarding their Governor Eyre, throw him out of window to a small loud group, small as now appears, and nothing but a group or knot of *rabid Nigger-Philanthropists, barking furiously in the gutter*, and threatening one's Reform Bill with loss of certain friends and votes. (1867, 13–14; my emphasis).

---

15. Trollope 1993, 123. The text's modern editor, David Skilton (in Trollope 1993, x–xvi), argues against a nonironic reading. For example, Trollope "is reported to have angrily told an enquirer, an 'intimate friend,' that he *meant* 'every word' of the *Fixed Period*. His retort is grandly unhelpful." Skilton is silent about Carlyle.

16. "His ideas were called 'democratic' or 'republican,' at a time when those words had a subversive connotation" (Grampp 1960, 128)."He came to be regarded as an opponent of the monarchy, and occasionally was spoken of, only half in humor, as the first President of Great Britain" (129).

Thus, we find a public health justification for exterminationism. Is there an earlier one?

Americans living months after the Civil War may have had a somewhat more intimate relationship with violence than British readers of that era. Here is a quote from an 1866 issue of the Boston reprint journal, the *Living Age*. The article, which originally appeared in the *Saturday Review*, is entitled "Philosophers and Negroes." In it, we are introduced sarcastically to Carlyle's position on human worth:

> And, though a Jamaica negro's life may be a sham from the point of view of the Immensities, still it is a sort of reality to the creature himself. But then, of course, Mr. Carlyle is a great humourist, and on the humouristic side there is a good deal to be got out of the noise and fuss that has been made about a few "two-forked radishes," black radishes, strung up in the air. If one is given up to listening to the Heavenly Sphere-Music, why the shrieks and yells of a score of niggers, under the lashes of a scourge made of pianoforte wire, naturally fall on deaf, inattentive ears. . . . Besides, Mr. Carlyle has propounded a universal poser which makes very short work of any tearful claim for sympathy on the part alike of negroes and white folk. Rights! he exclaims somewhere, Why what right had'st thou even *to be?* ("Philosophers and Negroes" 1866, 181)[17]

His disciple's characteristic position on the relative worth of black and white is then explained in the context of statements expressed at a meeting in support of Eyre. Blacks are afflicted with slavery; whites with a railroad. As we have already encountered Ruskin's "analysis" of the racial transformation wrought by the iron agent of industrialization, it is easy to guess which for Ruskin is the greater affliction:

> Mr. Ruskin's anger against the disfigurements inflicted on London and the suburbs by railways is very hot indeed. The connection between the London, Chatham, and Dover Railway and negroes was not easy for a plain man to see, but Mr. Ruskin is not to be baffled by any difficulties of this sort. So it appears that he began by saying that he hated all cruelty and injustice, by whomsoever inflicted or suffered, and from this he advances straight into the Metropolitan Extensions. "He would sternly reprobate," he said, "the crime which dragged a black family from their home to dig your fields; and more sternly the crime which turned a white family out of

---

17. I do not know the original source of Carlyle's "two-forked radishes" reference, but the Ruskin quotation is accurate.

their home, that you might drive by a shorter road over their hearth." That is to say, metropolitan extension is positively a worse crime than slavery. The promoter whose line obliges a working-man to go and live somewhere else is actually more guilty than if he were a slave-trader. The horrors of the Middle Passage were less worthy of reprobation than the horrors of having to move from here to the street round the corner. (182)

In 1869, a writer in *Putnam's* puts the specific statements justifying Eyre in the wider context of Carlyle's philosophy, linking his antieconomics with his proviolence:

It is always anti-democratic, anti-economical, and anti-philanthropic; its notes are force displayed in war or arbitrary government—a contempt for political economy and every thing akin to it—a readiness to shed blood. ("Thomas Carlyle as a Practical Guide" 1869, 522)

Then the target of the violence at home—the dogs of war—is suggested:

Mr. Carlyle and his chief imitators did not fail to exhibit their personal "force" on the occasion. Mr. Carlyle called the Jamaica Committee, the leading names on which were those of John Bright, John Stuart Mill, and Thomas Hughes, "a group or knot of nigger philanthropists, barking furiously in the gutter. . . ." Mr. Ruskin, who here displayed again the manly vigor which he had exhibited in applauding the butcheries which followed the Indian mutiny, published his "more than contempt" for men whose his contempt alone would scarcely crush. (528)

Check!

7. Pictures of the real John Bright are easy to find. The National Portrait Gallery has a lovely collection available for inspection. We see a representation of a broad-faced Bright with more forehead than hair, no beard, and no mustache, only an elegant set of mutton chops.

What if we require a Bright imagined in cartoon form?[18] That wish is easy to grant. In the *Pilgrimage*, Bright is identified as number 44 (*Cope's Key* 1878, 14). His broad, gruff face, vacant forehead, and wisp of mutton chops—this is how he is identified:

John Bright (44), always a man of peace—save when Ottoman barbarism calls for a new Crusade—is happy in a smoker's reverie of "auld lang-syne."

---

18. Wendy Motooka asked this question.

Fig. 3. Dr. Dulcamara in Dublin. (From *Punch* 1878.)

Perhaps an even more informative cartoon of Bright (fig. 3) was published in *Punch* on November 10, 1866 (*Punch* 1878). Here, portrayed as a vendor of patent medicines, he is hawking "Radical Reform" to Irish listeners. Note the apelike teeth and jaws. Nonhuman teeth we have seen before.

Check? If I did not think so, this section would not exist. However, the reader will have opinions on the matter of this correspondence between prediction and fact.

Conclusion

This solution I believe satisfies the Holden challenge: find the man. Bright, and as far as I know Bright alone, fits the symbols. This solution also satisfies James Buchanan's worry that the face—when one looks closely—does not match the cartoon stereotype, with which Buchanan, as an American of southern extraction, is all too familiar. Perhaps this is the cartoon of what Carlyle in his pleasant way labeled the "Nigger-philanthropist": one who carries with him the dismal science and has taken leave of his human status. Symbols of race and hatred merge in opposition to the dismal science.

THREE

Beginning with an Exchange or with a Command?

In the Beginning

> Some say the world will end in fire,
> Some say in ice.
> —*Robert Frost 1968, 220*

Although this book is about beginnings not endings I too have a bifurcation to propose. Some propose that the social world of persons begins with a command, and some propose that it begins with an exchange. Adam Smith surely holds with exchange, as he opens his 1776 analysis with an isolated couple, F. Y. Edgeworth's "catallactic atom," exchanging deer and beaver (Edgeworth 1881, 31).[1] Edgeworth's phrase of 1881 recalls Richard Whately's coinage, *katallactics*—"the science of exchange" from the Greek word describing exchange and reciprocity—offered in his 1831 *Introductory Lectures on Political Economy.* Just as surely, Carlyle holds with command, as he defines his Great Man in terms of the worship accorded him by the lesser.[2]

Does not exchange itself presume an ability to command things and thus at least a minimal sort of command over people? If something is mine to exchange, then can I command you to keep off? Is not, then, command foundational? No. Smith knew this answer because his friend David Hume modeled the process by means of which people obtain their right to command things as itself an exchange. In the Humean view, property—this right of a person to command a thing—requires a social exchange; property is a convention with which we buy social peace. Property is not foundational because if a thing were not scarce—and so my ability to command the thing does not

---

1. Following nineteenth-century transliteration conventions, Whately and Edgeworth used a *c* to represent the κ in the Greek word for exchange and reciprocity.
2. "Society is founded on Hero-worship. All dignities of rank, on which human association rests, are what we may call a Heroarchy (Government of Heroes),—or a Hierarchy, for it is 'sacred' enough withal!" (Carlyle 1993, 12).

conflict with your ability to command it—then there would be no reason for the exchange and hence no reason for property to exist.[3]

Is there any command that is not based in exchange? What about Jean Bodin's undivided and immortal sovereign? Not if the katallactic analysis is correct. Sovereignty is also part of the process of exchange. Although this, too, is an implication from Hume, perhaps this consequence could not be easily appreciated until Whately added a note in the second edition of his *Lectures* (1832) emphasizing that the science of exchange covers taxation as well. Subjects trade taxes for their government's protection.[4] Whately characteristically made his point pungently when he wrote:

> And it is worth remarking, that it is just so far forth as it is an exchange,—so far forth as protection, whether adequate or not, is afforded in exchange for this payment,—that the payment itself comes under the cognizance of this science. There is nothing else what distinguishes taxation from avowed robbery. (1832, 10–11)[5]

I shall let Carlyle's 1833 statement make the consequence as clear as can be:

> [W]hoso has sixpence is Sovereign (to the length of sixpence) over all men; commands Cooks to feed him, Philosophers to teach him, Kings to mount guard over him,—to the length of sixpence. (1987, 31)

The universalization of exchange turns hierarchy topsy-turvy. Kings command their intermediaries, and they in turn command the poor, but the poor, through the mechanism of exchange, command kings. How is *that* possible? How can kings command and be commanded? Is that not a logical absurdity?

Of course it is not. Kenneth Arrow created quite a stir in the intellectual world, winning a Nobel Prize in economics in the process, for his demonstra-

---

3. As far as I know, Hume's theory of property was first explained by Arnold Plant in series of articles collected in Plant 1974. Can society have property with abundance? The "Lockean proviso," the critical step to make property justifiable, requires abundance. In Hume's theory, absent scarcity there is no property (Levy 1992, 94–97).

4. "I had not thought it necessary to observe that, in speaking of exchanges, I did not mean to limit myself to *voluntary* exchanges;—those in which the whole transaction takes place with the full consent of both parties to all the terms of it. Most exchanges, indeed, are of this character; but the case of taxation,—the revenue levied from the subject in return for the protection afforded by the sovereign, constitutes a remarkable exception; the payment being compulsory, and not adjusted by agreement with the payer" (Whately 1832, 10). The argument is explained in detail the next year (Whately 1833, 63–73).

5. I am indebted to Sam Papenfuss for showing me this aspect in Whately (Papenfuss 1998).

tion that majority rule may be intransitive. That is, merely because policy A is selected pairwise over B by majority rule and policy B is selected pairwise over C by majority rule, there is good reason to believe that C can still be selected pairwise over A by majority rule.[6] James Buchanan's comment on Arrow's demonstration, that intransitivity is actually the point of democracy, as it, and it alone, guarantees the absence of hierarchy, has been insufficiently appreciated (1954). In some sense, all of this was intuitively obvious to Carlyle when he described the concept of consumer sovereignty.

One attraction so many "cultural critics of capitalism" feel for Carlyle's criticism of market exchange may be precisely that he recognized that when market exchange enters hierarchy exits. Consumer sovereignty is thus a dire threat to the notion of a political sovereignty in which orders are given from up the hierarchy to be obeyed by those below. We have command without hierarchy, command without foundation. And, for anyone who thinks that the state or society is simply a person writ large, a state or a society without a hierarchy of desires is nonsensical.

We are perhaps currently witnessing the last of the great debates over hierarchy. The hierarchy of race is embarrassed memory. The hierarchy of religion is gone. The hierarchy of government is going. The last hierarchy alive and furiously defended is the hierarchy of culture. And I, who before the Web selected a bookstore to patronize on the basis of the number of Loeb editions it stocked, will address this issue how? This book is about beginnings not endings. And if economics fails to teach us about cost there is nothing it does teach.

Market Egalitarianism

It is convenient to define a political direction to the debates we shall consider. I think it is completely nontendentious to orient the discussion this way: those who defend property in persons are to the right of those who oppose property in things. Thus, the economists we study who defend property in things and attack property in persons find disputes on both their left and their right. The centrality of economists is easiest to appreciate if one takes seriously Smith's normative assertion that each person ought to have command over his or her

---

6. The difficult proof in Arrow 1963 would be a triviality if he had supposed that the democratic process was one of random representation (e.g., as in the election by lot practiced at Athens). No random process can be supposed transitive. It is not therefore an impossibility that Plato's criticism of contemporary democracy reflects knowledge of policy cycles and the like (Levy 1992, 135–54). One might view Arrow's theorem model theoretically as a demonstration that both models of democracy—election by lot and election by vote—share intransitivity.

time and the things that can be acquired in exchange for that time.[7] This doctrine we might label market egalitarianism. This doctrine, property in things not property in persons, will involve those who follow Smith in controversy from two directions.

Market egalitarianism has an intimate relationship with a broad form of utilitarianism. For utilitarians, there is something deeper in the moral universe than existing property rights; there is human happiness. Property for a utilitarian is not part of the furniture of the world; some forms of property are helpful to human happiness while other forms are impediments. A utilitarian supports the former and opposes the latter.

Since there are two debates involving economists, one pointing right and one pointing left, is there an unambiguous way to come to a judgment of the net effect of these controversies? Not for the last time, I shall invoke, hypothetically, a principle that can be attributed to Karl Marx. If the point is to change the world, then the answer about the real importance of classical economics is clear as long as we get the real world right. And although there were models of socialist societies—the various utopian communities are a favored topic of scholarship—there were no socialist societies to change. The existing eighteenth- and nineteenth-century alternatives to markets were societies with racial slavery. Thus, to the extent that classical economics was used in the struggle to replace property in persons with market exchange, in the space of the real world the impact of classical economics was to move the world to the left. The fact that there are few alive to explicitly defend racial slavery is evidence only of how complete that triumph has been. Classical economics remade the world.

Also, and not for the last time, I shall involve an idea attributable to George Berkeley. If we unreflectively judge the past in light of our status quo, we are likely to take as "conservative" those forces that produced the status quo. Successful radicalism tends to be invisible. One chapter will examine Berkeley's argument that by ourselves we cannot tell the difference between a big thing and a small thing when these things stand at different distances from our status quo. If we cannot tell the difference between big and small, how can we tell the difference between right and left? Since we live in a world of markets,

---

7. "The property which every man has in his own labour, as it is the original foundation of all other property, so it is the most sacred and inviolable. The patrimony of a poor man lies in the strength and dexterity of his hands; and to hinder him from employing this strength and dexterity of his hands; and to hinder him from employing this strength and dexterity in what manner he thinks proper without injury to his neighbour, is a plain violation of this most sacred property. It is a manifest encroachment upon the just liberty both of the workman, and of those who might be disposed to employ him. As it hinders the one from working at what he thinks proper, so it hinders the others from employing whom they think proper. To judge whether he is fit to be employed, may surely be trusted to the discretion of the employers whose interest it so much concerns" (Smith 1976a, 138).

this we can reach out and touch. But the institution that the Carlyleans defended as superior to the market we understand from experience is found in the dim, distant past. What exactly was it? Would it stand to our left or to our right? Is it more or less constraining than market order?

The economist's debate with the proslavery right shows in the oblique method by which the economists responded to the authors of the antimarket novels, Charles Dickens and Charles Kingsley. The Dickens-Kingsley position on the dreadful fate of British workers is voiced by a kindly slave owner in Harriet Beecher Stowe's *Uncle Tom's Cabin*. When Richard Whately reviewed *Uncle Tom's Cabin*, statements of this character were singled out for attention. Literary scholars who write as if they believe attackers of markets and defenders of racial slavery had nothing in common seem not to have noticed that this is how an economist responds to the industrial novels.

Attack from Their Right

Market egalitarianism is inconsistent with a slavery that gives one person the right to command another person's time. Commanding time means commanding things; market egalitarianism is inconsistent with a slavery in which the slave's acquisitions are not his or hers to command.[8] Carlyle's life's work, as I read it, was an attempt to develop a system of hierarchical obedience to oppose that which he pilloried as the "cash nexus" of market exchange. Of course, the theorist of hierarchical obedience is no more compelled to defend existing hierarchical institutions (e.g., American racial slavery) than the theorist of competitive markets is compelled to defend existing market institutions. Adam Smith, to give the greatest example possible, claimed that all too many of the existing markets of his time were only grotesque parodies of what he would defend as ideal. The shortcoming he found was largely the failure to conform to market egalitarianism.

We can appreciate Carlyle's idealization of hierarchy best when we find his industrious disciple Charles Dickens offering plans to "reform" American racial slavery. In contrast, those who idealized exchange had no plan to reform slavery. Five letters, appropriately arranged around a space, would exhaust their insight as to how to bring existing slavery into correspondence with the ideal. These letters are END IT. Thus, in the debate between the abolitionists and the "reformers" of slavery, we can best see the idealized hierarchy; a slavery with-

---

8. One learns this from *Uncle Tom's Cabin*, as its best commentator explains: "You [Stowe] are careful to publish the fact that Mr. Legree took possession of the wardrobe of Tom, which, it seems, was rather abundant; that he made Tom divest himself of the handsome suit of clothes in which he bought him. . . . As a matter of course, if a slave owns not himself, he can own nothing else; and this is the truth, and is in exact accordance with the laws of slavery. Every thing pertaining to the slave is his master's" (Brimblecomb 1853, 102–3).

out "abuses." In the view of those who idealized exchange, slavery is an abuse of human nature itself.

It will be apparent, if it is not so already, that I view the world in competitive terms. Philosophers offering a vision of a world of exchange compete with those offering a world of hierarchy. So stated, this competition seems preposterous. Why would anyone trade a position as a free worker to become a slave? But that wasn't the actual deal on the table. Carlyle offered the chance to be a master. And how does it happen that we can all be masters?

Here is the trick. All *Christian white* people can be masters.[9] As long as there are enough black slaves to harvest the spices we want, what does it matter if there are few people higher still? And there would be black slaves for all if those beastly economists and their Christian allies did not muck up the natural order of things by going around and freeing the black slaves. Why do economists and their Christian allies care so much about people who do not look like us, who do not believe like us and are so far away?[10] Carlyle's pet phrase is "charity begins at home." Perhaps it needs to be said that it also ended there.

Attack from Their Left

What follows is an attempt to come to an understanding of how those who hold with market egalitarianism were attacked from their right. But of course market egalitarianism will not be satisfactory to those who hold with a more thoroughgoing egalitarianism. The command over things that property presupposes restricts the access of other persons to those things. This command over things William Godwin proposed to abolish. This debate has been heavily studied and is a matter of textbook record.

Five assertions underlie the textbook view of this debate, which informs far too many claims about the "fact" of the dismal science. (1) It begins when William Godwin proposed to abolish property and government as a way to bring about an egalitarian society. (2) T. R. Malthus's principle of population was a response to Godwin, as it made the claim that social hierarchy was natural; that is, that the condition of the poor is fixed by their choices. (3) In the context of the French Revolution, Malthus's doctrine served to defend social hierarchy as natural. (4) The later economists, David Ricardo in particular,

---

9. Just what it means to be "Christian" will be addressed later. It's not "man and brotherism."

10. The political use of racial doctrine explains the oddity that the racism presented was in avowedly stereotypical form, which admits of no exceptions to generalizations. It is not presented in statistical form, where of course there is a distribution of characteristics. Statistical form admits of outliers/exceptions that would ill serve the political purpose of justifying the slavery of the "Other." Perhaps an Other of ability is less destined for slavery than one of "us." That is a dangerous thought. I am indebted here to a clarifying conversation with Bryan Caplan.

used Malthus's fixed-wage theory as the central empirical regularity on which to build a distribution theory. (5) The dismal science is a judgment offered by egalitarians about the claim of the natural hierarchy of the type described in claims 2–4.

The textbook view of the debate has far-flung consequences. To offer one that is relevant to what follows, it can be used as evidence for the view that "art moralizes." Great art makes great human beings, so art ought to be in a hierarchical relationship with market activity. How does this follow from the textbook view? The *critics* of economists included the greatest literary artists of Victorian Britain: Carlyle, Dickens, Kingsley, and Ruskin. Their art gave them a vantage point from which the naughty policies of the economists could be exposed. The alternatives that these literary artists supported are vague in the textbook account.

Malthus's defense of property in a world without abundance seems to me to constitute a nice instance of Hume's theory of property. It ends the way such debates usually do: one does not get rich by betting against David Hume. By accepting as fact Malthus's account of American birth rates and choosing to save his dreams at the expense of life, Godwin gave up, his friends judged, and Malthus discontinued arguing against the nonproperty ideal in late editions of his *Population.* That argument ended (Levy 1999b). And this has absolutely nothing to do with the dismal science.[11]

The Malthusian controversy does, however, have an important feature in common with the debates over hierarchy that we shall study. It is very difficult for readers trapped in the present to see how radical the position of the economists was. Here is another instance in which successful radicalism is invisible. (Levy 1999b). Here, too, successful radicalism changes the status quo, from which we view the past. Just as it seems hard to understand why Protestant Christians would oppose birth control, it seems hard to understand why anyone without a financial interest would favor racial slavery. But if successful radicalism is invisible to someone who judges debates in terms of our status quo, what does that do to our understanding of the opponents of the radicals?

The antislavery coalition included both neo-Malthusians (the contemporary term for someone pro–birth control), utilitarians, and Christian thinkers. If we do not understand the depth of the coalition disagreement over the issue of sexuality, happiness, and divine commands, we will fail to wonder about the importance of an issue that would find evangelical Christians and utilitarians in alliance.

Consider the fact that when Harriet Beecher Stowe toured England what she wanted most was to meet with Lord Macaulay. Vast was his personal

---

11. The issues of getting classical distribution theory right, textbook claims 2 and 4, are technical (Hollander 1979, 1997; Levy 1992, 1999b).

stature, as befits one who with one speech slashed five years off the transition of black West Indian slaves to market freedom, but he also was connected by memory to both Wilberforce and the early days of the *Edinburgh Review*. Stowe talked about Kingsley's and Dickens's views on "white slaves" with Richard Whately, the Church of England's archbishop of Dublin. Needless to say, such a pious Christian would not have encountered John Stuart Mill. But after the American Civil War there would come a time when her coreligionists would find themselves in dire need of allies to defend the importance of the rule of law for people of all colors. Foundational debates would be set aside during the moral emergency.

The attack on economics with which I am concerned comes from those who put forward an idealization of command, property in persons when it comes to that, to combat the classical economist's idealization of exchange and market egalitarianism. Carlyle is the great name here. Those in an existing hierarchical society, the American South of the 1850s, could acknowledge him as a theorist who defended slavery because, and only because, he thought it best. He was not a bought advocate for the position. He was not a slave owner. As Mill said in his response to the "Negro Question," Carlyle's essay provided the slave owners with an unbelievably important gift—an honest man defending their institution. And Carlyle had many friends who would talk like him.

And how is this remarkable feat of defending racial slavery to be accomplished? First, one "proves" that the slaves or potential slaves are not fully human. Second, one acknowledges that, while there are certain abuses that existing racial slavery allows, a suitably reformed slavery could make the slaves or potential slaves more nearly human.[12]

The question that perhaps the previous paragraph raises is: what has this to do with economics then or now? How would an economist be involved in a debate over who is or is not human? This is as good a place as any to begin the explanation.

As a way of making sense of both Smith's language and our difficulty in reading it, I propose to first describe what I take to be Smith's vision. Over half a century ago, Joseph Schumpeter argued for the importance of describing the "preanalytic vision" of the thinkers we study.[13] I believe this is right because I

---

12. The defense of the system of slavery acknowledging the "abuses" is confronted in Hill, Whately, and Hinds 1852, 244–45.

13. "[A]nalytic effort is of necessity preceded by a preanalytic cognitive act that supplies the raw material for the analytic effort. In this book, this preanalytic cognitive act will be called Vision. It is interesting to note that vision of this kind not only must precede historically the emergence of analytic effort in any field but also may re-enter the history of every established science each time somebody teaches us to *see* things in a light of which the source is not to be found in the facts, methods, and results of the pre-existing state of the science" (Schumpeter 1954, 41).

think it is easier to let go of a model than a vision.[14] "Model" seems to be a more flexible description of what I think Schumpeter is after with his word *analysis.*[15] Whether or not Smith's vision can be represented as a model—is it consistent?—is an open question I shall address. Without consistency, a vision is little more than an optical illusion.

Smith's vision is one of fixed human beings whose continual exchange produces the world of flux. In this moving world, the human alone is the constant quantity. Over the long years since Smith wrote, an economist can almost be defined as someone who participates in Smith's vision. If we disagree with Smith, it is at the level of the model not the vision. Without considerable effort, it is difficult to recognize how someone like Carlyle could disagree at the level of vision but still use—or pervert—Smith's model.

In Smith's vision, the exchanging human is the one unchanging element. This raises an obvious question: what counts as human? Here Whately gave an extraordinarily interesting gloss on Smith's own answer: to be human is to exchange. It was in this context that Whately proposed katallactics as the right name for political economy.

There is for Carlyle something terribly empty in Smith's vision: there is no natural hierarchy in the social world. While modern economists quarrel with Smith for having too much structure in his model, Carlyle quarrels with Smith for having too little structure in his vision. Smith's vision does not encompass race in any "natural" sense. Of course, Smith used the word, for example, when he begins a famous sentence with "That unprosperous race of men commonly called men of letters," but, as the sentence suggests, *race* among humans for Smith is just a word, something conventional, not part of the nature of things. The differences among nations and peoples are the result of their experiences and incentives. What distinguishes Carlyle from his lesser followers is an ability to participate in Smith's model while denying the vision.

The Smith-Whately test for the human can be sketched as follows:

To be human is to accept an advantageous trade.

It is entirely in this spirit that Carlyle then proposes

---

14. "It does require maturity to realize that models are to be used but not be believed" (Theil 1971, vi).

15. Economic terminology seems to use *model* as the narrowest interesting aspect of language, for example, what one proposes to estimate by econometric methods. The terminology of logicians, on the other hand, uses *model* as the widest interesting aspect of language, that is, a model is a collection of sentences from which all the other sentences in the language cannot be deduced. This elegant definition rules out an inconsistent collection of sentences (Chang and Keisler 1973, 9).

Behold: X refuses trade α,

and then he draws the inference

X is not human,

whereas the economists—Mill and many others—drew the inference

Trade α is not advantageous.

Of course, much more was said, as we shall see. Carlyle wanted to tell a story about why races defined by X required slavery for their humanization. The economists wanted to talk about the trades $\beta \ldots \omega$, which were in fact accepted by the Xs. But all this in due course.

Races that fail the Smith-Whately test in Smith's *Wealth of Nations* are in fact dogs. Dogs don't trade because they do not have a language in which to express the concept "fair." Carlyle concluded that races of "humans" who failed his version of the test can be treated as if they were dogs. Thus, races that fail the Smith-Whately test lose the claim to a shared moral community with humans. When choosing between helping humans and nonhumans, it is hard to argue that we ought not to help the human. The slogan Carlyle and his friends used to combat a vision of moral universality is "charity begins at home." This was not meant as a joke.

Idealized trading of the sort supposed for market egalitarianism is a relation between moral or legal equals. The idealization of competitive exchange I shall label the "katallactic moment" in economics. It is easy to appreciate that from a vantage point that idealized trade between equals, slavery would be viewed as the ultimate perversion of a social order. It will then be obvious why there was contention between economists of this period and those who presented an idealized slavery as a paradigm of human relationships.

In Coalition with Biblical Literalists

Carlyle's attack on economics is framed as a lecture at Exeter Hall—the London center of organized evangelicalism. The public choice problem is to make sense of the coalition of Christian evangelicals and economists that (1) ended the Atlantic slave trade, (2) abolished slavery in the West Indies, (3) maintained British neutrality in the America Civil War, and (4) fought against the death of the rule of law for persons of color in Jamaica. There would be no public choice issue if all the economists were evangelical Christians. Precisely because I do not wish to make this case, I owe the reader the evidence I know that would be helpful in making such an argument.

One ought to focus on two figures in the Clapham sect. The first is everyone's idea of a great economist: Henry Thornton. He brings the same spare elegance in his *Family Commentary upon the Sermon on the Mount* that he did to *Paper Credit.* The second is Macaulay, who I am prepared to claim made important contributions to economics proper. And with all the new attention paid to Christian economics of the period, a sizable collection of interesting and important antislavery Christian economists could be collected across the century.[16] Whately would be important, and with Whately comes Nassau Senior (Schumpeter 1954, 483–84) and the Whately lecturers.

I do not take this approach because I see in the desperation of evangelical Christians to bring the rule of law to people of all races a willingness to cooperate with other moral universalists. The consequence of this cooperation was to bend the Christian understanding of sexual morality, and with this bending our language was remade. Important words have seen their meanings change drastically in the last century. For instance, in the language community in which I live the word *economist* can be said to mean something akin to "a student of markets, that is, someone of the right." In the language community that I study, the word *economist* can be said to mean something akin to "a student of markets, that is, someone of the left." Here *liberal* means "unambiguously promarket." Pregnant with deep consequence is a drastic switch in the meaning of *birth controller.* In the language community in which I live, it means "an advocate of responsible behavior, someone achingly dull." In the language community that I study, it has an entirely different flavor, that of "an atheist, someone not to be trusted in the company of young women" (Holden and Levy 2001).

Watching the meaning of a word flip-flop as we move among language communities gives independent evidence that difficulties are waiting for us. W. V. Quine's research into language and logic has forewarned us of this theoretical possibility by means of his holistic doctrine: the meaning of a word is defined in the whole of the language. This general equilibrium approach to language braces us for the confrontation with what mathematicians have taught us to call a "high-dimensional" problem.[17] Each of the difficulties I have mentioned, and the ones to come, are dimensions. High-dimensional problems are generally intractable. Thus, my (risky) simplification of the problem—focusing narrowly on racial slavery instead of broadly on race and slavery—buys tractability by lowering the dimensionality of the problem.

It is common knowledge that the evolutionary biologists Charles Darwin

---

16. The reader who wishes to pursue this line of inquiry will find the learned work of Salim Rashid and A. M. C. Waterman of enormous help (Waterman 1991).

17. Richard Bellman (1958) was enormously important in terms of focusing attention on the dimensionality of a problem. His dynamic programming procedure is a method by which a higher dimension problem can be reformulated as a sequence of lower dimension problems.

and T. H. Huxley had some disagreements, as to the origin of species, with Christian literalists. Faded from this stock of common knowledge is the unspeakability of birth control during much of the nineteenth century, signifying as it did the deepest form of atheism.[18] Before the decriminalization of the dissemination of birth control material in 1877, I know of only one thinker whose ideas live outside the memory of specialists who was willing to publicly support birth control: John Stuart Mill.[19] Mill's atheism was public and pungent: he dared God to send him to Hell in case the Divine Calculus did not, in fact, correspond to the utilitarian alternative. (The narrow Utilitarianism of the neo-Malthusians will be later distinguished from broad utilitarianism.)

The last of the antislavery coalition's battles was its long losing fight to bring Governor Eyre to justice. The vast majority of the members of the Jamaica Committee were Christian evangelicals, and 10 percent were clergymen.[20] These were the spiritual heirs to the biblical literalists, who, persuaded that the Word of God reveals Adam and Eve to be the parents of the black and the white, concluded that racial slavery is an entirely wicked thing. The questions the evangelicals asked on behalf of black slaves were "Am I not a man and a brother?" and "Are not Adam and Eve parents of us all?" That both Darwin and Huxley joined and aided the Jamaica Committee is a wonder to behold. More wonderfully still was the committee's unanimous vote to elect Mill its head.[21] Pious, respectable Christians of their own free will were electing the Utilitarian of their time to speak for them?[22]

This is where I think our language was bent. Of all the Christian churches, it was the ultrarespectable Church of England, not a backwoods American sect of snake handlers, that first accepted the Utilitarian doctrine that birth control

18. The dissemination of birth control material in Britain was not decriminalized until the 1877 Bradlaugh-Besant trial. The reader who is under the impression that all "progressives" supported birth control is misinformed. Marxist leadership was in permanent, announced opposition (Holden and Levy, 1993). For the neo-Malthusians, Darwin's theory of natural selection became *the* alternative to talking about preventive checks to population. Roger Manvell (1976, 100–101) gives texts in which Darwin's venture into "social Darwinism" is sharply criticized. The inability of textual specialists to understand the difference between a neo-Malthusian and a social Darwinist suggests strongly that the relative cost of reading and writing has not attained a social optimum.

19. His support of birth control as a teenager distributing Francis Place's pamphlets cost him an encounter with the police. One reads jokes about this in the magazines of the time. His support continued into the magisterial *Political Economy.*

20. "[T]he Jamaica Committee had *clergymen;* thirty-two of the original 300 members of the Committee were ministers" (Semmel 1962, 64).

21. The initial head of the Jamaica Committee, Charles Buxton, resigned over differences in tactics. Was it prudent to attempt to prosecute Eyre for murder? "To no one's surprise, and amid great applause, John Stuart Mill was unanimously elected" (ibid., 71). The fact that no one was surprised is worthy of reflection.

22. The four adjectives Semmel uses to describe the committee members are *sober, respectable, pious,* and *serious* (ibid., 64). I believe that the second and third were never used to describe a public advocate of birth control until deep into the twentieth century.

within marriage is a moral act.[23] The evangelical pro-contraception forces, when the votes were counted at the decisive Lambeth Conference in 1930, were led by H. H. Henson.[24] In 1936, Henson would write an introduction to the *Yellow Spot*, an early documented account of the murderous policy at Dachau.[25]

If economic theory, developed by those economists more Utilitarian than Christian, provided weapons to evangelicals, could these weapons be used without some effect upon their users? Settled doctrine it is among Zen martial artists that in mastery of a weapon the weapon and the master merge.[26] By their mastery of Utilitarian weapons were the Christians thereby mastered by Utilitarianism? So I would conjecture, and mastered by this conjecture I shall emphasize the importance of the non-Christian Utilitarians in the coalition.

What united the coalition, I shall argue, was a shared moral universality encapsulated in a reciprocity norm. The two most important reciprocity norms proposed at the time were the Golden Rule of Christianity and the Greatest Happiness Principle of Utilitarianism. It will be important in my argument that major thinkers in the coalition agreed that these versions were formally identical. The "formal" is necessary because it lets us ignore the substance of what we mean by happiness. Is happiness more than what is chosen? Over that issue, the coalition members debated heatedly among themselves. When the issue is slavery, where the range of choice is drastically attenuated, the coalition's disagreement over the substance of happiness will not matter.

If the reciprocity norm were followed, then what? As partial compensation for my inattention to Thornton elsewhere, I shall give his answer. First, markets work as the textbooks claim; second, slavery ends.[27] To get at the intra-coalition logic, I shall work through Smith's account of the type of morality requisite for a market order. Smith argues that one needs a reciprocity norm

---

23. John Noonan (1965, 409) emphasizes the importance of the Lambeth vote of 1930 precisely because the Church of England was so close theologically to the Catholic Church.

24. H. H. Henson (1942–43, 2:270–75) frames the debates at Lambeth in 1930 in terms of Evangelicals versus Anglo-Catholics. He had previously been involved in a dispute that threatened to turn into Gorham II (252–55).

25. *Yellow Spot* is back in the news in an important context. Did T. S. Eliot have a role in *Criterion's* dismissive review? That he did is vital to the argument in Julius 1996, 167–73.

26. The classic reference is Herrigel 1953, with D. T. Suzuki's authoritative commentary.

27. Here is what a reciprocity norm does for market transactions: "If the buyer and the seller would put themselves in the place of each other; then, the fraud and iniquity of trade would cease." Here is what it does for slavery: "If all those, who possess power, would imagine themselves to be in the condition of him who is subjected to that power; if the slave owner would imagine himself the slave; and the oppressor suppose himself the oppressed; and would endeavour to do unto others whatsoever he would that others (if they were in his place) should do unto him; how many millions of mankind would experience a termination of their sufferings" (Thornton 1837, 123). The reader will notice that Thornton has used a Smithian sympathetic move to explicate the Golden Rule of Christianity!

and not much else. Both parts of the argument are important because the conjunction tells us how "thick" the morality has to be to hold society together.

Race, Sex, Gender, and Belief

Midcentury debates over socialism will enter my account only obliquely because an occasional theorist viewed slavery and socialism as kindred alternatives to the market.[28] I shall deal with neither racial issues per se nor issues of slavery outside a racial context.[29] Rather, I focus on the narrow issue of racial slavery because, as the argument was made, some races were proposed as natural slaves and some as natural masters.

Racial slavery also had a gender component: masters could use slaves sexually, and slavery made marriage tenuous.[30] When writers compare the fate of "white slaves" under existing markets and black slaves under the existing alternative to markets, it makes a difference whether they talk about men or women. No allegations were made that the masters had an interest in sexually using male slaves. Then, as now, rape is hard to observe and easy to deny. But Malthusian theory gave economists rather subtle tools with which they could point to the observable consequences of sexual slavery.

Malthus himself, like Smith, followed European convention with the analytical supposition that a man could only have one family at a time. Conse-

---

28. Nassau Senior made the profound analogy between slavery and the Poor Law in an 1841 article for the *Edinburgh Review*. In either alternative to a market, one works for someone else. "But mischievous as slavery is, it has many plausible advantages, and freedom many apparent dangers. The subsistence of a slave is safe; he cannot suffer from insufficient wages, or from want of employment; he has not to save for sickness or old age; he has not to provide for his family; he cannot waste in drunkenness the wages by which they were to be supported; his idleness or dishonesty cannot reduce them to misery; they suffer neither from his faults nor his follies" (1865, 47). "We have shown that during the third period [of the English Poor Laws] an attempt was made to give to the labourer a security incompatible with his freedom; to provide for him and his family a comfortable subsistence at his own home, whatever were his conduct, and whatever were the value of his labour. And we have shown that this attempt succeeded in what have been called the pauperised districts, and placed the labourer in the condition, physically and morally, of a slave;— confined to his parish, maintained according to his wants, not to the value of his services, restrained from misconduct by no fear of loss, and therefore stimulated to activity and industry by no hope of reward" (115).

29. The problem of transportation of convicted prisoners to Australia was posed as a problem of slavery by Whately (1834). This example is actually quite elegant because it considers a pure slavery purged of injustice and racial hierarchy. Indeed, to the extent that crime is a voluntary act and slavery the known and settled punishment, then this sort of slavery could be seen as voluntarily chosen by the criminal on a probabilistic basis. Larry Moss asked about discussions of voluntary slavery in the period.

30. T. F. Buxton—Wilberforce's political wizard—judged that emancipation had succeeded this way: "The best news continued to arrive from the West Indies of the industry and excellent behavior of the negroes. Crime had rapidly diminished; marriages had considerably increased" (1925, 167).

quently, the marriage decision was modeled as essentially one of timing: early marriage or late? Smith himself had made the pretty point that the value of children in America was such that, unlike her situation in Europe, a young American widow with children could readily attract a new husband using their labor as dowry.

Harriet Martineau, an avowed Malthusian, pointed out that the institution of racial slavery allowed a man *multiple* families—one white and the others colored. Proslavery writers had pointed to the paucity of southern prostitution, vis-à-vis northern standards, to argue for the moralizing effect of slavery. This very evidence Martineau used to make her case. She patiently explained to the analytically challenged how the fact that colored children can be sold changes a man's sexual rental-purchase decision. Why would a man rent a woman by the hour when he can buy her for a lifetime and keep their children to sell? Thus, the relative infrequency of southern prostitution becomes, post-Martineau, the compelling evidence of the massive hidden economy of interracial forced sexuality.

I am at a loss to explain why modern economists not do take Martineau seriously. The kindest explanation I can provide is that she handled her tools better than her readers are able to appreciate.[31] To remedy this underestimation, all one need do is read those who wrote to protest that what she said was true. No, that sentence is correct as written: I did not omit a "not." That is *exactly* what her enemies said: she was horrid because she told the truth. When rhetorical flourishes like this are employed, one might suspect that things are starting to fall apart.

We read in *Revelation* that following the opening of the seventh seal there will be a silence; it will last for half an hour, and then the angels of destruction will remake the world. In America, the silence lasted closer to fifteen years until Harriet Beecher Stowe, who as a young woman had been compared to Martineau, told her stories of sexual slavery. Then the remaking began.

The dimensions we confront do not end here. The idealization of slavery we find in Carlyle supposed that society embodied a natural hierarchy of ability that was held together by shared belief. Carlyle's slogan is the "gospel of labor." One owed obedience to those up the hierarchy and charity to those down the hierarchy. This is a rather "thick" sort of belief—there are lots and lots of things in the belief claims. This requirement for a thick morality must be contrasted with a claim that a desire for approbation and a reciprocity norm are really all that are needed in a system of morality to hold a market order together.

---

31. George Stigler (1949, 26–36) argues persuasively that the classical economists were at their best when it came to specific problems. If we are not interested in Martineau's problem, then it behooves us to find someone who was.

It is helpful to consider the way in which Smith treats moral questions as public opinion taken in an equilibrium state.[32] If morality is nothing more than public opinion, appropriately conceived, then we have as "thin" an account of morality as can be. Everyone pays attention to public opinion, so if morality is built out of public opinion then we do not really have to worry about nonbelievers.[33] The morality need not be populated with gods, demons, essences, afterlives, or a chain of being.[34] In point of fact, it might have such entities. But then again it might not. Smith looks to America to see an idealized religion emerging from a competitive process (Levy 1992).

The thinness of the morality required in economic accounts for a market order is interestingly close to the sort of belief claims that one might find pressed by the founders of the English Reformation. If one believes that the Bible is the Word of God in its infinity, but one also has a reasonable view of finite human capacities, then it is an obvious inference that we are all going to come to different conclusions as a result of our encounter with the divine.[35] We are going to get it wrong because the finite cannot grasp the infinite. There will be many interpretations; what persuades you will not necessarily persuade me. All that one can hope for is a serious inquiry. The thinness of what a Christian evangelical can mandate for belief and the thinness of what a Smithian must assume in order to give stability to a market order give us insight into how the antislavery coalition was linked.

High-dimension problems are full of surprises. The doctrine required for inclusion in the Church of England is a political matter. To the extent that church politics are interwoven with antislavery coalition politics, startling things might happen. Those who had hitherto minimal interest in religious disputes might intervene massively on the side of their coalition partners.[36]

---

32. Wendy Motooka describes contemporary unhappiness with the thinness of Smith's account (1998, 198–230).

33. Even economists pay attention to our citations. Journals and economics departments are ranked by citations. It is an amusing empirical illustration of the principle of rational choice scholarship that the competing rankings of departments are sensitive to the current departmental address of the author (Feinberg 1998)! One behavioral move in economics of economics is to posit citation-maximizing behavior (Levy 1988a; Feigenbaum and Levy 1993).

34. There is a reason why Smith was Kant's favorite among the British moralists. The major difference between the two is that Kant allowed for a rich set of infinities that would be precluded to Smith as a follower of George Berkeley (Levy 1988b).

35. Exodus 33:20: "Thou canst not see my face: for there shall no man see me, and live."

36. Consider the helpful account of the Gorham judgment in Leavis 1989. While she stresses the importance of Whately (then archbishop of Dublin), she overlooks the role of John Bird Sumner as archbishop of Canterbury in forcing the decision. Whately and Sumner are of course the two premier Christian Malthusians of the period. Her judgment is "It must be added to the credit of the Church, and characteristic of its traditional desire, in opposition to Roman Catholic dogmatism, to leave as much freedom as possible as possible for individual interpretation of its theology, that though the case was adjudged to Gorham, the *subject* of it was never settled, and no the-

What Is So Hard about That?

All of this is, I claim, rather easy to see if one bothers to read the debates of the time. But most of this is impossible to find if one reads the modern scholarship on classical economics and its Victorian literary critics. Now why might that be? To this metatheoretical question we turn next.

---

ological ruling was given" (3:45). The case was never about whether Church doctrine was Catholic or Calvinist but whether it was Catholic or open. Here is the glossing of Gorham's advocates', which stresses that the issue was a metatheological one: "Real Argument of Mr. Gorham's Counsel, that the Reformers left the Doctrine of Regeneration an open question" (Moore 1852, 249). Whately (1850, 6–7) began his argument by pointing out that the Anglo-Catholics responsible for the celebrated Oxford *Tracts* claimed a toleration for their views that they would deny to Gorham's.

FOUR

A Rational Choice Approach to Scholarship

Answering the question of why economists do not *know* the material seems to me to require a different type of machinery than answering the question of why textual specialists do not *report* the material. I am fortified in my approach by some personal experience. The reaction of a colleague who is an economist when learning the history of "dismal science" is predictable: "Good God, we were the good guys!" After scribbling down the name of the Carlyle article—which actually can be mentioned in public—my colleague will not remain long in conversation about the textual issues but vanishes in search of an old argument. The reaction of a colleague who is a textual specialist is equally predictable: "Of course I know where *dismal science* came from. I'm not illiterate." Since I have provided no new information, this conversation continues, turning to Macaulay's unenlightened opinion of Indian culture or Mill's fierce moral absolutism or something equally deplorable about these two in whose memory candles burn in my mind.

Not Reporting What Is

Scholars ought not consider ourselves outside the thrall of rational choice calculations. I view this not so much as old-style University of Chicago economics methodology—although it is that[1]—but as an exercise in moral universality. If people inside the model are supposed to be rational choosers, then the makers of models ought to be supposed to be rational choosers. We ought not to consider ourselves as differing in structure from those we study. On the question of whether the origin of *dismal science* is of interest, I find that the desires of economists differ from the desires of students of literature. Conse-

---

1. I am not certain whether it was Harry Johnson or Don Patinkin who first said that he would believe economics was a science when the students at Chicago found that fiscal policy matters and the students at Yale found that money matters. Ronald Coase said that one tortures the data until they confess. Feigenbaum and Levy (1996) give the references and a model of this folk wisdom.

quently, I shall propose one rational choice explanation for why economists do not see the issues in the texts and another explanation for why textual specialists do not choose to report them.

What does the scholar want? In some contexts, for example, when the scholar acts as an expert witness for one party in litigation, the answer is obvious. Since the litigants get to pick their experts, it surprises no one that the experts will see things the same way as the party that writes the check. Just as litigants always prefer one outcome over another, the folk wisdom of applied econometrics is that ofttimes scholars have subtle versions of such preferences, which we reveal by reporting what is most pleasing for us to believe.

There has been considerable attention paid to the ways in which statistical workers affect such preferences without recourse to data falsification or fabrication.[2] Because the data-generating process is random, there is some amount of slack in what to report. Think about the following gamble. You win with "heads" and I win with "tails." Suppose, unbeknownst to you, that I get to look at more than one coin in search of my favorite outcome, tails. Even if each coin were fair, this gambling procedure is obviously unfair. I can force things to come out my way by searching over more and more coins. Since this possibility—*specification search* is the common term—is indeed something that econometric folk wisdom warns us against, the response of the sensible reader of econometrics articles is not to get too excited about the results of an isolated study and cautiously wait for the reports of other workers, especially those with differing preferences.

Here is one way of posing the problem. It is easy enough to believe that someone of the right who believes in natural hierarchy, in other words, that the elite ought to guide the masses, would be attracted to at least some aspects of Carlyle's work. Thus, it can hardly come as a surprise that F. R. Leavis, that candid defender of elites and articulate enemy of mass culture, singles out Dickens's 1854 *Hard Times,* inscribed to Thomas Carlyle, as the greatest of Dickens's achievements. How, then, do we explain why critics from the left who describe themselves as Marxist, Raymond Williams in particular, have also singled out Carlyle and his followers as offering an important "progressive" cultural criticism of market exchange?

I think there is a simple answer here: waste not, want not. If one wishes to *attack* markets without having to become an economist oneself, it is hard to do better than to use Carlyle as a critic. Knowledgeable? Quotable? Absolutely. But Carlyle as defender of racial slavery and, when slavery fails to humanize this

---

2. Plagiarism, falsification, and fabrication are conventionally regarded as the sum and substance of scientific misconduct. This view unfortunately ignores the possibility of substituting technical alternatives that effect the same end at lower cost (ibid.). The American Statistical Association Statement on Ethics (2000) is completely sensible about this.

race, genocide? Well, why need that matter? And it will matter even less if the reader does not know about it. As market egalitarians, the classical economists were stuck in the middle between those who hold with property in persons and those who oppose even property in things. Attacks from their right can—after a bit of rational choice scholarship—be presented as an attack from their left.

No interesting writer who lives to produce a number of articles or a sizable book reveals all of his or her thoughts in any ten pages. Ten-page chunks of text are something like coin tosses or econometric specifications: there is enough randomness among them to allow the interpreter to emphasize one aspect of the author's work, at the expense of another, by selecting which one to talk about. As a case in point, in the bulk of Carlyle's works racial issues occur as a passing matter or not at all. The question facing a scholar who prefers to see markets in an unfavorable light, and so presents Carlyle's pungent opinion on the matter, is whether those textual coins revealing an unambiguous belief that blacks can be improved through slavery are to be picked up and reported.

Let me put forward a counterfactual possibility that motivates my explanation of interpretative silence by means of the hypothesis of rational choice scholarship. Markets without hierarchy, and the economists who study them, are not well loved in many parts of the scholarly community. If the "dismal science" label had been applied because a major figure such as Smith or Mill, or even an important secondary figure such as Whately or Martineau, had defended racial slavery along the lines immortalized in *Birth of a Nation*, can one imagine anyone literate not knowing *precisely* why economists are dismal? Would there be the slightest confusion about this?

This explanation of the desires of literary scholars is disciplinary. Literary scholars prefer the Pegasus-eye view of great man accounts to invisible hand accounts. But how about economists? Certainly we prefer invisible hand accounts to Great Man accounts? Ought not disciplinary competition settle things?

Why Economists Cannot See the Issue

I shall approach the problem faced by economists in recovering the invisible context of Carlyle's attack on economics as one that adults face when learning a new language by trial and error. Here I propose to draw on the insights developed by Adam Smith's rational choice approach to linguistics. We can formulate his statement of the problem of adult language acquisition as a problem in what we now call *exploratory data analysis*.[3] Smith's approach encourages us to

---

3. This field of statistics was largely conceived by John Tukey (see, e.g., Tukey 1977 and Mosteller and Tukey 1977). The problem is to simultaneously develop an understanding of the structure and to test hypotheses about the structure. Traditional statistical theory had supposed a sequential approach wherein one brings prior knowledge of the structure of the problem to hypothesis testing. The possibility of exploratory data analysis has distributional consequences (Levy 1999–2000).

think of a language as a model for which grammatical structures have to be discovered. The difficulty with adult language acquisition is that languages differ wildly in their grammatical complexity: one cannot count on the grammatical structure of one's native language carrying over to the target language. English is everyone's favorite example of a language with a minimum of grammatical structures. Words in English are rarely gendered, the difference between object and subject is localized to rapidly vanishing distinctions in pronouns, and there is no specialized vocabulary in which one talks with one's mother-in-law.

If learning a language as an adult is akin to coming to understand the structure of a statistical process one intends to model, then it is easy to understand why modern linguistic scholars report how much more difficult it is to move *to* language with a novel grammatical structure than *from* a language with that structure. If one's native language inflects on number, that is, if it has a plural, then it occurs to one to look for the plural in the target language. But what English speaker would think to look for a specialized vocabulary with which to talk to one's mother-in-law (Dixon 1989)?

Modern economists do not see the context of the dismal science because the economics that descends from Smith has structures in it that neoclassical economics lacks. And it is these structures that are central to the debate between Carlyle and the classical economists. If this is so, then learning Smith's model will require discovering how the missing structures work. Linguists claim that it is possible to express any thought in any language, and in this spirit, to make operational my understanding of Smith's model, I shall employ the missing structure to address open problems in neoclassical economics.

Ofttimes, linguists who study dying languages find the most exotic grammatical structures in the memory of the oldest living native speakers. The younger speakers of a language have grown up side-by-side with another language, and the time learning one is time not spent learning another. This results in a loss of the finer points of their grandparents' languages. I find the memory of the debate between the classical economists and those to their right only in the books of neoclassical economists who knew little or no mathematics, scholars who were famous when even my now-departed teachers were yet students.[4] By and by, we shall encounter a passage in which Schumpeter explains Carlyle's importance to the economist in which it is obvious that he knows all about the Carlyle-Mill exchange (1954, 409–10). Instead of actually explaining the debate, he makes the sort of nasty joke with which the enormously erudite can laugh at the naive.[5] The joke works for a few because most will not catch the reference.

---

4. In Levy 1992, I report the memory of language-linked problems in the work of Frank Knight. I learned to see the language-linked aspects in *Wealth of Nations* through the eyes of Knight's student, George Stigler.

5. "This is not to say it is an easy book, or suitable for the kindergarten atmosphere in which so much college education proceeds. Nor is it in every respect a 'safe' book: the orthodox of any

Katallactics or Robinson Crusoe?

The critical aspect I find in Smith that is lacking in neoclassical economics is an emphasis on the desire for approbation from one's fellow humans. Approbation can be carried by human language, so there can be symbolic rewards of real importance.[6] Language is important for Smith's argument because it—and only it—allows the experience of one to be shared by others and because it allows approbation to extend beyond the reach of a caress. Science/technology and morality have natural representations as models in an agent's language, and, as I read Smith, he drew no fundamental distinction between the two sorts of models. Thus, language-directed choosing offers insight into a plethora of issues. And, as one might expect, when the attention of neoclassical economists returns to issues of science, we find Smith's insights to be valuable.

The decisive distinction is in one's attitude toward "Robinson Crusoe models." In the classical period, Whately claimed that what he understood as political economy could make no sense of an isolated individual. He named Robinson Crusoe explicitly, and that sticks in the mind. In our time, a dart hurled energetically at a stack of technical journals, such as those sitting on the floor by my desk waiting for me to finish this book and for the twentieth century to end, must pierce Robinson Crusoe a dozen times over.

What is the difference between a katallactic model starting with two and a Robinson Crusoe model starting with one? In the usual subjectivist account of Robinson Crusoe, there is no reason to believe that Robinson would view Friday any differently than he would view one of the island's goats. His preferences and perceptions are completely unrestricted in the subjective analysis. In a katallactic model, humans form a natural kind, as we can obtain the approbation we want from a fellow human not from a goat.[7] The argument to come will exploit this additional structure.

While language, the desire for approbation, and the human as natural kind may seem to be exotic inhabitants of an economic model, Smith makes one move that a modern economist will readily appreciate. In Smith's model, any

---

description must be prepared for constant shocks, and the literal-minded will miss much that is said only between the lines" (Hayek 1969, 340–41). Schumpeter charged Hayek with secret writing (Levy 1990a)! Schumpeter is not the only one with things to teach. Ludwig von Mises's *Human Action* has a opening polemic against one particularly virulent form of racism (1949, 74–78). When I read the book as an undergraduate, I could not understand why all the sensible things he said about "polylogism" would matter in the slightest to an economist.

6. When we take increasing returns to scale models of economic growth seriously, we must deal with the possibility that everyone cannot be paid their marginal product in terms of physical output. In Smith's account, poets and philosophers are paid mainly in approbation (1976a, 123). Willingness to accept payment in approbation might be necessary to any competitive increasing-returns model (Levy 1988a; Levy 1992, 155–74).

7. My friend Jack Wiseman spent the last years of his life attempting to construct a katallactic account from radical subjectivist roots. Would that he were here to disagree!

individual, when faced with the same set of incentives and information, will behave just like any other individual. When the agents in the model come to understand this, they give up any claim to uniqueness. In this reflective equilibrium, the individual judges himself or herself as others do. We have freed ourselves of the natural illusion imposed by our status quo. We have come to understand ourselves as the model understands us. For Smith, this insight is embodied in the moral injunction of reciprocity in action. Modern economists will see this as offering rational expectations insights in a somewhat unexpected context.

But for Smith the path to such a rational expectations outcome is difficult and contingent. Since we view the social world from our status quo, we are subject to the social equivalents of the optical illusions that Berkeley described. As Berkeley pointed out, without some learning we really do think that our thumb is bigger than the moon because we can cover the one with the other. The role of moral education in Smith's account is to combat the social equivalents of these natural illusions.[8]

Where Did Language Go?

As I read the historical record, over the long period in which neoclassical economists have been in conversation with Smith's model we have been attempting to travel more lightly. The human as a natural kind, a hardwired desire for approbation, and a language community in which approbation is carried have been seen as burdens carrying ontological commitments. To travel lightly is to travel efficiently. Or so it has seemed. But just how did this come about? I do not recall reading of a convention at which neoclassical economists got together and agreed not to "do" language.

In fact, it was during the classical period that a great mathematician, Charles Babbage, suggested that the assumption of homogenous agents be replaced with the assumption that the agents' abilities are randomly distributed. But Mill had little difficulty incorporating this suggestion within the general confines of Smith's model of the labor market in competitive equilibrium.

Smith, the rational choice linguist, can help us explain why structures of his economic model have been shrugged off. He noticed something very interesting about the collision of languages. When people of different language communities are thrown together, a new language with fewer grammatical structures than the parent languages emerges. Starting in the 1870s, economics as a language community collided with the mathematical language commu-

---

8. With competition in religion, society tends to go in one direction; lacking competition it tends to go in another (Levy 1992, 65–91).

nity. Here the mathematicians I would point to are Fleeming Jenkin, F. Y. Edgeworth, and John von Neumann.[9]

Neoclassical economic rethinking, informed by ever-deepening mathematical insight into the properties of the real numbers, offers a fundamental challenge to Smith's way of implementing our shared vision. An individual's preferences are supposed to share deep structure with the real numbers. If our preferences—and thus our perceptions—are as sharp as the relation greater than that over the real numbers, then we would not seem to need the help of others in order to optimize. Can we not remove the agent from the language community and still prove everything we want to know about the social order? (Levy 1992 asks "Really?") If we start with one, we need not worry about whether this one belongs to a natural kind. If the language community goes, then so goes concern about approbation which is carried by language.

Models as Sufficient Statistics of the Past?

To the extent that modern economics education confronts the past, it is through a collection of modern dress models—canonical growth models and the like. The prevailing attitude seems to be that these modern dress models are sufficient for our understanding of the past. In a important technical sense, models of the past have come to be viewed by modern economists as if they were sufficient statistics.

Sufficiency in a statistical context means roughly that this estimator is all one needs to know. With a sufficient statistic, one can throw away the raw data and be none the worse off for any decision one would make.[10] The textbook history of economics is, as a matter of necessity, an account or a model of a text or a collection of texts. Models must simplify if they are to be of use: a map of Nebraska in 1:1 scale does not fit in the glove compartment of any automobile I am likely to own. Simplification is not the issue. The issue is our tacit supposition that models are sufficient statistics, so the raw texts might as well be thrown away and forgotten.[11]

However, if it is true that we will have an easier time appreciating a structure in the past if this same structure is in our current theory, then this attitude

9. For Jenkin and von Neumann, see Levy 2000a.

10. A precise account of sufficiency is found in Lehmann 1986, 18–22, at which he explains importance of randomization to reclaim data as useful as the originals.

11. T. S. Kuhn (1962, 137) gets at this exactly: "More historical detail, whether of the science's present or of its past, or more responsibility to the historical details that are presented, could only give artificial status to human idiosyncrasy, error, and confusion. Why dignify what science's best and most persistent efforts have made it possible to discard?" See also: "Why, after all, should the student of physics, for example, read the works of Newton, Faraday, Einstein, or Schrödinger, when everything he needs to know about these works is recapitulated in a far briefer, more precise, and more systematic form in a number of up-to-date textbooks?" (164).

toward the past cannot be correct. A development in modern research that introduces a new structure might allow us to see more deeply into the past. If we do not see the structure of the past, then our models will not get the details right for the same reason that if one leaves out an explanatory variable in a regression problem one forces the coefficient to be zero.

One of the few noncontroversial aspects of Thomas Kuhn's *Structure of Scientific Revolution* is his remark that when major change occurs in a discipline it acquires new heroes (1962, 137). These are workers of the past whose insights could not be appreciated until some technical barrier had been overcome. For instance, in the modern foundation of mathematics Berkeley has become one of the heroes *avant la lettre.* This is an instructive example for us because Berkeley's new mathematical fame is a consequence of his twofold doctrine that we must learn to perceive and we will never perceive the infinitesimally small or the infinitely large. Not taking Berkeley seriously until recently, we have tended not to appreciate the consequences that follow from his argument. For instance, if we restrict ourselves to the finite, as Berkeley urged, transitivity joins infinitesimals as a ghost of departed relationships. As Henri Poincaré joked—perhaps *proved* is the right word—only in classical mathematics is equality transitive.

Transitivity of equality is critical to a series of substitution principles in neoclassical accounts. If you know α, and one can prove that α is the same as ß, then transitivity of equality says you know ß. And if transitivity fails? We shall have to consider this. Smith, avowedly following Berkeley, presents a related doctrine that we have to learn in order to perceive the importance of those around us. Importantly, Smith argues that we are especially prone to making errors when the state of those we judge is at a great distance from our situation.

I shall argue at some length that this worry about perception errors, which increase as distance from our status quo increases, is responsible for one structure in Smith's argument that is not present in the modern drill: median-based utilitarianism. I would wish that this method of evaluation were in the modern tool kit, but it isn't (Levy 2000b). Historically, utilitarianism has meant that the visionary slogan—not due to Jeremy Bentham—that we ought to seek is "the greatest happiness of the greatest number." It is important that the slogan was shown to be mathematical nonsense by Edgeworth at various times during the nineteenth century. The vision turned out to be a mirage. Edgeworth proposed that we simply drop "the greatest number" to protect the model from the vision. And he proceeded to construct an elegant theory that maximizes the average happiness of society. And in the fullness of time the Edgeworthization of utilitarianism has been accepted as the sufficient statistic of utilitarianism.

I shall propose, on the contrary, that pre-Benthamite utilitarianism is better modeled with the doctrine that one ought to seek the greatest happiness of the majority, that is, maximize the well-being of the median, than it is with the

Edgeworthian approach of maximizing average well-being. In addition to Smith, the Christian philosopher William Paley is a median-based utilitarian. In the nineteenth century, Malthus was perhaps the most important of the "robust utilitarians."

It goes without saying that without the massive attention that has been devoted to such estimators as the sample median in the last few decades I would never have seen what one might call the robust utilitarian aspects in Smith. The proposition that recent work lets one see more deeply into to the past is something I should wish to defend in contexts outside the history of economics. Indeed, it seems to be something implied by the technological externalities that arise from any sort of basic research.

This rethinking utilitarianism has a simple consequence: there is more to utilitarianism than Bentham and his "predecessors." There are different ways of utilitarianism. I shall argue at length that important members of the anti-slavery coalition understood themselves to be utilitarians in the sense that made Benthamite Utilitarianism formally equivalent to the moral center of Christianity.[12]

Protecting an Interpretation of Carlyle with a Bodyguard of Silence

Believing as I do that it is less useful to compare a model with reality than to compare competing models with reality, I shall here sketch what I propose to be the alternative interpretation of Carlyle and his various friends most deserving of attention. This is the interpretation of Carlyle as social progressive put forward in 1958 by Raymond Williams in his extraordinarily influential *Culture and Society*. Then I shall consider how this interpretation is protected by a bodyguard of silence.

To understand Williams's importance, it is helpful if we participate, if only for a little while, in the vision put forward by Karl Marx. As Marx looked across the ebb and flow of history, he saw feudalism succeeded by capitalism and capitalism becoming socialism. Both of these developments he judged to be progressive. It is a consequence of this account that those who spoke for capitalism were on the side of progress in the debate with those who spoke for feudalism. To understand, therefore, how the arrow of history points in any particular debate in which an economist was involved, one would actually have to read the work of the economist in question. Marx tried to read them all, and

---

12. "To place his books in their environment would mean giving an account in the 'seventies and 'eighties' between Orthodoxy and Free-thought, in which Leslie Stephen played so effective a part, and it would mean giving some historical account of that close alliance between Agnosticism and Puritanism, as noticeable in him as it was in Huxley, which has struck a later generation as curious" (MacCarthy 1937, 5–6).

as far I can judge he nearly succeeded. Of course, Marx wrote on Carlyle's defense of slavery. Not surprisingly, Marx's judgment might have been written by Mill himself.[13]

Progressive Carlyle

Williams succeeded in merging the antimarket position of feudalism—again using Marx's terms—with the antimarket position of socialism. This tour de force has been given an elegant name: "left-Leavism" (Eagleton 1976, 22). Thus, Leavis's conservative criticism of markets becomes merged with the socialist criticism of markets. This is how Williams proposes we read Carlyle as a critic of market relationships:

> He sees, with a terrible clarity, the spiritual emptiness of the characteristic social relationships of his day, "with Cash Payments as the sole nexus" between man and man " . . . and there are so many things which cash will not pay." The perception disqualifies him, wholly, from acquiescence in this construction of relationships; and he is therefore, without argument a radical and a reformer. (1958, 76)

Williams was a serious scholar, so he warns the reader about troubling aspects in Carlyle's work that must be distinguished from the valuable. The valuable part is the critical:

> The decisive emphasis is on the need to transform the social and human relationships hitherto dictated by the "laws" of political economy. This emphasis, humane and general, was in fact more influential than Carlyle's alternative construction of heroic leadership and reverent obedience. (76)

And here is the troubling part: those institutions that Carlyle proposed to replace markets:

> After *Chartism*, the balance, or comparative balance, of Carlyle's first position is lost. *Past and Present* is eloquent. . . . But, while it was possible to expose the deficiencies of Industrialism by contrast with selected aspects of a feudal civilization, the exercise was no help to Carlyle, or to his readers,

---

13. "Finally, spake the oracle, Thomas Carlyle. . . . In a short parable, he reduces the one great event of contemporary history, the American Civil War, to this level, that the Peter of the North wants to break the head of the Paul of the South with all his might, because the Peter of the North hires his labour by the day, and the Paul of the South hires his by the life. . . . The bubble of Tory sympathy for the urban workers—but no means for the rural—has burst at last. The sum of all is—slavery!" (Marx 1887, 255–56).

in the matter of perceiving the contemporary sources of community. . . . In the *Latter-Day Pamphlets* the decisive shift has taken place; it is to the existing holders of power—the Aristocracy, the "Captains of Industry"—that Carlyle looks for leadership in the reorganization of society; the call it only for them to fit themselves for such leadership, and to assume it. By the time of *Shooting Niagara* this call has become a contemptuous absolutism. (82–83).

First, let me state the major area of agreement: Carlyle's major argument is with the political economy of the time. Thus, my overall approach of comparing Carlyle and friends with the economists is in accord with William's interpretation. Second, I am not here directly interested in the issue of how government is structured, so I do not in fact deal with such topics as whether Carlyle was a democrat. He obviously was not. Williams is right. Finally, I find a good deal of coherence in Carlyle's work, so I will not worry about really distinguishing Carlyle at time i from Carlyle at time j except when it comes to the racial matters, which Williams does not discuss. Here again I am in agreement with Williams when he says that "the unity of Carlyle's work is such that almost everything he wrote has a bearing on his main questions" (Williams 1958, 77).

Having agreed to *this*, what do I propose as an issue to debate? I propose that Carlyle's work root and branch, early to late—pick your cliché—argues for the rule of the inferior by the superior. Carlyle attained great political influence when he turned "inferior" to "nonwhite" and "superior" to "white." Oblique this is in *Past and Present*; crude past belief this is in the "Occasional Discourse on the Negro Question." And it was in this venue that he attacked classical economics for standing in opposition to the claim that the white race ought to command. The natural order of the social world is a system of racial slavery.

Where I come into most direct conflict with Williams's interpretation is that I read Carlyle as claiming the "cash nexus" appropriate for a world of moral equals. Among equals, there is no command; among equals there is exchange. That is why the katallactic enterprise bears Carlyle's fury: there is nothing but exchange; there are only moral equals. And so, against Williams, the laws of market relationship, instead of being stigmatized are in fact offered as a template of human status.[14] If you obey the laws of political economy, that is to say, if you are willing to work for money wages, fine, you are fully human. If you will not work for money wages, you are subhuman. Slavery is your natural state. The enslavement of an inferior race by the superior may bring moral elevation. What if that slavery does not make you an economic man suitable to

---

14. Wendy Motooka wrote this sentence for me when she explained to me the consequences of my research.

exchange with your equals? What if it is not the case that "emancipation itself follows" from such slavery? We glanced at Carlyle's answer in chapter 1.

For evidence of Williams's importance, I appeal to a controversy that occurred almost simultaneously with the publication of *Culture and Society;* that is, the attack by C. P. Snow on the antimaterialist vision of the literary culture.[15] The failure to pass the test of World War II is a charge he reports:

> I remember being cross-examined by a scientist of distinction. "Why do most writers take on social opinions which would have been distinctly uncivilised and démodé at the time of Plantagenets? Wasn't that true of most of the famous twentieth-century writers? Yeats, Pound, Wyndhman Lewis, nine of out of ten of those who have dominated literary sensibility in our time—weren't they not only politically silly, but politically wicked? Didn't the influence of all they represent bring Auschwitz that much nearer?" (1959, 7)

Speaking for himself, Snow points to the reaction of nineteenth-century writers to the Industrial Revolution and in the process launches a moral attack on those who attack materialism when the material in question allows children to live (24–25).[16]

One of Leavis's responses made what seems to me to be the correct point: if one is concerned about the actual historical debate, *Hard Times* is an appropriate text with which to discuss the substantive issues.[17] And since I propose to discuss *Hard Times* in detail below I see no need to get that out of place. Snow's defenders against Leavis conceded an important point. Here is the judgment of Martin Green:

---

15. Rereading Snow one must remember the illusion propagated that the Soviet Union was less hierarchical than market economies. Snow was criticized for his inability to distinguish counterfactually between his quality of life in Britain and life in the Soviet Union (Wain 1962, 16–19). Stefan Collini, in Snow 1993, xxii–xxiii, locates the genesis of Snow's ideas in the progressive scientific commonplace of 1930s Cambridge.

16. Snow, in common with Macaulay's argument against the poet Robert Southey, uses a life expectancy norm. This would allow one to avoid the need to worry about how to value the contribution of government-provided goods, for example, cholera-free water, when the good is provided without user cost. Although I have worried about the econometric issues of estimating the impact of government-financed research and development (Levy 1990b), the problem is obviously more general than this.

17. "And to come back to *Hard Times:* the undergraduate—or the senior—who has taken the significance of the book, and recognized the finality with which it leaves the Benthamite calculus, the statistical or Blue Book approach, and the utilitarian ethos placed, can say why either a 'rising standard of living,' nor equality, nor both together, will do when accepted as defining the sufficient preoccupations and aims of thought and effort, and why to be able to posit *two* cultures is a dangerous form of unintelligence" (Leavis 1969, 177).

> When Snow says that the traditional literary culture did not notice the Industrial Revolution, or, when it did notice, didn't like what it saw, then he does expose himself to the sort of scornful reprimand which Leavis is administering. The tradition of culture-criticism, explored by Raymond Williams in *Culture and Society*, is one of the two or three great achievements of modern English thought, and it is predominately the work of the literary culture. (1964, 34)[18]

In his recent edition of Snow's lecture and his 1963 "A Second Look," Stefan Collini adds the following information:

> Snow had read Raymond Williams's *Culture and Society*, published in 1958 (the quotation from Coleridge on p. 62 below is surely taken from Williams, p. 77), but its complex discussions of the literary responses to industrialism does not seem to have modified that the champions of "culture" were all tainted with "Luddism." (quoted in Snow 1993, xxxv).

The only conclusion I wish to draw from this is a certification of the overwhelming importance of Williams's *Culture and Society* as a mediator of the cultural critics of capitalism. The attack by Snow on the literary culture is judged wrong to the extent that it conflicts with Williams's account.

In the wonderful index in *Culture and Society*, neither *slavery* nor *emancipation* appears. Nor do we find any of the usual and customary terms used to distinguish members of one "race" of humans from another. What do we make of this? In the detailed studies below, I shall call attention to some very recent work that has seen in the Eyre controversy the oddity that the critics of economics whom Williams revives—Carlyle, Ruskin, Dickens, and Kingsley—lined up with the side claiming that killing blacks did not count for much. And the Carlyle-Mill exchange is also being talked about by specialists again. The silence is ending.[19]

From an orthodox Marxist position, what Williams did was very strange. One can read the puzzlement in the challenge to Williams's interpretation pressed by Terry Eagleton in 1976 when he first called Williams's approach "left-Leavism":

---

18. In response to Lionel Trilling's essay, Snow himself says this: "Martin Green has taken up the argument, more adequately, eloquently and dispassionately than I could have done" (1993, 107).

19. Carlyle's views on race were well cited in the British discussions during World War II. Carlyle as a forerunner of Hitler was a fairly standard theme. H. Trevor-Roper (1947, 97) discusses which of Carlyle's books Hitler had read to him as Marshall Zhukov's army neared.

> For all its eloquence and engagement, then, *Culture and Society* . . . could sustain its thesis only by systematic inattention to the reactionary character of the tradition with which it dealt—an inattention evident in the drastically partial and distorted readings of particular writers (Carlyle, Arnold, and Lawrence in particular) who were wrestled from their true *foci* and manipulated by selected quotation and sentimental misconception into the cause of a "socialist humanism." (1976, 25–26)

Eagleton did not, however, provide texts.[20] Aside from quoting a few Carlylean phrases, for example, the "Gospel of Labor"—which one can hardly understand without discussing the "Negro Question" and Mill's response—there is no substantial textual material provided in Eagleton's dissent. Just why is Carlyle a "reactionary"? Moreover, Williams talked about so many writers that, even if he got a few wrong, then whatever the personal failures of Carlyle, Carlyle as a critic of market exchange or Carlyle as filtered through the novels of Kingsley and Dickens remains. Since Kingsley, about whom Eagleton does not write, was a founder of Christian socialism, he is obviously above reproach.[21] Finally, since the economists were the opponents of "reactionaries" like Carlyle, then are they not "progressive"?[22] Left-Leavism is an easier organizing principle than Marx's own doctrine. In left-Leavism, one knows without actually having to read them that economists are always wrong, always horrid. Such left-Leavism simply has to be more pleasant to believe than Marx's hard old doctrine that to understand economists you must sit in the British Library, decade following decade, and read them all.

Why the Silence about Race?

Is there any real excuse for failing to talk about such episodes as the Carlyle-Mill exchange? Of course. One may believe that this—and other race-linked statements—are so bizarre, so unrepresentative of Carlyle's true intention, that

---

20. And he regarded himself very much as working inside Williams's framework. "It is enough to say that any Marxist criticism in England which has shirked the pressure of Williams's work will find itself seriously crippled and truncated. Williams has been the pioneer, and like every pioneer must now submit to criticism from those he has enabled to speak" (Eagleton 1976, 24).

21. "Nothing is easier than to give Christian asceticism a socialist tinge. Has not Christianity declaimed against private property, against marriage, against the state? Has it not preached, in the place of these, charity and poverty, celibacy and mortification of the flesh, monastic life and Mother Church? Christian socialism is but the holy water with which the priest consecrates the heartburnings of the aristocrat" (Marx and Engels 1959, 31).

22. "The *progressive* elements of the bourgeois ideological tradition (a concept which Williams has consistently opposed from a 'humanistic' standpoint) were consequently passed over, with one or two lonely exceptions" (Eagleton 1976, 26).

there is no way to make sense of them. But if you talk about these texts nothing else will matter for the modern reader.

In statistics, there are observations that are called "influential." By this is meant fragments of the data set that, regardless of the other observations, can force the result. If the modern reader reflects overly much on the Carlyle-Mill exchange, a willingness to think kindly about any aspect of Carlyle's life's work burns away. Perhaps Williams neglects these texts because talking about them would destroy any hope of making sense of what he views as the valuable aspects of Carlyle's writings. And, as someone who has put forward a proposal to make economic utilitarianism more robust precisely because I think doubling the wealth of a politically connected elite really ought not to count for very much in social evaluation, I am under an obligation to take such a robust, public-spirited account of silence with all due seriousness.

What I think is the most generous construction that can be put upon the silence is that the left-Leavists suppose that Carlyle as a *critic* of market relationships is independent of Carlyle as a *defender* of racial slavery. Carlyle's criticisms of market relationships do not stand or fall on his own view of the ideal society. This is precisely how I read the statements from Williams quoted above.

While I take this possibility seriously, I think it is deeply false. The idea that one can read Carlylean criticism of markets independently of their advocacy of hierarchical alternatives falls apart upon examination. Suppose one claims, as the Carlyleans were wont to do, that the black slaves of America were happier than the "white slaves" of Britain. Should it matter to the reader whether the one who makes such a claim is committed to a slave system? Here I believe we need to think carefully about the basis on which the observer made such an inference. It is easy enough to imagine a line of argument in which the judgment "better off" can be separated from the observer's own ideal state and another line of argument in which it cannot. Economists like Richard Whately employed the choices of slaves themselves to ask: if slavery is such a happy state, why was it necessary to offer rewards for the recapture of runaways?[23]

But suppose, with the racists, that this logic of revealed preference will not work for black slaves; they are supposedly too "dull" to understand their own happiness. Then consider "white slaves." Suppose a large number of British workers had sailed westward to New Orleans to sell themselves into slavery. Perhaps they learned from Carlyle that the unemployment rate was lower

---

23. "[W]e are told on every side that slaves are the happiest people in the world. . . . Slaves, we are told, *like* slavery. And if this be meant to apply only to individual instances, we are ready to admit it to be true. But if it be meant to assert that such is the case universally, or even generally, we feel bound, before we can give our assent to the proposition, to make a few inquiries. What is the meaning of the countless advertisements, offering rewards for the apprehension of runaway slaves, to be recognised by marks sufficient to prove the 'happy' state they left, and which they were too dull or too ungrateful to appreciate?" (Hill, Whately, and Hinds 1852, 248–49).

under slavery and the retirement benefits considerable. The judgment "happier" or "better off" supported by such facts would then be made only in reference to the revealed preference of the workers themselves. Perhaps the workers were ill informed; nonetheless, this type of evidence would not seem to depend upon the critic's ideology.

It is easy to believe that a proslavery writer might find such evidence more readily than a promarket writer. It is even easier to believe that the proslavery writer would report it with far more glee than an opponent would. Nonetheless, if such evidence were found and checked, it would be independent of the views of its discoverer. But such unproblematic evidence seems sparse. Movement eastward across the Atlantic by escaping black slaves was frequent enough for Dickens to joke about it in *Hard Times.*

What about the claim that black slaves were well fed by European standards and that they seemed "happy" while "white slaves" grumbled a lot?[24] The value of this "evidence" depends upon what one wants to see. Food was surely cheaper on American plantations than in Europe, so caloric benevolence did not cost very much and just possibly the cost of grumbling was higher for a black slave than a "white slave." In this context, the truth-seeking scholar owes the reader information about the observer's ideology. What the rationally choosing scholar tells the reader is perhaps another matter.

This is why I think that we cannot, in fact, assert that the criticism of markets is independent of the defense of slavery. Nonetheless, many serious scholars seem to believe it possible. And this raises the following question: how does one distinguish between rational choice scholarship—selective reporting as a way to effect private ends—and "robustly seeking the truth"—keeping the modern reader from simply dismissing Carlyle's *criticisms* of markets out of hand? Both hypotheses give a coherent explanation of the silence about the "Negro Question." Perhaps we can develop an additional prediction from these two hypotheses that will allow us to decide between them.

The rational choice modeling procedure employed to explain how the Governor Eyre unpleasantness dropped out of the Ruskin literature depended upon changes in common knowledge. Scholars will discuss only such unpleasantness about their hero as is necessary. What about an aspect of the Carlylean enterprise that received little contemporary notice: the Carlylean problem with Jews?[25]

Consider this hypothetical question: what if the Carlylean *criticism* of market exchange claimed that competitive markets allowed those without the

---

24. Hill, Whately and Hinds (ibid.) confront the stupifying argument that the "dancing" on the Middle Passage is evidence of "happiness."

25. "In *Past and Present* the outsiders were Jews. . . . Distanced by both history and a closed narrative, Carlyle's treatment of Benedict the Jew in *Past and Present* has never stirred quite the controversy roused by his depiction of Quashee in the 'Occasional Discourse on the Nigger question,' though Carlyle implies it has present applications" (Spear 1984, 108).

appropriate religious beliefs the ability to exploit others.[26] If one's hierarchical obligations depend upon religious beliefs, then could not a religion that neglects to impose such obligations allow its adherents to act as social parasites? What if the problem the Carlyleans saw in market exchange was in part a Jewish problem? How would the scholar react?

The rationally choosing scholar would of course not mention such an unpleasant aspect of a cultural hero. The scholar who wished to separate the valuable criticism of markets from the abhorrent policies Carlyle avowed would, of course, mention this. I'm sure that an appropriately energetic scholar could denigrate its importance by asserting that *since* it is ghastly it *therefore* could not be important. Whatever one would make of it, as it is part of the *criticism* of market exchange it would be discussed by the robustly truth-seeking scholar.

To make the issue as sharp as can be, I propose, in table 1, alternative explanations of scholarship: rational choice scholarship, which I propose; and a robust, truth-seeking explanation, which I regard as the most plausible alternative. The hypothesis of rational choice scholarship I support explains the silence on the "Negro Question" by supposing that modern opponents of markets are uncomfortable pointing out that racial slavery was the existing alternative to markets in the 1850s. The implication I draw from the rational choice scholarly hypothesis is that anti-Semitism in the criticism of markets would also be treated with silence. Against this rational choice view, I propose as the alternative that truth-seeking scholars are concerned that the numbing grossness of the "Negro Question" or the statements made by major literary figures in the Eyre controversy would deflect attention from the bulk of the unproblematic literary culture. By contrast with a rational choice view, the implication

TABLE 1.   Why the Silence about the "Negro Question"?

	Alternative Hypotheses	
	Rational Choice Scholarship	Pursue the Truth Robustly?
Hypothesized goal of scholars	Promote hierarchical alternatives to markets	Seek the truth
Explanation for silence about the "Negro Question"	Racial slavery is the existing alternative to markets in the 1850s. Why give aid and comfort to the advocates of markets?	Carlyle's ideals are irrelevant to his criticism of markets
Predicted reaction to the Jewish Problem of markets	So? Carlyle's idealized slavery requires common belief. One no more reports this than the "Negro Question."	This would question the value of the criticism of markets and would be fully discussed

26. "As a people behaves, so it thrives; as it believes, so it behaves" (Kingsley 1864, xlviii).

of this truth-seeking view of textual interpretation is that any anti-Semitism in the criticism of markets would be called to the attention of the reader.

H. S. Chamberlain, who is cited in *Mein Kampf*, plays no role in English literature, but let us take another enthusiastic follower of Carlyle, Charles Kingsley, the author of *Alton Locke*, that classic industrial novel discussed favorably by Leavis, Williams, and other students of Victorian literature who hold that culture ought to trump markets. In *Alton Locke*, economics and a market without compassion take turns as the primary villain. But there are other villains in the piece, those horrid sorts who actually *implement* the economic doctrine of justice without compassion. These are the "sweaters," who are compared to and contrasted with honorable employers. The econometrician in me asks: how is the reader supposed to distinguish the honorable employer from the sweater?

One might think that I would have figured this out by now: the sweaters are Jews.[27] And the role of the Jew as economic vampire was clearly explained in one of the major contemporary reviews, which parsed the book for the not so well informed.[28] A generation of extremely well informed critics has passed over this in silence, presenting *Alton Locke* as a creditable criticism of market-based economic activity.[29]

These facts (first, there is anti-Semitism at the center of the cultural criticism of markets of a completely unsubtle nature in one of the Carlylean industrial novelists, which, second, is passed over in silence by modern literary opponents of markets) provide what I contend is compelling evidence for the practice of rational choice, humanistic scholarship. One only reports what is most pleasing to believe. As always, behind Kingsley there is Carlyle. Possibly,

---

27. Everyone at the time said such things? No. "Eusebia once went into a Jewish synagogue. She was grieved when she saw the inattention of the worshippers, and felt inclined to despise the solemn pomp of the service, when she was restrained by the following reflection. 'This,' she said to herself, 'was the ancient Church of GOD, and I now behold some imperfect traces of the worship ordained from Mount Sinai. The glory is, indeed, departed from it; but let me at least honour its antiquity, and reverence its divine original'" (Thornton 1846, 140–41).

28. Kingsley's novel was presented as an autobiography of a working man, not as a novel by a cleric of the established church. W. E. Aytoun (1850) patiently explained why the reader ought not to be taken in by the claim of autobiography. Having performed this service, he lays out for the reader *exactly* why the wicked people in the stories are Jews.

29. "Carlyle had pointed this out by declaring in *Past and Present* that in the *laissez-faire* state there was one sole link between high and low: typhus fever. Kingsley two years earlier [than Dickens's *Bleak House*] had found a novelistic form for Carlyle's ideas by showing in his terrible account of the tailors' sweat-shops how typhus and other diseases due to the disgusting conditions in which the tailors worked and lived were transmitted to the well-to-do via the clothes made for them there" (Leavis and Leavis 1970, 166). The Leavises seem uninterested in the aspect of the story that explains that the sweaters are Jews. F. R. Leavis's obliviousness to T. S. Eliot's anti-Semitism is noted in Julius 1995, 8.

the "Gospel of Labor" ought to suggest who will be unwelcome when the world comes to be remade.

To what, then, do I attribute the fact that Dickens's episodic anti-Semitism, if it is that, is widely discussed?[30] Too many people know Dickens *novels* well, while *Alton Locke* is a book known only by specialists.[31] The constraints facing scholars discussing Dickens differ from the constraints facing scholars discussing Kingsley. When we deal with unfamiliar aspects of the Dickens opus, then perhaps we shall find surprising things there, too.

Appendix. Toward Reflexive Closure, a Denial of Systematic Error Guarantees It

I can comfortably predict that some of my fellow economists, who have no firsthand knowledge of the actual textual issues, will be remarkably uncomfortable with my claim that gross systematic error pervades an entire literature. I shall demonstrate how a principled opposition to the possibility of systematic error can serve to guarantee it. The denial of the possibility of systematic error seems to be a paradigm of "best case" thinking. Perhaps not surprisingly, then, there is a fundamental nonrobustness in the system.

The argument is akin to the way a Ponzi scheme might work: the "investors" believe that because the scheme enriched those who came before it will enrich them as well. Only the investors here are scholars who are buying propositions from the believers. In the technical jargon of modern economics, this process has an elegant name: it is called an information cascade.

Consider some proposition τ. I suppose that we can talk sensibly about the expected utility of τ; that is to say, the concepts of the probability and utility of τ can be defined. The probability of the truth of τ is p_δ, and the probability of the falsity of τ is $1 - p_\delta$. The utility of τ given that it is true is $U(\tau|\text{true})$, and the utility of τ given that it is false is $U(\tau|\text{false})$. Then we can predict acceptance of τ in the following way:

---

30. Is Fagin offset by Riah? Anthony Julius (1995, 181–82) reaches no conclusion. Julius discusses neither Carlyle nor Kingsley and thus gives no context for Dickens. For what little it is worth, I think whatever anti-Semitism there is in Dickens is independent of his attack on market exchange. Unlike the characters in *Alton Locke*, the horrid capitalists in *Hard Times* are not Jews. In *Alton Locke*, Jews are condemned for following Judaism. Since in *Oliver Twist* Fagin is a thief and shares complicity for murder, he stands condemned by the Decalogue, to which he adheres. The distinction seems worth making.

31. Possibly, too, Alec Guinness's performance as Fagin in the David Lean film version (1948) has made it impossible for a generation of students of literature to think of *Oliver Twist* in any other way.

$A(\tau)$ if $p_\tau U(\tau|\text{true}) + (1 - p_\tau)U(\tau|\text{false}) > 0$.

Denial of τ is likewise predicted:

$D(\tau)$ if $p_\tau U(\tau|\text{true}) + (1 - p_\tau)U(\tau|\text{false}) < 0$.

Obviously, we could replace denial of τ with acceptance of the negation, ~τ, and $D(\tau)$ with $A(\sim\tau)$ if we wish to economize on notation. It will be easier if we buy the extra consonant.

All that I have asked for is that the symbols can be defined. Now let us give some content to the form. I suppose that $U(\tau|\text{true}) > 0$ and that $U(\tau|\text{false}) \leq 0$. That is to say that the truth is always useful and what is false can never be useful. The weak inequality, as the reader might suspect, will be important.

Consider a literature composed of N articles, which take a position on τ: A of the N accept and $D = N - A$ deny. The belief that the literature cannot be in systematic error motivates an easy way to obtain a probability: $p_\tau = A/(A + D)$. To find out what is reasonable to believe, one reads the literature and makes a judgment on the relative frequency of conclusions. It is of course important that we are not able to separate those who accept τ because they have looked into the matter and those who accept it because it is accepted.

Literatures begin somewhere. Two related cases are sufficient to make the point. First, suppose that the first scholar to think of τ has the following utility: $U(\tau|\text{false}) = 0$. Second, suppose that the first scholar to think of τ has the belief $p_\tau = 1$. Either case might suffice to describe what William James long ago described as "the will to believe."

Case 1: $U(\tau|\text{false}) = 0$. Without any information on probability other than $p_\tau > 0$, we know immediately that the expected utility is positive and that the scholar will accept τ. Thus: $A = 1$, $D = 0$.

Case 2: $p_\tau = 1$. This is equally obvious since, regardless of the value of $U(\tau|\text{false})$, since $p_\tau U(\tau|\text{true}) > 0$ and $(1 - p_\tau)U(\tau|\text{false}) = 0$, here, too, $A = 1$, $D = 0$.

Consider the second scholar, who reads the literature and makes a judgment on the basis of relative frequency. This scholar is not a true believer, as Eric Hoffer described the situation, merely someone who supposes that an entire literature cannot be wrong and computes as follows: $p_\delta = A/(A + D) = 1/(1 + 0) = 1$. Thus, he, too, accepts since $U(\tau|\text{true}) > 0$ and $(1 - p_\tau)U(\tau|\text{false}) = 0$. Now $A = 2$, $D = 0$, and so on. Everyone accepts τ because it was accepted.

Possibly the probability assumption is a little suspect for small values of N? Let us weaken it. Suppose that to get the Ponzi scheme going we shall need some number, K, of "independent" reports in the literature. But unless we have reason to believe that the conclusions are not just K individuals who will their belief—$U(\tau|\text{false}) = 0$ or $p_\tau = 1$—the argument above goes through after we have attained the first K believers. The believers need not collude; their action is generated by the fact that in either case it cannot cost anything to accept τ.[32]

Once the Ponzi scheme has been running for a while, one suspects that an occasional D—even when the scholar publishes the evidence for the denial—will not matter. However, this will depend upon the values of $U(\tau|\text{true})$ and $U(\tau|\text{false})$, and about this we cannot speculate except in the case in which we have some reason to believe that $U(\tau|\text{false})$ is small.

Thus, we have no reason to rule out the possibility of systematic error once we encounter a literature that denies its possibility as a matter of principle. Since we can document gross systematic error among neoclassical economists, and since I wish to remain a neoclassical economist, it is pleasing to know that this fact is not theoretically impossible on neoclassical economic grounds (Caplan 2000). Indeed, all that we require is the simplest of rational choice considerations.

The commonly accepted beliefs about our history by modern economists, who are not themselves historians of economics, might be a lovely area in which to explore gross systematic error. We know perfectly well (first) that there is a small cost to this sort of error—one does not risk tenure by misstating David Ricardo's claims—and (second) there is a presupposition within modern economics that gross systematic error cannot exist. Those two facts should guarantee gross systematic error whenever it is in the interest of some K that the error exists.

---

32. Robert Newton (1977, 161) announced the wonderfully appropriate "principle that we may call the immortality of error." This is explained with tongue only slightly in cheek: "Suppose that an error made by a writer A has somehow been published, and suppose further that a later writer B quotes and cites the error, accepting it as correct. The error then becomes immortal and cannot be eradicated from the scholarly literature."

Part 2
Market Order or Hierarchy?

FIVE

Debating Racial Quackery

I propose to fill two gaps in the common understanding of the debates between economists and their opponents in nineteenth-century Britain. The first gap is in our understanding of the British economic debates over market organization and hierarchy. That defensible hierarchy encompassed racial slavery became as clear as it could be in the 1849–1850 exchange between Thomas Carlyle and John Stuart Mill.[1] Carlyle morphed racial slavery into an idealized feudalism and bent the very language of American debates over emancipation. The second gap in our understanding is why the "scientific" racists of Britain of the 1860s found classical economics their natural enemy, just as the biblical literalists had previously found it their natural ally.

If we do not know this debate, we get the simplest things wrong. With modern economists of great distinction occupying much the same position on property as their classical forebears had, scholars who do not know the Carlyle-Mill debate and its context all too often infer that since modern economists occupy a rightist position the attack came on classical economics from their left. No. The attack on economics for which *dismal science* was coined came from their right. Imagine a policy space along the single dimension of ownership of property. I take it as completely noncontroversial to make the following orientation. On the left tail, we find such philosophers as William Godwin opposing all property, property in things as well as property in people. On the right tail, we find those who defend the ownership of both things and people. While Mill's attraction to socialism is well known, the classical British economists generally speaking favored property in things and opposed property in people. When slavery ended in America, and with it support for property in people, the classical economists moved to the right by standing still.

When Adam Smith and his followers took human nature as a fixed quantity and so attempted to explain all behavioral differences by appealing to variation in incentives and histories, they produced a theory of great use to biblical literalists, for whom black slaves were both men and brothers. Smith's doctrine

---

1. Iva G. Jones (1967), Joseph Persky (1990), and James P. Smith (1994) provide valuable discussions of the debate.

81

of human homogeneity and the universalization inherent in utilitarianism are consistent with the revelation in Genesis of ultimate human kinship. Proponents of racial slavery come to be "progressive" in secondary accounts because of the overwhelming importance twentieth-century scholars assign to the movement away from biblical literalism and toward, among other things, the "scientific" study of racial differences. It is this "science" that authorizes some to be master and some to be slave. I read classical economics in two-fold opposition to both theories of natural slavery and the "science" of racial anthropology.[2]

Theories of slavery tend not to be terribly complicated: the "better" always seem to be ruling the "worse." Racial anthropology dovetails with this enterprise, as it gives "scientific" testimony to who is "better" and who is "worse." The British debates might make less counterintuitive the well-known correlation in late-nineteenth-century American economics between "progressive" and "scientific" racists.[3] These words are commonly used—though not, perhaps, in the same sentence—to describe the critics of classical economics.

I find a theoretical commitment in the economic antiracism in the British debates that scholars find lacking in the American debates. We are told the devastating fact that American economists in the late nineteenth century would speak against racism only when they themselves had a personal stake.[4] In the earlier British debates, it was Mill himself who would speak for the Irish and the black. I see no reason to believe that Mill was a saint; he was just the best economist of his time. Why this put him in permanent opposition to racist theorizing needs to be explained.

Let me begin by noting an objection to my enterprise. Who could possibly defend racial slavery in Britain after emancipation? In fact, many did.[5] Even if they did, how could this have an impact? Part of the difficulty, I believe, is that Carlyle's December 1849 "Occasional Discourse on the Negro Question" is so offensive to modern sensibilities that the natural tendency of many readers is to

---

2. The best study I know of the attack on economics from British anthropology is that by Ronald Rainger (1978). The importance of his focus on James Hunt, whose quarrel with the egalitarianism of classical economics is both explicit and persistent, will be brought out in the material that follows.

3. The important essays of Mark Aldrich (1979) and Robert Cherry (1995) are now easy to find. "The early AEA economists combined a peculiar mixture of progressivism . . . with scientific racism. Their enthusiasm for eugenics was consistent with their broad *anti-laissez-faire* posture" (Darity 1995, xv).

4. "And while in America, the defenders of the immigrants often were scholars who shared the immigrants' ethnicity . . . no comparable coterie of intellectual defenders of 'the Negro' existed" (Darity 1995, xx).

5. The sudden proslavery popularity in early 1850s Britain is noted in the open letter to Harriet Beecher Stowe and attack on Charles Dickens's opinions on slavery by Lord Denman (1853, iii–iv), which I discuss in chapter 7.

discard it as an outlier in the career of an otherwise creditable critic of market economics.[6]

For Britain, the answer of influence is well known to specialists—Carlyle helped turn a Jamaican racial massacre in the mid-1860s into a politically appealing cause.[7] In spite of this ghastly triumph, Carlyle's influence on British policy, as I read the record, was bounded. Whenever he would thunder for slavery and racial extermination, we find the greatest economist of his time in opposition, speaking on behalf those for whom Carlyle would prescribe enslavement or genocide. If the seriousness of a belief can be measured by how much one is prepared to pay, Mill's belief was very serious indeed.[8]

Carlyle had creative command of classical economic doctrine. Perhaps he found the idea in Edward Wakefield's commentary on the *Wealth of Nations* or perhaps he thought it through himself, but he twisted a claim, which Smith had used to argue for the fundamental equality of all language users, into one that would deny human status to blacks and Irish.

Carlyle, of course, is not the only one with an ideology of racial slavery to press. We shall consider two of his capable disciples, Charles Kingsley and James Hunt. Racism developed in Britain, but it did not stay there. When one of the founders of the American Economic Association (AEA) spouts Teutonic nonsense in the 1890s, it is useful to recognize that he is regurgitating

---

6. The article was enlarged and separately published as *Occasional Discourse on the Nigger Question* (hereafter *ODNQ*) in 1853. Because the pamphlet was published in Carlyle's *Works* with the assertion that *it* was the 1849 article, there has been some confusion about the name; thus, the OED entry for *dismal* has the date right but the title wrong. Simon Heffer (1995, 275) revives David Alec Wilson's (1927, 215) claim that the title was changed from "Negro" to "Nigger" in response to Mill's criticism. Neither Heffer nor Wilson consider the response to economists in "Present Time." On the contrary, I believe that Carlyle had this title in mind when he wrote it, so it was *Fraser's* that suppressed it. The appendix to this chapter contains my conjecture. James A. Froude (1885, 2:17) quotes Carlyle's February 7, 1850, journal entry: "Nigger article has roused the ire of all philanthropists to a quite unexpected pitch. Among other very poor attacks on it was one in 'Fraser;' most shrill, thin, poor and insignificant, which I was surprised to learn proceeded from John Mill. . . . He has neither told me nor reminded me of anything I did not very well know beforehand. No use in writing that kind of criticism." As we shall see, this is the line he takes in "Present Time."

7. A riot that turned into an administrative massacre initially inflamed British public opinion because George William Gordon, the Baptist minister—suspected of having had a leadership role in the riot—after presenting himself to the authorities, was promptly hanged. Holt 1992 is a valuable account from the Jamaican side. Semmel 1962 remains definitive on the British debates. Scholars of the present day, Catherine Hall (1992) and Robert J. C. Young (1995), who have begun to wonder why murdering blacks was such a "progressive" cause, have gone back to the Carlyle-Mill debate of 1849–50. Thomas Prasch (1989) gives useful background for the religious dimension of the debate.

8. "The unpopular cause of the Jamaica Committee probably lost John Stuart Mill his parliamentary seat. He was the only Liberal defeated in metropolitan London in the election of 1868" (Green 1976, 400).

what Kingsley was writing in the 1860s about the Teuton as natural master.[9] Hunt, who is known mainly to students of "scientific" racism, was its public face in the 1860s. His persistent criticism of the antiracist egalitarianism of classical economics helps contextualize the Carlyle-Mill exchange. By the strangest coincidence, Kingsley and Hunt found themselves buying and selling a "cure" for stammering. This cure, and here we leave coincidence behind, had the property of never "failing." The label for such promissory medicine, then, was "quackery."

How does a theorist respond to factual counterexamples?[10] This is an aspect of the Mill-Carlyle debate that has an importance well outside of economics. An economist like Mill is aware that he theorizes about averages when individuals deviate from the average as a matter of course. The racists theorized with the assertion that the average is all there is. There is no difference between the average and the individual. This procedure might be called "stereotypical" thinking when we understand that the stereotype is *not* allowed to change with the evidence.[11] T. H. Huxley called James Hunt a quack.[12] While little seems to have been made of Huxley's judgment other than disapprobation; there is

---

9. Cherry 1995, 17. Cherry quotes "Amasa Walker," but the references say "Francis A. Walker." Amasa Walker has a featured role in the appendix to this chapter, which addresses the morphing of *dismal science*.

10. Ali Khan asked how I propose to distinguish the quackery of which I evidently disapprove from the sort of immunization strategies that make the utility-maximizing hypothesis little more than a law of logic (I defend *that* practice in Levy 1992). Is quackery the same as specification search or exploratory data analysis (EDA)? I see two issues: a technical one and an ethical one. Many econometricians have a technical problem with EDA. When formalized, the possibility of EDA implies that errors in a linear regression context are nonnormal (Levy 1999–2000). I find this a more plausible outcome than the supposition that a finite model is fixed as the sample size goes infinite. The ethical issue for me about specification search is not that it is a biased estimation procedure—all sorts of widely used and plausible estimators are biased—but that the reader does not know how the procedure is biased (Feigenbaum and Levy 1996). If so, the researcher's hidden preferences, not the public data, can force the result. If the procedure is transparent—so the reader knows all about the specification search—I see no ethical problem. An ethic of transparency is supposed in the statement of the American Statistical Association (2000). My membership on the committee is duly noted.

Darity (1995, xvi–xvii) documents some racists' statistical claims that surely result more from their preferences than from the data they employ. Gould 1981 is a classic text on this matter.

11. The economic account of stereotypical thinking put forward by Edmund Phelps (1972) and Kenneth J. Arrow (1972) supposes that new observations will change the stereotype. The procedure described in the text supposes that the stereotype is protected from revision. Phelps and Arrow consider a context in which an unrevised stereotype imposes personal costs on the one who makes a decision. The discussion in the text supposes that the stereotype functions as a perverse "public good," that is, a public bad.

12. "But don't have anything to do with the quacks who are at the head of the 'Anthropological Society' over here. If they catch scent of what you are about they will certainly want to hook on to you" (Huxley 1900, 1:295). This is discussed in Desmond 1994, 320.

much more to it than that.[13] This wholesome medical term of reproach suggests that a stereotype will be protected from revision by a bodyguard of ad hoc devices because in medicine we know a quack by his or her claim that the cure being hawked never fails.

But individuals are not averages, and cures often fail. How can the theory be maintained? The quack tells a story to distract us from the factual counterexample. The story Carlyle told is of such transcendent quality that, if we know how to listen, we can hear its echoes even today.

Quackery Requires Science and Literature

Here is the problem facing a quack or the dispenser of racial stereotypes. How can one maintain the stereotype that all members of group X have a characteristic, α—the very characteristic that condemns them to the role of slave—in the presence of a member of X who lacks α? The quack must persuade others that the individual is not a "real" X. To stereotype swans as white, we need a story in which the inexorable black swan becomes something else entirely, for example, an elongated raven. This transparent piece of silliness dramatizes the problem. One has to have a *creditable* explanation of why we ought not to attend to this fact, and such a pathetic story obviously will not do.

Facts have no compassion. Once admitted, they come in their remorseless way, bringing death to theory. Quackery needs a story, such as Scheherazade herself might tell, which will let the theory live just one more night. One night more is all we need. If we can tell a good story this night, then there is no reason why we cannot tell its equal tomorrow night. By such means, death by fact can be postponed into a time without end.

Quackery needs both storytellers and scientists. Thus, we must listen when those learned about Victorian British racism tell us of two communities of *racists:* one community composed of storytellers and another of scientists. The question of whether there are therefore two forms of *racism* is addressed below, but let us agree for now that their approaches separate along community lines. There is, for want of a better term, the "literary racism" associated with Car-

---

13. Desmond (1994, 320–25, 343–53) gives a biting characterization of the man and his influence without examining Hunt's line of argument in any detail. While Hunt's claims about scientific practice are discussed in Rainger 1978, Hunt's method of practice is not. Ivan Hannaford (1996, 278) confuses a book Hunt translated, Vogt 1864, with something Hunt himself wrote. This is a mistake with the potential for ghastly consequences. H. S. Chamberlain was Vogt's pupil (Baker 1974, 48), and Vogt is not himself cited by Hannaford. What confuses the influences on Chamberlain muddles the linkage to the Nazi regime. Peart and Levy (2000) provide reasons to take Hunt *very* seriously, even more than I suggest here.

lyle, Kingsley, Anthony Trollope, *The Times*, and James Froude.[14] There is also what is universally referred to as "scientific racism." While the label "scientific" in an anthropological context traditionally meant "statistical,"[15] scientific racism today has been loosened from its statistical moorings to include the flamboyant Dr. James Hunt and, as he insisted upon calling himself, the *Anthropological Review*.[16] While Hunt did no statistical work, he thrust himself and his self-proclaimed "scientific" cause far into the public eye.

Scholars who have looked into the matter judge that for ordinary British people the literary influence was vastly more important than the scientific.[17] This judgment is surely right if only because of Carlyle's overwhelming importance. Mill responded so quickly to Carlyle for fear that the progression of abolition in America might be influenced. Sir Arthur Conan Doyle prepares the reader for Sherlock Holmes's willful ignorance of the solar system by having him first confess ignorance of Carlyle.[18] Hard as this is to appreciate from our

---

14. "*The Times*, truly representative of British opinion in this respect, heaped continual derision upon the Celtic character, which it assured its readers was the real cause of outrages in Ireland" (Lebow 1976, 48). "The view I took of the relative position in the West Indies of black men and white men was the view of *The Times* newspaper at that period; and there appeared three articles in that journal, one closely after another, which made the fortune of the book" (Trollope 1947, 110). Useful work on Kingsley includes that of John O. Waller (1963), Michael Banton (1977), and Douglas Lorimer (1978). Racial aspects in Carlyle's writing are discussed most helpfully by Persky (1990), Vanden Bossche (1991), and Young (1995).

15. "The anthropologists of the later period pursued the quest for certainty in the science of man by means of Number. Anthropology became the science of measuring the parts of the human body, principally the skull, but also the features, the limbs, the genital organs, the stature, the diameter of the heart or of the buttocks. Logic required that the measurements be made on large groups of specimens in order to find the common characteristics of the races. This process yielded statistical data" (Barzun 1937, 160–61).

16. Ashley Montagu (1942, 22) points to Hunt's influence. Haller, whose 1971 work made considerable use of publications in the *Anthropological Review*, does not mention Hunt himself, focusing on the statistical studies of Sanford Hunt and Samuel Morton (1995, 30–35). Gould (1981) also considers only statistical studies and consequently does not discuss Hunt. Hunt's importance is stressed in the work of L. P. Curtis (1968), Banton (1977), Lorimer (1978), Rainger (1978), Nancy Stepan (1982), Desmond (1994), and Young (1995). Frank Spencer (1986, 154) reports that Hunt's *The Negro's Place in Nature* served as the "model for 'scientific' writing on the subject for the remainder of the century." Peart and Levy (2000) argue that Hunt converted Francis Galton and so had an enormous albeit hidden impact on the discussion of race for the next fifty years.

17. "Scientific racism gave some weight to the belief in black inferiority, but the popular and literary sources were just as significant as scientific ones in the formation of the 'nigger' stereotype, and the concomitant conviction of English superiority. The mid-Victorians viewed the Negro as a happy-go-lucky, singing, dancing simpleton, who was perversely indolent, at times even deliberately and obstinately stupid, and on occasion ferociously cruel. This image, the *Daily News* noted, owed less to refinements in craniology or the definition of species, than to Thomas Carlyle, Charles Kingsley, and other less notable spokesmen for the West India interest" (Lorimer 1978, 160).

18. "Upon my quoting Thomas Carlyle, he inquired in the naïvest way who he might be and what he had done. My surprise reached a climax, however, when I found incidentally that he was

distance, their contemporaries seemed to have been on a familiar, first-name basis with both Carlyle and Kingsley.[19]

The scholarly distinction between literature and science supposes that in a vital sense these trades are different. A crude but serviceable distinction might be that in literature one can make everything up but in science one cannot. Facts cannot be manufactured out of wishes. But in quackery literature and science merge. Let the scientific hypothesis be as complicated as it can be, what the quack does is make up a reason—he tells a story—why a fact does not bear upon the theory. The black swan really is not a swan. And Carlyle might just number among the greatest storytellers of his age. It was not that long ago that his opposition to utilitarianism was a set text in Victorian literature. Perhaps it still is.

In quackery, we will find both real literature and real science. I am encouraged, therefore, that both Kingsley and Hunt publicly attest to Carlyle's great scientific stature.[20] Bringers of facts will find it perilous to laugh when Scheherazade begins her tale.

A Market for Racial Stereotypes

Carlyle cast American slave society as an instance of feudalism. Here is Froude's defense of this position—the explanation of the "Occasional Discourse on the Negro Question"—in his *Life of Carlyle:*

---

ignorant of the Copernican Theory and of the composition of the Solar System" (Conan Doyle 1930, 21). Barzun (1937, 57) quotes the Holmes stories as providing evidence for attitudes toward phrenology.

19. Using the OED on CD, we discover that "T Carlyle" is quoted 9 times; "Carlyle" is quoted 6,618 times. "C Kingsley" is quoted 95 times; "Kingsley" is quoted 2,959 times. "J Hunt" is by contrast quoted 16 times; none of the "Hunt" quotations are from his work.

20. "Scientific method is no peculiar mystery, requiring a peculiar initiation. It is simply common sense, combined with uncommon courage. . . . And let me say that the man whose writings exemplify most thoroughly what I am going to say is the present Lord Rector of the University of Edinburgh, Mr. Thomas Carlyle. As far as I know, he has never written on any scientific subject. For aught I am aware of, he may know nothing of mathematics or chemistry, of comparative anatomy or geology. For aught I am aware of, he may know a great deal about them all, and, like a wise man, hold his tongue, and give the world merely the results in the form of general thought. But this I know, that his writings are instinct with the very spirit of science; that he has taught men, more than any living man, the meaning and end of science; that he has taught men moral and intellectual courage; to face facts boldly, while they confess the divineness of facts; not to be afraid of nature" (Kingsley 1866, 24).

Hunt takes the events in Jamaica as the opening salvo in Knox's permanent racial war "He would have that latest of all ethnological puzzles to some—the present 'insurrection in Jamaica;' an insurrection, however, which he, as we have already seen, foretold upon scientific principles, which Carlyle, in his on 'The Nigger Question,' hinted at as probable on grounds of social economy" (1866a, 25–26). Young (1995) has an extensive discussion of Knox and his doctrine that "race is all."

> He did not mean that the "Niggers" should have been kept as cattle, and sold as cattle at their owners' pleasure. He did mean that they ought to have been treated as human beings, for whose souls and bodies the whites were responsible; that they should have been placed in a position suited to their capacity, like that of the English serfs under the Plantagenets. (1885, 2:15)

To appreciate the role that racial stereotypes play in the debates, it is helpful to consider Carlyle's presentation of an idealized hierarchical society in the days before the "Negro Question."[21] This will help to prepare us for the essay's importance in the American debates.

Although many things are obscure in Carlyle's exercise in metafiction, the 1833–34 *Sartor Resartus*, the claim that society is founded on obedience is as clear as can be:

> Thus is there a true religious Loyalty for ever rooted in his heart; nay, in all ages, even in ours, it manifests itself as a more or less orthodox *Hero-worship*. In which fact, that Hero-worship exists, has existed, and will for ever exist, universally among Mankind, mayst thou discern the corner-stone of living rock, whereon all Polities for the remotest time may stand secure. (1987, 190)

While Carlyle combats the notion of genetic equality,[22] his tribute to George Fox's antislavery crusade is as striking as anything he ever wrote.[23]

In the 1839 *Chartism*, Carlyle proposes *a* feudal system—not, of course, *the* feudal system, which actually existed—as an ideal to oppose a market economy:[24]

---

21. A conversation with Bryan Caplan is responsible for this section. He asked why statistical racism of the modern variety would not have sufficed for Carlyle's purposes.

22. "It is maintained, by Helvetius and his set, that an infant of genius is quite the same as any other infant, only that certain surprisingly favourable influences accompany him through life, especially through childhood, and expand him, while others lie close-folded and continue dunces. Herein, say they, consists the whole difference between an inspired Prophet and a double-barrelled Game-preserver. . . . 'With which opinion,' cries Teufelsdröckh, 'I should as soon agree as with this other, that an acorn might, by favourable or unfavourable influences of soil and climate, be nursed into a cabbage, or the cabbage-seed into an oak'" (Carlyle 1987, 72–73).

23. "Stitch away, thou noble Fox: every prick of that little instrument is pricking into the heart of Slavery, and World-worship, and the Mammon-god. . . . there is in broad Europe one Free Man, and thou art he!" (ibid., 159–60).

24. Thus, Carlyle's disciples can be seen as offering proposals to "reform" slavery in opposition to the abolitionist proposals of the antislavery coalition. Chapter 6 discusses some episodes and Richard Whately's attack on the idea of a reformable slavery.

O reader, to what shifts is poor Society reduced, struggling to give still some account of herself, in epochs when Cash Payment has become the sole nexus of man to men! On the whole, we will advise Society not to talk at all about what she exists for; but rather with her whole industry to exist, to try how she can keep existing! That is her best plan. She may depend upon it, if she ever, by cruel chance, did come to exist only for protection of breeches-pocket property, she would lose very soon the gift of protecting even that, and find her career in our lower world on the point of terminating!—For the rest, that in the most perfect Feudal Ages, the Ideal of Aristocracy nowhere lived in vacant serene purity as an Ideal, but always as a poor imperfect Actual, little heeding or not knowing at all that an Ideal lay in it,—this too we will cheerfully admit. (1904, 29:164–65)[25]

This is not to say that a market economy did not have its place:

—In those entirely surprising circumstances to which the Eighteen Century had brought us, in the time of Adam Smith, *Laissez-faire* was a reasonable cry;—as indeed, in all circumstances, for a wise governor there will be meaning in the principle of it. To wise governors you will cry: "See what you will, and will not, let alone." To unwise governors, to hungry Greeks throttling down hungry Greeks on the floor of a St. Stephen's, you will cry: "Let *all* things alone; for Heaven's sake meddle ye with nothing."

How *Laissez-faire* may adjust itself in other provinces we say not: but we do venture to say, and ask whether events everywhere, in world-history and parish-history, in all manner of dialects are not saying it, That in regard to the lower orders of society, and their governance and guidance, the principle of *Laissez-faire* has terminated. (157)

And who should be the master? Who shall rule and be ruled? Look around:

That *Laissez-faire* has as good as done its part in a great many provinces; that in the province of the Working Classes, *Laissez-faire* having passed its

---

25. A similar argument is found earlier: "'The Soul Politic having departed,' says Teufelsdröckh, 'what can follow but that the Body Politic be decently interred, to avoid putrescence? Liberals, Economists, Utilitarians enough I see marching with its bier, and chaunting loud pœns, toward the funeral-pile, where, amid wailings from some, and saturnalian revelries from the most, the venerable Corpse is to be burnt'" (Carlyle 1987, 177). The argument that government is an exchange of protection for taxation is found in Whately 1832, 10; 1833, 63–73. The reader who does not know Whately's argument that government is founded in exchange will have a hard time appreciating Carlyle's craft.

New Poor-Law, has reached the suicidal point, and now, as *felo-de-se*, lies dying there, in torchlight meetings and suchlike, that, in brief, a government of the under classes by the upper on a principle of *Let-alone* is no longer possible in England in these days. . . . The Working Classes cannot any longer go on without government: without being *actually* guided and governed. (155)

That Carlyle's proposal of domination is meant for English subjects is clear in his ringing tribute to the authors of the New Poor Law:

[We] are far from joining in the outcry raised against those poor Poor-Law Commissioners, as if they were tigers in men's shape; as if their Amendment Act were a mere monstrosity and horror, deserving instant abrogation. They are not tigers; they are men filled with an idea of a theory: their Amendment Act, heretical and damnable as a whole truth, is orthodox and laudable as a *half*-truth; and was imperatively required to be put in practice. To create men filled with a theory, that refusal of out-door relief was the one thing needful: Nature had no readier way of getting out-door relief refused. . . .

Any law, however well meant as a law, which has become a bounty on unthrift, idleness, bastardy and beer-drinking, must be put an end to. In all ways it needs, especially in these times, to be proclaimed aloud that for the idle man there is no place in this England of ours. (1904, 29:131–32)

In a joking metaphor, Carlyle compares the workers to horses. The metaphor will remain as the jokes vanish, as we shall see later:

New Poor-Law! *Laissez faire, laissez passer!* The master of horses, when the summer labour is done, has to feed his horses through the winter. If he said to his horses: "Quadrupeds, I have no longer work for you; but work exists abundantly over the world: are you ignorant (or must I read you Political-Economy Lectures) that the Steamengine always in the long-run creates additional work? . . . Ah, it is not a joyful mirth, it is sadder than tears, the laugh Humanity is forced to, at *Laissez-faire* applied to poor peasants, in a world like our Europe of the year 1839! (142)

However, mixed with these stern words about the English, both upper and lower classes, are messages of another sort about the Other: improve or face extermination.[26]

---

26. "The time has come when the Irish population must either be improved a little, or else exterminated" (Carlyle 1904, 29:139). Carlyle makes a list of political issues that distract parlia-

The most systematic discussion of an idealized slavery is found in Carlyle's 1844 *Past and Present:*

> True enough, man *is* forever the "born thrall" of certain men, born master of certain other men, born equal of certain others, let him acknowledge the fact or not. It is unblessed for him when he cannot acknowledge this fact; he is in the chaotic state, ready to perish, till he do get the fact acknowledged. (1965, 249).

The point of life is to find one's natural master, to be directed to one's dynamic optimum:

> Sure enough, of all paths a man could strike into, there *is*, at any given moment, a *best path* for every man; a thing which, here and now, it were of all things *wisest* for him to do,—which could he be but led or driven to do, he were then doing "like a man," as we phrase it; all men and gods agreeing with him, the whole Universe virtually exclaiming Well-done to him! His success, in such case, were complete; his felicity a maximum. This path, to find this path and walk in it, is the one thing needful for him. (217)

When it comes to that, one might have to be whipped to be free:

> Liberty? The true liberty of a man, you would say, consisted in his finding out, or being forced to find out the right path, and walk thereon. To learn, or to be taught, what work he actually was able for; and then, by permission, persuasion, and even compulsion, to set about doing of the same! . . . If thou do know better than I what is good and right, I conjure thee in the name of God, force me to do it; were it by never such brass collars, whips and handcuffs, leave me not to walk over precipices! (211–12)

In *Past and Present*, we find a continuation of Carlyle's complaint about the attention paid to other races far away and, something that is critical to the

---

mentary attention from the condition of the workers, which contains the following items: Canada question, Irish appropriation question, West-Indian question, Queen's bedchamber question, game laws, usury laws, African Blacks, Hill Coolies, Smithfield cattle, and dog-carts (120–21). Four "other" races, three animals and three other questions serve to distract. One must note that Carlyle's Hero crosses racial lines (164): "Society, it is understood, does not in any age prevent a man from being what he *can be*. A sooty African can become a Toussaint L'Ouverture, a murderous Three-fingered Jack, let the yellow West Indies say to what they will." Since Carlyle proposes "extermination" as a policy option, presumably the reader ought not to read "murderous" as serious disapprobation.

argument of the "Negro Question," an infallible method of distinguishing masters and slaves:

> if I had a Twenty Millions, with Model-Farms and Niger Expeditions, it is to these that I would give it! Quashee has already victuals, clothing; Quashee is not dying of such despair as the yellow-coloured pale man's. Quashee, it must be owned, is hitherto a kind of block-head. The Haiti Duke of Marmalade, educated now for almost half a century, seems to have next to no sense in him. Why, in one of those Lancashire Weavers, dying of hunger, there is more thought and heart, a greater arithmetical amount of misery and desperation, than in whole gangs of Quashees. (275)[27]

Consider Carlyle's problem as a supplier of the ideology of slavery. How does he go about persuading someone in a market economy—LF denotes that status quo—to favor the institution of slavery, S? As Carlyle explains, although the point probably did not require explanation, in slavery there are masters and there are slaves. Suppose further that the free worker believes that *his* hypothetical conditions could be compared to the status quo as follows:[28]

$$U(S|\text{master}) > U(LF) > U(S|\text{slave}).$$

If acceptance of the ideology of slavery depends upon the expected utility of S relative to LF, then the problem is to persuade men to believe that they are destined to be masters.

When Mill responds to the "Negro Question," he notes that Carlyle's Gospel of Labor has been refashioned to make it more appealing to whites:

> Your contributor incessantly prays Heaven that all persons, black and white, may be put in possession of this "divine right of being compelled, if permitted will not serve, to do what work they are appointed for." But as this cannot be conveniently managed just yet, he will begin with the blacks, and will make them work *for* certain whites, those whites *not* working at all. (1850, 27)

This is precisely the reading I would urge.

---

27. The 20 million pounds are part of the price the British taxpayer absorbed for West Indian emancipation. Judging from my reading of the British debates, no one would miss the reference. It is somewhat harder to find in modern literary discussions of Carlyle, as JSTOR can verify.

28. *His* is emphasized to note the sexual usage of slaves. If married male masters use their slaves sexually but married female masters do not, slave-owning wives might not be as pleased with the arrangement as their husbands are.

Carlyle's Economic Quackery

In the late 1840s, the former slaves in the West Indies were devastated by a fall in the price of produce brought about by the abolition of protective tariffs.[29] Liberal philanthropy—which had been so important in the emancipation—raised money to help ameliorate the distress. Carlyle was persuaded that their unemployment was the result only of their refusal to work. From this refusal to work—a characteristic of both Irish and blacks—Carlyle attempted to prove their subhuman status. There are three important essays in the public Carlyle-Mill exchange. The first is Carlyle's December 1849 *Fraser's* "Negro Question," in which he proposed reenslavement of Jamaicans.[30] The second is Mill's response in January 1850.[31] The third is Carlyle's reply in the February 1850 essay "The Present Time," the first of the *Latter-Day Pamphlets.*[32]

What Carlyle said about his command of economics on this occasion is correct: he had a firm grasp of the relevant line of thinking. The defining characteristic of the human race, in the classical economics of Adam Smith and Richard Whately, is that humans trade. Smith used this approach to argue for the analytical equality of humans. The analysis was also used by Edward

---

29. "The compensation for this loss was partly the money awarded by parliament to the slave-holders; much more, the pledge of the government that slave-grown sugar should be subject to a higher duty than that produced by free labour" (Denman 1853, 35).

30. "[M]anful industrious men occupy their West Indies, not indolent two-legged cattle, however 'happy' over their abundant pumpkins! Both these things, we may be assured, the immortal gods have decided upon, passed their eternal act of parliament for: and both of them, though all terrestrial Parliaments and entities oppose it to the death, shall be done. Quashee, if he will not help in bringing out the spices, will get himself made a slave again (which state will be a little less ugly than his present one), and with beneficent whip, since other methods avail not, will be compelled to work" (Carlyle 1849, 675).

31. In response, Mill puts forward the Afrocentric hypothesis that "It is curious withal, that the earliest known civilization was, we have the strongest reason to believe, a negro civilization. The original Egyptians are inferred, from the evidence of their sculptures, to have been a negro race: it was from negroes, therefore, that the Greeks learnt their first lessons in civilization; and to the records and traditions of these negroes did the Greek philosophers to the very end of their career resort (I do not say with much fruit) as a treasury of mysterious wisdom" (1850, 30). Testifying as to how far the Carlyle-Mill debate is from common knowledge, this statement was unknown to Martin Bernal (1987). Young (1995, 128) sees it.

32. "Negro Question" purports to be a report of a lecture at Exeter Hall. In "The Present Time" we are presented with "*Speech of the British Prime Minister to the floods of Irish and other Beggars, the able-bodied Lackalls, nomadic or stationary, and the general assembly, outdoor and indoor, of the Pauper Populations of these Realms*" (Carlyle 1850b, 46). After the speech goes on for some time, we read what follows.

Carlyle (53–54): "[Here arises indescribable uproar, no longer repressible, from all manner of Economists, Emancipationists, Constitutionalists, and miscellaneous Professors of the Dismal Science, pretty numerously scattered about; and cries of 'Private Enterprise,' 'Rights of Capital,' 'Voluntary Principle,' 'Doctrines of the British Constitution,' swollen by the general assenting hum of all the world, quite drown the Chief Minister for a while. He, with invincible resolution, persists; obtains hearing again:]

Wakefield and then by Carlyle to argue for the subhuman condition of some humanlike races: if the members of a race will not trade, then they are not fully human.

Quackery enters when we observe members of race X not trading in circumstance α, but when they trade in circumstance ß we tell a story to distract attention from this fact.[33] Or it enters when we observe members of race X "not trading" in circumstance δ but we tell a story to distract attention from the fact that members of race Y also do not trade in the same circumstance δ.

Commentary on the racial aspects of Carlyle's work sometimes focuses exclusively on the Jamaican-centered debates, ignoring the extensive Irish debate.[34] Mill's response to the "Negro Question" was written in anger and in haste. His attack on the vulgarity of racial explanations in the 1848 *Political*

"Respectable Professors of the Dismal Science, soft you a little! Alas, I know what you would say, For my sins, I have read much in those inimitable volumes of yours,—really I should think, some barrowfuls of them in my time,—and, in these last forty years of theory and practice, have pretty well seized what of Divine Message you were sent with to me. Perhaps as small a message, give me leave to say, as ever there was such a noise made about before. Trust me, I have not forgotten it, shall never forget it. Those Laws of the Shop-till are indisputable to me; and practically useful in certain departments of the Universe, as the multiplication-table itself. Once I even tried to sail through the Immensities with them, and to front the big coming Eternities with them; but I found it would not do. As the Supreme Rule of Statesmanship, or, Government of Men,—since this Universe is not wholly a Shop,—no. . . . But beyond and above the Shop-till, allow me to say, you shall as good as hold your peace. Respectable Professors, I perceive it is not now the Gigantic Hucksters, but it is the Immortal Gods, yes they, in their terror and their beauty, in their wrath and their beneficence, that are coming into play in the affairs of this world! Soft you a little. Do not you interrupt me, but try to understand and help me!—"

33. Arguments for the subrationality of workers because they worked less when wages were higher were met by the classical economists, who emphasized the importance of knowing whether the workers were really paid higher wages or not."Some workmen, indeed, when they can earn in four days what will maintain them through the week, will be idle the other three. This, however, is by no means the case with the greater part. Workmen, on the contrary, when they are liberally paid by the piece, are very apt to over-work themselves, and to ruin their health and constitution in a few years" (Smith 1976a, 99–100). David Ricardo emphasized that happiness is the goal of all people. Moreover, the worker had to be certain that extra wages would in fact be forthcoming for extra work: "Happiness is the object to be desired, and we cannot be quite sure that provided he is equally well fed, a man may not be happier in the enjoyment of the luxury of idleness than the enjoyment of the luxuries of a neat cottage, and good clothes. After all we do not know if these would fall to his share. His labour might only increase the enjoyments of his employer" (1951, 7:184–85). Sam Hollander gave me this reference.

34. While Hall (1992, 288) is completely clear on the racial issue—in terms of black and white—between Carlyle and Mill, she attributes their debate to different conceptions of masculinity. Indeed, she has a "problem" whether Mill might not have a doctrine of "a *natural* division of labour between the races." She seems not to be aware of the decade-spanning racial debates in a Celtic context. Curtis (1968, 47–48) discusses an 1868 review in the *Quarterly Review*, which "pointed out that it was foolish for the political economists to prescribe remedies for the Irish question until the character of the Irish people had completely changed. J. S. Mill's [1848] mistake, he maintained, was to treat Irish cottiers as though they were Englishmen. It was time Mill learned

Economy is a technical set piece in which he walks the reader through a precise delineation of the quackery.[35] How can the "Celtic race" be the explanation for Irish poverty and unemployment? This can only be accomplished by ignoring the fact of the Irish working in America, where they were actually being paid for their work. If modern commentators do not know Mill's official position on the vulgarity of racial explanations, Carlyle certainly did. Mill gave him a copy of *Political Economy*, and his marginal note on the vulgarity paragraph has survived.[36] If one does not know the science, then it will be hard to understand why the story is told the way it is.

To see the science, we must know the *Wealth of Nations*. For Adam Smith, the problem is to explain trade and all things that result from trade. To this end, he appeals to a language-linked instinct to truck and barter. This he explains as a characterization of our race alone:

> Whether this propensity be one of those original principles in human nature, of which no further account can be given; or whether, as seems more probable, it be the necessary consequence of the faculties of reason and speech, it belongs not to our present subject to enquire. It is common to all men, and to be found in no other race of animals, which seem to know neither this nor any other species of contracts. (1976a, 25)

The race of humans is set apart from the other races of animals by language because language, not physical differences, is the key to cooperation. Dogs have more physical differences than people, but lacking language in which to

---

that the Irishman was 'not an average human being—an idiomatic and idiosyncratic, not an abstract man.'" The author of the attack on Mill is W. R. Greg, one of the founders of eugenics (Peart and Levy 2000). It is in this context that one ought to read Nassau Senior's 1841 *Edinburgh Review* discussion of the English Poor Law (1865, 2:98): "The redundancy [of population] vanished with its causes. The able-bodied pauper is the result of art; he is not the natural offspring of the Saxon race." Please note: Senior is applying the "giggle test" to racism.

35. The argument is mentioned but not used in reply to Carlyle: "[I]f he had not disdained to apply the same mode of investigation to the laws of the formation of character, he would have escaped the vulgar error of imputing every difference which he finds among human beings to an original difference of nature" (Mill 1850, 29).

36. "Is it not, then, a bitter satire on the mode in which opinions are formed on the most important problems of human nature and life, to find public instructors of the greatest pretensions, imputing the backwardness of Irish industry, and the want of energy of the Irish people improving their condition, to a peculiar indolence and *insouciance* in the Celtic race? Of all vulgar modes of escaping from the consideration of the effect of social and moral influences on the human mind, the most vulgar is that of attributing the diversities of conduct and character to inherent natural differences. What race would not be indolent and insouciant when terms are so arranged? . . . It speaks nothing against the capacities of industries in human beings, that they will not exert themselves without motive. No labourers work harder, in England or America, than the Irish; but not under a cottier system" (Mill 1965, 319). "Yes, but what kind of 'race' is it that has *made* such arrangements?" (Carlyle, quoted in Baumgarten 1980, 87).

express the notion of "fair" they cannot trade (30). In 1831, Whately put Smith's point this way:

> Man might be defined, "An animal that makes *Exchanges*:" no other, even of those animals which in other points make the nearest approach to rationality, having, in all appearance, the least notion of bartering, or in any way exchanging one thing for another. (6)

A rich source of information about the development of economics in the nineteenth century can be found in the commentary appended by successive editors to the nineteenth-century editions of the *Wealth of Nations*. In particular, the widely employed edition by Edward Wakefield challenges Smith's doctrine of human uniqueness. Wakefield argued that the sharp distinction between humans and animals that Smith and Whately supposed is actually fuzzy.[37] There are some races that will not trade and therefore are closer to animals than they are to the fully human. Here is what we shall call the Wakefield claim:

> The savages of New Holland never help each other, even in the most simple operations; and their condition is hardly superior, in some respects it is inferior, to that of the wild animals which they now and then catch. (Smith 1835, 1:27)

Having made this claim, it is not surprising that Wakefield objects to Smith's foundational claim that there is a language-linked human propensity to exchange. The New Hollanders are language users, so any language-linked propensity to trade would predict that they trade even if we do not observe it easily. Rather, he argues against Smith proposing that dogs don't trade because there is nothing they want that they do not already have:

> The highly ingenious illustrations of the alleged principle, which it is the object of this chapter to establish, have kept out of view some considerations from which it will appear that, in truth, there is no such principle; that division of employments does not arise from a mere trucking propensity in man, but from certain human peculiarities which give occasion to the exchange itself.

---

37. We know that Wakefield encountered Whately's doctrine of human uniqueness because he cites Whately's proposal, made on the same page, to change *political economy* to *science of exchange* (Smith 1835, 1:77). Whately in fact proposed a Greek coinage—*katallactics*. The Greek carries connotations of reciprocity. This proposal, which embodies the Smith-Whately doctrine of the uniqueness of human exchange and the analytical irrelevance of the isolated individual, is discussed in chapter 10. The importance of a norm of reciprocity for the evangelical-economic coalition is considered in chapter 6.

The wants of every inferior animal are extremely limited. No inferior animal wants more than food and shelter; the quantity and kind of food, and the kind of shelter, being always the same with respect to each race of animals. . . . The wants of man, on the contrary, are unlimited. (Smith 1835, 1:59)

Thus, in Wakefield's argument, humans will trade because they are insatiable whereas animals are easily satiated.[38]

At the center of classical economics, therefore, we have a test for the human status of a particular race. If they will trade, they are human; if they will not trade, they are not. The Wakefield claim removes language from the argument and substitutes unsatisfied desires. Dogs—and semihumans—in Wakefield's account don't trade because they are not in want.

It is in this context that I suggest we read the Carlyle-Mill debate. In it, Carlyle argues for the fundamental identity of the Irish, blacks, and horses on the ground that neither horses, blacks, nor Irish will voluntarily trade leisure for wages. The Carlyle material will be read out of order so that we can separate, as much as we can, the Carlyle version of the Wakefield claim—the science required for the quackery—from the story Carlyle told to distract attention from Mill's facts. The story has two characters in it. After we see the science, we can appreciate what each character does in the story Carlyle tells.

For Carlyle, contractual relationships with horses are as promising as contractual relationships with blacks or Irish. Before, horses stood for all workers, indeed, those with whom we were invited to sympathize. They have a new role to play. They are now the image of the Other. Here is the Carlyle version of the Wakefield claim; motivation by incentives will not work for the subhuman, as they have no reason to exchange. Want not work not:

West-Indian Blacks are emancipated, and it appears refuse to work: Irish Whites have long been entirely emancipated; and nobody asks them to work, . . . Among speculative persons, a question has sometimes risen: In the progress of Emancipation, are we to look for a time when all the Horses also are to be emancipated, and brought to the supply-and-demand principle? Horses too have "motives;" are acted on by hunger, fear, hope, love of oats, terror of platted leather; nay they have vanity, ambition, emulation, thankfulness, vindictiveness; some rude outline of all our human

---

38. In fact, the foundations of modern neoclassical economics are much closer to Wakefield's ideas than to Smith's. Nonetheless, the recent experimental work on animal economics ought to have shattered the illusion that animal preferences differ in structure from those of humans. A reconsideration of Smith's argument in light of this research is undertaken elsewhere (Levy 1992, 17–33 and chap. 10).

> spiritualities,—a rude resemblance to us in mind and intelligence, even as they have in bodily frame. . . . I am sure if I could make him "happy," I should be willing to grant a small vote (in addition to the late twenty millions) for that object!
>
> Him too you occasionally tyrannise over; and with bad result to yourselves among others; using the leather in a tyrannous unnecessary manner; withholding, or scantily furnishing, the oats and ventilated stabling that are due. Rugged horse-subduers, one fears they are a little tyrannous at times. "Am I not a horse, and *half*-brother?" (1850b, 30–31)

What is the consequence of treating horses as if they were human?

> So long as grass lasts, I dare say they are very happy, or think themselves so. And Farmer Hodge sallying forth, on a dry spring morning with a sieve of oats in his hand, and agony of eager expectation in his heart, is he happy? Help me to plough this day, Black Dobbin: oats in full measure if thou wilt. "Hlunh, No—thank!" snorts Black Dobbin; he prefers glorious liberty and the grass. Bay Darby, wilt not though perhaps? "Hlunh!"— Grey Joan, then, my beautiful broad-bottomed mare,—O Heaven, she too answers Hlunh! Not a quadruped of them will plough a stroke for me. (31–32)

Attempting to contract with the subhuman has predictable consequences that correspond exactly with attempts to contract with two-legged subhumans.

> Corn-crops are *ended* in this world!—For the sake, if not of Hodge, then of Hodge's horses, one prays this benevolent practice might now cease, and a new and better one try to begin. Small kindness to Hodge's horses to emancipate them! The fate of all emancipated horses is, sooner or later, inevitable. To have in this habitable Earth no grass to eat,—in Black Jamaica gradually none, as in White Connemara already none;—to roam aimless, wasting the seedfields of the world;—and be hunted home to Chaos, by the due watchdogs and due hell-dogs. (32)

The Wakefield claim is the science. Now the story. An unnamed speaker appears at Exeter Hall to tell the evangelicals ever so bluntly what they need to know. The voice speaks as if that of destiny itself.[39] Here is the comparison of white and black claims on our compassion:

---

39. Thus, Mill opens his response with what would later become his official position in such a case, that we would be under obligation to oppose the gods themselves: "If 'the gods' will this, it is the first duty of human beings to resist such gods" (1850, 25).

> [T]he British Whites are rather badly off; several millions of them hanging
> on the verge of continual famine; and in single towns, many thousands of
> them very sore put to it, at this time, not to live "well," or as a man should,
> in any sense temporal or spiritual, but to live at all:—these, again, are
> uncomfortable facts; and they are extremely extensive and important ones.
> But, thank Heaven, our interesting Black population,—equalling almost in
> number of heads one of the Ridings of Yorkshire, and in *worth* (in quan-
> tity of intellect, faculty, docility, energy, and available human valour and
> value) perhaps one of the streets of Seven Dials,—are all doing remarkably
> well. "Sweet blighted lilies,"—as the American epitaph on the Nigger child
> has it,—sweet blighted lilies, they are holding up their heads again! (Car-
> lyle 1849, 670–71)

The "Negro Question" has been judged a great piece of comedy that readers
are too humorless to grasp.[40] I use a footnote to parse one of the jokes that
indeed escaped the commentators.[41]

Now, we meet the first character, the black unemployed. Can anyone
imagine that this character is related to the white unemployed? Why would
one even think of making factual comparisons across such racial divides?

> Sitting yonder with their beautiful muzzles up to the ears in pumpkins,
> imbibing sweet pulps and juices; the grinder and incisor teeth ready for
> ever new work, and the pumpkins cheap as grass in those rich climates:
> while the sugar-crops rot round them uncut, because labour cannot be
> hired, so cheap are the pumpkins. (Carlyle 1849, 671)

Possibly, it is unnecessary to belabor the point that this character in the story
has lost some appeal. But, behold, there is another character in the story, one
who walks among the living. This is the economist, who brings facts. So
enthralled is the economist by the satanic mills of the imagination, that he or
she cannot tell the difference between the black and the white and from this
failure argues for emancipation for all:

---

40. "Carlyle constructs a brilliant parody of an Exeter Hall meeting, with an unnamed speaker
spelling out unpalatable truths to an audience driven deeper and deeper into shock. Philanthropy
in general he parodies. . . . Carlyle did not feel he was attacking the blacks; his targets were the liberals who were destroying them" (Heffer 1995, 276).

41. The modern editor of "Negro Question" could not find the reference to "sweet blighted
lilies" (Eugene August in Carlyle 1971, 8). Carlyle's friend Martineau visited America to confront
slavery in person. She reports: (1837, 3:101): "Even in their ultimate, funereal courtesies, the
coloured race imitate the whites. An epitaph on a negro baby at Savannah begins, 'Sweet blighted
lily!'" Carlyle laughs at a dead baby's parents' hope of the final Resurrection. Martineau's influence
is everywhere; Craft (1860, 109) acknowledges her help.

> Truly, my philanthropic friends, Exeter Hall Philanthropy is wonderful: and the Social Science—not a "gay science," but a rueful—which finds the secret of this universe in "supply-and-demand," and reduces the duty of human governors to that of letting men alone, is also wonderful. Not a "gay science," I should say, like some we have heard of; no, a dreary, desolate, and indeed quite abject and distressing one: what we might call, by way of eminence, the *dismal science*. These two, Exeter Hall Philanthropy and the Dismal Science, led by any sacred cause of Black Emancipation, or the like, to fall in love and make a wedding of it,—will give birth to progenies and prodigies; dark extensive moon-calves, unnameable abortions, wide-coiled monstrosities, such as the world has not seen hitherto! (672–73)

How confident must one be to condemn a race to death for its failure to match one's understanding. As was said long ago on a kindred occasion, one must be either a god or very wicked. Carlyle forces his readers to make this choice about who he is:

> —Work, was I saying? My indigent unguided friends, I should think some work might be discoverable for you. Enlist, stand drill; become, from a nomadic Banditti of Idleness, Soldiers of Industry! I will lead you to the Irish Bogs, to the vacant desolations of Connaught now falling into Cannibalism. . . .
>
>   To each of you I will then say: Here is work for you; strike into it with manlike, soldierlike obedience and heartiness, according to the methods here prescribed,—wages follow for you without difficulty; all manner of just remuneration, and at length *emancipation itself follows*. Refuse to strike into it; shirk the heavy labour, disobey the rules,—I will admonish and endeavour to incite you; if in vain, I will flog you; if still in vain, I will at last shoot you,—and make God's Earth, and the forlorn-hope in God's Battle, free of you. (1850b, 54–55; emphasis added)

The bulk of Mill's response deals with the normative questions raised by Carlyle's assumption of heavenly form and his Gospel of Labor—which exempts whites from labor and Carlyle from doing more than providing "guidance"—but he takes the time to sketch the fact that Carlyle's story must deflect:

> I have so serious a quarrel with him about principles, that I have no time to spare for his facts; but let me remark, how easily he takes for granted those which fit his case. Because he reads in some blue-book of a strike for wages in Demerara, such as he may read of any day in Manchester, he draws a picture of negro inactivity, copied from the wildest prophecies of the slavery party before emancipation. (1850, 27)

It is only the failure to compare workers in Demerara to those in Manchester that allows Carlyle to draw the conclusion that those in Demerara are unusual. If British workers are sometimes unemployed, then it is quackery to argue from Jamaican unemployment to Jamaican subhuman status without making the parallel case for the British workers.

Carlyle Comes to America

While British proslavery opinions of the 1850s might surprise nonspecialists, if Mill were correct one would expect that Carlyle's opinions would find an appreciative audience in the American South. Using the Making of America data set, we can document Carlyle's impact on America and test Mill's hypothesis that "Negro Question" would bend the debate.[42]

Doing searches on "dismal science" and "Carlyle ∧ emancipation," we find "Negro Question" reprinted twice:[43] first in the June 1850 *Commercial Review* and second in the 1851 compendium *Negro-Mania*.[44] We find a massive review of *Past and Present* and "Negro Question" in the *Southern Quarterly Review* of 1853 under the illuminating heading "British and American Slavery." We find proslavery voices seizing on the breaking of British antislavery hegemony:

> We are able, however, to point with satisfaction to distinguished exceptions: to the London Times, the ablest newspaper in the world; and to Thomas Carlyle, the greatest, the wisest, and the bravest living English author, with whose words of deep and solemn import . . . we will close this article. ("British and American Slavery" 1853, 410)

The Making of America data allow us to transcend mere reading and accomplish something more to the liking of modern economists: counting and testing. To this we turn.

The "Negro Question" in its forthright way emphasizes the important fact of the coalition between biblical literalists and utilitarian economists. By framing his essay as a lecture at Exeter Hall—the London center of organized evan-

---

42. Cynthia Earman told me about the Making of America data base. The searches were conducted October 1–4, 1999. Only the University of Michigan site <http://moa.umdl.umich.edu> was then searchable; the Cornell University site <http://edl.library.cornell.edu/moa/> was not yet operational. I leave the Cornell site as an exercise for the reader.

43. "Carlyle emancipation" produced 42 hits when restricted to the same page and 171 in the same work. The immediate American reception of "Negro Question" argues for its importance relative to *ODNQ*.

44. Variations on "Negro-Mania" turned up twenty-three hits, with several large reviews mentioning Carlyle.

gelicalism—Carlyle attempts to localize the opposition to slavery as that of a narrow sect. After all, Carlyle's opposition to biblical literalism earned him the persistent label "progressive." "Exeter Hall" might be an odd reference to find in an American discussion of slavery.

Indeed, in the period 1800–45, in the 987 works in which the word *slave** appears precisely 2 also contain the term *Exeter Hall*.[45] In the period 1850–65, in the 3,970 works in which the word *slave** appears 62 contain *Exeter Hall*. Conducting a simple test for the equality of the two proportions gives us a normally distributed test statistic of -3.38. This allows us to reject the hypothesis of the equality of two proportions at any conventional level. While correlation does not imply cause, what alternative is there to the conclusion that Carlyle bent the debate in America? Mill's hypothesis resists falsification.

Of course, Carlyle was not the only racist to be imported into America. Consider how attractive in predictable parts of America the words of Carlyle's disciple Kingsley published in 1864 were, identifying American slave owners with Teutonic knights and explaining how the condition of the slave depends on the race of the master. Such words came from the center of the British intellectual world. They are found in the printed version of his lectures—*The Roman and the Teuton*—which Kingsley delivered as the Regius Professor of Modern History at Cambridge:

> Roman domestic slavery is not to be described by the pen of an Englishman. And I must express my sorrow, that in the face of such notorious facts, some have of late tried to prove American slavery to be as bad as, or even worse than, that of Roman. God forbid! Whatsoever may have been the sins of the Southern gentleman, he is at least a Teuton, and not a Roman; a whole moral heaven above the effeminate wretch, who in the 4th and 5th centuries called himself a senator and a clarissimus. (1864, 20)

Kingsley in America? The early AEA Teutonic racism came from somewhere. Here?

Speech and Anthropological Quackery as Practiced

We leave the realm of high art to consider two of Carlyle's capable thralls. Kingsley and Hunt were vigorous critics of contemporary economics. Kingsley's 1850 *Alton Locke* is cited even today as a substantial criticism of the condition of the "white slaves" of Britain.[46] The problem with capitalism, as

---

45. The use of the asterisk allows us to catch *slave, slaves,* and *slavery* in one search.

46. Modern scholars prefer to use the term *wage slave,* although it is rarely found in the Making of America's University of Michigan data set: between 1800 and 1865, I counted 5 uses of *wage** *slave**. *White slave* is the common term employed in the debate. In the same 1800 and 1865 period, I found 216 uses of *white slave** in 119 works.

Kingsley explains, is that Jews get to be masters. Unlike Teutons, Jews are not a race one trusts with mastership.[47] Hunt proposed "anthropology" as a replacement for the egalitarian-influenced economics.[48] Contemporary scholarship classes Kingsley and Hunt as belonging to different communities of racism. Here I propose to document quackery common to speech therapy and racial anthropology.

I have used the market metaphor, the market for ideology, to describe Carlyle's recasting of slavery to make white men immune from the role of slave. However, the market for speech therapy is a real market. "Cures" are bought and sold with real money. We can, I propose, better understand the market metaphor by considering a real market transaction. In particular we can observe the same argumentative strategy that was used in a context to persuade men to part with their money being used in another context to persuade men to part with their antislavery egalitarian beliefs.

Hunt's first book is a response to the *Lancet's* charge of quackery against his father's speech practice. Here Hunt quotes from the *Lancet* about quacks in general:

> *Nothing but perfect cure and unparalleled success is ever heard of in the practice of the empiric.* Charles Lamb in the country churchyard, seeing the virtues set forth upon every tombstone, wondered "where all the bad people could have been buried." So we wonder where all the bad cases of the quacks can get to. (1854, 36; emphasis added)

This provides textual warrant for the assertion that in the judgment of the community we study a quack practices without failure. When Kingsley reviews James Hunt's speech therapy for *Fraser's,* the perfect cure claim for average stammerers is put forward:

> And now one word as to Dr. Hunt, son of the worthy old Dorsetshire gentleman, and author of the book mentioned at the head of this article. I could say very much in his praise which he would not care to have said, or the readers of *Fraser's* perhaps to hear. But as to his power of curing the

---

47. Chapter 6 studies how the secondary literature, in which Kingsley is "progressive" in the *Alton Locke* period, deals with the equation of Jew and sweater.

48. Hunt's promotion of anthropology as the racists' economics is discussed in Rainger 1978. Here is a characteristic statement "This assumption of human equality was first heard of in the latter half of the last century, and since then it has been industriously taught in our universities; and at the present day it has become a part and parcel of the systems of political economy on which we rear our legislators" (Hunt 1867, lix). One can date the open hostility to economics in the *Anthropological Review* to its October 1865 review of Henry Thomas Buckle's *The History of Civilization in England,* in which Buckle quoted with approbation Mill's *Political Economy* doctrine that racial "explanation" was the height of vulgarity (1914, 29). Then Hunt figured out who the real enemy was (1866b).

average of stammerers, I can and do say this—that I never have yet seen him fail where as much attention was given as a schoolboy gives to his lessons. Of course the very condition of the cure—the conscious use of the organs of speech—makes it depend on the power of self-observation, on the attention, on the determination, on the general intellectual power, in fact, of the patient; and a stupid or volatile lad will give weary work. (1859, 10)

Whatever failure there might be is only the failure of the patient. The story of the stupid patient—even when the patient is Kingsley himself—protects the therapy from fact.[49] How could the cure bear the responsibility for the stupidity of the patient? I return to the details of speech therapy in the following section when I report unpublished correspondence from Kingsley to Hunt. Because Kingsley will write about racial matters in which Hunt was involved, we should read the public debates before the private correspondence.

To this end, we consider Hunt's *The Negro's Place in Nature*, presented in 1863 and republished in New York in the following year. Hunt asserts that blacks are their stereotype. The average is the individual:

In the negro race there is a great uniformity of temperament. In every people of Europe all temperaments exist; but in the Negro race we can only discover analogies for the choleric and phlegmatic temperaments. The senses of the Negro are very acute, especially the smell and taste; but Pruner Bey says that there has been much exaggeration as to the perfection of the senses of the Negro, and that their eye-sight, in particular, is very much inferior to the European. The most detestable odors delight him, and he eats everything. (1864, 11)

Now and forever, they are a people unchanging:

We now know it to be a patent fact that there are races existing which have no history, and that the Negro is one of these races. From the most remote antiquity the Negro race seems to have been what they are now. We may be pretty sure that the Negro race have been without a progressive history;

---

49. In a letter to Hunt dated January 4, 1860, six months after the review, Kingsley reports that the stammering is worse and that he "can give no cause." In a letter of November 15, 1859, on the black-bordered paper that announced the death of his child, Kingsley writes about dining with the prince consort and his terror of stammering in front of his new pupil, the prince of Wales. While Kingsley describes either heartbreak or tension, he continues to seek an explanation for the worsening stammering elsewhere. The *Lancet,* cited in Hunt 1854 (37–38), gives an interesting explanation of testimonials: "We hardly know which is the greatest puffer and charlatan, the writer of the puff, or the party who procures it to be written."

and that they have been for thousands of years the uncivilized race they are at this moment. (13)

If this is so, then observing one is the same as observing all. Literature is science:

> In conclusion, let me observe that it is not alone the man of science who has discerned the Negro's unfitness for civilization, as we understand it. Here is Mr. Anthony Trollope, who is certainly quite guiltless of ever having examined the evidence of the distinction between the Negro and European, and yet truly says of the Negro:—"Give them their liberty, starting them well in the world at what expense you please, and at the end of six months they will come back upon your hands for the means of support. Everything must be done for them; they expect food, clothes and instruction as to every simple act of life, as do children." (27)

One might think that, as defined, neither medical quackery nor racial quackery would be very long-lived. The first failure to cure or the first black who diverges from the stereotype provides a fact that falsifies the claim that the cure *always* works or the group is *nothing but* the stereotype. Here comes the story explaining why a cure seems to "fail"? We have read Kingsley blaming the failure on the stammerer's lack of intelligence. The failure is the responsibility of the patient, not of the cure. The black who diverges from the stereotype is dealt with in exactly the same way. The story is told that he is not a real black but from some other race. Quoting Hunt:

> The many assumed cases of civilized Negroes generally are not of pure African blood. In the Southern States of North America, in the West Indies and other places, it has been frequently observed that the Negroes in places of trust have European features; and some writers have supposed that these changes have been due to a gradual improvement in the Negro race which is taking place under favorable circumstances. It has been affirmed that occasionally there are seen Negroes of pure blood who possess European features. Some observers have assumed that improvement has taken place in the intellect of the Negro by education, but we believe such not to be the fact. It is simply the European blood in their veins which renders them fit for places of power, and they often use this power far more cruelly than either of the pure-blooded races. (1864, 12)

The three sentences next quoted each have a complicated context. The jibe at "philanthropists" is explained by Carlyle's "Negro Question." The importance of Hunt's denigration of the ability to acquire languages in the third sentence will be clear immediately:

> The exhibitions of cases of intelligent Negroes in the saloons of the fashionable world by so-called "philanthropists," have frequently been nothing but mere impostures. In nearly every case in which the history of these cases has been investigated, it has been found that these so-called Negroes are the offspring of European and African parents. We admit, however, that the African Negro occasionally has great powers of memory, in learning languages. (16)

This quackery is responsible for one of Hunt's least attractive public moments.[50] When the doctrine of uniform intellectual incompetence was publicly challenged by William Craft—an escaped slave whose intelligence in his abolitionist lectures or his writings (1860) ought to have been evident to the slowest anthropologist—his first concern was to provide evidence that he was "black enough" to count.[51] Hunt, of course, waved this off—since Craft was not a pure black, the evidence provided by his intelligence is irrelevant.[52] A later speaker who put forward a doctrine similar to Hunt's, Henry Guppy—including the critical exclusion of "the mixed race" (1864, ccix)—seems to have realized that if Craft himself is ruled out as evidence of black intelligence then

---

50. Montagu (1942, 22) discusses the rudeness of the "egregious and insolent Dr. Hunt" at this meeting without bothering to describe how his dismissal of Craft's evidence works. Lorimer (1978, 47–48) discusses Craft and the confrontation with Hunt. Desmond (1994, 353) and Young (1995, 136) comment on the "mixed blood" exclusion principle.

51. "Mr. Craft said that though he was not of pure African descent he was black enough to attempt to say a few words in reference to the paper which had just been read. Many scientific gentlemen present would probably dispute that; but at any rate, supposing Adam to have been the founder of a race of men, white men had no stronger claim to him as their father than black men, as it was admitted that owing to the climate in which he commenced his existence, he could have been neither black nor white, but copper coloured. . . . With regard to his not being a true African—his grandmother and grandfather were both of pure Negro blood. His grandfather was a chief of the West Coast; but, through the treachery of some white men, who doubtless thought themselves greatly his superiors, he was kidnapped and taken to America, where he (Mr. Craft) was born" (Craft 1863, 388).

52. "Dr. Hunt in reply said he was sorry that some speakers had attempted to draw away the attention of the audience from the great facts under discussion. . . . He would leave his scientific friends to judge of the value of Mr. Craft's remarks. He was sorry, however, that the speaker had not confined himself to uttering exploded theories, but had accused scientific men of wasting their time when discussing this subject. He for one thought it was a great pity that scientific men in this country had so long delayed to bring these facts prominently before the public, and thus explode some of the popular delusions on the subject. It was not at all necessary for Mr. Craft to tell anyone at all acquainted with the subject that he was not a pure Negro, although there were many present who were deluded with the idea that he was. As to the statement that Britons did not make good slaves, he was quite ready to admit the fact; and he knew of no European race that would make good slaves. In this respect Negroes were certainly far superior. . . . All he asked was that scientific evidence of this character should be met by scientific argument, and not by poetical claptrap, or by gratuitous and worthless assumptions" (Hunt 1863, 390–91).

his *argument* must be taken as seriously as any other "white" man's.[53] No one telling the "mixed race" story seems to have responded to Craft's point that American slavery was not restricted to the racially pure.[54]

Hunt's discussion of language acquisition is quackery of a more subtle variety, which shows that he was well aware of the defense of black intelligence on the basis of observed language acquisition. Not only could Africans acquire many inflectionally rich local languages, but they could acquire the grammatically impoverished English.[55] Unlike Hunt's *Anthropological Review*, the Anthropological Society was open to speakers of vastly different points of view.[56] Consider the account of the Bunu Tribe presented by Valentine Robins, in which he discusses a boy emancipated from slavery:

> He is very intelligent, speaks the Hausa, Nufi, Bunu, and Igbirra tongues fluently, and these are not acquired by tuition, but through their unsettled state of life, being frequently sold from one tribe to another. (1867, cxi)

The first comment from the floor (cxii) asked the perfectly sensible question whether these four languages were closely related dialectics. The response to this was the withering:

> Mr. Bendyshe observed, that as it had been stated by Mr. Robins that the boy could speak English, and sing English songs, it was evident that he was capable of learning different languages. (cxiii)

---

53. "In the discussion that ensued on the reading of Dr. Hunt's paper, Mr. Craft observed that the agricultural labourers in England were bent (in figure) as well as the negro" (Guppy 1864, ccxi).

54. "It may be remembered that slavery in America is not at all confined to persons of any particular complexion; there are a very large number of slaves as white as any one" (Craft 1860, 2).

55. The quackery here is this: isolated languages would tend to be much more heavily inflected than English, and it is easier for native speakers to move from a highly inflected language to a language with a lower inflectional dimension. Admitting that African languages are grammatically as complicated as Greek or Latin would expose the argument for exactly what it was worth. The link between grammatical complication and cross-language trade was developed by Adam Smith, as I discuss in Chapter 11. Baker (1974, 501) wonders at Smith's ability to predict features of language two hundred years before they were observed by other professional linguists.

56. The *Journal of the Anthropological Society* seems to give a perfectly fair account of the papers and the floor discussion of the Society's meetings. Craft's comments on Hunt's paper are reported in the *Anthropological Review*, which was owned and edited by Hunt, only, I believe, because it was a floor discussion at the British Association. Galton's comments on Hunt precede Craft's (Peart and Levy 2000). Craft's own paper was refused republication in the *Anthropological Review* (Young 1995, 199). Complications arose because the two magazines were part of a financial package to which one subscribed. (The *Popular Magazine of Anthropology* was another Hunt venture. It lasted only for a year.) Rainger (1978) tries to sort out the relationship between Hunt and the society. Hunt was charged but acquitted of financial impropriety that took the form of cross-subsidization of his magazines.

With no one wishing to make the case that English and Igbirra are dialects of a common language, it was time for quackery to save the hypothesis of black inferiority. Here is the story:

> Dr. Beigel said he should like to hear more particulars indicative of the intelligence of the boy. If it were proved that the boy was as intelligent as boys of his age usually are, then it would become a question who his father and his grandfather were, and whether there was any white blood in him. (cxiii)

After a speaker claimed to see webs between the boy's fingers (cxiii)—a silliness that puts the "elongated raven" story to shame—the racial purity story came back:

> Mr. Mackenzie remarked upon the receding lower jaw of the boy. Though the brow and the face were well developed, he did not think he looked like a pure negro.
> Mr. Mill said he had seen boys in Africa like the one then present. He considered he belonged to the Houssa tribe, which was a pure negro tribe, as far as that tribe were concerned. He had seen one of them who was six feet two inches high. They inhabit a country, the chief town of which is the head centre of Mohammedanism, and where the archives of the town were written in Arabic. (cxiii)

Hunt closed his comments with this story:

> He should like to know whether there was any evidence of there being Arab blood in the boy's veins. (cxix)

Robins responded to the comments with claims that (1) the four languages were in fact different, (2) the boy himself did not know who his father was, and (3) "the boy was not more intelligent than other boys of his tribe" (cxiv).

When presented with a young slave's ability to acquire languages, which would do credit to a young John Stuart Mill, the story is told that the boy obviously is not a real black: he is partly white, perhaps partly Arab.

The Kingsley-Hunt Connection

The Huntington Library holdings of the letters from Kingsley to Hunt allows us to more easily see how science and literature blend for quacks.[57] The oddity

---

57. The letters date from September 1855 until Hunt's death in 1869. They also include the letter of condolence that Kingsley sent to Hunt's widow. The extracts quoted subsequently will

that central members of the distinct racist communities knew each other pro-
fessionally has been noted and important questions asked.[58] These letters let us
see more clearly the link between quackery in speech therapy and racial matters. The first question we can answer is why Kingsley contacted Hunt. When,
on September 22, 1855, Kingsley first wrote to Hunt, he described his
difficulty as stammering in private:

> I am a clergyman; I never stammer in the reading desk or in the pulpit. I
> am, I suppose, superior in "elocutional" prowess to most of my brethren in
> the country. (Kingsley Collection, HM 32205)

Then he explained why he was writing Hunt:

> The true cause (& this fact sends me to *you*, from what I have seen of your
> papers) is anatomical. My lower jaw is much too narrow for the tongue os
> hyoides; and in speaking, I am always "*conscious*" of the os hyoides. (HM
> 32205)[59]

While Kingsley is completely candid about the mental aspect of his affliction,
he stammers when he worries about stammering, and he describes his youth as
filled with ridicule of his disability, he seeks a physical explanation. Why he
thinks the relationship between tongue and jaw changes as he moves from private to public is not explained. Nonetheless, this letter sends us to Hunt's first
published work, in which he explains why the relationship between teeth and
jaw changes as we move from savagery to civilization:

---

perhaps suggest why these would repay study. The Hunt side of the correspondence is not at the
Huntington Library. The report of Kingsley's correspondence with Hunt (Jutzi 1971) mentions
only speech issues. Consequently, Styron Harris (1981, 133) is silent on racial issues. Nevertheless,
without Harris's meticulous scholarship I would not have visited the Huntington to read the letters. The library's card catalog calls attention to racial matters most helpfully.

58. "It would be interesting to learn how Kingsley's views about race were influenced by his
relations with England's brashest exponent of the theory of permanent racial types. For worries
about his stammering took him to the leading authority on its treatment, none other than Dr.
James Hunt, a young man of great energy who was soon to be founder of the Anthropological
Society of London. Kingsley seems to have consulted him in the mid-fifties. We are told that in
January 1857 he spent ten days in London visiting 'Hunt the stammering man' and that he passed
a fortnight at Hunt's house in Swanage. Hunt became notorious for his views on Negro inferiority" (Banton 1977, 77). Lorimer (1978, 154–56) discusses Kingsley's attitudes in terms of contemporary anthropology. Arthur Keith writes (1917, 18): "The Rev. Charles Kingsley joins [the Eth-
nology Society] at the same time [1856] as Hunt."

59. I gratefully acknowledge help from (first) Christine Holden and (second) Nicola Tynan
and Andrew Farrant in reading the manuscripts. Words that we read with shaky confidence are
enclosed in brackets, the addition of a question mark suggests that there is more shake than
confidence, and empty brackets indicate no confidence whatsoever. The spelling is not "corrected,"
and the emphasis is in the original, although we have changed underscores to italics.

It may appear strange to allude to civilization as increasing the number of stammerers, but the fact can hardly be doubted.

Savages do not stammer; in them the human animal remains unchanged. In the civilized world, on the contrary, refinement has materially altered the physical man. Robustness yields to delicacy, and the very structure of organs undergoes metamorphosis. The ample jaw of the wild Indian, for instance, has room for the full dentition of the species; whilst the contracted jaw, the result of civilization in the features of more elevated beings is insufficient for the reception of the numerical providence of the teeth. Hence the almost universally needed assistance of experienced dentists, to limit the number and train what are left to their necessary functions. Other organs have undergone similar changes, and the issue has been to render attention to the education and management of the voice at least as expedient and important as it is the preservation of the eyes or the cultivation and management of the teeth. (1854, 25)

This made sufficient sense to Kingsley for him to risk therapy with Hunt.

The second question we can answer is whether Kingsley shared Hunt's racial quackery, so evident in *The Negro's Place in Nature*. The critical document here is Kingsley's letter of September 20, 1863:

I have just been reading in the Reader a resumé of your paper on the negro. . . . If you said that the negro was as much a diff't species from us, as a donkey is from a zebra, you said what I as a [Darwinite] firmly believe. I believe that donkeys & zebras split off from each other ages since & that Whites & negros did. I believe that they had common parents: but are 2 varieties & have become now fixed & that the White man is by far the higher. I believe that we both spring from a common dark ancestor, with probably strait hair, & that the negro [sprouted wool] & also [st?] a stout [manly?] physique, without improving his brain.

As for bringing in Philanthropic & political practices it is a sham. Science really must not be meddled with & Mr. Kraft [has a] hiccup to set up [ ]—confusing himself as instance, because he is *not* a pure black.

People cannot see that even if a negro here & there can be taught to *imitate* White civilization, that proves nothing—He has not *originated* the civilization or added elements? of his own to it. I don't doubt that something may be made of the negroes under European influence. & I [hold] that you are bound to the negro by the same Moral Laws as to the White— But to tell me that he is my equal, is to outrage fact—*& the negro himself knows it* [well enough]. (Kingsley Collection, HM 32247)

The signature of quackery—a perfect cure, a perfect fit of the stereotype and the group—is evident in Kingsley's dismissing Craft.[60] The jab at "Philanthropic . . . practices" is pure Carlyle. Quacks in correspondence echo their great master.

Conclusion

Carlyle's literary gifts have never been questioned. Although he claimed to know a good deal of the economic theory of his contemporaries, scholars tend not to take this seriously.[61] Nonetheless, his inference from an inability to exchange to the conclusion of subhuman status is warranted by either the Smith-Whately approach to economic foundations or the Wakefield approach. When this command over the theory is combined with an ability to tell a compelling story, which distracts one's attention from the facts, we have a quack of the highest order.

We observe how much the Hunt-Kingsley speech quackery resembles their racial quackery. But the Hunt-Kingsley racial quackery is not such a work of art as Carlyle's. The story they tell to distract us is fairly transparent. Perhaps this why Hunt and Kingsley are remembered mainly by specialists while Carlyle bent the English language itself with his devastating and doubtless immortal characterization of economics as the dismal science. The fact that this occasion was intended to bring forward facts that would make blacks and whites equals has somehow slipped out of memory.

Appendix: Three Problems

1. Why was there a name change between article and pamphlet? Speculation about why Carlyle's article was called the "Negro Question" and the pamphlet wasn't seems not to notice that for someone with as good an ear for language as Charles Dickens had the pamphlet would convey a lower-class Americanism. Here is Dickens discussing improved editions of the classics:

> Imagine a Total abstinence edition of Robinson Crusoe, with the rum left out. Imagine a Peace edition, with the gunpowder left out, and the rum left

---

60. On August 4, 1864, he discusses the *Anthropological Review*, mentioning his belief that the Negroes' "chances of subsistence depended on their becoming more like the white man." On January 28, 1865, he acknowledges receipt of Hunt's translation of Carl Vogt's lectures.

61. Who first called attention to the principle of consumer sovereignty? The reader—who must suspect what the answer will be—cannot be more surprised than I was (Carlyle 1987, 31).

in. Imagine a Vegetarian edition, with the goat's flesh left out. Imagine a Kentucky edition, to introduce a flogging of that 'tarnal old nigger Friday, twice a week. Imagine an Aborigines Protection Society edition, to deny the cannibalism and make Robinson embrace the amiable savages whenever they landed. (1853b, 97–98)

Perhaps the editors of *Fraser's*—a journal of sufficient respectability that a decade later Mill would publish "Utilitarianism" in its pages—shied away from this breach of decorum in the title?

2. When did the "dismal science" become associated with Malthus? The earliest instance I find in the Making of America data base is the following passage from Amasa Walker in 1866:

The question of population has been invested, by the treatment of British writers, with a great mystery and terror. The glut, famine, and death theories of Malthus have done much to impress upon political economy the shape it has today in the world's estimation. Rightly enough, if they are correct, is it called a dismal science. Malthus exhausted the direct horrors of the subject; but the effect was greatly heightened by the benevolent efforts of many subsequent writers to provide some way of escape from this fatal conclusion,—efforts which, as they resulted in palpable failure, made the outlook of humanity more dreary and hopeless. The fact is, all this British philosophy of population is perverted and diseased from its root. (452)

Waste not, want not. If the Civil War ended the popularity of the cause for which Carlyle opposed the dismal science, that was hardly reason to abandon such a useful slogan. It is worthy of note that Walker's son's views on race are notorious.

3. If any part of what I have written so far is true, why were economists not told about it by our greatest teachers? The answer is that we *were* told: we just did not listen properly. Consider Joseph Schumpeter, who from his Harvard position taught generations, his students and their students to follow, how to understand economics past. Listen to the way Schumpeter explains Carlyle's importance to the economist:

For economists [Carlyle] is one of the most characteristic figures in the cultural panorama of that epoch—standing in heroic pose, hurling scorn at the materialistic littleness of his age, cracking a whip with which to flay, among other things, our Dismal Science. This is how he saw himself and how his time saw and loved to see him. (1954, 409–10)

Schumpeter knows, but, contemptuous of the reader, among others, he will not mention that the "other things" that Carlyle proposed to flay were black people. The joke is at the expense of a reader who cannot match Schumpeter text for text. If Schumpeter is right in thinking that classical political economy came to share the strokes of the lash with victims of the hierarchy for which it had provided the opposition—and it was partly for this reason that classical political economy passed away—it was a good way to die.

SIX

Economic Texts as Apocrypha

Introduction

Samuel Hollander asked me to explain how the classical economists came to be considered "reactionaries." The otherwise appealing answer—that they *were* reactionaries because of Malthusian wage theory— has the difficulty of being demonstrably false. Hollander himself has demolished the lynchpin of such an interpretation—the fixity of the condition of the working class—in his decades in the making *Economics of Thomas Robert Malthus*. But if Hollander, and those of us who have come to similar conclusions, are correct, then how do we explain the nearly unanimous view to the contrary?[1]

One question can determine who bears the blame for the error. In what context did economics become the "dismal science"? The predictable answer—we became the dismal science precisely because of Malthus's theory of the fixed condition of the working class—demonstrates what is so odd about seeing the classics as reactionary.[2] The correct answer is that we became the dismal science as the result of our classical predecessors' role in the abolition of British racial slavery. As we have seen, this claim is not a conjecture; it is a matter of the historical record. We have read more than once of the long-forgotten context in which Thomas Carlyle first used the phrase "dismal science" in the December 1849 article in *Fraser's*, "Occasional Discourse on the Negro Question."

As Frank Knight is reported to have said on such occasions, it is not ignorance that gets us into so much trouble but knowing so much that simply isn't true.[3]

---

1. George Stigler asked precisely this question when I proposed my version of the "new" view of Malthus and Ricardo. It has taken me close to thirty years to find an answer worth even taking seriously. My stubbornness on this issue was largely influenced by a lesson I learned from Earl Hamilton.

2. For some dismal results of an electronic survey of the economics literature, see the appendix to this chapter. The reader will then appreciate why Earl Hamilton mattered so much to my education.

3. "I have personally heard Knight repeat many times the Josh Billings aphorism: 'It ain't what we don't know that hurts us. It's knowing so darned much that ain't so'" (James M. Buchanan in Knight 1982, xi–xii).

Widespread error is easy to explain since the truth is very costly.[4] But how is it possible that so many careful scholars make the *same* error? It is completely improbable that such a large literature would have fallen into common error *if* there had been independent research behind the erroneous conclusion.

What might cause a violation of independence of research efforts? I shall argue that there are two violations. First, there is an omitted common factor in research. This will be the topic of the first section of the chapter. What has fallen out of our common knowledge is the fury aimed at economic models of a free society by nineteenth-century defenders of slave society. That Carlyle was *the* British theorist of an idealized slave system was absolutely clear to those who found themselves in need of a justification for the existing slave system in America. Consequently, when George Fitzhugh introduces *Cannibals All!* he defers to the great man across the waters:

> At the very time when we were writing our pamphlet entitled "Slavery Justified," in which we took ground that Free Society had failed, Mr. Carlyle began to write his "*Latter Day* Pamphlets," whose very title is the assertion of the failure of Free Society. The proof derived from this coincidence becomes the stronger, when it is perceived that an ordinary man on this side [of] the Atlantic discovered and was exposing the same social phenomena that an extraordinary one had discovered and was exposing on the other. The very titles of our works are synonymous—for the "Latter Day" is the "Failure of Society." (1857, xx).

How surprising can it be that the American debates in the 1850s, with war impending, provide a vantage point from which oblique British defenses of slavery attain transparency?

There is a second violation of research independence. Literary scholars of various persuasions seem to be enamored of a view of literature, attributed to Carlyle's great disciple, John Ruskin, that literary art moralizes or, as Matthew Arnold put it: "In thus making sweetness and light [S&L] to be characters of perfection, culture is of like spirit with poetry."[5] What does the scholar, for whom this identification of culture and poetry makes sense, do in the presence of great art akin to *Birth of a Nation*? The trick seems to be that S&L does not always come in fixed proportions; one can obtain more S out of the texts by shedding less L in some corners.

The first section of this chapter deals with what seems to be hard to see.

---

4. This is so if for no other reason than that we must combat our inclination to believe that which is most pleasing to us (Feigenbaum and Levy 1996).

5. On Ruskin, see Belsey 1980, 8; and Arnold 1993, 67. Arnold criticizes Carlyle's "aristocracy" for insufficient L (90). Denise Albanese gave me these references.

The second deals with that which is easy enough but which all too many scholars seem to prefer not to see.

What Has Not Been Seen

We study the past to make sense of the present.[6] Included in the present is some notion of that which distinguishes then from now. This notion, which we call "progress," is not in the past; rather, it is a theoretical claim with which we organize events imposed upon the past in service of the present. Importantly, the notion of progress tells scholars which texts are vital to read and which texts are not.

It is in the context of the independence of research efforts that I propose we think about the canon in economics. Let us call "canonical" the texts one is expected to know to be in the discipline. "Progress" gives us a reason to consider some texts more important than others. Of course, there is a good economic reason to have a limited canon at some moment in time—the day only has twenty-four hours and one can only read so many words per minute. The debates on the canon have paid insufficient attention to another economic way of making disciplinary demands consistent with one's life. This is to mark off some texts as irrelevant, texts that need be read by no one. Just as the deepest economic theory tells us that every market is connected to every other market, the most persuasive philosophy of language tells us that every text is connected to every other. But these are councils of perfection for a better world.[7] In our world, in which time is scarce, it is helpful, perhaps even necessary, to suppose that there is a boundary across which these connections are remote enough to neglect.[8] Without a convention that there are texts that everyone can ignore—whatever it is they mean, this does not bear upon the important texts—the number of texts can swamp the time available for reading them.

---

6. Lawrence Levine (1993, 5) writes that historical research "involves not changing interpretations of well-agreed-upon standard events but changing notions of which events—and which people—should constitute the focus of the historian's study." Levine (1996, 96–97) continues the argument.

7. "[W]e impoverish our understanding of the past if we chop it up into little bits labelled 'constitutional history', 'economic history,' 'literary history,' 'political history' and so on" (Hill 1993, 436).

8. The philosophical correlative to an economic general equilibrium point of view is W. V. Quine's (1961) doctrine that "The meaning of words is defined in the whole of the language." The correlative to a partial equilibrium point of view is found in Hilary Putnam's "linguistic division of labor." Not everyone in a language community is knowledgeable about what the various words we all use actually mean. As Putnam notes, "in giving up my right to be the authority on the denotation of my own words, I give up, often, the ability to give any satisfactory description of my own denotations. I can refer to elms as well as the next man; but I probably couldn't tell an elm from a beech if my life depended upon it" (1975, 2:274–75).

We need a name for the books that, as a disciplinary convention, are excluded. Since *canon* is used to name what all need to know, let us use *apocrypha* to name what none are expected to know. *Apocrypha* is Greek for "hidden"; that seems right.

With such notation in hand, let us return to the problem of systematic common error. Suppose that the meaning of a canonical text depends upon a text in the apocrypha.[9] Since knowledge of the apocrypha is at best second-hand, there is no reason to believe that scholarly conclusions will be independent. Without independence, there is no reason to believe that the discipline will correct even gross common errors.

Broad Utilitarianism

As an overview to my reading of the larger debate, the missing piece in the equation—the information that neither modern economists nor others have—is the utilitarian basis of the antislavery coalition that united Christian evangelicals and Utilitarian political economists.[10] As there is a mathematical issue involved at the center of the matter, economists ought not expect much guidance from innumerate textual specialists.[11] I propose to distinguish a "narrow" (capitalized) Utilitarianism, as formulated in the position of Jeremy Bentham

---

9. This problem occurs even in a biblical context in which canonical books contain citations to the noncanonical (Charlesworth 1983).

10. When John Stuart Mill responded to Carlyle's "Negro Question" he began by making clear who was the majority partner in the coalition (1850, 26): "But I must first set my anti-philanthropic opponent right on a matter of fact. He entirely misunderstands the great national revolt of the conscience of this country against slavery and the slave-trade, if he supposes it to have been an affair of sentiment. It depended no more on humane feelings than any cause which so irresistibly appealed to them must necessarily do. Its first victories were gained while the lash yet ruled uncontested in the barrack-yard and the rod in schools, and while men were still hanged by dozens for stealing to the value of forty shillings. It triumphed because it was the cause of justice; and, in the estimation of the great majority of its supporters, of religion. Its originators and leaders were persons of a stern sense of moral obligation, who, in the spirit of the religion of their time, seldom spoke much of benevolence and philanthropy, but often of duty, crime, and sin." His tribute is all the more striking coming from perhaps the greatest opponent Christianity faced in the nineteenth century. James Hunt (1866c)—the driving force behind midcentury British racial anthropology—testifies to this coalition.

11. Indeed, even the modern student of the evangelicals and economists does not see the coalition in utilitarian terms."They supported slave emancipation because slavery was obviously incompatible with free will individualism, but were notoriously much less concerned about wage [*sic*] slavery, and the other social evils of their own land" (Hilton 1988, 98). Some classics are hopeless. For example, Leslie Stephen finds it incomprehensible that slavery could be defended: "The conflict with morality, again, was so plain as to need no demonstration. It seems to be a questionable logic which assumes the merit of a reformer to be proportional to the flagrancy of the evil assailed" (1900, 1:113). Questionable it is, but one might have thought that an authority on the history of Utilitarianism would recognize the principle of attacking the worse evils first.

and his associates, and a "broad" utilitarianism, which encompasses multiple interpretations of the Greatest Happiness Principle.[12]

Multiple interpretations of the defining slogan of utilitarianism—Francis Hutcheson's "the greatest happiness for the greatest number"—exist. A Platonist knows this as a logical matter. The slogan is mathematically inconsistent: all sentences follow from it.[13] To make coherent policy on the basis of the

---

12. The adjective *broad* I hope resonates with the celebrated description of the Church of England as "not High, or Low, but Broad." Credit is claimed for this coinage by Arthur Stanley (1870, 8) in his 1850 *Edinburgh Review* article on the "Gorham Controversy." This controversy generated—by *Dictionary of National Biography* (DNB) count—over fifty pamphlets, all forgotten even before the DNB was printed. Forgotten or not, Gorham shows the hand of the broad utilitarian coalition playing real power politics. The flavor of the coalition was caught in the *Christian Remembrancer,* which noted (1850, 13–14): "and we see hoary liberals, who have all their life been sneering at kings, and scoffing at Churches, gravely rise up in their place in Parliament, to interrogate the Prime Minister, whether he has done his duty in upholding the endangered prerogative of her gracious Majesty, as the 'Supreme Head of the Church.'"

At issue was whether an Anglo-Catholic bishop [Henry Phillpotts] could deny an office to an otherwise qualified candidate [George Gorham] because of Gorham's evangelical views on the sacraments. Phillpotts blamed the Privy Council's decision—evangelical views must be tolerated—on John Bird Sumner, who held office as archbishop of Canterbury (Phillpotts 1850). Richard Whately weighed in as archbishop of Dublin with a subtle explanation of why one would expect variation in interpretation of hard texts (1850). Sumner and Whately have been studied by Boyd Hilton (1988), Anthony Waterman (1991), and Donald Winch (1996). Only Hilton's research extends through the 1850s, but he does not study the Gorham decision.

The rowdy world of seventeenth-century evangelicalism (see Hill 1993) was alive and well in the Gorham controversy, as we learn from William Bennett: "I wish to inform you, my Lord, that on Sunday the 10th of November, while I was performing the duties of Divine service in the church of S. Barnabas, a tumultuous crowd assembled in the streets round about the church, and that a band of persons who had congregated together no doubt for this purpose within the very church walls, was guilty of violent outrage against all decency, in uttering hisses, and exclaiming, 'No mummery! No popery!' and other similar cries, alarming the decent worshippers" (1850, 1–2). William Tyndale, whose views on sacraments were cited in the controversy (Maskell 1850), dramatically characterizes evangelical views and suggests why Anglo-Catholics would find them unhappy: "Testament here, is an appointment made between God and man, and God's promises. And a sacrament is a sign representing such an appointment and promises: as the rainbow representeth the promise made to Noe, that God will no more drown the world. And circumcision representeth the promises of God to Abraham . . . as baptism which is come in the room thereof, now signifieth" (Tyndale 1992, 82–83). Tyndale's view of sacraments—Judaism is in Tyndale's representation a sacramental religion—helps predict on which side of the debate anti-Semitism will be found.

13. "The principle of greatest happiness may have gained its popularity, but it lost its meaning, by the addition '*of the greatest number.*'" (Edgeworth 1881, 118). Here is a way to see the technical issue without appeal to the calculus of variations. Utilitarianism proposes to move from facts of individual happiness to claims about social happiness. Consider the same three individuals in two possible states of the world. Each state of the world is described in terms of the ordered triple of the individuals' happiness. Consider the case of $A = \{1,2,9\}$ and $B = \{2,3,4\}$. Which has the "greater happiness of the greater number"? A has the higher *mean* happiness [4 > 3]—and since the population is fixed the higher *total* happiness—but B has the higher *median* happiness [3 > 2]. Hutcheson's slogan encourages one to believe, wrongly, that a utilitarian will never have to choose between a higher mean *and* median of happiness.

imperative, one must select one of an infinity of models, of which infinity Bentham's maximizing total happiness approach is just one.[14] And, as a matter of fact, pre-Benthamite utilitarianism seems to have made judgments on the basis of the happiness of the median individual.[15]

Broad utilitarianism is of necessity a universalist philosophy. One's moral obligations do not stop at an inconsequential border imposed by race, nationality, or belief. It is entirely in this spirit that we can find the evangelicals, for whom Adam and Eve were part of the real past, asking on behalf of the slaves: "Am I not a man and a brother?"[16] As any form of utilitarianism must do, it judges overall well-being on the basis of individual well-being. The decisive step to make the evangelical-Utilitarian coalition function is the twofold agreement that (1) the well-being of those at the bottom of the distribution of happiness merit our immediate attention and (2) the greatest happiness principle of Utilitarianism is *formally* equivalent to the Golden Rule of Christianity. By focusing exclusively on the condition of slavery, the intracoalition disagreement as to the nature of happiness was obviated. Utilitarians, then and now, are divided as to whether happiness is anything other than what we, in fact,

---

14. Francis Hutcheson emphasizes the *number* of those benefiting: "In comparing the *moral Qualities* of Actions, in order to regulate our *Election* among various Actions propos'd, or to find which of them has the greatest *moral Excellency*, we are led by *our moral Sense* of *Virtue* to judge thus; that in *equal Degrees* of Happiness, expected to proceed from the Action, the *Virtue* is in proportion to the *Number* of Persons to whom the Happiness shall extend; (and here the *Dignity*, or *moral Importance* of Person, may compensate Numbers) and in equal *Numbers*, the *Virtue* is as the *Quantity* of the Happiness, or natural Good; or that the *Virtue* is in a *compound Ratio* of the *Quantity* of Good, and *Number* of Enjoyers. In the same manner, the *moral Evil*, or *Vice*, is as the *Degree* of Misery, and *Number* of Sufferrers; so that, *that Action* is *best* which procures the *greatest Happiness* for the *greatest Number*" (1726, 177).

Darwall 1995 is in my opinion the single most important work treating utilitarianism in broad terms. The accounts of Stephen (1900) and Halévy (1955), for all their erudition and sympathy, take utilitarianism in the narrow sense of Bentham and his school, relegating Francis Hutcheson, Adam Smith qua moral philosopher, and William Paley to the role of predecessors *avant là lettre*. The decisive test for the analytical seriousness of a study of utilitarianism is whether it recognizes the incoherence of the "greatest happiness of the greatest number." The fact that neither Stephen nor Halévy seem even to know of Edgeworth's work hints at a failure to understand why there must be more than one kind of utilitarianism.

15. I read Smith as supposing a utilitarianism based on medians (see chapter 10). William Paley's utilitarian calculus is based on a *count* of those who benefit and those who lose from policy: "It may be useful to rob a miser, and give the money to the poor; as the money no doubt would produce more happiness, by being laid out in food and cloathing for half a dozen distressed families, than by continuing locked up in the miser's chest" (1785, 62). But, as Paley adds in his defense of general rules: "a disposition of affairs which would presently fill the world with misery and confusion; and ere long put an end to human society, if not to the human species." (64). Hollander (1997, 830–31) points out how Malthus's welfare arguments depend upon the well-being of the *majority* of society.

16. "Wedgwood, the celebrated potter, had made another effective contribution to the cause. He designed a cameo showing, on a white background, a Negro kneeling in supplication while he utters the plea to become so famous, 'Am I not a man and a brother?'" (Howse 1952, 40–41).

choose. In the nineteenth century, a heatedly debated topic concerned the relationship between freely chosen sexuality and happiness.[17] When one focuses on the happiness of slaves—those for whom the range of all choice is radically attenuated—debates over choice vanish and utilitarians unite.[18]

The belief in the formal identity of the Golden Rule of Christianity and the Greatest Happiness Principle of Utilitarianism seems to have passed without notice among twentieth-century commentators.[19] Nonetheless, the texts are exactly where one would expect to find them: in the great debate between T. B. Macaulay and the Utilitarians over James Mill's *Government*.[20] Macaulay found nothing to dispute in the Utilitarian formula because it was also a Christian formula:

> The "greatest happiness principle" of Mr. Bentham is included in the Christian morality; and, to our thinking, it is there exhibited in an infinitely more sound and philosophical form, than in the Utilitarian speculations. . . . "Do as you would be done by: Love your neighbour as your-

---

17. Levy (1999b) identifies four major positions taken by Christians and Utilitarians in the Malthusian controversy, three of which were publicly defended in the nineteenth century. Only in the twentieth century would we see publication of the fourth position, sexually liberated Utilitarianism. Stephen (1900, 1:326) knows that the manuscript of *Not Paul, but Jesus* has Bentham's defense of the decriminalization of homosexuality, but he is not going to tell the reader anything about that. I conjecture that the vote reconciling Anglican Christianity to neo-Malthusianism at the 1930 Lambeth Conference was a consequence of the utilitarian coalition. I have two independent reasons to think so. First, there is a simple public choice calculation: Anglo-Catholics separated themselves from the Church of England after Gorham and so changed the distribution of votes on the issue. Second, no one of any evangelical sympathies could doubt J. S. Mill's moral seriousness; hence, his neo-Malthusian views earned reflection and consideration.

18. Thus, I disagree with Marcus Cunliffe, who reads the larger debate as one in which the participants viewed chattel slavery and "white slavery" as composed of the same fundamentals: "Moreover, if slavery in general were evil, and if chattel slavery were arguably the most ominous form, then the abolitionists had a good case for attacking the problem on this particular front. . . . Reform must begin *somewhere*. . . . their crusade would have been altered out of all recognition if they had endeavored to direct a dual assault, on both chattel slavery and wage [*sic*] slavery" (1979, 26–27). Working for money wages instead of approbation is a choice in both Smith's and Mill's models of utilitarianism.

19. The accounts by Halévy (1955) and Stephen (1900) would not suggest that such a formal identity exists. Indeed, although Stephen (3:300) notes Mill's identification of the Golden Rule with the Greatest Happiness Principle, he ignores this agreement in the Macaulay-Mill exchange, (2:85–98). Moreover, he neglects Bentham's own Utilitarianization of Christ when he dismisses *Not Paul, but Jesus* as irrelevant to his concerns (1:323–24).

20. The papers in the debate are most conveniently available in Lively and Rees (1978; hereafter L&R), from which source I cite. The debate is rather more central to various open public choice problems than standard accounts suggest (see, e.g., Schumpeter 1954, 432). Scholars have long speculated about the reasons why Macaulay declined to republish his attack on Mill. Stephen, for example (1900, 2:85), suggests "gratitude for Mill's generosity in regard to the Indian appointment." Perhaps the importance of the solidarity of the antislavery coalition dominated the importance of old intracoalition debates? In any event, Macaulay's arguments are not forgotten in Mill 1861.

self;" these are the precepts of Jesus Christ. Understood in an enlarged sense, these precepts are, in fact, a direction to every man to promote the greatest happiness of the greatest number. (quoted in Lively and Rees 1978, 175). [21]

Macaulay's Utilitarian opponent affected surprise that this needed to be mentioned:

Nobody ever thought of denying, that the author of Christianity was the first of Utilitarians. . . . Mr. Bentham has demonstrated that for individuals, societies, nations, to "do as they would be done by," is sound earthly policy. The bigots keep a close lock on their Elysium; but whenever the time comes for the *second* Utilitarian to present himself at the gate, it is presumable the *first* will not wait for their leave, to greet him with "Well done." (191)[22]

John Stuart Mill, offering his most considered statement of Utilitarianism, found the true spirit of this philosophy in the teachings of Christ.[23] This establishes the coalition agreement on the formal issue.

What evidence is there of agreement that slavery was the worst case? The leader of the "Clapham sect," William Wilberforce, put forward a series of considerations as to why we should regard West Indian slavery as the worst state possible for a human. While there may have been other reasons for thinking this,[24] he offered three strong ones. The first two appeal to all universalists;

---

21. Paley (1785) gave definite form to the Christian version of utilitarianism. William Wilberforce (1823, 18) refers to Paley as a "most sagacious observer of human nature."

22. The critical Bentham text is *Not Paul, but Jesus,* in which the non-Utilitarian aspects of Christianity are blamed on Saint Paul's teaching: "Not so Jesus: no harm did he see in eating and drinking, unless with the pleasure it produced greater pain. With this reserve, no harm . . . did he see in any thing that gives pleasure" (1823, 394). The role of this text in the intracoalition debate is discussed in Levy 1999b.

23. "I must again repeat, what the assailants of utilitarianism seldom have the justice to acknowledge, that the happiness which forms the utilitarian standard of what is right in conduct, is not the agent's own happiness, but that of all concerned. As between his own happiness and that of others, utilitarianism requires him to be as strictly impartial as a disinterested and benevolent spectator. In the golden rule of Jesus of Nazareth, we read the complete spirit of the ethics of utility. To do as you would be done by, and to love your neighbour as yourself, constitute the ideal perfection of utilitarian morality" (Mill 1861, 401).

24. Evangelicals such as Wilberforce are under obligation to oppose any system restricting access to the Word of God. The proslavery writers were sensitive to the charges that the slaves were kept from the Bible and thus their salvation itself was jeopardized. John Fletcher (1852, 23) confronts an argument from Francis Wayland that slavery "renders the eternal happiness of the one party subservient to the temporal happiness of the other." Edward Pringle (1852a, 20; 1852b, 482) cites "the taunt that we should not boast of the education of the slave as long as the reading of the Bible is shut out from him by our laws." He responds: "The slave's inability to read has given

the third appeals to all Christians. Here are the claims he put forward. One ought not treat a person as a horse:

> Not being supposed capable of being governed like other human beings, by the hope of reward, or the fear of punishment, they are subjected to the immediate impulse or present terror of the whip, and are driven at their work like brute animals. Lower than this it is scarcely possible for man to be depressed by man. (1823, 12)

One ought not to treat a woman as a sexual object without will:

> No one who reflects on the subject can be at a loss to anticipate one odious use which is too commonly made of this despotism, in extorting, from the fears of the young females who are subject to it, compliances with the licentious desires of the drivers, which they might otherwise have refused from attachment to another, if not from moral feelings and restraints. It is idle and insulting to talk of improving the condition of these poor beings, as rational and moral agents, while they are treated in a manner which precludes self-government, and annihilates all human motives but such as we impose on a maniac, or on a hardened and incorrigible convict. (13)

---

rise to a more kindly feeling, and to a closer connection between the races, than if each slave could read his own Bible. It has induced oral teaching; and the effect of this upon both races no man at the North can conceive." The always illuminating "Nicholas Brimblecomb" (1853, 80) emphasizes how orality restricts the *slave's* ability to select which biblical texts on slavery to read as well as to learn other lessons.

Evangelicals, for whom the Bible was the Word of God, would be vastly unhappy with a secondhand encounter with the Word. If orality suffices, then what exactly is wrong with having a priest explain the Latin Bible? Wilberforce (1982, 3) compares two systems of belief: real Christianity versus one in which "The Bible lies on a shelf unopened." William Tyndale, in his *Letter to Fryth,* explains translation as an act for which *his* salvation was at risk: "I call God to record against the day we shall appear before our Lord Jesus, to give a reckoning of our doings, that I never altered one syllable of God's Word against my conscience." I modernized the spelling and quote the epigram of Tyndale's nineteenth-century biographer (Demaus 1871, iv). Tyndale's moral seriousness was of great consequence. Gerald Hammond (1983, 44ff.) establishes just how Tyndale's translation attains the stupendous feat of preserving *both* semantics and syntax of the Hebrew original by bending English itself, as when he introduced the syntactical form "X-of-X" as an English superlative, for example, the "Song of Songs."

The antislavery movement's link to Reformation controversy is suggested by Nassau Senior when he poses the puzzle: "If we did not know that 'Uncle Tom' has been prohibited by the Pope, we should have supposed that there was no form of Christian faith in which it would not find grateful admirers" (1864, 434). He suggests an answer : "It is possible, too, that the Papal authorities were alarmed by hearing of one of the effects produced by the work in Paris—a general demand, among the ouvriers, for bibles. . . . All the stalls were full of them; and the purchasers, to most of whom the book was unknown, asked anxiously whether what they were buying was the 'real bible,'—'Uncle Tom's bible?'" (435).

One ought not to make marriage impossible for men and women:

> I have dwelt the longer, and insisted the more strongly on the universal want of the marriage institution among the slaves, because, among the multiplied abuses of the West Indian system, it appears to me to be one of the most influential in its immoral and degrading effects. . . . Alas! the injustice with which these poor creatures are treated accompanies them throughout the whole of their progress; and even the cordial drops which a gracious Providence has elsewhere poured into the cup of poverty and labour, are to them vitiated and embittered. (16)

When challenged with an argument that we shall meet below, Wilberforce selects the sexual slavery argument as the most powerful. Here is the proslavery challenge:

> Indeed, the West Indians, in the warmth of argument, have gone still farther, and have even distinctly told us, again and again,—and I am shocked to say that some of their partizans in this country have re-echoed the assertion,—that these poor degraded beings, the Negro slaves, are as well or even better off than our British peasantry. (33–34)

Here is Wilberforce's response:

> Let me therefore ask, is there, in the whole of the three kingdoms, a parent or a husband so sordid and insensible that any sum, which the richest West-Indian proprietor could offer him, would be deemed a compensation for his suffering his wife or his daughter to be subjected to the brutal outrage of the cart-whip—to the savage lust of the driver—to the indecent, and degrading, a merciless punishment of a West-Indian whipping? (35)

The Utilitarians were in agreement that slaves are at the bottom of the distribution of happiness. This is made abundantly clear in the debate over Mill's *Government*. Mill's worst-case model of government specified it as if it were a slave driver. Mill asked how English gentlemen behave when given slaves in the West Indies:

> The world affords some decisive experiments upon human nature, in exact conformity with these conclusions. An English Gentleman may be taken as a favourable specimen of civilization, of knowledge, of humanity, of all the qualities, in short, that make human nature estimable. . . . In the West Indies, before that vigilant attention of the English nation, which now, for thirty years, has imposed so great a check upon the masters of slaves, there was not a perfect absence of all check upon the dreadful propensities of

power. But yet it is true, that these propensities led English Gentlemen, not only to deprive their slaves of property, and to make property of their fellow-creatures, but to treat them with a degree of cruelty, the very description of which froze the blood of those of their countrymen, who were placed in less unfavourable circumstances. (quoted in Lively and Rees 1978, 67)

[I]f one man has power over others placed in his hands, he will make use of it for an evil purpose; for the purpose of rendering those other men the abject instruments of his will. If we, then, suppose, that one man has the power of choosing the Representatives of the people, it follows, that he will choose men, who will use their power as Representatives for the promotion of this his sinister interest. (78)

Macaulay's response takes up several themes, none of which deny slavery its position as the worst case. Rather neatly, he seems to have encountered a paradox of the worse case. If one is thinking of government with the potential to emancipate slaves, what sense does it make to model the government in worst-case slave-driving terms?[25] Consequently, Macaulay defends models of government under which the self-interest of the governors needs to be filled in empirically before conclusions can be drawn.[26] Moreover, he asks why Mill's democratic conclusions follow from the axioms of the model.[27] Won't the majority have a sinister interest in exploiting the minority?[28]

---

25. Worst-case theorizing has a long and distinguished history. "Political writers have established it as a maxim, that, in contriving any system of government, and fixing the several checks and controuls of the constitution, every man ought to be supposed a *knave,* and to have no other end, in all his actions, than private interest" (Hume 1987, 42). The modern revival of this Humean point of view comes in Buchanan and Brennan 1980. The analogue in mathematical statistics is that developed in the various robust schools of thought (see. e.g., Mosteller and Tukey 1977 and Huber 1981). The worst-case paradox *seems* to be avoided when one describes the decision abstractly, for example, by minimizing the maximum loss, and not concretely, for example, by supposing that the government "is" a slave driver. One must be cautious here because I am not aware of any attention that has been paid to the possibility of this paradox in the theoretical literature.

26. "When we see the actions of a man, we know with certainty what he thinks his interest to be. But it is impossible to reason with certainty from what *we* take to be his interest to his actions. One man goes without a dinner, that he may add a shilling to a hundred thousand pounds: another runs in debt to give balls and masquerades. One man cuts his father's throat to get possession of his old clothes: another hazards his own life to save that of an enemy. One man volunteers on a forlorn hope: another is drummed out of a regiment for cowardice. Each of these men has, no doubt, acted from self-interest. But we gain nothing by knowing this, except the pleasure, if it be one, of multiplying useless words. In fact, this principle is just as recondite, and just as important, as the great truth, that whatever is, is" (Macaulay in L&R 1978, 125).

27. And Macaulay asks why Mill excludes women since the same reasoning that argues for universal manhood suffrage argues for universal suffrage (ibid. 116).

28. This exchange might be central to Jeremy Bentham's attack on what seems to be utilitarianism based on medians (see chapter 10). Macaulay's demonstration of the importance of time preference to Utilitarian claims—a point that one can find in Mill (L&R 1978, 75)—may have had something to do with Bentham's *Auto-Icon* (Levy 1992). Andrew Farrant found the point in Mill for me.

It may perhaps be said that, in the long run, it is for the interest of the people that property should be secure, and that therefore they will respect it. We answer thus:—It cannot be pretended that it is not for the immediate interest of the people to plunder the rich. Therefore, even if it were quite certain that, in the long run, the people would, as a body, lose by doing so, it would not necessarily follow that the fear of remote ill consequences would overcome the desire of immediate acquisitions. Every individual might flatter himself that the punishment would not fall on him. Mr. Mill himself tells us, in his Essay on Jurisprudence, that no quantity of evil which is remote and uncertain will suffice to prevent crime. (quoted in Lively and Rees 1978, 119)

Surely, Macaulay argues, approbation is desired and this might offset the desire for wealth at what we would say the margin: "the love of approbation, and other kindred feelings, always tend to produce good government" (127).

In response, the Utilitarians averted again to racial slavery as a model of despotic government and while conceding the formal "unrealism" of the account defended the value of worst-case models in familiar Humean fashion:

It is true that there are partial exceptions to the rule, that all men use power as badly as they dare. There may have been such things as amiable negro-drivers and sentimental masters of press-gangs. . . . But it would be as wise to recommend wolves for nurses at the Foundling, on the credit of Romulus and Remus, as to substitute the exception for the general fact, and advise mankind to take to trusting to arbitrary power on the credit of these specimens. (quoted in Lively and Rees 1978, 135)

On the strength of this debate, Macaulay came to such prominence as to become a member of Parliament, where he spoke vigorously for the emancipation of the slaves in the British West Indies. His parliamentary role in the emancipation of West Indian slaves in 1833 is wonderfully told in George Trevelyan's *Life*. The government proposed giving 20 million pounds to the slave owners and voiced a commitment to a twelve-year transition between slavery and freedom, an "apprenticeship." The money was easy; consenting to even temporary slavery was not.[29] Macaulay found himself, as Trevelyan tells, caught between the hard duty to principles that argued for immediate liberation and the politically possible.[30] He spoke in qualified support for the gov-

---

29. A useful test for any edition of a Carlyle text designed for students is whether the editor glosses Carlyle's customary grumping at the "wasted" 20 million pounds.

30. His principles were announced in the great essay on Milton: "There is only one cure for the evils that newly acquired freedom produces; and that cure is freedom. When a prisoner first leaves his cell he cannot bear the light of day; he is unable to discriminate colours, or recognize faces. But the remedy is, not to remand him into his dungeon, but to accustom him to the rays

ernment after handing in his resignation. First, he argues for the importance of competition:

> In free countries the master has a choice of labourers, and the labourer has a choice of masters; but in slavery it is always necessary to give despotic power to the master. This bill leaves it to the magistrate to keep peace between master and slave. Every time that the slave takes twenty minutes to do that which the master thinks he should do in fifteen, recourse must be had to the magistrate. Society would day and night be in a constant state of litigation, and all differences and difficulties must be solved by judicial interference. (quoted in Trevelyan 1978, 1:284–85)

Holding firm to his position in the debate with Mill, Macaulay trusts the government more than he trusts slave owners:

> He did not share in Mr. Buxton's apprehension of gross cruelty as a result of the apprenticeship. "The magistrate would be accountable to the Colonial Office, and the Colonial Office to the House of Commons, in which every lash which was inflicted under magisterial authority would be told and counted. My apprehension is that the result of continuing for twelve years this dead slavery,—this state of society destitute of any vital principle,—will be that the whole negro population will sink into weak and drawling inefficacy, and will be much less fit for liberty at the end of the period than at the commencement. My hope is that the system will die a natural death; that the experience of a few months will so establish its utter inefficiency as to induce the planters to abandon it, and to substitute for it a state of freedom. I have voted," he said, "for the Second Reading, and I shall vote for the Third Reading; but, while the bill is in Committee, I shall join with other honourable gentlemen in doing all that is possible to amend it." (285)[31]

---

of the sun. The blaze of truth and liberty may at first dazzle and bewilder nations which have become half blind in the house of bondage. But let them gaze on, and they will soon be able to bear it. . . .

"Many politicians of our time are in the habit of laying it down as a self-evident proposition, that no people ought to be free until they are fit to use their freedom. The maxim is worthy of the fool in the old story, who resolved not to go into the water till he had learnt to swim. If men are to wait for liberty till they become wise and good in slavery, they may indeed wait for ever" (Macaulay 1961, 1:179–80). Macaulay uses the analogy of people adjusting to inexpensive alcohol to make the case (178–79). The reader who does not know the tacit reference to the *Wealth of Nations* (Smith 1976a, 492) will not catch the division of labor within the coalition.

31. A view of Buxton from *Fraser's* is found in May 1831.

In a day, the government weakened and proposed a seven-year transition to freedom. The abolitionists, perhaps fearing to give up a great attainable good, accepted.

"Progressive" *Fraser's*

If economists do not know the racial texts as a matter of disciplinary convention, what about textual specialists? Physicists report that there is a wraithlike particle, the neutrino, which could pass through a block of lead a light year thick without collision. Imagine how much more difficult it would be to find a neutrino if the atom that it finally encountered claimed upon inquiry that it was actually visiting the Balkans at the time! The Utilitarian-evangelical agreement of the identity of the Greatest Happiness Principle and the Golden Rule has not only sailed neutrinolike through a century of humanistic texts, but one "fact" that everyone knows, Charles Dickens's testimony in *Hard Times* of the opposition of Utilitarian and Christian beliefs, is a falsification of the historical record.[32] As a consequence, perhaps, the debate over whether policy ought to be focused on black or "white slaves" has not been seen as a debate over just who is at the bottom of the distribution of happiness. Nor has it been appreciated how the issue of slavery obviated debate over choice and happiness.

What is important for humanists is not what is important for economists. "Progress" in the humanistic disciplines involves the triumph of science over traditional Christianity. A defining episode in the warfare of science with theology in Christendom—to recall the title of A. D. White's classic study—is the question of whether Adam and Eve were real people from whom all the human inhabitants of the world descend. In service to this vision of progress, historians have singled out for special attention a group of Christians who reconciled their beliefs with the emerging scientific consensus that Adam and Eve were not real.[33] In addition to Carlyle himself, these include S. T. Coleridge, Charles Kingsley, and James Froude.[34]

---

32. "[A]fter eight weeks of induction into the elements of Political Economy, she had only yesterday been set right by a prattler three feet high, for returning to the question 'What is the first principle of this science?' the absurd answer, 'To do unto others as I would that they should do unto me'" (Dickens 1972, 95).

33. Thus, Willey (1956, 144–47) defines "liberal" Christians in terms of their denial of "uncritical bibliolatry" and their acceptance of Darwin's theory.

34. "A liberal effort to free the mind from these 'Hebrew old clothes' seemed to many thinkers the major need of the age. Only then could religious truth be reembodied in a believable form. 'It was clearly the part of every noble heart,' said Carlyle, thinking of himself and his work, 'to expend all its lightnings and energies burning-up without delay, and sweeping into their native Chaos' these 'incredible uncredited traditions'" (Houghton 1957, 49).

Emphasis on the universal in evangelical Christianity is replaced with emphasis on the local in progressive Christianity; claims of truth are replaced with claims of belief.[35] At the limit, we find progressive religious thinkers asserting that, the quantum of familiarity being equal, Pan is as good as Christ.[36] The Victorian periodical that perhaps most closely identified itself with such progressive Christianity was *Fraser's Magazine for Town and Country*. It is worthy of reflection that, with the possible exception of Coleridge, this list of religious thinkers is the same list that recent scholars have compiled of Britain's most important "literary" racists.[37] Humanistic scholars have no theoretical explanation for the progressives' racial brutalism.[38] In localized reli-

---

35. "Carlyle is remembered, and his influence was felt, as an upholder of the spiritual view of the world in an age of increasing materialism and unbelief. Yet he is the most remarkable example of a phenomenon which I take to be typical of the nineteenth century, that of the religious temperament severed from 'religion'" (Willey 1949, 105). "The strength of Carlyle lay in the passionate sincerity with which he believed in his own 'God'" (117).

36. Here is an extract from Froude's *Nemesis of Faith:* "Whatever after evidence we may find, if we are so happy as to find any, to strengthen our religious convictions, it is down in childhood their roots are struck, and it is on old association that they feed. Evidence can be nothing but a stay to prevent the grown tree from falling; it can never make it grow or assist its powers of life. The old family prayers, which taught us to reverence prayer, however little we understood its meaning; the far dearer private prayers at our own bedside; the dear friends for whom we prayed; the still calm Sunday, with its best clothes and tiresome services, which we little thought were going so deep into our heart, when we thought them so long and tedious" (1849, 28).

"Pan, almighty Pan! Had the water-nymphs forsaken their grottoes where the fountains were flowing as of old? Were the shadows of the deep woods less holy? Did the enchanted nightingale speak less surely the tale of her sorrow? As it was in the days of their fathers so it was in theirs—their fathers had gone down to the dust in the old ways, and so would they go down and join them. . . . Who shall say that those poor peasants were not acting in the spirit we most venerate, most adore"(32).

37. The texts are discussed in chapter 5, where I propose "quackery" as the unifying principle of "literary" and "scientific" racists. J. J. Thomas caught the spirit of quackery: "Here we are reminded of the dogma laid down by a certain class of ethnologists, to the effect that intellectuality, when displayed by a person of mixed European and African blood, must always be assigned to the European side of the parentage" (1889, 134–35). "Racism" is not simply a retrospective judgment from the comfortable vantage point of the passing of our ghastly twentieth century. Nineteenth-century attacks on racial aspects of Carlyle, Froude, and Kingsley, respectively, are found in Mill 1850, Thomas 1889, and Robertson 1897. Cunliffe (1979, 13) describes Carlyle's *Latter-Day Pamphlets* as "radically conservative" and as far as I can see never mentions his opinions on race. This is odd because he sees John Campbell's *Negro-Mania* for exactly what it is (22), "a vehemently anti-black compendium." Carlyle's "Negro Question" is reprinted in *Negro-Mania*. Kingsley's *Alton Locke*—which Cunliffe (14) describes as one of a list of novels with "socially conscious titles"—will later be considered in detail.

38. Willey's analysis of Carlyle does not comment on the racism (Willey 1949, 128–29). According to Houghton (1957, 213): "Sadistic brutality of this kind is pathological, and no doubt the desire to 'smash 'em good' in Carlyle and Froude as well as Kingsley had personal origins. But nationalism and racism, sanctioned by Old Testament Puritanism and social Darwinism, created an atmosphere in which the normal control of the beast in man could be seriously weakened." One stares at such claims. Does Houghton mean to blame the antislavery evangelicals for Carlyle's

gion, the equivalence of the Greatest Happiness Principle and the Golden
Rule breaks down. The only "Others" who matter are those near at hand; those
who look like us and believe like us.

To see how humanistic scholars have come to grips with the racially
charged texts on this issue, consider the judgment of scholars on the status of
Fraser's, the locus for the dismal science label. It appears that there is one, and
only one, book-length scholarly treatment of this magazine in its early days,
Miriam Thrall's 1934 "meticulous" *Rebellious Fraser's*.[39] Thrall tells us in great
detail (129–45) how, under the leadership of William Maginn, *Fraser's* stood
against the economists and for humanity. Here is her judgment, which links
Maginn's "anti-antislavery" with Carlyle's attack on economists:

> In condemning the cupidity, heartlessness, and hypocrisy of those political
> economists who were smirched by the child slavery of the factories, Mag-
> inn was as unsparing as Carlyle was later in his *Nigger Question*. An
> instance of the kind of slur to which they were subjected. . . .
>
> Maginn did not wish it thought that he favored the institution of slav-
> ery because he opposed emancipation propaganda. The question in the
> abstract, he said he was not concerned with. His sole contention was that
> the economists and their supporters by the policies of free trade and anti-
> slavery were striking at the prosperity of the colonies, weakening the ties
> which bound them to England, and in consequence operating to the detri-
> ment to the empire. (145)

Thrall seems to propose that the "child slavery" of the factories is of greater
concern than that of real slavery. The impartial *Wellesley Index* says this about
why *Fraser's* became important:

---

racist brutality? Even that makes more sense than blaming post-1859 texts (didn't social Darwinism have to wait for Darwin?) for arguments in the late 1840s and early 1850s. Williams (1958)
mentions neither racial issues nor slavery. Hall (1992) thinks different conceptions of masculinity
motivate the debate between Carlyle and Mill. Stephen has a characteristically dense version of
this argument: "His feelings, however, were I take it, as tender as a woman's. They were wanting,
not in keenness, but in the massiveness which implies more masculine fibre. And this, indeed, is
what seems to indicate the truth. Mill could never admit any fundamental difference between the
sexes. That is, I believe, a great but natural misconception for one who was in character as much
feminine as masculine. He had some of the amiable weaknesses which we at present—perhaps on
account of the debased state of society—regard as especially feminine. The most eminent women,
hitherto at least, are remarkable rather for docility than originality" (1990, 3:72–73). The parallel
"masculinization" of Harriet Martineau is documented later.

39. "Sixty years after it was written, Thrall's book remains the only full-length study of the
magazine. Her scholarship was so meticulous, and many of her sources now so irrecoverable, that
anyone who writes anything at all about *Fraser's* must be deeply indebted to her work" (Leary 1994,
123).

Whatever else "a magazine" may be, wrote the editor in 1879, "it is primarily an organ of literary expression." That, indeed, was the basic reason for *Fraser's* initial success in the 1830s and its establishment as a major periodical. In the second place, from start to finish, it was an outstanding organ, if not of open revolt, as Thrall would have it (*Rebellious Fraser's*), at least of progressive thought. (Houghton 1972, 303)[40]

In the first volume of *Fraser's Magazine for Town and Country,* which was published in 1830, there is a response by this humane, progressive Maginn to Macaulay, who had written in part as an economic historian in the *Edinburgh Review* challenging the poet laureate Robert Southey's reflections on society. Macaulay was young when he reviewed Southey, so Maginn introduced him to *Fraser's* readers as part of the great Christian antislavery crusade, the voice of Wilberforce:

Our judgment on him for the article which we have just mentioned is not too severe, as the following extract will shew; and, reader, remember, whilst you are enjoying its beauties of diction, and giving the author all credit for the mild spirit of Christianity which it breathes, that that author is the same youth whose existence Mr. William Wilberforce would have involved in the economy of all-gracious Providence, and who is not only the son and heir to the shining virtues of Zachary Macauley [*sic*], the friend of humanity and of the *nigger* portion of the creation, but has himself spouted at anti-slavery meetings in favour of all black populations, until he received the *accolade paternelle* of the old and enthusiastic Mr. Wilberforce, on account of the fervour and zeal with which he pleaded the cause of universal charity,—and good will and affection towards the *niggers* in particular, *not* of Sierra Leone, but of our West Indian islands. (Maginn 1830, 584)[41]

---

40. Houghton (1972, 305–8) considers in detail Maginn's wickedly unkind attack on the economist Francis Place, then the founder of neo-Malthusianism and later the author of the People's Charter. Maginn's untrue attack on Harriet Martineau for neo-Malthusianism is considered in chapter 6. Patricia Marks (1986, 29) is puzzled that the attack is in personal not intellectual terms. Rather systematic personal attacks on Martineau will be documented later in a context that is easy to explain. When facts or law could be quoted against her, the argument was completely polite by the standards of the time. James Austin (1839, 45) calls her "this intrusive stranger," gives his evidence, and then proceeds to his next point.

41. Please note that these are not my italics; they are there in the original. Macaulay's speech is quoted in Trevelyan (1978, 1:103–5); *Fraser's* attack is not discussed at all. Contemporary judgments of the antislavery movement often characterize it as Wilberforce & Co. Here is testimony from the industrious proslavery American publisher responsible for considerable reproduction of British racial anthropology (van Evrie 1868, 27): "And if the Father of Lies, Lucifer himself, had plotted a plan or scheme for concealing a great truth, and embarrassing a great cause, he could have accomplished nothing more effective than the movement that Wilberforce inaugurated for the

The contrast drawn between "humanity and of the *nigger* part of creation" by someone who is paid to use the English language suggests that, for Maginn, humanity was exclusively white.[42] The fact that *Fraser's* "from start to finish" is judged "progressive" by the standard reference work in Victorian periodical literature—the very one that I gratefully employ to assign attributions to the *Fraser's* articles—hints, one might say, that there is something very interesting about the authoritative understanding of Victorian literature. But, before we leap to any such substantive conclusions on the basis of one article—actually a few sentences from one article—we should read further.

What seems to be missing in the standard readings of *Fraser's* role in the great debate over emancipation is its persistent denial that slaves occupy the bottom level in the distribution of happiness. For example, *Fraser's* in the February 1831 issue explained that opposition to slavery was based in an ignorance of the science of philology:

> The West Indians, at the very outset, labour under a serious disadvantage. In no country is liberty so highly extolled, and so little understood, as in Great Britain. And consequently the word *slave*, is associated in the mind of the great mass of the people with every thing that is debasing and cruel. If, however, we examine the origin of the term, much of this cause of offence, this stumbling-block to the uninformed, will vanish. "From the *Sclavi*," observes Sir Walter Raleigh, "came the word, *slave . . .* which is in their language 'glorious.'" (114)

After providing tables comparing the penalties of slaves and soldiers for various offenses and concluding that the slaves were punished less harshly, *Fraser's* offers evidence from the slaves' cash balances to demonstrate that at least some were richer than some free laborers.

Then, in the March 1831 issue, *Fraser's* put forward a real argument that there is reason to believe that slaves do not occupy the bottom of the scale of happiness. Slaves will be well-treated by profit-maximizing masters for the same reasons that profit-maximizing farmers treat their horses well:

---

professed benefit of the negro and other subordinate races of mankind, which, masked under the form of religious duty, and appealing to the conscience, the love of proselytism, the enthusiasm, and even the bigotries of the religious world, has, for more than half a century, held in thrall the conscience as well as the reason of Christendom."

42. It also suggests that Carlyle's contribution to the language is rather less original than recently urged. Hall (1992, 275) thinks Carlyle's use of the emphasized word in 1853 to be worthy of note: "It was the Mutiny which brought the term 'niggers' into common parlance. This was the term that Carlyle had seen fit to use publically in 1853." In *Alton Locke*, the word is used only by characters without pretensions to education (Kingsley 1850a, 190, 246). The "author," speaking in his own behalf, does not descend to this vulgarity. For example, he uses negro or black man at p. 343 and elsewhere.

It is manifest, by the comparison of their sleekness to that of our English horses, they must be in no bad condition. I have often thought it might occur to anti-slavery writers and speakers, that if there were no higher motive to restrain the planters from whipping their slaves to death, they might be induced to refrain by the consideration that the slaves were their property. What horse-dealer whips his horse to death? (205)[43]

Did *Fraser's* really believe this or was it simply a convenient argument? Perhaps we can see the answer to this question by considering an episode that might serve both to illustrate what was meant by good treatment of slaves and to demonstrate just how *Fraser's* earned its reputation for wit:[44]

After this, he goes on to describe a West Indian execution, as it was set down by Dwarris:

"On conviction, sentence of death must be passed without an appeal. The execution takes place without delay; and, there being no assigned place for the execution, the wretched convict is fastened to the nearest tree, unless, which frequently happens, the owner of the soil is at hand to prevent it. In such cases, the miserable culprit is dragged from tree to tree—from estate to estate; and in one case of then recent occurrence, the constable was at last forced to throw the exhausted sufferer off the town-bridge, securing the rope by a lamp-post."

This speaks to the necessity of an established gallows instead of trusting to the casual hospitality of the planter. A West Indian proprietor may occasionally be a man of such taste as to object to ornamenting his plantation with hanging negroes. I submit, that no tree owners, even in this country, would like to have the culprits of the neighborhood exhibited as pendants on their estates. George Robins, or one of his tribe (I fear the story is in Joe Miller[45]), was so ingenious as to describe, in an advertisement of an estate

---

43. One can find this argument in Stearns 1853, 46. J. G. Lockhart, in the *Quarterly Review*, made the perfectly correct observation that this sort of argument assumes that the *owner* of the slaves is directly responsible for punishment: "Absenteeism all the world over is the greatest of evils that can befall a labouring population; and it is impossible not to admit that if the West India proprietors had generally visited their estates in person, and endeared themselves, as Lewis did, to their dependents, it would have been a hard matter indeed for all the fanatics, backed by all the liberals, and all the East India sugar-dealers, to consummate their ruin" (1833, 397).

44. Testimony to *Fraser's* wit is well-nigh universal (see, e.g., Houghton 1972, 304). "At Maginn's death *Punch* claimed him as its own by donning for the first time in its as yet brief course the black border, which has ever since been famous as its symbol of mourning for the passing of those who have had the wit to make the world laugh at folly" (Thrall 1934, 10).

45. The *Dictionary of National Biography* (1997) informs us: "Joe Miller's name has long been a synonym for a jest or witty anecdote of ancient flavour."

to be sold, some half dozen gibbets in prospect, as "an agreeable view of hanging woods;" but the story does not say that the purchaser was much delighted with such an ornament to his new estate when he discovered what it really was. (*Fraser's,* March 1831, 206–7)

The line of argument that Wilberforce encountered, and that we read in *Fraser's* in the context of British West Indian slavery, will be recycled for use in an American context.

The Sexual Use of Slaves: Arrows "Poisoned by Truth"

Fraser's appeal to profit-maximizing considerations to argue that slaves will be well treated might seem an argument to which the stereotypical "free market economist" of the time might assent. This is of course fatuous. Adam Smith thought it obvious that slave owners abuse their slaves precisely because they are not profit maximizing. They get a thrill out of dominating, a thrill for which they are willing to pay:

> The pride of man makes him love to dominere, and nothing mortifies him so much as to be obliged to condescend to persuade his inferiors. Wherever the law allows it, and the nature of the work can afford it, therefore, he will generally prefer the service of slaves to that of freemen. (1976a, 388)

Perhaps the attitude of later economists is best summarized by Richard Whately in a letter to Nassau Senior proposing cannibalism to humanize slavery:

> Only t' other day I heard a man repeat the argument of the "Times" that self-interest is a sufficient security; as in the case of cattle, where, by-the-bye, it is so little a security that we have a law against cruelty to them. But even the most humane master of cattle treats them in a manner which one could not approve towards men, *e.g.* selling most of the calves that a cow bears; and knocking on the head a horse that is past work. I suggested that it would be an advantage to slaves if the masters could acquire a taste for human flesh. When a negro grows too old to be worth keeping for work, instead of being killed by inches by starvation and over-work, he would be put up to fatten like an ox. (1868, 313)[46]

Harriet Martineau during her 1830s visit to America found, as Wilberforce had before, the compelling piece of evidence with which to distinguish

---

46. This argument—purged of the pungent suggestion of cannibalism—appears in Hill, Whately, and Hinds 1852, 245.

the treatment of slaves and horses.[47] Horse owners do not use them sexually. As a Malthusian, Martineau attends to the tradeoff between sex and material income. Unlike Smith and Malthus, who confined themselves to contexts in which the Christian convention of one man–one family is generally enforced, she finds in America an instance in which a man can have more of both sex and material income by acquiring additional families, only one of which will be white:

> Every man who resides on his plantation may have his harem, and has every inducement of custom, and of pecuniary gain,* [*The law declares that the children of slaves are to follow the fortunes of the mother. Hence the practice of planters selling and bequeathing their own children.] to tempt him to the common practice. (Martineau 1837, 2: 222)

Then she proposes a test for moral motivation:

> Those who, notwithstanding, keep their homes undefiled may be considered as of incorruptible purity. (223)

Martineau is here responding to the claim that the morality of slavery can be judged by the relative infrequency of prostitution in southern cities. So it can, Martineau argues, but not in the way the slavery apologists thought. Why, she asked, would a man rent a woman for an hour when he can buy her and keep the children to sell?[48] Thus, the relative infrequency of prostitution in slave cities can provide evidence that slaves were used sexually in sufficient numbers to affect the market demand for irregular sex.[49]

---

47. If modern economists have heard of Harriet Martineau, it is as the preeminent popularizer of classical economics (Blaug 1958, 129–38). Blaug suggests that she should be judged as a journalist rather than an economist because she bears some responsibility for our discipline becoming the "dismal science" (138–39). By this, Blaug does not mean the possibility that her willingness to discuss interracial sex in public made economics "dismal." If there is a Malthusian link, the references to interracial sexuality in Carlyle's "Negro Question" suggest this would be it. There is a recent account of Martineau that takes the charming line that since she is too radical to be a real economist she must be something else, the first woman sociologist! (Hoecker-Drysdale 1992).

48. The lease-purchase analysis is easy to find. Here it is expounded by someone writing as Amor Patriæ: "A highly civilized, intelligent and refined society, cannot exist without servants of some kind—and the difference between purchase and hiring, is just about the difference between buying and hiring a horse; the former is generally the best used" (1858, 14–15). Karl Marx was quoted above attacking Carlyle for just such an argument (1887, 255–56).

49. "It is a common boast in the south that there is less vice in their cities than in those of the north" (Martineau 1837, 2:325). She then goes on to develop the argument that owning a sexual object as a slave is a good substitute for renting one in a brothel. The argument to which Martineau refers can be found in the anonymous 1844 *Slavery* together with an added homosexual twist (1844, 27): "[W]ho, on entering any large Northern city, is not made painfully aware of the low state of moral feelings, in noting the innumerable evidences of prostitution that meet his eye on

Let me pause to dwell on the simple implication of Martineau's point, which differs in subtle ways from Wilberforce's related claim.[50] Martineau's argument that American slavery is a system of sexual exploitation establishes that the relative well-being of free and slave labor will differ between men and women. Thus, when in the great debates over American slavery the well-being of *male* "white slaves" and *male* black slaves is compared, a claim is being made. The reader who knows neither Wilberforce nor Martineau may not see the evasion for what it is.

But Carlyle did know Martineau and her works extremely well. Indeed, "Negro Question" gives evidence of close acquaintance with Martineau's *Society in America*, in which these arguments are pressed. Thus, we do not have to read too far to discover what Carlyle means when he links economics, evangelicals, and interracial sexuality. The issue is common to Wilberforce and Martineau.

It was another woman who brought new weapons into the war of words over American slavery. As witness to their novelty, we may read from the long version of Senior's *Edinburgh* review of *Uncle Tom's Cabin:*

> Mrs. Stowe came like a heavenly auxiliary, like the divine Twins at the battle of the Lake Regillus, or St. Jago in the van of Cortez, using weapons such as they had never thought of, wielded with a skill which they did not possess. She showered on the supporters of the Fugitive Slave Law and of the extension of slavery, invective, ridicule, contempt, and defiance, with arrows winged by genius, and barbed and pointed, and poisoned by truth. (Senior 1864, 437).[51]

Senior stressed what was uniquely horrible about American slavery. It was

> the breeding and exporting system,—the system under which the principal use made of men and women is to produce and bring up children, to be

---

every side? What visitor of New York city, has failed to notice with what unblushing effrontery prostitutes of both sexes make Broadway their place of assignation?" Wendy Motooka asks whether the Martineau procedure for estimating the hidden economy of interracial sex might not be applicable here, too? Responding to *Uncle Tom's Cabin*, Stearns (1853, 82–83) discusses prostitution and concubinage as substitutes.

50. As a Christian, Wilberforce is bound by the *Book of Common Prayer's* injunction to marry early to avoid fornication. As a Malthusian, Martineau would allow people to choose *when* to marry to find happiness as they perceive it. Christian Malthusians had a very narrow line to walk between competing conceptions of happiness.

51. The long version of the review is available as the very rare *American Slavery* (Senior 1862), which is in turn reprinted in Senior 1864. Thomas Gosset (1985, 240–43) emphasizes the importance of this review. Leslie Fiedler (1979, 37) cannot see why there was so much fuss about *Uncle Tom*, but then he shows no interest in the actual debates over slavery and sexuality.

torn from them as soon as they attain the age of sale, and never to be seen or heard of again. (409)[52]

Stowe's attack is on the institution of slavery, regardless of the moral qualities of the slave owners, so she populates her story with slave owners of different moral qualities.[53] This is important for the polemic because in her account the rational slave will prefer freedom to slavery under even the kindest and most upright master. One never knows what the future will bring: who might next master be?[54] And we the reader are to judge the morality of a slave owner how? Following Martineau, the test for moral stature seems to be whether one will use a slave sexually or sell her for such a purpose.[55] Interracial concubinage serves many purposes in the plot. It provides a moment of irony as it explains how it comes to be that an escaping slave *darkens* himself.[56] More importantly, the inclusion of characters with parents of different races establishes on the crudest biological level possible that we are of one species.[57]

To appreciate how Stowe uses concubinage as a weapon in the argument against slavery, we ought to compare her discussion with Wilberforce's, quoted earlier, or with what the escaped slave and abolitionist William Craft would

---

52. Senior's demographic analysis argues that child selling is important. His role in this debate is unremarked in economic scholarship even by Marion Bowley (1937).

53. "Mrs. Stowe has taught us generous sympathy for these [honorable slave owners], while she has revealed to us the uncontrollable necessities of a *system* which is an incubus on the moral energies of the western world, and deliverance from which is become a matter of death. Her book leaves the conviction that the evil lies in the *essence* of the system and not in its *accidents*" (Hill, Whately, and Hinds 1852, 236).

54. See Stowe 1982, 30, and then, in case the reader missed it the first time, page 512.

55. Stowe (ibid., 14–15) begins *Uncle Tom's Cabin* with a respectable owner, reflecting upon his wife's reaction, refusing to a sell a woman for sexual usage even though it is clear that he "might make your future on that ar gal in Orleans, any day. I've seen over a thousand, in my day, paid down for gals not a bit handsomer." Simon Legree, the embodiment of all evil, has a old concubine, Cassy, and has recently acquired the fifteen-year-old Emmeline as her replacement. Obviously, I disagree with Josephine Donovan (1991, 40), who writes: "Most wrongdoing and evil behavior in the novel are shown to have monetary motives. In this Stowe links slavery with capitalism, and her critique of the profit motive therefore remains relevant today." But surely it is Mrs. Shelby who puts the iron in Mr. Shelby's spine about selling Eliza for sexual use, and she is certainly the more competent capitalist. Donovan testifies how sturdy is the faith of any progressive who opposes markets. Emancipation would put the former slaves in what institution?

56. "[George's] mother was one of those unfortunates of her race, marked out by personal beauty to be the slave of the passions of her possessor, and the mother of children who may never know a father" (Stowe 1982, 133). "It may be remembered that slavery in America is not at all confined to persons of any particular complexion; there are a very large number of slaves as white as any one" (Craft 1860, 2). It is possibly relevant that in *Hard Times* Tom Grandgrind darkens himself to escape (Dickens 1972, 298–99).

57. Gossett emphasizes Senior's claim that many Britons had never seen a black person, (Gossett 1985, 242). Carlyle detested that part of *Uncle Tom's Cabin* that he read (247). Carlyle's argument that blacks and whites are a species apart is considered in chapter 6.

write in 1860.[58] When these men write about sexual slavery, they use spectator language to ask how a *man* would feel about having his wife, sisters, or daughters used sexually.[59] They do not pretend to enter into a *woman's* situation. But Stowe enters into the heart of this darkness.[60] She has Simon Legree's past (and perhaps current) concubine, Cassy, talk to her presumptive successor, Emmeline, about how to deaden the inevitable sense of violation:

> "He wanted to make me drink some of his hateful brandy," said Emmeline; "and I hate it so—"
>
> "You'd better drink," said Cassy. "I hated it, too; and now I can't live without it. One must have something;—things don't look so dreadful, when you take that." (Stowe 1982, 438)[61]

---

58. "For instance, it is a common practice in the slave States for ladies, when angry with their maids, to send them to the calybuce sugar-house, or to some other place established for the purpose of punishing slaves, and have them severely flogged; and I am sorry it is a fact, that the villains to whom those defenceless creatures are sent, not only flog them as they are ordered, but frequently compel them to submit to the greatest indignity. Oh! If there is any one thing under the wide canopy of heaven, horrible enough to stir a man's soul, and to make his very blood boil, it is the thought of his dear wife, his unprotected sister, or his young and virtuous daughters, struggling to save themselves from falling a prey to such demons!" (Craft 1860, 8). Craft's mixed-race status, which kept him from falsifying the racists' claim that "all blacks were stupid"—he was too smart to be black—did not exempt him from black slavery (see Young 1995 and chapter 5). The spectator move is found elsewhere (*Suppressed Book* 1864, 128).

59. Wendy Motooka (1998, 213) argues from Adam Smith's texts that spectating is gendered. I only saw the connection here as a result of a conversation with Gordon Wood. The general principle in Smith's account is that we imagine new situations in which our current consciousness is placed (see chapter 10). Thus, without reflection we get many things wrong in our judgments, as Smith explains. For example, we think that the problem with being dead is the cold and the gnawing vermin.

60. Senior explained the importance of *Uncle Tom's Cabin* as partly resulting from the fact that there are no unmarried lovers with whom the reader is invited to sympathize (1864, 441–42). He notes that it was a novel that the evangelicals were permitted to read: "Even in this country in some classes, particularly among the Dissenters, novel reading is forbidden, and here, as in America, 'Uncle Tom' is excepted from the general prohibition" (436). Most of the unmarried sexuality, lacking consent, is deeply sinful on broad utilitarian grounds.

61. Tom's murder at Legree's hands results from his assistance in Cassy and Emmeline's escape (Stowe 1982, 479). In a famous essay, Fiedler (1979, 35–36) reads unproblematical rape into the story. But Stowe insists that bought concubinage as a long-term relationship can have strange effects on the owner-rapist: "The influence of Cassy over [Legree] was of a strange and singular kind. He was her owner, her tyrant and tormentor. . . . the most brutal man cannot live in constant association with a strong female influence, and not be greatly controlled by it. When he first bought her, she was, as she had said, a woman delicately bred; and then he crushed her, without scruple, beneath the foot of his brutality. But, as time, and debasing influences and despair, hardened womanhood within her, and waked the fires of fiercer passions, she had become in a measure his mistress, and he alternately tyrannized over and dreaded her" (1982, 466).

As I read the historical record, just as one economist, Smith, provided Macaulay with the analysis of how one adjusts to new possibilities of intoxication for Macaulay's metaphor of intoxication and freedom, it was another who provided Stowe with the poisonous truth.[62] Merely because Martineau's texts are hidden from us, we ought not conclude that Stowe's contemporaries were equally uninformed. It is, I take it, no coincidence that in 1852 and 1853, in the midst of the debate over *Uncle Tom's Cabin,* three massive American attacks on Martineau's claims regarding slavery and sexual exploitation, published at various times and places, were collected with an unrelated essay into a volume called *The Pro-Slavery Argument.*[63] From the words of these attacks, we can document the origin of this fatal mix of poison and truth.

The first line of argument from William Harper tacitly assumes that the sex is uncoerced. On the basis of this clever postulate, he gives a cogent cost-benefit explanation for why Martineau's account is true:

> In such communities, the unmarried woman who becomes a mother, is an outcast from society—and though sentimentalists lament the hardship of the case, it is justly and necessarily so. She is cut off from the hope of useful and profitable employment, and driven by necessity to further vice. Her misery, and the hopelessness of retrieving, render her desperate, until she sinks into every depth of depravity, and is prepared for every crime that can contaminate and infest society. She has given birth to a human being, who, if it be so unfortunate as to survive its miserable infancy, is commonly educated to a like course of vice, depravity, and crime.

62. Hedrick (1994, 264) documents that the teenage Harriet Beecher had been compared to Harriet Martineau even when the latter was on her famous American tour.

63. Two of the three authors are mentioned in the *Suppressed Book:* Hammond (1853, 26) and Harper (1853, 34). The 1852 collection claims to have been published in Charleston, the 1853 in Philadelphia. Spot comparison of the two suggests that the same type was used for both editions. Indeed, the page number 132 is transposed in both editions to 231 and page number 120 is set in broken type in both editions, although that of the 1853 version seems less damaged. The margins of the Philadelphia edition are more generous, which suggests that it was a more expensive edition. It seems odd that a more expensive edition would be printed with the same type after a less expensive edition.

Uncle Tom's Cabin had the property of reviving classics. Leander Ker (1840, 1842) attained a decade-delayed third edition with the addition of a discussion of *Uncle Tom* (Ker 1853). Ker provides a treasure chest of the commonplace defense of slavery, which might be useful to read in conjunction with Carlyle, for example, on the 20 million pounds needed to ransom the West Indian slaves (34–35): "[F]rom her oppressed, starving and over-wrought population at home, to emancipate her slaves in the West Indies, which slaves labored less, and were better fed, clothed and lodged, than half the operatives of England." We find Carlylean moral localism in the new material (vi)—"There *was* a time, when philanthropy, like charity, began at home"—and on why despots so like *Uncle Tom* (iv): "[T]hey can get a club by which they will be able to dash out the brains of the young Western Lion of Liberty. . . . [They] prefer *white* slaves to *black.*" On Ker, see the *Suppressed Book* 1864, 75–76.

Compare with this the female slave under similar circumstances. She is not a less useful member of society than before. If shame be attached to her conduct, it is such shame as would be elsewhere felt for a venial impropriety. She has not impaired her means of support, nor materially impaired her character, or lowered her station in society; she has done no great injury to herself, or any other human being. Her offspring is not a burden but an acquisition to her owner; his support is provided for, and he is brought up to usefulness; if the fruit of intercourse with a freeman, his condition is, perhaps, raised somewhat above that of his mother. Under these circumstances, with imperfect knowledge, tempted by the strongest of human passions—unrestrained by the motives which operate to restrain, but are so often found insufficient to restrain the conduct of females elsewhere, can it be matter of surprise that she should so often yield to the temptation? (Harper 1853, 42–43)

Harper attempts to make the case that it is better to have a black concubine than engage a white prostitute (43–45), which is, of course, Martineau's point, although she would say "more profitable" not "better." Harper is not content to respond to—or ratify—Martineau's model. He draws on Coleridge to attack the motives of utilitarians concerned with distant people:

Are we not justified then in regarding as criminals, the fanatical agitators whose efforts are intended to bring about the evils I have described? It is sometimes said that their zeal is generous and disinterested, and that their motives may be praised, though their conduct be condemned. But I have little faith in the good motives of those who pursue bad ends. It is not for us to scrutinize the hearts of men, and we can only judge of them by the tendency of their actions. There is much truth in what was said by Coleridge. "I have never known a trader in philanthropy who was not wrong in heart somehow or other. Individuals so distinguished, are usually unhappy in their family relations—men not benevolent or beneficent to individuals, but almost hostile to them, yet lavishing money and labor and time on the race—the abstract notion." The prurient love of notoriety actuates some. (93)[64]

John Henry Hammond levels the charge of sexual hysteria against Martineau:

---

64. The reference in *Table Talk* is to Coleridge (1990, 14:416). Perhaps it is not a surprise that Harper (1853, 92) cites Coleridge's racist reading of *Othello:* "[A]s Coleridge has said, we are to conceive of him not as a negro, but as a high bred Moorish chief." *Fraser's* in September 1849 proposed to amend the established text of *Anthony and Cleopatra* to rid it of the blackness of Cleopatra.

> But your grand charge is, that licentiousness in intercourse between the sexes, is a prominent trial of our social system, and that it necessarily arises from Slavery. This is a favorite theme with the abolitionists, male and female. Folios have been written on it. It is a common observation, that there is no subject on which ladies of eminent virtue so much delight to dwell, and on which in especial learned old maids, like Miss Martineau, linger with such an insatiable relish. They expose it in the slave States with the most minute observance and endless iteration. Miss Martineau, with peculiar gusto, relates a series of scandalous stories, which would have made Boccaccio jealous of her pen, but which are so ridiculously false as to leave no doubt, that some wicked wag, knowing she would write a book, has furnished her materials—a game too often played on tourists in this country. The constant recurrence of the female abolitionists to this topic, and their bitterness in regard to it, cannot fail to suggest to even the most charitable mind, that "Such rage without betrays the fires within." (1853, 117)

To quiet concerns about the truth of Martineau's model, Hammond asks what it is edifying to believe:

> But I do not intend to admit that this charge is just or true. Without meaning to profess uncommon modesty, I will say that I wish the topic could be avoided. I am of opinion, and I doubt not every right-minded man will concur, that the public exposure and discussion of this vice, even to rebuke, invariably does more harm than good; and that if it cannot be checked by instilling pure and virtuous sentiments, it is far worse than useless to attempt to do it, by exhibiting its deformities. (118)

But he does respond to the sharp implication of the model. It is true. And as such it provides evidence of the love of slave owners for their slaves; hence, slaves really aren't thought of as cattle. They are so lucky:

> One of your heavy charges against us has been, that we regard and treat these people as brutes; you now charge us with habitually taking them to our bosoms. I will not comment on the inconsistency of these accusations. I will not deny that some intercourse of the sort does take place. (119)

What is "ridiculous" is *avowedly* buying a slave for sexual use from a woman.

> What Miss Martineau relates of a young man's purchasing a colored concubine from a lady, and avowing his designs, is too absurd even for contradiction. No person would dare to allude to such a subject, in such a manner, to any decent female in this country. (120)

With arguments like this, one can certainly appreciate why attacking Martineau's motivation was an attractive use of one's time.

But possibly the high point of personal attack comes from a Dr. W. Gilmore Simms Esq. of South Carolina, who opens his essay by attacking Martineau's motives on the basis that, although she is deaf, she makes light of her difficulty, pointing to the beneficial silence in which to think. In this, Simms finds her denial of the providential order.[65] Simms charges her with intellectual dishonesty, forcing the evidence to fit her preconceptions. How so? Carlyle's opinion of slavery is different than hers, and if Carlyle says so who is she to disagree?

> Had it not been for this name of odium, and that Slavery had been assimilated with those features of government policy which it was her cue to obliterate, we shou'd have seen her, as we have in latter days seen Carlyle, boldly looking through all the mists and mystifications of the subject, and probing it with an independent analysis, with which neither prescription, nor prejudices, nor selfish policy, could be permitted to interfere. Her self-relying nature would have sufficed for this, had she not determined against Slavery, before acquiring any just knowledge of that condition which has received this name. (Simms 1853, 198)

The example in which this dishonesty shows is as follows:

> Alleged rapes, by negroes upon white girls, are frequently stated by Northern journalists. We refer to Mr. Tappan for such particulars as resulted from the examination of the Commissioners of the Magdalen Asylum into the morals of New-York; and we regret that Miss Martineau had not looked more closely into the negro quarters, and into the various police trials of negro offenders in the different cities of the free States. Had she done this, she would have spared us the entire chapter on the morals of Slavery. (210–11)

The reason why it would have been good if Martineau had not included this chapter on the morals of slavery is explained a little later. Her charges are true:

> There is one painful chapter in these two volumes, under the head of "Morals of Slavery." It is painful, because it is full of truth. It is devoted to the abuses, among slaveholders, of the institution of slavery; and it gives a

---

65. "What person beside herself would undertake to argue for the advantages of being deaf? To prove that the ears are but surplusage, is certainly to suggest to the deity a process of improvement, by which the curtailment of a sense will help the endowments of a philosopher" (Simms 1853, 188–89).

collection of statements which are, no doubt, in too many cases, founded upon fact, of the illicit and foul conduct of some among us, who make their slaves the victims and instruments, alike, of the most licentious passions. Regarding our slaves as a dependent and inferior people, we are their natural and only guardians; and to treat them brutally, whether by wanton physical injuries, by a neglect, or perversion of their morals, is not more impolitic than it is dishonorable. We do not quarrel with Miss Martineau for this chapter. The truth—though it is not all truth—is quite enough to sustain her and it; and we trust that its utterance may have that beneficial effect upon the relations of master and slave in our country, which the truth is, at all times, most likely to have every where. (228–29)

So, when arguments fail, attack the person:

Still, we are not satisfied with the spirit with which Miss M. records the grossness which fills this chapter. She has exhibited a zest in searching into the secrets of our prison-house, in the slave States, which she does not seem to have shown in any other quarter. (229)

Simms's testifies to Martineau's power. The power comes from her command of language and her willingness to apply economics to such matters as sex:

Miss Martineau is a monstrous proser. She has a terrible power of words, and is tyrannical as she is powerful, in the use of them. We have no doubt she is herself free from stain or reproach; but her tongue is wretchedly incontinent. . . . She scruples at no game, fears no opponent, and, whether the meat be washed or unwashed, hawk or heron, it is all the same to her. She discusses the rights of man, and—heaven save the mark!—the rights of women too, with her chambermaid, when she cannot corner a senator. Smart exceedingly, well practised in the minor economies of society, and having at her tongue's end all the standards of value in the grain, cotton, beef and butter markets, she does not scruple to apply them to the mysterious involutions of the mind and society. (246)[66]

---

66. Simms's masculinization of Martineau is rather more interesting than the later Stephen-Hall feminization of Mill, if only because it helps Simms see the robust utilitarianism that underlies the economics Martineau wields as a weapon of terror: "With her, as with most European philosophers of her order, they are assumptions only—specious or imposing—which have been taken on trust; according, perhaps, with the particular temperament of the individual. To a woman of the bold, free, masculine nature of Miss Martineau, impatient of the restraints of her sex, and compelled to seek her distinction in fields which women are rarely permitted to penetrate, democracy is one of the most attractive of social philosophies, as conservatism must be necessarily the most offensive. With her, the doctrine of the majorities is the voice of God." (1853, 247). F. C. Adams (1853, 38–41) responds to Simm's attack on *Uncle Tom's Cabin*.

What One Prefers Not to See

If the "antiprogressive" economists defended competition, what alternative did their opponents point to as superior? The answer is easy: slavery. Of course, it was a slavery supposed to be lacking certain "abuses." We now consider a series of three episodes in which the issue of competition or slavery is raised. The criterion by which I selected these episodes is simply that each of them has been extensively discussed by literary scholars. In this way, we can see how the judgment of "progressive" is applied. What, I would like to ask, does it take for opponents of markets to lose their progressive credentials?

I have stressed above the difficulty that many have had in seeing the coalition of economists and evangelicals in terms of their shared utilitarianism. A coalition that includes J. S. Mill and biblical literalists is not, as a matter of fact, the easiest group to explain. But there is another aspect of the hidden nature of the debate in which the texts are crude and their meaning becomes all too clear. There is a story that literary historians like to tell about how great art moralizes. The conclusion drawn is that great Victorian literary artists were led to question market relationships. This is doubtless a very comfortable story since, among other things, it suggests that art provides a vantage point that is above markets.

Consider the edition of Carlyle's *Past and Present* that was produced in 1965 by that formidable scholar, Richard Altick. Altick spends his introduction belaboring the horrors of unrestricted markets while noting that Carlyle's own solution looks like "Prussian authoritarianism."[67] In this text, Carlyle uses the phrase "Jew Harpies."[68] One presumes that the use of such an adjective is part and parcel of the historical dehumanization of Jews. Reflect, then, upon the note that Altick places after "Jew Harpies," which says this: "Rapacious monsters, half women, half birds." That is all he says.[69] He sees the Harpies, but that is all he will see. Turn *Prussian* into *Nazi* and the truth value of "art moralizes" attains transparency.

The first of the three episodes I shall consider is Poet Laureate Southey's

---

67. "[T]hese made the lot of the industrialized masses brutal beyond anything ever before experienced in England, and unmatched anywhere in the western world. . . . The intellectual rationalization of the get-rich-quick, dog-eat-dog, and devil-take-the-hindmost spirit that dominated British economic life in the age of *Past and Present* was supplied by Benthamite utilitarianism" (Altick in Carlyle 1965, x). "[T]he cure, for its part, strikes one as being a substitution, for the justly maligned Morison's pill, of something uncomfortably like Prussian authoritarianism. But if Carlyle's remedy fails to satisfy us, the acuteness with which he recognized the symptoms of a diseased society compels our imagination" (xvii).

68. Carlyle (1965, 91): "Jew Harpies"; (96): "harpy Jews." Carlyle (95) is ecumenical: "ravening flights of Jew and Christian creditors, pouncing on him like obscene harpies."

69. Altick in Carlyle 1965, 91. Altick's gloss on page 95 gives a reference to the *Aeneid*. One might have expected Apollonius, but then he misses the 20 million pounds.

reflections on slavery and competition and Macaulay's attack. (This attack pro-voked *Fraser's* illuminating outburst, which was quoted earlier.) The second is Carlyle's idealization of slavery in *Past and Present* in which the cash nexus is replaced with religious belief carrying moral obligation. The obvious question arises of what to do with those who do not share the particulars of the required belief and thus escape moral obligation. Jews are the particular menace. This Carlylean theme continues in Charles Kingsley's "novel" *Alton Locke,* in which the fault of a competitive order is laid on the Jews as outsiders to the religious-moral order. *Alton Locke* is also the focus of the third episode because it con-tains an enormously influential description of the condition of the "white slaves" of England vis-à-vis the black slaves of America. Its influence may have extended to the making of *Uncle Tom's Cabin.*[70]

Southey and Macaulay

Southey's *Sir Thomas More* (1829) seems to have been calculated to maximally offend evangelical sensibilities.[71] Defending More against the "libel" of "good old John Fox" (88), Southey implicitly sides with More in his persecution and with the judicial murder of William Tyndale, the first translator of the Hebrew scriptures into English.[72] "More" describes the benefits of feudalism for the workers secure in their "station." They had attained the state of happy cattle:

---

70. In *Uncle Tom's Cabin,* Stowe's character St. Clare, who sometimes sounds a great deal like Carlyle in "Negro Question" (Stowe 1982, 261), makes the following assertion: "Well, I've trav-elled in England some, and I've looked over a good many documents as to the state of their lower classes; and I really think there is no denying Alfred, when he says that his slaves are better off than a large class of the population of England." (270). Morley and Dickens's review singled out St. Clare for special praise (1852). Needless to say, the comparison drew comment (see Arthur Helps 1852a, 6; 1852b, 238). "[T]here is, I am sorry to say, an exaggeration in the statements which are made in the course of the volume, and are not contradicted, respecting the condition of the Eng-lish laborer" (Gossett 1985, 243–45). Stowe's response to Helps was twofold: (1) this is how the slave owners in fact defended themselves and (2) this is what she learned from "the works of Charles Dickens and Charles Kingsley" and others (Hedrick 1994, 243). Stowe talked to an econ-omist about this "evidence": "When Stowe broached the subject with Richard Whately, the Eng-lish archbishop of Dublin, he assured her that her literary evidence was suspect, especially her use of Charles Kingsley: 'He, & a Profr Maurice, & some others, are what are called Christian Social-ists; giving such a representation of Christianity as would have justified the Roman Emperors in putting it down by force, as leading straight to anarchy'" (Hedrick 1994, 243). Hill, Whately, and Hinds (1852, 254–56) confront St. Clare's argument.

71. Macaulay did not take the bait, treating More as saint and statesman.

72. Explicitly, Southey claims that such things as persecution are morally random: "Had it been my fortune to have associated with Bilney, or Tindal and Frith, I might have partaken their zeal and their fate. On the other hand, had I been acquainted with you and Cuthbert Tonstal, it is not less likely that I should have received the stamp of your opinions" (1829, 245–46). On More, Bilney, and Tyndale, see Foxe 1829, 117–19. See also David Daniell (1994, 1): "William Tyndale gave us our English Bible. The sages assembled by King James to prepare the Authorised Version of 1611, so often praised for unlikely corporate inspiration, took over Tyndale's work. Nine-tenths of the Authorized Version's New Testament is Tyndale's. The same is true of the first half of the

> The practical difference between the condition of the feudal slave, and of the labouring husbandman, who succeeded to the business of his station, was mainly this, that the former had neither the feeling nor the insecurity of independence. He served one master as long as he lived; and being at all times sure of the same sufficient subsistence, if he belonged to the estate like the cattle, and was accounted with them as part of the live stock, he resembled them also in the exemption which he enjoyed from all cares concerning his own maintenance and that of his family. (68–69)

After comparing this fixed status to the "vicissitudes" of the modern age, More points to the virtue of their masters that provides room for hope:

> They had nothing to lose, and they had liberty to hope for; frequently as the reward of their own faithful services, and not seldom from the piety or kindness of their lords. This was a steady hope depending so little upon contingency, that it excited no disquietude or restlessness. They were therefore in general satisfied with the lot to which they were born, as the Greenlander is with his climate, the Bedouin with his deserts, and the Hottentot and the Calmuck with their filthy and odious customs. (69–70)

Southey's spokesman argues with More: "I am sure it is not your intention to represent slavery otherwise than as an evil, under any modification." More responds:

> That which is a great evil in itself, becomes relatively a good, when it prevents or removes a greater evil. . . . But it led immediately to nefarious abuses; and the earliest records which tell us of its existence, show us also that men were kidnapped for sale. (70–71)

In spite of the stern words about the "abuses" of slavery, as one can easily imagine, the vision of the kindly slave owner seemed to resonate in certain districts of America.[73]

Old Testament, which is as far as he was able to get before he was executed outside Brussels in 1536." Daniell (262ff.) demonstrates that the dispute between Tyndale and More is alive and well.

Kingsley testifies to the importance of the Hebrew scriptures for nineteenth-century evangelicals: "As for the Bible, I knew nothing of it really, beyond the Old Testament" (1850a, 12). Hill expresses his surprise that his study of the biblical basis of seventeenth-century radicalism ended up almost exclusively focusing on the Hebrew Bible (1993, 440). On Foxe's importance: "All East India vessels carried the Bible as reading matter, together with Foxe's *Book of Martyrs* and Hakluyt's *Voyages*" (18).

73. Thus, one of the responses to *Uncle Tom's Cabin* passed along the following intelligence: "What says Southy [*sic*], the English poet, of the great mass of the English poor? He says that 'they are deprived, in childhood, of all instruction, and enjoyment. They grow up without decency—without comfort—without hope—without morals, and without shame'" (Woodward 1853, 25).

Before we consider Macaulay's response, let us reflect upon a secondary literature, which considers nineteenth-century economics to be dismal because of an alleged "fixed condition" claim. Here we have one of the more energetic critics of nineteenth-century economics *defending* a system in which the status of the worker is as fixed as the average weather of his neighborhood.[74]

We have quoted Macaulay's statement of the importance for the worker of a choice of masters, so let us consider how in 1830 Macaulay tackles the question raised by Southey of whether the condition of the working class has improved over the last three centuries. For Smith, the state of the well-being of the working class, the majority of the population, is critical to his evaluation of the well-being of society. Macaulay (1961, 216) notes that Southey does not "even pretend to maintain that the people in the sixteenth century were better lodged or clothed than at present."[75] Southey claims that the workers were better fed in the sixteenth century, so Macaulay (216) cites evidence from household expenditure records to dispute this. Then he does something quite remarkable; he proposes a novel method of measuring well-being:[76]

> The term of human life is decidedly longer in England than in any former age, respecting which we possess any information on which we can rely. All the rants in the world about picturesque cottages and temples of Mammon will not shake this argument. No test of the physical well-being of society can be named so decisive as that which is furnished by the bills of mortality. That the lives of the people of this country have been gradually lengthening during the course of several generations, is as certain as any fact in statistics; and that the lives of men should become longer and longer, while their bodily condition during life is becoming worse and worse, is utterly incredible. (217)

Houghton's judgment is that Macaulay's response to Southey is a "tissue of evasions," in particular that "he never comes to grips with the central charge that the poor are being exploited by the rich" (1957, 415). Kenneth Curry (1975, 87–88) thinks that the portrayal of More "contributes to the charm of the book" and that Southey is clearly the "progressive" in the debate, as he attacks competition. Neither explains what is the matter with using life expectancy as a welfare norm and why the conclusions aren't as Macaulay

---

74. Winch (1996, 290–91) has a discussion of Southey's *More* that does not mention the idealization of slavery.

75. "It is but equity, besides, that they who feed, cloath, and lodge the whole body of the people, should have such a share of the produce of their own labour as to be themselves tolerably well fed, cloathed, and lodged" (Smith 1976a, 96).

76. The Smithian roots of the idea of using life expectancy as a measure of well-being is discussed in chapter 10. It has been revived by A. K. Sen (1993).

argues. What is remarkable is that neither scholar appears to notice that an inability to switch masters—to regard one's station with the same fatality as one regards the weather—is a more plausible ground for exploitation than a competitive system in which the worker has a choice of masters. Possibly the reading that *Fraser's* offered at the time was more to the point. Macaulay's defense of competition represents a dire threat to the system of slavery in the British West Indies, and his attack on Southey's defense of feudal slavery, slavery without "abuses," is just a skirmish in the space of historical memory in the long struggle of a competitive system against a variety of slave systems.

"Just" Slavery and the Jewish Menace

Carlyle's *Past and Present* has long enjoyed unimpeachable "progressive" credentials because it was so enthusiastically greeted by Frederick Engels.[77] In *Past and Present,* Carlyle introduced his notion of "economic chivalry" in which the permanence of one's social state is anchored by an unquestioned moral imperative. Here he reflects on the need for despotism:

> A question arises here: Whether, in some ulterior, perhaps, some not far-distant stage of this "Chivalry of Labour," your Master-Worker may not find it possible, and needful, to grant his Workers permanent *interest* in his enterprise and theirs? So that it become, in practical result, what in essential fact and justice it ever is, a joint enterprise; all men, from the Chief Master down to the lowest Overseer and Operative, economically as well as loyally concerned for it?—Which question I do not answer. The answer, near or else far, is perhaps, Yes;—and yet one knows the difficulties. Despotism is essential in most enterprises; I am told, they do not tolerate "freedom of debate" on board a Seventy-Four! Republican senate and *plebiscita* would not answer well in Cotton-Mills. (1965, 278)

To reconcile slavery and freedom? Easy! the voice of the master is the voice of God:[78]

---

77. When one views the world through traditional Marxist preconceptions, one tends not to see much racial conflict. Engels's opinion signifies one thing for a world split on class among white people; perhaps it implies something else when we introduce racial considerations. Léon Poliakov (1974, 244–46) discusses Engels and Marx's racism, emphasizing Engels's claim that "Blacks were congenitally incapable of understanding mathematics." The problem for friends of Carlyle is explained this way. "Yet the Carlyle who kindled the enthusiasm of Emerson and Engels and Whitman . . . is not another creature from the Carlyle who brought tears of hope to the eyes of Hitler" (Rosenberg 1985, 117).

78. Carlyle lives as a "progressive" in textbook accounts because of his impact on religious thinking. It is remarkable, though, how many "Hebrew old clothes" Carlyle presupposes. God in Carlyle's account does not want to use His slaves sexually—or in any other way for that matter.

> And yet observe there too: Freedom, not nomad's or ape's Freedom, but man's Freedom; this is indispensable. We must have it, and will have it! To reconcile Despotism with Freedom:—well, is that such a mystery? Do you not already know the way? It is to make your Despotism *just*. Rigorous as Destiny; but just too, as Destiny and its Laws. The Laws of God: all men obey these, and have no "Freedom" at all but in obeying them. (278)

There was obviously a contemporary demand for the doctrine that "real freedom" is slavery to one's betters, as we see from a participant in the debate over *Uncle Tom's Cabin* who found this, and similar doctrines, edifying.[79]

A consequence of the doctrine of "just" slavery is that one's moral obligation is relative to one's status within the hierarchy. One has the obligation of obedience toward those up the hierarchy and the obligation of charity to those down the hierarchy. The slogan of this view of the moral world is that "charity begins at home." It also ends there. Those outside the hierarchy, people in a distant land or with different beliefs, have no claim on us. We have read the passage in *Past and Present,* complete with reference to the ill-spent 20 million pounds, in which the universalism of the antislave coalition is contrasted with Carlyle's moral localism.

Carlyle's doctrine of moral localism is represented in Kingsley's "novel" *Alton Locke.* Here Kingsley has the voice of Carlyle localize moral obligation:

> "What do ye ken aboot the Pacific? Which is maist to your business? That bare-backed hizzies that play the harlot o' the other side o' the warld, or these—these thousands o' barebacked hizzies that play the harlot o' your ain side—made out o' your ain flesh and blude? You a poet! True poetry, like true charity, my laddie, begins at hame." (1850a, 85)

"Alton Locke" learns this lesson for his examination:

This presupposes the God of Abraham and not Pan and the old Homeric crew of raping optimizers. Charles Gore made the point with perfect clarity: "There was an old dilemma invented I think at the time of the Reformation: 'either Jesus was God or He was not a good man'; and the modern critic often laughs at it as ridiculous. I do not think I can laugh at it as ridiculous. What is, after all, the worst kind of spiritual crime? Is it not spiritual arrogance? What makes men hate with a profound hatred the wrong sort of sacerdotalism? It is that it exercises tyranny over human souls. Every man has the right to be himself; he ought not to be dominated or mastered by any other except God" (1922, 18–19). For an account of the Homeric divinity as optimizers who differ from mortals only in their constraints, see Levy 1992, 108–34.

79. "[I]f there is any inalienable right of another class, it is that so ably set forth by Carlyle,—the right of every man to be compelled to do what he is fit for, if he won't do it voluntarily; and this brings us back to Quashy" (Stearns 1853, 21).

"I've fearful misgivings about it, just because Irishmen are at the head of it."

"Of course they are—they have the deepest wrongs; and that makes them most earnest in the cause of right. The sympathy of suffering, as they say themselves, has bound them to the English working-man against the same oppressors."

"Then let them fight those oppressors at home, and we'll do the same: that's the true way to show sympathy. Charity begins at home. They are always crying 'Ireland for the Irish;' why can't they leave England for the English?" (292)

While the utilitarian coalition supported emancipation regardless of the religion of the slaves, the moral localism of Carlyle and Kingsley, by locating obligation in a hierarchy embodied in religious belief, finds differences in religion to be a threat. Thus, in *Past and Present*'s medieval fantasy Carlyle's Abbot Samson expels the Jews.[80] As Carlyle says: "Time, Jews, and the task of Governing, will make a man's beard very gray!" (1965, 104). If anything, the theses that Jews threaten the moral economic order is pursued more vigorously in *Alton Locke* than it is in *Past and Present*.[81]

In *Alton Locke*, when the old employer dies, the new owner changes his policy to emulate that of the Jews, who pursue wealth at the expense of all moral obligation in excess of market-based obligation. Jewish economic practice embodies economic doctrine perfectly:[82]

His father had made money very slowly of late; while dozens, who had begun business long after him, had now retired to luxurious ease and suburban villas. Why should he remain in the minority? Why should he not get rich as fast as he could? Why should he stick to the old, slow-going, honorable trade? . . . Why should he pay his men two shillings where the government paid them one? Were there not cheap houses even at the

---

80. "In less than four years, says Jocelin, the Convent Debts were all liquidated: the harpy Jews not only settled with, but banished, bag and baggage, out of the *Bannaleuca* (Liberties, *Banlieue*) of St. Edmundsbury,—so has the King's Majesty been persuaded to permit. Farewell to *you*, at any rate: let us, in no extremity, apply again to you! Armed men march them over the borders, dismiss them under stern penalties,—sentence of excommunication on all that shall again harbour them here: there were many dry eyes at their departure" (Carlyle 1965, 96).

81. Styron Harris (1981, 16) describes two letters to the *Times* in 1862 protesting Kingsley's views on Jews.

82. "[H]is wages, thanks to your competitive system, were beaten down deliberately and conscientiously (for was it not according to political economy, and the laws thereof?) to the minimum on which he could or would work" (Kingsley 1850a, 245).

West-end, which had saved several thousands a year merely by reducing their workmen's wages? And if the workmen chose to take lower wages, he was not bound actually to make them a present of more than they asked for! They would go to the cheapest market for any thing they wanted, and so must he. . . .

Such, I suppose, were some of the arguments which led to an official announcement, one Saturday night, that our young employer intended to enlarge his establishment, for the purpose of commencing business in the "show trade;" and that, emulous of Messrs. Aaron, Levi, and the rest of that class. (Kingsley 1850a, 96–97)

The chapter "The Sweater's Den" contains Alton's misadventures among the Jewish "sweaters."

As I had expected, a fetid, choking den, with just room enough in it for the seven or eight sallow, starved beings, who, coatless, shoeless, and ragged, sat stitching, each on his truckle-bed. . . ."Oh! blessed saints, take me out o' this!—take me out, for the love of Jesus!—take me out o' this hell, or I'll go mad intirely! Och! will nobody have pity on poor sowls in purgatory—here in prison like negur slaves?" (190)

The Jews threatened Christian workers both in this world and the next:

"Och! Mother of Heaven!" he went on, wildly, "when will I get out to the fresh air? For five months I haven't seen the blessed light of sun, nor spoken to the praste, not ate a bit o' mate, barring bread-and-butter. Shure it's all the blessed sabbaths and saints' days I've been a-working like a haythen Jew, and niver seen the insides o' the chapel to confess my sins, and me poor sowl's lost intirely." (191)

And, in what has to be one of the great surprises in literature, we learn that Jews don't fight fairly:

At last, as Downes's life seemed in danger, he wavered; the Jew-boy seized the moment, jumped up, upsetting the constable, dashed like an eel between Crossthwaite and Mackaye, gave me a back-handed blow in passing, which I felt for a week after, and vanished through the street-door, which he locked after him. (193)

The role of Jew as menace to the moral economy is worthy of remark if only because a generation of well-informed critics have passed over it in silence.[83] The question naturally should occur: how could *this* be in *Alton Locke* if no one else has read it? Indeed, I would agree that if no one caught the Jewish references they might as well not be there. But then let us reflect upon how a contemporary reader, W. E. Aytoun, reviewing *Alton Locke* for *Blackwood's*, parses the relationship between Jews and the competitive order. First, one must make a distinction between honor and competition:

> This is intended, or at all events given, as an accurate picture of a respectable London tailoring establishment, where the men receive decent wages. Such a house is called an "honourable" one, in contradistinction to others, now infinitely the more numerous, which are springing up in every direction under the fostering care of competition. (1850, 598)

Second, the competitive establishments employ "sweaters" so that they need not deal with workers on a face-to-face basis:

> These sweaters are commonly Jews, to which persuasion also the majority of the dishonourable proprietors belong. Few people who emerge from the Euston Square Station are left in ignorance as to the fact, it being the insolent custom of a gang of hook-nosed and blubber-lipped Israelites to shower their fetid tracts, indicating the localities of the principal dealers of their tribe, into every cab as it issues from the gate. These are, in plain terms, advertisement of a more odious cannibalism than exists in the Sandwich Islands. (598–89)

The moral course of action naturally suggests itself:

> Very often have we wished that the miscreant who so assailed us were within reach of our black-thorn cudgel, that we might have knocked all ideas of fried fish out of his head for at least a fortnight to come! In these days of projected Jewish emancipation, the sentiment may be deemed an

---

83. "In part, *Alton Locke* is in the orthodox sense an 'exposure': an informed, angry and sustained account of sweated labour in the 'Cheap and Nasty' clothing trade. Much of it can still be read in these terms, with attention and sympathy. It is fair to note, however, that in respect of this theme the Preface is more effective than the novel" (Williams 1958, 100). There is no preface in the first edition. Houghton (1957) has an extensive discussion of *Alton Locke* without mentioning the role of Jews as "sweaters." David Lodge continues in the tradition, even as he emphasizes that Kingsley late in life took a "right-wing line" on the American Civil War and Eyre (1967, xviii). Elizabeth Cripps's notes in her edition of *Alton Locke* (Kingsley 1983, 409) helpfully explain that *guanaco* is a "reddish-brown wool from the South American llama," but she doesn't explain why Jews might be "sweaters." This is obvious to the reader? John Hawley (1986) also reads the Jews out of the story.

> atrocious one, but we cannot retract it. Shylock was and is the true type of his class; only that the modern London Jew is six times more personally offensive, mean, sordid, and rapacious than the merchant of the Rialto. And why should we stifle our indignation? Dare any one deny the truth of what we have said? It is notorious to the whole world that these human leeches acquire their wealth, not by honest labour and industry, but by bill-broking, sweating, discounting, and other nefarious arts. (599)

The Jewish link to economics is trivial:

> Talk of Jewish legislation indeed! We have had too much of it already in our time, from the days of Ricardo, the instigator of Sir Robert Peel's earliest practices upon the currency, down to those of Nathan Rothschild, the first Baron of Jewry, for whose personal character and upright dealings the reader is referred to Mr Francis' Chronicles of the Stock Exchange. (599)

Aytoun provides a possible British context for H. S. Chamberlain's pregnant rantings:

> Read the following account by a working tailor of their doings, and then settle the matter with your conscience, whether it is consistent with the character of a Christian gentleman to have dealings with such inhuman vampires. (599)[84]

"White Slaves" and Black Ones

Charles Kingsley's name does not appear on the title page of the first edition of *Alton Locke*. This is how it reads: *Alton Locke, Tailor and Poet. An Autobiography*. Of course, there is an "Ed.," who makes various footnote appearances, hardly surprising as the book ends as Alton lays dying, far too weak to bundle the manuscript off to the printer. Readers of later editions who know that it is a novel, might know something that the readers in the 1850s might not. "Alton Locke" laments his status as a "white slave" (Kingsley 1850a, 179). The working men Alton Locke encounters view themselves as "nigger slaves" or "negur slaves." What does this mean to the reader?[85] A reader who knows

---

84. The reader ought not to think that *vampire* refers to the suave, elegant, highly erotic creatures of late Victorian fiction or modern movies, with whom one might well spend an enchanting evening. Paul Barber (1988) describes the loathsome folkloric monster as a belief evolved to rationalize the nasty facts of bodily decomposition.

85. This problem, an example of reader-response criticism (Stanley Fish 1967), seems not to have been noted by literary commentators. The reviews in *Fraser's* (November 1850) and *Blackwood's*, (Aytoun 1850) warn readers that it isn't really what it purports to be. The extract reprinted in *Harper's* has this preface (1850b, 803): "It was an error to call this work the autobiography of an

Alton Locke to be a novel might conclude that the *author* views the condition of English workers and black slaves as comparable. A reader who does not know *Alton Locke* to be a novel might conclude that the *English workers* themselves were ready to migrate to America to sell themselves in the New Orleans slave market.

The identification of white slaves with black slaves—which we saw in Thrall's commentary on the economists—seems to be a contestation for the role of the minimum of the happiness distribution. This is important to Kingsley, as a Christian, in a way that it isn't important to Carlyle. While for Carlyle blacks and Irish are not morally human, so they can be exterminated if they object to their remaking, Kingsley contends with the coalition on its own grounds by putting forward the British working man as a contender for the position at the minimum of the distribution of happiness.[86]

The great crisis in slavery, in the form of *Uncle Tom's Cabin*, was published as an invitation to readers to imagine the fate of mothers seeing their children sold to strangers. In the debate that followed, we find readers who cite *Alton Locke* as offering creditable testimony that the white slaves viewed themselves and the black slaves as being in comparable positions. If modern scholars are correct in thinking that Stowe's view of British laboring conditions comes at least in part from Kingsley, perhaps even from *Alton Locke* itself, then *Uncle Tom's Cabin* authorizes this very response. Here is one attack:

---

individual. It is a picturing—faithful, minute, and eloquent—of the hardships, the suffering, and the miseries endured by a large mass of our fellow men. It is an earnest and honest exposure of the hollowness that infests English society." The reviewer in the American *Southern Quarterly* considers it an "auto-biography" that testifies truthfully (1851, 120–21): "There is a vivid reality about his descriptions which too well vouches for their truth, and touches us home—we of these Southern United States—by the great contrast which such a state of society presents, with the far happier, and every way more elevated, position of *our* labouring classes. Aye—negro and slave though these be—the white slave of England—great, proud, glorious England—has sunk far lower than they, in the weltering abyss of misery and hopeless wretchedness." Westward the course of rationalization? However, the extensive reprinting of extracts from *Alton Locke* by John Cobden (1859, 193) contains this information: "In Charles Kingsley's popular novel, 'Alton Locke,' we find a vivid and truthful picture of the London tailor's workshop, and the slavery of the workmen." Cunliffe (1979, 43) cites a 1853 edition of Cobden 1859 that I have not seen.

86. Even though Kingsley asserts in *Alton Locke,* and everywhere else the question comes up, the doctrine of racial hierarchy, his social theorizing is constrained by Christian doctrine. "Abstract rights? They are sure to end, in practice, only in the tyranny of their father—opinion. In favored England here, the notion of abstract right among the many are not so incorrect, thanks to three centuries of Protestant civilization; but only because the right notions suit the many at this moment. But in America, even now, the same ideas of abstract right do not interfere with the tyranny of the white man over the black. Why should they? The white man is handsomer, stronger, cunninger, worthier than the black. The black is more like an ape than the white man— he is—the fact is there; and no notions of an abstract right will put that down: nothing but another fact—a mightier, more universal fact—Jesus of Nazareth died for the negro as well as for the white" (Kingsley 1850a, 343–44). Kingsley wrote to Stowe, agreeing with her doctrine of racial differences (Gossett 1985, 246).

> In bringing forward the condition of the English labouring class, then, I do it from no vile motive of recrimination. I do it, because the subject is introduced into the work I am commenting on, and because my *argument* requires it. (Stearns 1853, 81)

Stearns takes note of Helps's *Letter*. He brings up the question of women working in gangs:

> "White slaves," in the words of the London Times, . . . "of a sex and age least qualified to struggle with the hardships of their lot—young women, for the most part, between sixteen and thirty years of age, *worked in gangs* in ill-ventilated rooms . . ." sewing "from morning till night, *and night till morning*." (87)

Then "Alton Locke" is offered as testimony:

> And these things are done in "*merry* England!" Ay, and not these alone. The milliners and dressmakers are not the only ones who thrive on the miseries of their fellows; the keepers of "furnishing" shops are in the same category,—witness the "song of the shirt;" and so are the "fashionable tailors," as many an Alton Locke could testify. (89)

A second attack occurs in a pamphlet reprinted in *Fraser's*,[87] which mixes statistics and fiction promiscuously:

> This power that slavery gives to one man over another is met with everywhere in society. Caleb Williams! Alton Locke! Mary Barton! Parliamentary Blue Books! Mining Districts! Manufacturing Districts! Combinations of Workers! Combinations of Masters!—to which shall we point especially? In all is the lesson of one man's power over another. (Pringle 1852a, 20; 1852b, 481)

If all work is slavery and we are interested in those who are the worst off, then what difference is there between "white slavery" and black slavery?[88]

---

87. The attack was bracketed by an earlier most favorable review (Helps 1852b) and an favorable discussion of the Beecher family ("Some Account" 1852). Pringle's attack was prefaced by editor John Parker's announced policy of publishing both sides. Parker calls attention to the exchange over the "Negro question." Modern authorities on *Fraser's* pass Parker's policy over in silence. Both the Helps and Pringle articles are reprinted from pamphlets. Ashton (1977) only catches the Helps reprint.

88. Economists ought to have learned from the Soviet era to be cautious of claims that the standard of living in an area people flee *from* is higher than the standard of living in an area people flee *to*. Some particularly embarrassing "data" are considered in Levy 1993. Hill, Whately, and Hinds (1852, 248–49) employ the revealed escaping argument to confront the "happy" slave assertions.

Moral localism would not in fact contradict universalism since the "white slaves" of Britain would merit our concern as much as do the black slaves of America. But there is a trap in this line of argument: all those who lament their status as "white slaves" in *Alton Locke* are male.

And we see the trap sprung in the response to the critics of *Uncle Tom's Cabin* taking withering variations on the sexual slavery theme of Wilberforce and Martineau. Writing with an ink capable of etching steel, "Nicholas Brimblecomb" retold the story from a "proslavery" point of view:[89]

> He sought to secure Harry's young and beautiful mother, as judging her suitable to accommodate and please one of those numerous southern gentlemen who not only have field and house servants, but also certain house servants of a peculiar character. (Brimblecomb 1853, 13–14)

> Slavery gave him power to compel such slaves to be his concubines as he saw fit; he acted accordingly, and when he was weary of one, he would buy another for his particular purpose. . . .
>   Whosoever would see slavery—see it in its genuine nature, operations, and character—must not look at such an awkward case as that of St. Clare; but he must look at Legree. (115)

F. C. Adams explicitly challenges Pringle's doctrine that slavery moralizes:

> In all our intercourse with Southerners, we never heard one claim moral caste for the institution of slavery; but not unfrequently have we heard them denounce instances of outrage upon chastity, sustained in the rights of the master, and beyond the remedy of laws made to govern the outraged. With our knowledge of social life in Charleston, we feel no hesitation in saying, that Mr. P——'s erudition in behalf of the divine precepts of slavery will prove as novel to Southern readers, as it will be forcible to those of more Northern sensibility. (1853, 15–16)

The conflict between universality and "progressive," localizing moralizing is clearly explained:

> But the reader must remember that the quality, depth, and attributes of Christianity, according to the rule of progress, are at the present day measured by a scale of locality. That which is made the medium of an accommodating morality in Charleston, would be rejected as unwholesome by the sterner judgment of the New Englander. (16)

---

89. Ashton (1977, 10) regards this as "possibly satire." It is possible that I am an economist.

Literary scholars who restrict their attention to British publications, and who take seriously neither economists like Martineau nor evangelicals like Wilberforce, evidently do not see what is so odd about comparing "white slaves" to black slaves on the basis of male well-being.[90] Slavery was not the same burden for men and women.[91] This was the contention of the broad utilitarian coalition, and to silently suppress this issue is to take a position in the debate.

Conclusion

The real past is complicated. British economists not only studied the world, but they helped to change it. Indeed, they helped to change it so radically that without considerable effort we cannot see what is so radical about their views. The "reactionary" status of the classical economists, it seems to me, comes from the lazy habit of making a judgment from the comfortable vantage point of the status quo.

The mathematician-philosopher A. N. Whitehead said that a science that hesitates to forget its past is lost. I think this is precisely wrong—it is by remembering our past that we shall deserve to be saved. The past has always been contested ground. "Who controls the past controls the future." George Orwell told us that.

> The mutability of the past is the central tenet of Ingsoc. Past events, it is argued, have no objective existence, but survive only in written records and in human memories. The past is whatever the records and the memories agree upon. (1961, 176)

If we do not remember our past, others with no love for the sort of market or political organizations that economists study will be all too willing to provide a "past" for us. It ill becomes economists, of all people, to have our understanding of our place in the world depend on the kindness of strangers.

Appendix: Some Dismal Results

Thanks to the generosity of the Mellon family, economists and others have the capability to do on-line searches of the content by character strings of major

---

90. As far as I can see this is even the case for Cunliffe (1979), who carefully attends to the interrelations between the American and British discussions. His references to Martineau are decorative and to Wilberforce nonexistent.

91. This issue has not vanished, as the debate over the Thomas Jefferson–Sally Hemings affair testifies (Foster et al. 1998).

journals for the entire period of their run in the data base JSTOR.[92] The ten economics journals so accessible at the time of the study were as follows: *American Economic Review, Econometrica, Journal of Economic History, Journal of Industrial Economics, Journal of Money, Credit, and Banking, The Journal of Political Economy, Quarterly Journal of Economics, Review of Economics and Statistics, Journal of Applied Econometrics,* and *Journal of Economic Perspectives*.

A search of the articles in these journals uncovered sixty-nine uses of the term *dismal science*. Searching for *dismal science* $\wedge$ (*Malthus* $\vee$ *Malthusian* $\vee$ *wage*) found forty-seven. Searching for *dismal science* $\wedge$ (*nigger* $\vee$ *negro*) found exactly two germane articles.[93] These are Hamilton 1952 and Persky 1990.

---

92. The Web address is <www.jstor.org>. The search was conducted in September 1998 and was replicated with a wider list of journals on September 1, 2000.

93. A third "article" was actually a series of independently authored comments. One author used *dismal science* and another used *Negro*. JSTOR can search the whole of journals, including such things as the table of contents, lists of publications received, and the like. Needless to say, searches in such heterogeneous material turn up many such illusory hits.

SEVEN

Hard Times and the Moral Equivalence of Markets and Slavery

The Novelist as Rational Chooser

Charles Dickens's novel *Hard Times* gives definitive form to Thomas Carlyle's opposition to the "cash nexus" of market exchange. As we have seen, when Carlyle coined the term *dismal science* he juxtaposed it to the "gay science" of poetry. The debate to which he pointed, economics versus poetry, continues in our own time. The literary critics and philosophers influenced by these literary critics, whom we shall encounter soon, seem to take it for granted, as befits such a great work of art as *Hard Times*, that the story Dickens told is "true" and so can serve as opposition to the truth claims of economic models.[1]

The truth claims on behalf of *Hard Times* are twofold. Not only are claims about the world outside the novel a serviceable approximation of that reality (first), but (second) the acts described in the story are consistent with the laws of the world imagined. I propose to question this tradition root and branch. I shall venture the claim that it is precisely where the novel is "false" in both of these directions—one critical claim about the world outside the story is a transparent falsification and the characters's actions deviate from the laws of Dickens's world to serve Dickens's polemic purpose—that we can see what message *Hard Times* has to convey.

To make my case that we can observe false choices in *Hard Times*, I need to identify a law of Dickens's world independent of the acts of the agents. But

---

1. "Theorists of poetry (or literature more generally) have continued to argue that this form of writing offers a unique solution to the problem of induction either because the literary text constitutes what W. K. Wimsatt called 'a concrete universal' or because, as Steven Knapp has more recently contended, 'the object of literary interest is a special kind of representational structure, each of whose elements acquires, by virtue of its connection with other elements, a network of associations inseparable from the representation itself'" (Poovey 1998, 326–27). In the period we study, Charles Kingsley (1864, xli) offers a kindred explanation for the conflict between Great Man accounts and what today are called "invisible hand explanations" and explains the literary basis of the Great Man stories.

in *Hard Times* this is easy. The law of the world is that the self-described eco-
nomic-Utilitarian agents seek to maximize their happiness without regard for
the happiness of others. The problem with Utilitarianism is its hardness and
inhumanity. This is the first of many things that F. R. Leavis, the modern
scholar most responsible for *Hard Times'* contemporary fame, writes:

> But in *Hard Times* he is for once possessed by a comprehensive vision, one
> in which the inhumanities of Victorian civilization are seen as fostered and
> sanctioned by a hard philosophy, the aggressive formulation of an inhu-
> mane spirit. The philosophy is represented by Thomas Gradgrind,
> Esquire, Member of Parliament for Coketown, who has brought up his
> children on the lines of the experiment recorded by John Stuart Mill as car-
> ried out on himself. What Gradgrind stands for is, though repellent, nev-
> ertheless respectable. (1990, 341)

Attacking Modern Economics by Means of Victorian Novels

It is in the spirit of the doctrine of authorial infallibility in great works of art
that we might read Martha Nussbaum's recent lecture on economics past and
present in light of *Hard Times*. Here she contrasts economic with novelistic
accounts:

> Mr. Gradgrind knows that storybooks are not simply decorative, not sim-
> ply amusing—though this already would be enough to cause him to doubt
> their utility. Literature, he sees, is subversive. It is the enemy of political
> economy, as Mr. Gradgrind knows that science. It expresses, in its struc-
> tures and its ways of speaking, a sense of life that is incompatible with the
> vision of the world embodied in the texts of political economy; and
> engagement with it forms the imagination and the desires in a manner that
> subverts that science's norm of rationality. (1991, 878)[2]

Nussbaum asserts—on the basis of her personal experience of life among "the
econ"—that the criticism of economics in *Hard Times* is fundamentally fair.

---

2. Nussbaum makes her obligations to Leavis and Williams clear (1991, 907). It is important
for what follows that she cites not a single nineteenth-century economist. Leavis and Williams do
discuss John Stuart Mill, albeit in Leavis's case in a rather bizarre fashion (Fielding 1956). Moreover, Nussbaum makes the following assertion: "The antagonist throughout will be not sophisti-
cated philosophical forms of utilitarianism, and not the political economy of the greatest philosophical political economists, such as Adam Smith—but the cruder form of economic
utilitarianism that is actually used in many areas of public policy-making, and is commended as a
norm for still others. (1991, 880). Since one of the little Gradgrinds is named "Adam Smith Gradgrind," Nussbaum's exemption raises questions too obvious to belabor.

The novel is more nearly true than the competing economic models with which it contends.[3]

While Nussbaum's conflation of the target of *Hard Times,* early- and mid-nineteenth-century economics, with that with which she has personal knowledge might seem to be debatable essentialism, I have no quarrel with at least one central theme in her argument. ChicagoSchool economics does indeed assume a fixed human nature of a fairly simple form. Change incentives, change behavior. That's rational choice theory. Obviously, there are technical details to fuss over, but indeed the critical step is the assumption that human nature is fixed. And the economic teaching that provoked Dickens made a similarly simple claim about human rationality in terms of fixed human nature.

It is the next step I worry about. Nussbaum makes the following claims against modern economics:

> It does not even tell us about life expectancy and infant mortality—far less about health, education, political functioning, the quality of ethnic and racial and gender relations. (1991, 904–5)

And this bears on the target of Dickens how? Nussbaum is vague here, and since she does not cite the texts of past economists I shall attempt to reconstruct an argument to fill the gap. She writes as if one need not actually read the past to know what cannot be found there. This seems to me to be as pure an instance of presentism as one could hope to find. This surely means to say that if a concept is not found in modern economics—that economics she knows, with all its high mathematical and statistical technology—it cannot be found in the past. If modern economists do not worry about life expectancy, such concerns are not found in the past. If modern economists of undoubtedly respectable views on race and politics are not concerned in their technical work about "the quality of ethnic and racial and gender relations," surely those

---

3. "What I am about to say here may seem in some respects obvious. For it is part of the novel's design that the economist's way of thinking, seen in the full context of daily life, should look extremely strange, and the opposing way natural. What I hope to bring out here, however, is that the economic opponent is not a straw man: it is a conception that even now dominates much of our public life, in a form not very different from the form presented in this novel. Once, focusing on the subtle modifications of utilitarianism that one finds in recent philosophy, I felt that the satire of *Hard Times* was unfair. But now that I have spent time in the world of economics, . . . reading the prose and following the arguments, I am convinced that the criticisms in the novel are both fair and urgent. The simple utilitarian idea of what rational choice consists in dominates not only economic thought and practice, but also—given the prestige of economics within the social sciences—a great deal of writing in the other social sciences as well, where 'rational choice theory' is taken to be equivalent to utilitarian rational choice theory as practiced in neoclassical economics" (Nussbaum 1991, 882).

blasted souls of economics past could not have been so concerned. Economics present is an upper bound to economics past.

On the contrary, I should argue that the content of economics past serves as a lower bound to economics future. If it was in the past, then as long as we persist in holding to our rational choice vision it can be in our future. Thus, while I think some of Nussbaum's criticisms of economics present are sensible, the defects she points out are not inevitable in a rational choice model of the future precisely because they were dealt by those who worked in the rational choice tradition of the past.[4]

The quarrel I have with Nussbaum is that by using economics present to bound economics past she completely misses the context of the larger debate in which *Hard Times* is but one set piece. A vast amount of classical economics is intertwined with controversies over racial slavery. And, as economic theory is a public good, it was seized upon by noneconomists in the antislavery movement and so entered a great public debate.

Socrates, as represented in the *Meno*, claims that all knowledge is recollection. This chapter is an attempt to remember. In recollection, we discover what we were and thus what we might be again.

Reading the Silence over Carlyle versus Mill

Let us recall that *Hard Times*, published in 1854, is "Inscribed to Thomas Carlyle" and ask what this might mean to Dickens's contemporaries. The Carlylean twofold doctrine, fully explained in a pair of essays published in 1849–50, is (first) that people of color can be improved to approach human status through enslavement to whites and (second) without this improvement genocide is a policy option. These we have read. Dickens's inscription signifies at a bare minimum his nonrevulsion in the face of this doctrine.

Today, who writes about the Carlyle-Mill debate? Who wants to talk about Carlyle's attack on the role of classical economic theory for its role in black emancipation? Who wants to talk about the fact that this was the same economic theory that Dickens attacked?

As an aid in developing a hypothesis, let us first look at the data. Here is a data collection procedure anyone at a modern research institution can conduct by means of that most magical of scholarly devices, JSTOR. With JSTOR, one can read the relative silence: what is not in one discipline but is in another. Put the following four items in "full-text" mode in the default search engine: Carlyle and Mill and negro question and nigger question. First, restrict the search

---

4. Two words on Nussbaum's technical criticisms. The replacement of a scalar measure of well-being—inflation adjusted money income—with a vector approach to well-being has been a topic of conversation among economics for decades. See, for example, Terleckyj 1975.

to literature journals in JSTOR. What do you find? The search I conducted turned up nothing.[5] No hits. Funny that. Possibly, the words I used have no meaning in the material world? Second, change the search to journals in the field of African American studies. Two hits. Perhaps the words do mean something after all.[6]

One might remember, however, that every now and again someone calls attention to the unhappy fact that there are aspects of the Dickens *opera* that are completely out of tune with the ordered harmony in his hagiography.[7] In particular, there are articles in Dickens's weekly magazine, *Household Words*, that his admirers then and now would wish unwritten. From 1853, here is Lord Denman's linkage of that character in *Bleak House*, concerned more about the well-being of distant slaves than her own children with those words Dickens was publishing in his weekly magazine.

> [U]nluckily we cannot disassociate her [Mrs. Jellyby] from some papers in the "Household Words," which appear to have been written for the taste of slave traders only. (Denman 1853, 11)[8]

And this is related to *Hard Times* how? Since Denman's time, scholars have learned the names of the authors of *Household Words* articles. In Kate Flint's introduction to the newest Penguin edition of *Hard Times*, she notes that if

---

5. The literature journals as of October 11, 1999 are *American Literature, ELH, MLN, Negro American Literature Forum, Shakespeare Quarterly, Speculum, Yale French Studies, Black American Literature Forum, Modern Language Notes, Callaloo, Representations,* and *African American Review.*

6. I commend the work of Iva Jones (1967) and James Patterson Smith (1994) to the reader.

7. The reader might wish to consult the work of Michael Goldberg (1972a, 1972b) and William Oddie (1972). The Carlyleanization of Dickens was noted in an unattributed article in *Fraser's* of 1850 ("Charles Dickens and David Copperfield," 709): "The coincidence of opinion between the two authors is the more remarkable, as they are probably divided in opinion upon every other subject, secular or sacred. We even remember a passage in *Dombey and Son* which looks like an overt declaration of war against the great priest of Hero-worship. However this may be, it is certain that no one has been more instrumental than Dickens in fostering that spirit of kindly charity which impels a man to do what he can, however narrow his sphere of action may be, to relieve the sufferings and to instruct the ignorance of his brethren; while Carlyle, on the other hand, treats all such efforts with lofty disdain, and would call them mere attempts to tap an ocean by gimlet-holes, or some such disparaging metaphor." This article is reprinted in Collins 1971, 243–48. Oddie (1972, 131) disagrees with the *Fraser's* judgment.

8. The reader might wish to consider how the Dickens Protective Agency (DPA) deals with Denman's perfectly correct discussion of what was being published in *Household Words.* According to Edgar Johnson (1952, 2:760): "Lord Denman's violence was partly the result of declining health—he died the following year—of which his son sent Dickens an apologetic explanation." The reader who disbelieves in the existence of a DPA might wish to consult Claire Tomalin (1991) on the lengths to which many have gone to conceal the existence of the friendship between Dickens and the woman to whom his wife first applied the label "your actress." Harry Stone describes how recent scholarship has broken through old barriers and the way his work (1994, xix) draws "upon this checkered and fluctuating interest in a darker, more concealed Dickens."

words Dickens wrote in that text are juxtaposed against what he wrote in *Household Words,* their meaning lurches in unexpected directions. There is

> an amusing quirkiness in hearing that Coketown was "a town of unnatural red and black like the painted face of a savage" until one recollects Dickens's hysterical attack in an [*Household Words*] article of 1853 on "The Noble Savage." (Dickens 1995, xix)

We shall encounter the noble savage by and by.

That the Carlyle-Mill debate, which we encountered earlier, frames Denman's attack on Dickens we learn by reading what Denman says in the open letter to Harriet Beecher Stowe that prefaces the reprinting of his letters to the *Standard:*

> [I]n England there are symptoms calculated to mislead. First, the open defence of Slavery by some of our most popular and influential writers. For the unaccountable part they have been induced to take in the great process now going on between mankind and the owners of and traders in Slaves, we, the public, feel the deepest grief, but no alarm as to the ultimate result. (1853, iii–iv)

Sissy Jupe Passes Her Exam

When Nussbaum writes about Dickens's attack on economics, she does not consider his attacks on the Christian evangelicals. That these groups ought to be taken as one target is the considered judgment of a modern specialist:

> If Dickens was in the main an environmentalist, he could number among the moralists, two of his least favorite groups: evangelicals and political economists. Indeed, these two groups often overlapped in the nineteenth century to produce writers who, in the tradition of Malthus, "preached what might be called evangelical economics." (Schacht 1990, 78)[9]

We know from the Carlyle-Mill exchange that the cause of black emancipation united Utilitarian and evangelical. As we have seen, the antislavery coalition between Utilitarians and evangelical Christians functioned because in part it was agreed that there is a formal identity between the Golden Rule of Chris-

---

9. The quotation is from Richard Altick (1973, 127). The reader will note that the names of the offensive evangelicals are not given. I shall suggest one name below, that of T. B. Macaulay, whose work illustrates the thesis that Dickens thought of evangelicals and economists as a package.

tianity and the Greatest Happiness Principle of Utilitarianism, thus forging what one might label "broad utilitarianism."

This agreement on foundations requires a further stipulation to turn it into an effective antislavery coalition; that is, the agreement among the partners that black slaves are at the bottom of the distribution of happiness and that their lot deserves immediate attention. Lord Denman's attack on Dickens's views on slavery, as revealed in the *Household Words* review of *Uncle Tom's Cabin,* comes from the point of view of a biblical literalism raging against the coming of progressive religion, which would, by denying the imperative to raise the worst off, deny the Gospel:

> But it is only of late years that small wits have found the sentiment a proper theme of ridicule. They have all become ashamed of their dark-complexioned brother, and would fain disclaim the relationship. They cannot do so without renouncing that of Him who spoke of the whole family of man as one brotherhood, without distinction of class or colour, and proclaimed eternal happiness or misery to the great ones of the earth, according to the deeds that they shall have done to the least of His brethren. (1853, 12)[10]

Now this raises a series of interesting questions about what to make of *Hard Times* and Leavis's interpretation of that text, precisely the inconsistency between Utilitarianism and Christianity that forms the philosophical claim in the text for which Leavis vouches "finality." Consider that celebrated passage in which Sissy Jupe first encounters political economy:

> [A]fter eight weeks of induction into the elements of Political Economy, she had only yesterday been set right by a prattler three feet high, for returning to the question "What is the first principle of this science?" the absurd answer, "To do unto others as I would that they should do unto me." (Dickens 1972, 95; 1995, 60)

Since the economists in *Hard Times* are supposedly Utilitarian, the "absurd" answer is nothing of the kind. Among those qualified to grade such an examination—the founders of Utilitarianism and the opponent they took with most seriousness, as we have seen—her answer has been certified as the correct answer. The Golden Rule of Christianity is an equivalence of the Greatest Happiness Principle of Utilitarianism. Nonetheless, as far as I know, profes-

---

10. Matt. 25:40: "And the King shall answer and say unto them, Verily I say unto you, Inasmuch as ye have done [it] unto one of the least of these my brethren, ye have done [it] unto me." The cult of Pan as religious localism is glanced at in chapter 6.

sional students of *Hard Times* follow Leavis in accepting Dickens's claim of the inexorable opposition of Utilitarianism and Christianity.[11]

Only in the very recent (1997) *Companion to Hard Times* is Mill's identification of the Golden Rule with Utilitarianism juxtaposed against Sissy Jupe's answer.[12] As the *Companion* aims to provide "annotation [that] is factual rather than critical," no inference is drawn.[13] Could one fault a naive reader who makes the inference that since *Hard Times* dates from 1854 and Mill's statement from 1861 Dickens had an effect on Mill in a sense other than to protect the record from falsification.

And this connects to the issue of racial slavery how? Perhaps things will be clearer if we appeal to one of the proslavery tracts written in opposition to *Uncle Tom's Cabin* by admirers of Carlyle, here the American Rev. E. J. Stearns.[14] Here we find a context in which it makes some sense that the Greatest Happiness Principle of Utilitarianism is morphed to the My Happiness Principle. What temerity the abolitionists have in attacking their betters! Stearns writes that

> the slave-holders generally are the *elite* of society,—the picked men . . . far, very far, in advance of "the majority in our world," in both "consideration" and "self-control." As to "an enlightened regard to their own interest," if by that is meant, minding the main chance, i.e., looking out for the greatest good of the greatest number, meaning thereby, as Thelwell has it, "number one," I am very much afraid that they would have to yield the palm to us Yankees. (1853, 47)

---

11. The Utilitarian-Evangelical antislavery coalition is hidden even from a Dickens scholar who works explicitly with the racial texts I discuss later and systematically questions the Leavis tradition: "Until textual or other evidence for such a suggestion is available, it will surely seem more likely that *Hard Times* refers to a general atmosphere of neo-Benthamite theory and practice, and to the wide-spread popular debate engendered by it and available equally to those who had and had not read Bentham" (Oddie 1972, 55). By "neo-Benthamite," Oddie presumably means those who would turn the "Greatest Happiness Principle" into the "My Happiness Principles" and thus turn Utilitarianism into egoism.

Uncritical acceptance of the Leavis reading of Dickens's truthfulness is found in Earle Davis in Gray 1969, 71; Easson 1973, 21; David Lodge in Dickens 1990, 385; Juliet McMaster in Dickens 1990, 412; Samuels 1992, 86; and Nussbaum 1991, 904.

12. Simpson 1997, 117–18. Because Simpson's valuable commentary is keyed to the older Craig Penguin Library edition of *Hard Times,* not the newer Flint Penguin Library edition, I give citations to both the Craig and the Flint editions.

13. Shatto and Paroissien in ibid., 1997, xi.

14. "[I]f there is any inalienable right of another class, it is that so ably set forth by Carlyle,—the right of every man to be compelled to do what he is fit for, if he won't do it voluntarily; and this brings us back to Quashy" (Stearns 1853, 21).

In answer to the supposition that the Atlantic provides a barrier to ideas, this pamphlet was noted in *Household Words*.[15]

"Inscribed to Thomas Carlyle"

I propose to discuss four aspects of the Carlyle-Mill debate and ask what they tell us about Leavis's interpretation of Utilitarianism and the Utilitarian economists. These are (1) the "hardness" of Utilitarianism as revealed in this debate and the linked Governor Eyre controversy; (2) the Snow-Leavis controversy, in which the real world reasons for the existence of a Dickens Protective Agency are made clear; (3) John Ruskin's detailing of the moral equivalence of markets and slavery as a clarion call to the defense of Governor Eyre; and (4) Dickens as a reformer of slavery and his opposition to abolitionism.

1. Utilitarianism, Spices versus Leisure, and the "Beneficient Whip"

Although there is a tendency for commentators to attribute the inscription of *Hard Times* to a particular Carlyle book, (i.e., *Past and Present*), no evidence is cited to warrant such particularization.[16] We have quoted Leavis on the "hardness" of Utilitarianism. Now we read his words about human dignity, spontaneity, and Utilitarianism:

> Representing human spontaneity, the circus-athletes represent at the same time highly-developed skill and deftness of kinds that bring poise, pride and confident ease—they are always buoyant, and ballet-dancer-like, in training. . . .
>
> Their skills have no value for the Utilitarian calculus, but they express vital human impulse, and they minister to vital human needs. The Horse-riding, frowned upon as frivolous and wasteful by Gradgrind and malignantly scorned by Bounderby. . . . It brings to them, not merely amusement, but art, and the spectacle of triumphant activity that, seeming to contain its end with itself, is, in its easy mastery, joyously self-justified. (1990, 344–45)

Let us see what "Inscribed to Thomas Carlyle" tells us about these important questions:

---

15. Lynn and Wills 1856, 137: "The Rev. E. J. Stearns, of Maryland, shows by an elaborate calculation, in his criticism of Uncle Tom's Cabin . . ." The Dickensian opposition to fact was intermittent.

16. Easson 1973, 31. Dickens's letter to Carlyle about the dedication only talks about Carlyle's work in general terms, stating that "no man knows your books better than I" (Dickens 1938, 2:567).

If Quashee will not honestly aid in bringing out those sugars, cinnamons, and nobler products of the West Indian Islands, for the benefit of all mankind, then I say neither will the Powers permit Quashee to continue growing pumpkins there for his own lazy benefit; but will sheer him out, by and by, like a lazy gourd overshadowing rich ground; him and all that partake with him,—perhaps in a very terrible manner. For, under favour of Exeter Hall, the "terrible manner" is not yet quite extinct with the Destinies in this Universe; nor will it quite cease, I apprehend, for soft sawder or philanthropic stump-oratory now or henceforth. No; the gods wish besides pumpkins, that spices and valuable products be grown in their West Indies; thus much they have declared in so making the West Indies:—infinitely more they wish, that manful industrious men occupy their West Indies, not indolent two-legged cattle, however "happy" over their abundant pumpkins! Both these things, we may be assured, the immortal gods have decided upon, passed their eternal act of parliament for: and both of them, though all terrestrial Parliaments and entities oppose it to the death, shall be done. Quashee, if he will not help in bringing out the spices, will get himself made a slave again (which state will be a little less ugly than his present one), and with beneficent whip, since other methods avail not, will be compelled to work. (1849, 675)

Here is Mill's response along several dimensions. First, Carlyle exempts whites from his Gospel of Labor:

Your contributor incessantly prays Heaven that all persons, black and white, may be put in possession of this "divine right of being compelled, if permitted will not serve, to do what work they are appointed for." But as this cannot be conveniently managed just yet, he will begin with the blacks, and will make them work *for* certain whites, those whites *not* working at all; that so "the eternal purpose and supreme will" may be fulfilled, and "injustice," which is "for ever accursed," may cease. (1850, 27)

Second, why is work per se valuable?

This pet theory of your contributor about work, we all know well enough, though some persons might not be prepared for so bold an application of it. Let me say a few words on this "gospel of work." . . .

Work, I imagine, is not a good in itself. There is nothing laudable in work for work's sake. To work voluntarily for a worthy object is laudable; but what constitutes a worthy object? On this matter, the oracle of which your contributor is the prophet has never yet been prevailed on to declare itself. He revolves in an eternal circle round the idea of work, as if turning up the earth, or driving a shuttle or a quill, were ends in themselves, and

> the ends of human existence. Yet, even in case of the most sublime service to humanity, it is not because it is work that it is worthy; the worth lies in the service itself. (27–28)

Third, why are material goods so valuable as to overwhelm the goods of life and freedom?

> In the present case, it seems, a noble object means "spices." "The gods wish, besides pumpkins, that spices and valuable products be grown in their West Indies"—the "noble elements of cinnamon, sugar, coffee, pepper black and grey," "things far nobler than pumpkins." Why so? Is what supports life, inferior in dignity to what merely gratifies the sense of taste? Is it the verdict of the "immortal gods" that pepper is noble, freedom (even freedom from the lash) contemptible? (28)

Thus, Carlyle represents in the crudest imaginable terms the type of materialism—"sugars, cinnamons, and nobler products of the West Indian Islands" are everything, leisure and human dignity are nothing—with which Leavis whenever possible saddles Utilitarianism. The real Utilitarian in the debate responds by defending the rights of *black* people to leisure and their dignity as human beings.

These are not subtle texts. But the next round is less subtle still. This is from the February 1850 "Present Time"—one month after Mill's response—wherein Carlyle considers the possibility that slave labor will fail to emancipate. Destiny itself decrees the sentence for a race's failure to conform to its standards: death by shooting. But this we have read before.

Ruskin's statement opening the literary sage's defense of Governor Eyre will have some importance for our understanding of *Hard Times.* One of the delicate moments in the modern Dickens hagiography is explaining just why he sided with Carlyle. But this really ought not be much of a mystery. Here is an extract from Dickens's 1853 article "The Noble Savage," which was published in *Household Words:*

> All the noble savage's wars with his fellow-savages (and he takes no pleasure in anything else) are wars of extermination—which is the best I know of him, and the most comfortable to my mind when I look at him. He has no moral feelings of any kind, sort, or description; and his "mission" may be summed up as simply diabolical. (1853a, 338)[17]

---

17. Here and elsewhere I depend upon the attributions based on the *Household Words* office book published by Anne Lohrli (1973). The "Noble Savage" results in Oddie's ranking of Dickens and Carlyle made Oddie 1972, 138: "Carlyle, even in 'The Nigger Question,' appears much more benevolent than Dickens about non-whites."

There is a frantic wickedness in this brute's manner of worrying the air, and gnashing out ". . . O how charmingly cruel he is! O how he tears the flesh of his enemies and crunches the bones! O how like the tiger and the leopard and the wolf and the bear he is! O, row row row row, how fond I am of him!"—which might tempt the Society of Friends to charge at a hand-gallop into the Swartz-Kop location and exterminate the whole kraal. (339)

Is Dickens writing about a character in fiction whose existence need not be a matter of concern? A quick trip to the *Encyclopedia Britannica* entry for *kraal* explains just who it is that shall be exterminated. These are real people. And in Dickens's closing words we can see his characteristic opposition to cruelty in juxtaposition to his belief that some races ought not to exist:

To conclude as I began. My position is, that if we have anything to learn from the Noble Savage, it is what to avoid. His virtues are a fable; his happiness is a delusion; his nobility, nonsense. We have no greater justification for being cruel to the miserable object, than for being cruel to a WILLIAM SHAKESPEARE or an ISAAC NEWTON; but he passes away before an immeasurably better and higher power than ever ran wild in any earthly woods, and the world will be all the better when his place knows him no more. (339)

How should this be read? For an economist, this raises an inevitable question: what happens when one cannot get rid of an offensive race without cruelty? What happens when these two goals of Dickens come into conflict? The test of how practice bears upon theory comes with the Eyre Controversy of the mid-1860s and the question of what one makes of murderous cruelty as policy? We can observe how Dickens revealed which of the goals was the more important in a letter, complete with a reference to Exeter Hall, which reads as if he had just finished rereading Carlyle's "Negro Question" from fifteen years early:

That platform—sympathy with the black—or the Native, or the Devil— afar off, and that platform indifference to our countrymen at enormous odds in the midst of bloodshed and savagery, makes me stark wild. Only the other day, here was a meeting of jawbones of asses at Manchester, to censure the Jamaica Governor for his manner of putting down the insurrection. So we are badged about New Zealanders and Hottentots, as if they were identical with men in clean shirts at Camberwell, and were bound by pen and ink accordingly. So Exeter Halls holds us in mortal submission to missionaries. (Dickens 1938, 3:445)[18]

---

18. This is quoted by Goldberg (1972a, 147). Carlyle's opinion on state terror had been there from the beginning. Here is the *French Revolution* on the merits of order by desire for "mammon" and terror: "Mammon, cries the generous heart out of all ages and countries, is the basest of known

2. Leavis on Snow and Hard Times

Leavis was famously involved in a controversy in which the merits of the pur-
portedly distinct literary and scientific cultures were intertwined with competing visions of British government support for higher education. One might
have thought that the historical record of the literary sages as guides to public
morality would have been at the heart of the Snow-Leavis controversy. Indeed,
this was precisely the charge mentioned to C. P. Snow by one of his intellectual betters:

> I remember being cross-examined by a scientist of distinction. "Why do
> most writers take on social opinions which would have been distinctly
> uncivilised and démodé at the time of the Plantagenets? Wasn't that true
> of most of the famous twentieth-century writers? Yeats, Pound, Wyndham
> Lewis, nine out of ten of those who have dominated literary sensibility in
> our time—weren't they not only politically silly, but politically wicked?
> Didn't the influence of all they represent bring Auschwitz that much
> nearer?" (Snow 1959, 7)

But this is of course not how the Snow-Leavis controversy played out. Snow
was an undisciplined thinker and a slovenly scholar.[19]

There is no sentence that I should willingly write in which the words
undisciplined or *slovenly* appears modifying "F. R. Leavis." And it happens that
Leavis wrote on *Hard Times* in the aftermath of his attack on Snow. Leavis
offered the following claims for Dickens. First, against Dickens's "friends":

Gods, even of known Devils. In him what glory is there, that ye should worship him? No glory discernible; not even terror: at best, detestability, ill-matched with despicability" (Carlyle 1956, 611).

19. Consider Snow's scholarship as revealed in his study of Trollope: "He had every [nonlin-
guistic] gift for a good traveller . . . unusual lack of national or racial prejudice" (1975, 97). [Snow
claims the same immunity for the scientific culture (1959, 45).] In particular, *West Indies and the
Spanish Main* is described as "one of the most splendid travel books of the nineteenth century." To
pick a passage more or less at random from Trollope's chapter "Black Men": "I do not think that
education has as yet done much for the black man in the Western world. He can always observe,
and often read; but he can seldom reason. I do not mean to assert that he is absolutely without
mental powers, as a calf is. He does draw conclusions, but he carries them only a short way. I think
that he seldom understands the purpose of industry, the object of truth, or the results of honesty"
(Trollope 1860, 57). Trollope's views were well known. For example, in James Hunt's notorious
Negro's Place in Nature, Trollope is cited as an authority (Hunt 1864, 27): "In conclusion, let me
observe that it is not alone the man of science who has discerned the Negro's unfitness for civilization, as we understand it. Here is Mr. Anthony Trollope, who is certainly quite guiltless of ever
having examined the evidence of the distinction between the Negro and European, and yet truly
says of the Negro:—'Give them their liberty, starting them well in the world at what expense you
please, and at the end of six months they will come back upon your hands for the means of support. Everything must be done for them; they expect food, clothes and instruction as to every simple act of life, as do children.'" Jones (1967) discusses racial attitudes in Trollope, Carlyle, and Mill
in considerable detail.

I can best explain with brevity what I mean in terms of Dickens. And that will enable me to do at the same time something that badly needs doing, which is to make an indignant protest against the established attitude to that very great writer. . . . Dickens is of course a genius, but "as soon as he begins to think he is a child": there you have the attitude. . . . Moreover, Dickens wasn't capable of understanding Bentham. (1969, 174–75)

Second, Leavis testifies for *Hard Times* as the refutation of all Utilitarian teaching:[20]

And to come back to *Hard Times:* the undergraduate—or the senior—who has taken the significance of the book, and recognizes the finality with which it leaves the Benthamite calculus, the statistical or Blue Book approach, and the utilitarian ethos placed, can say why neither a "rising standard of living," nor equality, nor both together, will do when accepted as defining the sufficient preoccupations and aims of thought and effort. (177)

Think again of the consequence of students reading the Carlyle-Mill exchange while they read Dickens's attack on Utilitarianism. Just how does *Hard Times* refute Mill's response to Carlyle? Perhaps an explanation would be requested as to just why Dickens takes the side he does. All of this awkwardness can be avoided by the simple expedient of not mentioning such unpleasantness.

3. *Ruskin on* Hard Times

As Leavis's representation of Utilitarianism has been so helpful, perhaps there is more that he has to teach. What about his representation of the reception of *Hard Times?* As point of reference, this is how Leavis begins his famed appendix to the *Great Tradition:* "'Hard Times's: An Analytical Note" from which we have quoted him on the hard inhumanities of Utilitarians:[21]

---

20. Behind Dickens, Carlyle lurks. "Carlyle had pointed this out by declaring in *Past and Present* that in the *laissez-faire* state there was one sole link between high and low: typhus fever. Kingsley two years earlier [than Dicken's *Bleak House*] had found a novelistic form for Carlyle's ideas by showing in his terrible account of the tailors's sweat-shops how typhus and other diseases due to the disgusting conditions in which the tailors worked and lived were transmitted to the well-to-do via the clothes made for them there" (Leavis and Leavis 1970, 166).

21. It was retitled when it was reprinted in ibid. as "'Hard Times's: The World of Bentham." The older title is used in the version included in the *Norton Critical Edition of Hard Times,* with the editors assuring us (Ford and Monod in Dickens 1990, 340) that "The 1970 version is virtually identical with the 1948 except for a modification of the final sentence of the first paragraph." Oddie (1972, 55) protests the new title's "extravagance."

> *Hard Times* is not a difficult work; its intention and nature are pretty obvi-
> ous. If, then, it is the masterpiece I take it for, why has it not had general
> recognition? To judge by the critical record, it has had none at all. If there
> exists anywhere an appreciation, or even an acclaiming reference, I have
> missed it. (1970, 187)

But, notoriously, Leavis did in fact miss one admiring discussion, that of John
Ruskin, mentioned so prominently in John Forster's *Life of Dickens,* which the
Leavises themselves commend to the reader.[22] But perhaps this was not all that
Ruskin said on the matter.

It may bear repeating that it was John Ruskin who, first among the literary
sages, alerted his peers to Eyre's importance to their common cause. Ruskin's
December 20, 1865, letter to the *Daily Telegraph* was quoted earlier but repays
careful rereading. Ruskin opens with compliments to J. S. Mill and Thomas
Hughes. He declares himself to be a "King's man" in opposition to the "Mob's
men" and then gets down to the business at hand. That business is slavery in
America and Europe. I shall proceed line by line:

> Not that I like slavery, or object to the emancipation of any kind or num-
> ber of blacks in due place and time. (Ruskin 1903–12, 18:551)

The letter is dated December 20, 1865. It bears repeating that the agreement
of April 9, 1865, at the Appomattox Court House settled one dispute regardless of whether the time and place was right. Ruskin continues, charging that
those objecting to Eyre's actions are unaware of the full dimensions of "slavery." This gives some context to the "due place and time":

> But I understand something more by "slavery" than either Mr. J. S. Mill or
> Mr. Hughes; and believe that white emancipation not only ought to pre-
> cede, but must by law of all fate precede black emancipation. (551)

The "law of all fate" is of course the standard Carlylean appeal to as-if divine
revelation. Then, perhaps conscious of the need to address the unbelievers in

---

22. John Ruskin, quoted from *Unto This Last* by John Forster (1966, 2:120–21): "But let us
not lose the use of Dickens's wit and insight, because he chooses to speak in a circle of stage fire.
He is entirely right in his main drift and purpose in every book he has written; and all of them, but
especially *Hard Times,* should be studied with close and earnest care by persons interested in social
questions. They will find much that is partial, and, because partial, apparently unjust; but if they
examine all the evidence on the other side, which Dickens seems to overlook, it will appear, after
all their trouble, that his view was the finally right one, grossly and sharply told." Leavis and Leavis
(1970, x): "Professor Edgar Johnson's biography of Dickens cannot claim to have superseded or
even to rival Forster's."

his audience, Ruskin, employing the literary gifts that continued to charm all but the hardest heart, launches an argument by parallel construction:

> I much dislike the slavery, to a man, of an African labourer, with a spade on his shoulder; but I more dislike the slavery, to the devil, of a Calabrian robber with a gun on his shoulder. (551)

African slaves have men with spades—no better or worse than other men—as masters. And this bears on America and England how?

> I dislike the American serf-economy, which separates, occasionally, man and wife; but I more dislike the English serf-economy, which prevents men being able to have wives at all. (551)

To a sensible scholar like Bernard Semmel, this sentence must make no sense whatsoever. He does not quote it.[23] What kind of attack on British capitalism is the argument that "English serfs" do not have wives? And in any event how are we to read "occasionally"? Are American husband and wife upon an occasion temporarily separated or is it upon an occasion that American husband and wife are permanently separated? We continue:

> I dislike the slavery which obliges women (if it does) to carry their children over frozen rivers; but I more dislike the slavery which makes them throw their children into wells. (551)

At least one reference is crystal clear: Eliza pursued by dogs is carrying little Harry across the ice.[24] But then to what does Ruskin refer by "the slavery which makes them throw their children into wells"? Is it a novel, the *Uncle Tom's Cabin* of the English serfs? In the hope of enlightenment, we continue:

> I would willingly hinder the selling of girls on the Gold Coast: but primarily, if I might, would the selling of them in Mayfair. (551)

As we take leave of Ruskin, the letter continues with the Carlylean trope of the importance of masters and the politics of administrative massacre.

We have to be careful reading Ruskin because he makes the case that the kidnaping and serial rape of black girls—prostitution compelled by the

---

23. Semmel 1962, 108–9. Let me thank Wendy Motooka, who provided a bracing correction for my temptation to rely upon even this best of all secondary sources!

24. E. T. Cook and Alexander Wedderburn (in Ruskin 1903–12, 18:551) and the editor of *Arrows of the Chace* (Ruskin 1880, 2:345) give *Uncle Tom's Cabin* as referenced.

lash[25]—is less of a moral issue than that of white girls prostituting themselves for money. The critical step in what passes for argument is that in which Ruskin denies the possibility of imputing material gain from exchange.[26] The violence of kidnap and rape is morphed into voluntary prostitution. It is just sex taken instrumentally. Thus, for Ruskin there may be no interesting difference between being thrown into a well and falling into one. It is just a hole in the ground. Is this a reference to *Hard Times* and Stephen Blackpool's fatal fall into the Old Hell mine shaft? How can this be? Stephen is in no chronological sense a child. But for a paternalist—the kindest description of the Carlyleans of which I know—are we not all children of our betters?

The line in Ruskin's letter that Semmel does not quote—English serfs without wives—seems to me to make sense in and only in the context provided by *Hard Times*. Stephen and Rachael are doomed by Dickens's plot to pass their lives in separate bedrooms. Is it necessary to stress the fact that Stephen and Rachael find themselves in such a fix because Dickens has given him a wife and the laws of England make divorce impossible for the poor?

Ruskin makes it as clear as can be that "white slavery" is worse than black.[27] The interesting distinctions are racial—whites being "fated" to be more important—and in the details of the masters: blacks being blessed by "men" as masters and whites being cursed by "devils" as masters. This is transparent. The interesting question is whether Ruskin reads *Hard Time* as making this very case.

I do not think Dickens makes the case that black slavery is morally superior to "white slavery"; rather, I think he makes the case that there is a moral equivalence of the two. To establish the moral equivalence of markets and slavery with the argument that there is nothing but the kindness of masters in all institutions, Dickens "mistold" the story of capitalism. There is nothing in the logic of capitalism that would prevent a man and woman of mature years from contracting marriage. Even by the iron logic of Malthusian norms, Stephen and Rachael have delayed marriage sufficiently to support their family. What there is is a legal impediment to recontracting because Dickens rigged the story

---

25. A convenient example is found in an article by George Stephens that is included with Lord Denman's republished attack on Dickens's views on slavery: "The national conscience was awakened to inquiry, and inquiry soon produced conviction. Could it be otherwise than a sin to enslave the soul by enchaining the body? Could it be otherwise than sinful to compel prostitution by the lash?" (Denman 1853, 56).

26. While there is no material gain in exchange, there can be "advantage." The difference seems to be in what is evaluated by the choosing agent—material gain—and what is evaluated by the poet—advantage. This is discussed in chapter 1.

27. Here is that passage in the 1853 "Nature of the Gothic" that emphasizes the irrelevance of the fate of black people on the Middle Passage: "Men may be beaten, chained, tormented, yoked like cattle, slaughtered like summer flies, and yet remain in one sense and the best sense, free" (Ruskin 1997, 85).

so that Stephen already has a wife. If my reading of Ruskin is correct, then that would suffice.

But perhaps I am not reading Ruskin right. No matter, there is more. To this we turn now.

4. *Dickens on* Uncle Tom's Cabin *and the "Reform" of Slavery.*

Fortunately for later scholars, many of the basic facts connecting Dickens and *Uncle Tom's Cabin* have been reported by Harry Stone (1957). In particular, Stone draws attention to the newspaper attack on Dickens's views on slavery by Lord Denman—some of which has been quoted—which was quickly republished under the title *Uncle Tom's Cabin, Bleak House, Slavery, and Slave Trade.* Denman distinguished between those who favored slavery and those who opposed the attempts to abolish it. Dickens he put in the camp of what we might consider the anti-antislavers:

> We have a still heavier charge against Mr. Dickens. In one particular instance, but the most important of all at this crisis, he exerts his powers to obstruct the great cause of human improvement—that cause which in general he cordially advocates. He does his best to replunge the world into the most barbarous abuse that ever afflicted it. We do not say that he actually defends slavery or the slave-trade; but he takes pains to discourage, by ridicule, the effort now making to put them down. We believe, indeed, that in general terms he expresses just hatred for both; but so do all those who profit or wish to profit by them, and who, by that general profession, prevent the detail of particulars too atrocious to be endured. The disgusting picture of a woman who pretends zeal for the happiness of Africa, and is constantly employed in securing a life of misery to her own children, is a laboured work of art in his present exhibition. (1853, 9)

Denman characterized the program of those who would use slavery for "education" of the slave and compares this with the real antislavery of the evangelical Clapman sect variety:

> The "Times" Reviewer is quite justified in comparing the relation which the present slaveholders in America bear to this question to that of the planters in Jamaica before the great act of emancipation. But those planters and their advocates against the natural rights of the negro were loud in denouncing the experiment of giving freedom to the slave. They declared him unfitted to receive that blessing, urged that he be required to be educated into that capacity. . . . These views were . . . discussed by Mr. Macaulay (as we understood) in an able paper which appeared in the

"Edinburgh Review." He ridiculed the notion that such preparation was requisite, comparing it to the prudence of the father who advised his son not to bathe until he could swim. (19–20)

Can slavery make one fit for freedom? Here is where the assumption of a fixed human nature becomes a weapon in the war against human bondage. Thirty years had passed, but Denman recalls T. B. Macaulay's argument against the delay of emancipation. There is no harder rationality principle than that which Macaulay learned from Smith. The institution of slavery cannot remake one's nature, not for good nor for ill. Here is evangelical-economics policy in one lesson: release the slaves and they grope in freedom to become the same as their masters.[28] This is so even though the masters are white and the slaves are black. Human nature is one and the same everywhere.

Macaulay and his parliamentary associates were unable to effect immediate emancipation. Even with a 20 million pound ransom paid to the West Indian slaveholders by the British taxpayers, emancipation required an additional "apprenticeship" on the part of the slaves. Macaulay himself seems to bear personal responsibility for shortening the period of transition.[29]

Stone, who draws our attention to Denman on Dickens and slavery, also points out the importance of Henry Morley and Dickens's review of *Uncle*

---

28. Macaulay (1961, 1:178–79) uses the analogy of wine consumption to argue that it takes time for revolutions to find their equilibrium: "It is the character of such revolutions that we always see the worst of them first. Till men have been some time free, they know not how to use their freedom. The natives of wine countries are generally sober. In climates where wine is a rarity intemperance abounds. A newly liberated people may be compared to a northern army encamped on the Rhine or the Xeres. It is said that, when soldiers in such a situation first find themselves able to indulge without restraint in such a rare and expensive luxury, nothing is to be seen but intoxication. Soon, however, plenty teaches discretion; and, after wine has been for a few months their daily fare, they become more temperate than they had ever been in their own country. In the same manner, the final and permanent fruits of liberty are wisdom, moderation, and mercy. Its immediate effects are often atrocious crimes, conflicting errors, scepticism on points the most clear, dogmatism on points the most mysterious."

The modern reader will probably not hear Smith's plain speech behind Macaulay's cadence (Smith 1976a, 492): "Though in every country there are many people who spend upon such liquors more than they can afford, there are always many more who spend less. It deserves to be remarked too, that, if we consult experience, the cheapness of wine seems to be a cause, not of drunkenness, but of sobriety. . . . When a French regiment comes from some of the northern provinces of France, where wine is somewhat dear, to be quartered in the southern, where it is very cheap, the soldiers, I have frequently heard it observed, are at first debauched by the cheapness and novelty of good wine; but after a few months residence, the greater part of them become as sober as the rest of the inhabitants."

29. Trevelyan 1961, 1:284–85. See also Morley 1851, 402: "In 1833 the great Act passed, emancipating all the negro slaves in British Colonies and decreeing payment of twenty million in compensation to the slave-owner." One persistent Carlylean trope is the wasted 20 million pounds. Question: would an undergraduate reader in the late twentieth century know what this number represents? Question: does the rationally choosing editor of Carlyle's *Past and Present* gloss the number? Yes, this will be on the final exam.

Tom's Cabin in an 1852 issue of *Household Words*. Several things are made clear in this review. First, just as Denman suggested, Morley and Dickens propose to reform slavery, to delay emancipation until the black slaves are "suited" for freedom. Slavery, which has mutilated black people, can also, when suitably reformed, heal them. Morley and Dickens describe in detail the hideously cruel treatment visited upon slaves. Cruelty is bad, but intellectual development is good. How shall we choose when the two goals might conflict?

> We think, too, that it is possible to combine with the duty of emancipation the not less important duty of undoing the evil that has been done to the slaves' minds and of doing them some good service by way of atonement. When we have clipped men's minds and made them slavish, it is poor compensation that their bodies should be set at large. (Morley and Dickens 1852, 5)

Morley and Dickens appeal to the importance of kind masters; those who would guide by words and not the lash.[30] The reformed slavery would be one without cruelty:

> The stripes! Though slavery be not abolished promptly, there can be no reason why stripes should not cease. Though there *may* be little of lashing and wailing in the slave system, as it is commonly administered in North America, yet men are degraded by being set to work by a coarse action of their fears, when the same men are far more capable of being stimulated by an excitement of their love of honour and reward. (5)

Then Morley and Dickens reflect upon innate racial differences and how the newly reformed slavery could make blacks nearly white. The educational prospects of the new model slavery are compared in detail to those of the existing model of slavery. In the existing system, the slaves are too stupid to figure out that they ought to resent their situation. This is why Christianity cannot be preached in full:

> The negro has what the phrenologists would call love of approbation very strongly marked. Set him to work for the hope of distinction, instead of the fear of blows. No doubt it has been true that negroes, set to work by any motive which called out their higher feelings as men, would become ambitious and acquire a thirst for freedom in the end. So it is, so let it be. Edu-

---

30. And just where are these kind, new model masters supposed to come from to replace the really existing masters? The fundamental nonseriousness of Dickens as a social reformer is remarked upon by an unknown reviewer in the *Dublin Review* of 1871. The "stupidity" interpretation of Dickens is there pressed ("Two English Novelists: Dickens and Thackery" 1871).

cate the negroes on plantations, make them intelligent men and women, let them imbibe in their full freedom the doctrines of Christianity. It has been true that it was not safe to give knowledge to men who were placed in a position which the faintest flash of reason would resent. (5)[31]

Under reformed slavery, this defect will be mended and with it the slaves will be remade:

We have been told by a Christian minister, who laboured in his way to elevate the minds of negroes in some North American plantations, that his permission to preach was clogged with many stipulations that he was expressly forbidden to teach anything which might induce a slave to question his position or wish to be free; and that, in consequence, he found himself unable to preach even man's duty to his neighbour. So it has been and must be; the slave who acquires education and religious principle must desire to be free: let it be so. (5)

As a matter of racial destiny, blacks could never really compete with whites, so after the period of beneficent slavery they would leave for lands for which their nature is suitable. Slavery is not essential, Morley and Dickens assure us, *if:*

The time is not far distant when the demand for negroes will be confined wholly to those districts in which the climate appears to be unsuited for field labour by white men: even to those districts whites will become acclimatised, but in those, for some time at any rate, negroes will be needed. *It is not essential that the negroes should be slaves. If, step by step, the degraded race be raised, their higher impulses awakened, their minds developed,* their moral ties religiously respected, there will arise out of the present multitude of slaves, by slow degrees, a race of free labourers far more efficient than the present gangs, while the yearly increasing surplus of black population educated into love of freedom would pass over to Liberia. (5)[32]

---

31. Nicholas Brimblecomb's "attack" on *Uncle Tom's Cabin* points to the biblical texts of Moses leading the slaves out of Egypt as abolitionist forgeries: "It is by no means certain but that this whole account of the slavery of the Israelites in Egypt, and their running away from their masters, is a sheer fabrication, having been foisted, it may be, into the Bible by some lying and wicked abolitionists" (1853, 153). Motooka notes the "love of approbation" here racializes Adam Smith.

32. I have added the emphasis. One of the issues in Dickens's continual sniping at Harriet Beecher Stowe was her treatment of blacks as members of a rather superior race. Blacks, in her account, are noticeably closer to God than are whites. Stone (1957) gives the references to Dickens's correspondence. Stowe's eccentric racism—inconsequential in terms of the contemporary policy debates—was duly noted as a matter of amusement by Nassau Senior, who reviewed *Uncle Tom's Cabin* for the *Edinburgh Review.*

As we reflect upon how one is supposed to "reform" slavery—by means of what magic wand are the whips to be banished and the Bible uncensored?—it is helpful to recall George Orwell's reading of the Dickens program to "reform" capitalism:

> Bounderby is a bullying windbag and Gradgrind has been morally blinded, but if they were better men, the system would work enough—that, all through, is the implication. And so far as social criticism goes, one can never extract much more from Dickens than this, unless one deliberately reads meaning into him. His whole "message" is one that at first glance looks like an enormous platitude: If men would behave decently the world would be decent.
>
> Naturally this calls for a few characters who are in positions of authority and who *do* behave decently. Hence that recurrent Dickens figure, the Good Rich Man. This character belongs especially to Dickens's early optimistic period. He is usually a "merchant" (we are not necessarily told what merchandise he deals in), and he is always a superhumanly kind-hearted old gentleman who "trots" to and fro, raising his employees' wages, patting children on the head, getting debtors out of jail and, in general, acting the fairy godmother. (1968, 1:417)

In a competitive market economy, why does the kindness of masters especially matter? If one's conditions of employment can be raised by seeking alternatives, then what is so special about the kindness of one's employer in comparison, say, to the cleanliness of the workplace? There is an enormous number of nonpecuniary forms of compensation that one weighs in considering the net advantages of different employment.[33] If one's master is unkind and there is nothing offered by way of compensation, move across the street. What if there is no one across the street? Then we question the competitive assumption and need to think hard.

By contrast, in a system of slavery, surely, the kindness of one's master is of overwhelming importance. And in Dickens's *Household Words*, both in what he himself wrote and in what he published that was written by others, he emphasizes over and over again the dreadful fate of slaves who are cursed with unkind masters.[34] But still the question is: what shall be done? The choices Dickens

---

33. The canonical treatment is found in *Wealth of Nations*, book 1, chapter 10, in which the equalization of the net advantages of employment within a labor market are described. In this chapter, Smith describes in detail how the desire for approbation of all people influences their calculation of individual agents. Dickens's falsification works by ignoring such elements in the economist's bag of tools. Chapters 9 and 11 demonstrate how they work.

34. The evils of slavery seem easier to appreciate when the slave owners are not British. "A shriek was heard, suddenly, and horrible; another yet more frightful pierced the thunder of the breakers; the sea-water became purple. Those unhappy wretches had made their choice between

seems to imagine are freeing the slaves or removing the cruel masters. In *Uncle Tom's Cabin,* the rational slave is seen as preferring freedom to slavery under the most benevolent master because one never knows who the next master might be.[35] The reading of *Hard Times* for which I shall argue next is that Dickens responds to this by making the case that there is no difference between markets and slavery—everything is just a question of the kindness of the masters.

The Moral Equivalence of Markets and Slavery

We now take leave of Dickens's journalism, where the Carlylean defense of beneficent slavery and extermination of races has been duly documented in the literature (Oddie 1972; Goldberg 1972a, 1972b). Here I turn to *Hard Times* itself. There are two parts to the argument. First, in the present section I point out a series of odd parallels between *Hard Times* and *Uncle Tom's Cabin* that for various reasons seem not to have occurred to the commentators on *Hard Times.* These parallels have the effect, I shall argue, of making a case for the moral equivalence of market capitalism and racial slavery. With kindly masters, market capitalism is well suited for the white, and with kindly masters racial slavery is well suited for the black.

The reader will note that I do not count as evidence that to which I believe Ruskin points as a critical opposition between *Hard Times* and *Uncle Tom's Cabin.* As I read Ruskin, he proposes that the permanent separation of Stephen and Rachael under capitalism stands in opposition to the temporary separation of George and Eliza under slavery. If I am reading Ruskin right, I think he has made my case. As there is more opposition than this, I shall set this separation aside and consider other aspects of the plot.

In the next section, I compare Dickens's views on the dehumanization of slavery, as they were published in his *American Notes,* to his assertions in *Hard Times* about the dehumanization of workers under industrialization. Again, we find an argument for the moral equivalence of markets and racial slavery.

It is easy to think of two reasons why *Hard Times* and *Uncle Tom's Cabin*

---

the Spaniards and the ground-sharks" (Von Goetznitz 1858, 112). On the other hand, when are the masters kind? John Hollingshead's (1858) treatment of the kindly slave ship captain reads like *Springtime on the Middle Passage.* Lohrli quotes Dickens's policy on some topics: "Let Hollingshead do it. . . . He's the most ignorant man on the staff, but he'll cram up the facts, and won't give us an encyclopaedical article" (Lohrli 1973, 306).

35. "'O, but master is so kind!' 'Yes, but who knows?—he may die—and then he may be sold to nobody knows who'" (Stowe 1982, 30). This is not the only episode. "'No, Mas'r,' said Nathan; 'you've always been good to me.' 'Well, then, why do you want to leave me?' 'Mas'r may die, and then who get me?—I'd rather be a free man.' After some deliberation, the young master replied, 'Nathan, in your place, I think I should feel very much so, myself. You are free'" (512).

are not customarily read together. First, *Uncle Tom's Cabin* is American. By means of a disciplinary convention I find rather odd, British books attacking markets are read in isolation from contemporary American books attacking slavery. But Stowe and Dickens read and wrote about each other's work. Indeed, some of the dialogue in *Uncle Tom's Cabin* about the conditions of the lower classes in Britain's market capitalism seems to reflects the opinions common to the Carlyleans Kingsley and Dickens.[36] Second, under the conventional interpretation *Hard Times* is about market capitalism and *Uncle Tom's Cabin* is about racial slavery. What does the one have to do with the other? Isn't socialism the alternative to market capitalism?

While one can indeed point to episodes of socialism in the nineteenth century—the Oneida community and the Shakers stand out in the historical record[37]—these episodes were attempts to model a new society. They were not societies themselves on the scale of Britain or America. The real existing alternative to market capitalism was racial slavery.

In addition to the inscriptions to Carlyle, I find five linkages between the two texts that I propose to discuss. For ease of reference, I present these links in table 2. The table gives the short versions of the textual aspects, the factual background I find important, the interpretation of the texts for which I shall argue, and, when I know of one, a plausible alternative interpretation of the texts. In the following sections, I give my reasons for favoring my own interpretation over the alternative.

1. To Freedom in Blackface

Mr. Gradgrind's son Tom is in flight for his crime. We get a glimpse of him before he catches a ship for the Americas:

> "Look at 'em again," said Sleary, "look at 'em well. You thee 'em all? Very good. Now, mith;" he put a form for them to sit on; "I have my opinionth, and the Thquire your father hath hith. I don't want to know your brother'th been up to; ith better for me not to know. All I thay ith, the Thquire hath thtood by Thethelia, and I'll thtand by the Thquire. Your brother ith one o' them black thervanth." (Dickens 1972, 298–99; 1995, 282)

---

36. Morley and Dickens (1852) praise the character of St. Clare, whose views on the condition of the British working class seemed to reflect the Carlylean views expressed in Kingsley's *Alton Locke*. Chapter 6 cites the scholarship on the British abolitionists' criticism of Stowe using such sources. As Oddie (1972, 150–51) points out, *Alton Locke* offers an even more slavish adherence to the Carlylean line than does *Hard Times*. One point of difference is Dickens's support in *Hard Times* of divorce in the face of Carlyle's emphasis on the permanence of human relationships. This is easy to explain on the basis of the My Happiness theory of belief.

37. "All the possessions and revenues of the [Shaker] settlement are thrown into a common stock, which is managed by the elders" (Dickens 1985, 258–59). He was not impressed.

The image of an escape to freedom in blackface, *westward* across the Atlantic, has a certain undeniable element of robust mirth of the entirely nonpolitically correct variety for which Dickens had a wonderful gift. He is, authorities tell us, and here I do not disagree, the greatest comic novelist in the language.

Might the joke refer to the general flight of black people escaping slavery for market capitalism *eastward* across the Atlantic or to that particularly telling episode in *Uncle Tom's Cabin* in which George *darkens* himself to pass for Spanish?

> "I am pretty well disguised, I fancy," said the young man, with a smile. "A little walnut bark has made my yellow skin a genteel brown, and I've dyed

TABLE 2.   Decoding Hard Times

Textual Aspect	Factual Background	My Maintained Interpretation	An Alternative Interpretation
Inscription to Thomas Carlyle in 1854	1849–50 Carlyle-Mill debate: 1853 *Nigger Question*	Carlyle's racist antieconomics; hence, the dedication is merited	Carlyle's antieconomics; hence, the dedication is merited
Fleeing in blackface to freedom	Black slaves flee to freedom	Joke about escaped black slaves or of George's darkening to pass for Spanish	What joke?
Utilitarianism inconsistent with Christianity	Evangelicals-Utilitarians have opposition to racial slavery in common	Emancipation of black slaves not a moral issue	
Unstable marriages under capitalism; Utilitarian sells woman into sexual servitude	Unstable marriages under slavery; selling women into sexual servitude	Moral equivalence of racial slavery and market capitalism	Dickens has a problem with women
Opposition to facts (or averages), that is, increased life expectancy	The fact of increased life expectancy from serfdom to market economy	Attempt to change the subject	Stupidity or ignorance
Terrible consequences of unkind masters	Kindness of masters important for slaves	Moral equivalence of racial slavery and market capitalism	

my hair black; so you see I don't answer to the advertisement at all." (Stowe 1982, 133)

Stowe pauses to explain the sexual facts of American racial slavery:

> We remark, *en passant,* that George was, by his father's side, of white descent. His mother was one of those unfortunates of her face, marked out by personal beauty to be the slave of the passions of her possessor, and the mother of children who may never know a father. (133)

We shall return to the issue of sexual slavery in due course.

2. Utilitarianism Is Inconsistent with Christianity

Sissy Jupe's answer has been discussed sufficiently. In case the reader is wondering whether Dickens is exercising authorial irony,[38] let me document two additional slurs:

> The Gradgrind party wanted assistance in cutting the throats of the Graces. (Dickens 1972, 157; 1995, 128)

> He sat writing in the room with the deadly-statistical clock, proving something no doubt—probably, in the main, that the Good Samaritan was a Bad Economist. (1972, 238; 1995, 215)

If Dickens could not distinguish between evangelicals and economists, what does this suggest? Reflect upon the Wedgwood cameo of the bound black slave and the question it asks on his behalf: "Am I not a man and a brother?" This is parodied by Carlyle in what I take to be his response to Mill[39] and cited by Denman in response to Dickens. Surely, in Dickens's understanding, Christianity would answer "no." From this, I conclude that for Dickens the emancipation of black slaves is not a moral issue. Of course, Dickens believed in improving the condition of black slaves. How one does this *without* emancipation was described earlier in the review of *Uncle Tom's Cabin.* Unkind mas-

---

38. Richard Watts (1981) brings the apparatus of modern critical theory to bear on *Hard Times.* Judging by his citations, he evidently thinks that sufficient knowledge of Dickens's language community is available in the text itself.

39. "Him too you occasionally tyrannise over; and with bad results to yourselves among others; using the leather in a tyrannous unnecessary manner; withholding, or scantily furnishing, the oats and ventilated stabling that are due. Rugged horse-subduers, one fears they are a little tyrannous at times. 'Am I not a horse, and *half*-brother?'" (Carlyle 1850b, 31).

ters are to be replaced with kind masters. Easy, isn't it? Why didn't the dismal scientists think of that?

3. Selling Women into Sexual Service

Recent attention paid by scholars to the sexual aspects of *Hard Times* seems to be responsible for some interpretative instability in the commentary on the novel included in the successive Penguin editions. In David Craig's 1972 introduction, following Leavis and Williams, he takes the novel to be mainly about the market economy and industrialization. In Flint's 1995 introduction, she takes it to be mainly about family instability.[40]

The impossibility of a stable Christian marriage among slaves is a standard trope of the antislavery evangelicals. What kind of a marriage could one expect under an institution in which, whenever it suited their master's interests, husband and wife might be sold separately?[41] Is Dickens asserting that marital instability is no different in markets than in slavery?

Marital instability is a hopelessly broad topic. Consequently, I consider only the most narrow aspect of the sexual issues in *Hard Times*, Tom's pandering of Louisa. It is completely nonobvious just how Tom manages to pander his sister to Mr. Bounderby.[42] Here is the transaction:

---

40. "To put it in this way is not to beg the question of whether or not *Hard Times* is really an 'industrial novel.' My opening discussion of its title should already have shown that Dickens's concern entailed his dealing in the same breath, continually, with both the immediate facts of mill-town life and the less direct, the all-pervasive *cultural* effects of the new intensive production" (David Craig in Dickens 1972, 16). "Dickens's concerns in the novel are far from being entirely with the public world, however. Rather, *Hard Times* is increasingly taken over by an examination of the family, showing how damaging and limiting an upbringing which allows no place for imagination and fancy can be, and how an education and social philosophy based on the recognition of the necessity of looking after one's own interests can blind one to the needs of others" (Kate Flint in Dickens 1995, xii). "In all respects *Hard Times* is more like the work of William Blake than of Friedrich Engels" (Ackroyd 1990, 705).

41. *Suppressed Book* (1864, 57) quotes the Kentucky form of marriage: "until death . . . *or as long as circumstances will permit*." The acute "Nicholas Brimblecomb" writes this about *Uncle Tom's Cabin* (1853, 23): "The male slave has no duties towards a wife: his duties are to his owner. The female slave has no duties to a husband: she belongs body and soul, to her master. A slave child has no duties to parents: he owes nothing to any one but to his master. Marriages among slaves are an absurdity. . . . It is true that in many cases a male and female slave 'take up together,' as it is termed, but not by marriage. . . . the connection is a merely temporary one, solely for the purpose of propagation, and for the master's benefit alone."

42. "His grovelling sensualities leads him to pander his sister to a man she finds repulsive" (McMaster in Dickens 1990, 419). And she agrees to the contract because? "The psychology of Louisa's development and of her brother Tom's is sound. Having no outlet for her emotional life except in her love for her brother, she lives for him, and marries Bounderby—under pressure from Tom—for Tom's sake ('What does it matter?')" (Leavis in Dickens 1990, 352). Leavis's notion of "sound" escapes me. Richard Fabrizio (1987, 76–77) usefully discusses Tom and Louisa in terms of sibling incest.

What a game girl you are, to be such a first-rate sister, Loo!" whispered Tom.

She clung to him, as she should have clung to some far better nature that day, and was a little shaken in her reserved composure for the first time.

"Old Bounderby's quite ready," said Tom. "Time's up. Good-bye! I shall be on the look-out for you, when you come back. I say, my dear Loo! AN'T it uncommonly jolly now!" (Dickens 1972, 143; 1995, 111)

This is Tom's explanation of the episode later in the story:

"You know our governor, Mr. Harthouse," said Tom, "and therefore you needn't be surprised that Loo married old Bounderby. She never had a lover, and the governor proposed old Bounderby, and she took him."

"Very dutiful in your interesting sister," said Mr. James Harthouse.

"Yes, but she wouldn't have been as dutiful, and it would not have come off as easily," returned the whelp, "if it hadn't been for me."

The tempter merely lifted his eyebrows; but the whelp was obliged to go on.

"*I* persuaded her," he said, with an edifying air of superiority. "I was stuck in old Bounderby's bank (where I never wanted to be), and I knew I should get into scrapes there, if she put old Bounderby's pipe out; so I told her my wishes, and she came into them. She would do anything for me. It was very game of her, wasn't it?" (1972, 167; 1995, 138–39)

Of course, Harthouse attempts to buy her from Tom, but that transaction does not work so smoothly.[43]

Is Dickens making the claim that all Utilitarians would prostitute their family members if the price were right? Of course not.[44] Mr. Gradgrind—who was not raised as a Utilitarian—passes on Bounderby's proposal of marriage to his daughter, reviews the costs and benefits of the transaction, and encourages her to make the decision *she* thinks best. Gradgrind is a creditable feminist, so the same *choice* that was given to him will be given to her. He treats his daughter as

---

43. "The whelp went home, and went to bed. If he had any sense of what he had done that night, and had been less of a whelp and more of a brother, he might have turned short on the road, might have gone down to the ill-smelling river that was dyed black, might have gone to bed in it for good and all, and have curtained his head for ever with its filthy waters" (Dickens 1972, 169; 1995, 141). Thus, Tom finds it necessary to be out of the way when Harthouse puts the moves on Louisa. "'This is a device to keep him out of the way,' said Mrs. Sparsit, starting from the dull office window whence she had watched him last. 'Harthouse is with his sister now!'" (1972, 233; 1995, 209).

44. "Although Mr. Gradgrind did not take after Blue Beard, his room was quite a blue chamber in its abundance of blue books" (Dickens 1972, 131; 1995, 98).

a competent optimizing agent, but as both a caring father and an experienced economist he wants to verify the solution by means of standard algorithms:

> "I now leave you to judge for yourself," said Mr. Gradgrind. "I have stated the case, as such cases are usually stated among practical minds; I have stated it, as the case of your mother and myself was stated in its time. The rest, my dear Louisa, is for you to decide." (Dickens 1972, 135; 1995, 102)

Moreover, upon discovering the truth about the marriage, he protects his daughter with a quiet fierceness that puts the fright in Bounderby (1972, 259–62; 1995, 240–43).

The weirdness of a woman making this critical sexual decision on the basis of what best suits her brother's pecuniary interest—and her brother's evident belief that even after she was married he can repander her—evaporates if one supposes that *Hard Times* was written in opposition to *Uncle Tom's Cabin*. Stowe opens her book with a portrait of two slave owners—the decent Shelby and the loutish Haley. When Haley catches sight of the fetching Eliza, guess what transaction first pops into his mind?

> "By Jupiter," said the trader, turning to him in admiration, "there's an article now! You might make your fortune on that ar gal in Orleans, any day. I've seen over a thousand in my day, paid down for gals not a bit handsomer." (Stowe 1982, 14)

Shelby, motivated by fear of his wife's reaction, refuses to discuss such a trade. Here and elsewhere, Stowe seems to propose this test for the morals of slave owners: will they sell or buy a woman for sexual service? Some pass, some fail. In all institutions there are good people and bad people. What is important is how institutions bend behavior. Or at least that is how the promarket abolitionists saw the case, as they proposed to end the possibility of such sales by ending the ownership of other humans.[45]

I read Dickens as posing the Martineau-Stowe test in market capitalism.[46] Those who would sell or buy a woman for sexual service are moral monsters; those who would not live in hope of their redemption. Gradgrind Sr. is a unlucky man saved by his pre-Utilitarian upbringing. Dickens seems to make

---

45. See Hill, Whately, and Hinds 1852, 244–45, on the evils of the system in contrast to the decency of individual slave owners.

46. Dickens regarded Martineau 1837 as the best book on America (Lohrli 1973, 358). If there is truth in the gossip that Lohrli reports (359)—"According to contemporary report, Miss Martineau herself had served Dickens as the model for Mrs. Jellyby"—then we have an easy explanation for the fury at Dickens expressed by Denman (1853) as well as Mill's famous characterization of Dickens as "that creature" (Collins 1971, 297). Martineau had no children to neglect.

the case that institutions like market capitalism or slavery are neither good nor bad; all that matters is the quality of the people inside the institutions. Thus, capitalism and slavery are morally equivalent, morally neutral.

4. Opposition to Facts

Save for Leavis, and perhaps Nussbaum, even Dickens's warmest friends have some difficulty in explaining just why one would be opposed to the use of statistical methods for social policy. Indeed, one reads in generally admiring accounts that such an attitude would be, to be blunt, simply stupid, so Dickens could not have really believed this.[47] Moreover, anyone who has read Mill's *Autobiography*, and is willing to make a distinction between theory and fact, realizes that Utilitarians like James Mill were more theory entranced than fact entranced.[48] As was described earlier in their debate with Macaulay over Mill's *Government*, it was the Utilitarians who stood for a priori worst-case models of government against the empirical model of government defended by Macaulay. Could it be that Dickens could not tell the difference between an evangelical like Macaulay and a Utilitarian economist like Mill? And perhaps from our point of view this is exactly right?

Perhaps there is one particular aspect of Dickens's opposition to facts that can be given context. Consider the exchange between Louisa and her father in light of one particular fact to which Mr. Gradgrind—Dickens's best of Utilitarians—is particularly attentive:

> "Father, I have often thought that life is very short."—This was so distinctly one of his subjects that he interposed:
>
> "It is short, no doubt, my dear. Still, the average duration of human life is proved to have increased of late years. The calculations of various life assurance and annuity offices, among other figures which cannot go wrong, have established the fact."
>
> "I speak of my own life, father."

---

47. "The very journal in which the novel appeared is itself a complete answer to any man, who, treating in a hard-fact spirit all the fanciful allusions of the novelist, should accuse Mr. Dickens of attacking this good movement and the other hand of opposing the search after statistical and other information by which only real light can be thrown on social questions. What is *Household Words* but a great magazine of facts?" (John Forster in Collins 1971, 302). "But we are missing Dickens point if we fail to see that in condemning Thomas Gradgrind, the representative figure, we are invited also to condemn the kind of thinking and the methods of enquiry and legislation which in fact promoted a large measure of social and industrial reform" (Williams 1958, 94).

48. This is the burden of the argument advanced by Alan Ryan as quoted by Sylvia Manning (1984, 201). Let me acknowledge how much Manning's work helped me to find my way around the scattered scholarship. Kate Flint's edition of *Hard Times* has helped with the more recent scholarship.

> "O indeed? Still," said Mr. Gradgrind, "I need not point out to you, Louisa, that it is governed by the laws which govern lives in the aggregate." (Dickens 1972, 135; 1995, 103)

The context in which I argue this might be read is the attack on Robert Southey's defense of feudal "slavery"—the term is Southey's—by Macaulay. Macaulay's argument against Southey depended upon his claim that the life expectancy of British workers had increased since feudal times and thus it could hardly be the case that the well-being of the workers had declined.[49] We need not presume that Dickens had direct knowledge of this article because Carlyle has a perfectly competent summary of the debate in *Chartism*. Here Carlyle emphasizes the important of this critical fact in the debate about the worth of the movement from feudal slavery to a market economy:[50]

> Twice or three times have we heard the lamentations and prophecies of a humane Jeremiah, mourner for the poor, cut short by a statistical fact of the most decisive nature: How can the condition of the poor other than good, be other than better; has not the average duration of life in England, and therefore among the most numerous class in England, been proved to have increased? Our Jeremiah had to admit that, if so, it was an astounding fact: whereby all that ever he, for his part, had observed on other sides of the matter was overset without remedy. If life lasts longer, life must be less worn upon, by outward suffering, by inward discontent, by hardship of any kind; the general condition of the poor must be bettering instead of worsening. So was our Jeremiah cut short. (1840, 10)

Carlyle finds the evidence mixed and concludes:

> The condition of the working man in this country, what it is and has been, whether it is improving or retrograding,—is a question to which from statistics hitherto no solution can be got. Hitherto, after many tables and statements, one is still left mainly to what he can ascertain by his own eyes, looking at the concrete phenomenon for himself. (11)

---

49. "The term of human life is decidedly longer in England than in any former age, respecting which we possess any information on which we can rely. All the rants in the world about picturesque cottages and temples of Mammon will not shake this argument. No test of the physical well-being of society can be named so decisive as that which is furnished by bills of mortality. That the lives of the people of this country have been gradually lengthening during the course of several generations, is as certain as any fact in statistics; and that the lives of men should become longer and longer, while their bodily condition during life is becoming worse and worse, is utterly incredible" (Macaulay 1961, 2:217).

50. Poovey (1998, 315), who cites *Chartism*, does not tell the reader the "fact" at issue.

If one renounces statistics and uses one's "own eyes," what results?[51] This may partly explain why the debate between the Carlyleans and the economists often involved racial stereotypes versus averages. When Carlyle and crew offered racial explanations for the poverty in Ireland or unemployment in Jamaica, the economists produced facts. If Ireland's problems are those of the Celtic race, why is it a *fact* that on average the Irish in America, where they actually get paid for their efforts, work so hard? If Jamaican unemployment is the result of the racial characteristics of blacks, why is it a *fact* that the workers in Manchester are unemployed as a result of a strike for wages?

When an aggregation is required, a Utilitarian might think of the mean or median of a group. When Dickens aggregates, he seems to think of the race or class.[52] When Dickens published Eliza Lynn's article on the effect of the liver on the intellectual development of negroes, she announced the doctrine that "what is true of individuals is also of races."[53] Perhaps this resonated with readers familiar with Robert Knox's or and Benjamin Disraeli's doctrine that "Race is all."[54]

5. The Terrible Consequences of Unkind Masters

Dickens's master-centric view of the social order is clearly explained by Stephen Blackpool in *Hard Times:*

> "Of course," said Mr. Bounderby. "Now perhaps you'll let the gentleman know, how you would set this muddle (as you're so fond of calling it) to rights."

51. A powerful case for the "stupidity" interpretation of this argument would be to think through how one might compare the well-being of thirteenth-century workers to that of nineteenth-century workers using only one's "own eyes." The renunciation of statistical methods may explain why impressionistic comparisons were continually being made between the well-being of the "white slaves" of Britain and the black slaves of America.

52. Michael Hollington (1992) develops an interesting reading of *Hard Times* in terms of the hierarchy of body language.

53. "A man with a diseased or torpid liver never works heathfully, or with the full power of his mental organization. And what is true of individuals is also of races. Thus, the inactive liver of hot climates creates a smaller, less energetic, less finely organized, and more basely developed brain than is found in the temperate latitudes; passing gradually from the elliptical skull of the Caucasian—the ideal man—to the pyramidal head of the red or copper-coloured man, down to the lowest type of all, the prognathous, or jaw-protruding skull of the negro; as the lines fall near or more distant from the equator. So, by this showing, poor Quashie owes, not only his skill, but his skull to the unsuspected liver of his: not only the brand of Cain and the sign of slavery on his hide, but the cerebral development and ape likeness which ignorance seizes hold of, as the cause and excuse of cruelty" (Lynn 1857, 528). The correspondence of Kingsley and Hunt, discussed in chapter 5, is equally illuminating.

54. Robert Young (1995) has an extensive discussion of Knox and his doctrine that "race is all." L. J. Rather discusses Disraeli's doctrine that "race is everything." Robert Knox (1850, 91) directs his doctrine that "race is everything" against Macaulay.

> "I donno, sir. I canna be expecten to't. 'Tis not me as should be looken to for that, sir. 'Tis them as is put ower me, and ower aw the rest of us. What do they tak upon themseln, sir, if not to do't?" (1972, 181; 1995, 153)

There is, in Dickens's view, only one master for each of us in the market:[55]

> "You can finish off what you're at," said Mr Bounderby, with a meaning nod, "and then go elsewhere."
> "Sir, yo know weel," and Stephen expressively, "that if I canna get work wi' yo, I canna get it elsewheer." (1972, 183; 1995, 155)

Blackpool cannot get work under his own name, so he must leave his name and the community in search of employment elsewhere.[56] As a result of this, he leaves himself vulnerable to Tom's machinations, is falsely suspected of theft, and falls, upon his return, into the fatal mine shaft.

Again, taking *Uncle Tom's Cabin* as a comparison, we see a case being made for the moral equivalence of market capitalism and racial slavery. When we first meet Eliza's husband George, he is saying goodbye to his family prefatory to his flight to Canada. And why is he risking his life and the happiness of his much-loved family? The answer is an unkind master (Stowe 1982, 27–31).

An Evaluation of These Episodes

Dickens has morphed the Greatest Happiness Principle of Utilitarianism into the My Happiness Principle of the unsocialized. Dickens can, when he so desires, present completely coherent characters operating on the My Happiness Principle.[57] Consider as evidence Mr. James Harthouse, who would make a perfectly fine example of the professional expert witness:

> Mrs. Bounderby, no: you know I make no pretence with you. You know I am a sordid piece of human nature, ready to sell myself at any time for any reasonable sum, and altogether incapable of any Arcadian proceeding whatever. (1972, 198; 1995, 172)

---

55. In *American Notes,* Dickens (1985, 266) is flummoxed by the possibility that one could change not only masters but occupations!

56. "[H]e sent me the only letter I have had from him, saying that he was forced to seek work in another name." (Dickens 1972, 271; 1995, 253).

57. Charles Duffy in conversation with Carlyle: "I suggested that the difference between his men and women and Thackeray's seemed to me like the difference between Sinbad the Sailor and Robinson Crusoe." "Yes, he said, Thackeray had more reality in him and would cut up into a dozen Dickenses" (Collins 1971, 204).

Similarly, Bitzer's sticking mom in the workhouse as an economizing device, and then being berated for giving her tea rather than selling it to her, is a lovely touch:

> Having satisfied himself, on his father's death, that his mother had a right of settlement in Coketown, this excellent young economist had asserted that right for her with such a steadfast adherence to the principle of the case, that she had been shut up in the workhouse ever since. It must be admitted that he allowed her half a pound of tea a year, which was weak in him: first, because all gifts have an inevitable tendency to pauperize the recipient, and secondly, because his only reasonable transaction in that commodity would have been to buy it for as little as he could possibly give, and sell it for as much as he could possibly get; it having been clearly ascertained by philosophers that in this is comprised the whole duty of man— not a part of man's duty, but the whole. (1972, 150; 1995, 120)

I believe that two of the episodes I point to—selling women into sexual service as a test of moral motivation and the terrible consequences of unkind masters—are compelling internal evidence that *Hard Times* ought to be read juxtaposed to *Uncle Tom's Cabin*. They stand out in the text precisely because they make no sense as narrowly defined self-interested behavior within a market economy. The disasters in the episodes I have pointed out happen because agents *fail* to maximize their own well-being in some material sense. They are not operating on the My Happiness Principle. The best way I see to explain their behavior is that they have been endowed with a sufficiently perverted sense of the Greatest Happiness Principle for Dickens to let go of the law that Utilitarian agents act in their own narrow interests to make his polemical point against markets.

Need one stress that British market capitalism circa 1850 gave no one the legal right to sell others into sexual service? Louisa marries Mr. Bounderby to make Tom happy. She is not marrying to find her own happiness or even to suit the interests of her parents. Her father certainly tries to help her find her own happiness in marriage. He asks her to consider all the right, self-regarding, cost-benefit calculations. It would never occur to this best of all possible Utilitarians—although the same might be said if he were a well-watered houseplant—that she would marry to make her brother happy. But marrying to make her brother happy is how the story goes.

Wendy Motooka—who has helped so much in my work—suggests an alternative interpretation. Dickens views women as beings outside material motivation. Louisa does not act in a self-interested manner because in Dickens's view woman cannot.[58] I do not have evidence against this reading, only a

---

58. Hill, Whately, and Hinds (1852, 239) quote an attack on Harriet Beecher Stowe for trading "the natural feminine instincts for peace" for "that snug country place."

feeling that Dickens's abilities as a maker of characters is unlimited. It is worthy of notice, perhaps, that Mr. Gradgrind evidently sees no reason why his daughter should be treated any differently than he was. All Dickens would need to do is present her as her father imagines her to be. And, since "her father" is a character in Dickens's book, this ought not to be impossible for him.

The firm owners in *Hard Times* all seem to be male. Bounderby embodies the My Happiness Principle wonderfully. But he is not the only firm owner. Those who collude to attain monopsonistic power in a labor market are of course conceivable. When Bounderby fires Blackpool, Dickens describes an employer firing a competent worker for purely personal reasons. Why would Bounderby's private reasons make Blackpool less attractive to other employers?[59] Dickens is not describing something like an industrywide downturn in demand, which would, of course, lead to industrywide layoffs. If other employers—presumed to be interested in maximizing their own individual profits—turn down a profit-making employee out of a sense of moral community with Bounderby, then Dickens has again fallen into incoherence. Indeed, the image of the social solidarity of the terminally selfish has a fatuousness exceeding that of Louisa marrying to serve Tom's pecuniary desires. At least Louisa was related to Tom.[60] There has to be some Greatest Happiness Principle at work among the masters for them to turn down a profit opportunity by rejecting a capable worker.

These two episodes I regard as evidence that *Hard Times* echoes *Uncle Tom's Cabin because* the acts of Dickens's Utilitarian agents make no sense in their own severe logic. Their choices are exempted from Dickens's law of the My Happiness Principle for the sake of his polemic matching the horrors of slavery with the horrors of the market. Motooka's alternative reading would have us attend particularly to the behavior of the males in the plot.

Dickens's statement of the inevitable opposition of Utilitarianism and Christianity denies the meaning of their joint opposition to racial slavery. This seems to me compelling evidence of his denial of the moral content of abolitionism. To use Carlyle's phrase, he denies that the "cause of black emancipation" is "sacred." In this denial, he stands in opposition to *Uncle Tom's Cabin* and much much more.

But Dickens's denial takes the form a historical falsification. Utilitarians and at least an important part of British Christianity were allied. A finding of falsification in *Hard Times* is hardly original with me. Such a charge, without

---

59. "He was a good power-loom weaver, and a man of perfect integrity" (Dickens 1972, 103; 1995, 69).

60. Can we get Dickens out of the box by appealing to a game-theoretic reciprocity strategy (Tit-for-Tat) upon which the masters act? We can't because this strategy is formally one way of stating the Golden Rule! Chapter 10 has the details.

details, was made while Dickens lived by W. B. Hodgson. Hodgson is important because he was a very well informed economist[61] who knew Carlyle.[62] I
believe Dickens engaged in knowing misrepresentation; Hodgson only alleged
unwillinging misrepresentation in *Hard Times:*

> And here I cannot but express my deep regret that one to whom we all
> owe, and to whom we all pay, so much gratitude, and affection, and admi-
> ration, for all he has written and done in the cause of good—I mean Mr.
> Charles Dickens—should have lent his great genius and name to the dis-
> crediting of the subject whose claims I now advocate. Much as I am
> grieved, however, I am not much surprised, for men of purely literary cul-
> ture, with keen and kindly sympathies which range them on what seems
> the side of the poor and weak against the rich and strong, and, on the other
> hand, with refined tastes, which are shocked by the insolence of success
> and the ostentation incident to newly acquired wealth, are ever most apt to
> fall into the mistaken estimate of this subject which marks most that has
> yet appeared of his new tale, *Hard Times.* Of wilful misrepresentation we
> know him to be incapable; not the less is the misrepresentation to be
> deplored. (1917, 191)

What Hodgson does not know about Dickens's humanitarianism—he is writing as it is happening—is explained by Oddie, who notes that

> the admirer of Dickens must face the unpalatable fact that his views about
> black and brown, though humanitarian at the beginning of his career, grew
> progressively more illiberal, and that his utterances on the subject on more
> than one occasion reached depths of savagery never plumbed by Carlyle
> even in "Model Prisons." (1972, 135).

The joke about escaping to freedom in blackface is amusing only if one
laughs. I think most readers do not find the episode funny.[63]
     Why did Dickens oppose the use of facts? Dickens does emphasize the

---

61. Evidence for my judgment "well-informed" is provided in the lecture itself; he knows
Samuel Bailey and Richard Whately (Hodgson 1917, 170–72). These are serious thinkers, as a
quick tour of Schumpeter 1954 will attest. A more pointed claim of misrepresentation is made by
Edwin Whipple, who is quoted in Watts 1981, 135. But Whipple shows no evidence of actually
knowing any real economists (Collins 1971, 315–21). Nor, in Whipple's defense, does Watts, who
fails to cite everyone who would matter.
     62. Hodgson 1883, 371: "He is an unsatisfactory man."
     63. "Black, as with Tom in blackamoor make-up, does have some of its customary associa-
tions with evil; but it is characteristically a pigmentation applied from without, and connotes a
social degradation rather than innate evil." If black equals evil what are we to make of black slaves?
(McMasters in Dickens 1990, 413). There is no mirth here.

importance to Gradgrind of the fact of increasing life expectancy. Carlyle explains in great detail why this fact is central to the debate over the condition of the country. Although Carlyle does not explain this to the reader, Southey was defending the claim that feudal slavery was better for the worker than was the market economy. Macaulay's citation of a fact, the fact of increasing life expectancy, was the death of that argument. I'm not sure this is a compelling explanation for the opposition to facts per se. But I would defend it against the alternative explanation, that of Dickens's stupidity.

Human Malleability—Deformed by Choice

After a lengthy detour, we return to the question of rational choice models and their presupposition of a fixed human nature. If the antislavery coalition held to a fixed nature for all humans, what did those who wrote against them hold?

Not surprisingly, the answer is human malleability. Of course, humans can be remade for the worse as well as for the better. Perhaps the most dramatic example of Dickens's belief in the ability of slavery to remake human nature for the worse is the following passage from *American Notes*. The cruelty of their masters has turned slaves in America into beasts more closely resembling Swift's "humans":

> To those who are happily unaccustomed to them, the countenances in the streets and labouring places, too, are shocking. All men who know that there are laws against instructing slaves, of which the pains and penalties greatly exceed in their amount, the fines imposed on those who main and torture them, must be prepared to find their faces very low in the scale of intellectual expression. But the darkness—not of skin, but mind—which meets the stranger's eye at every turn; the brutalizing and blotting out of all fairer characters traced by Nature's hand; immeasurably outdo his worst belief. That travelled creation of the great satirist's brain, who fresh from living among horses, peered from a high casement down upon his own kind with trembling horror, was scarcely more repelled and daunted by the sight, than those who look upon some of these faces for the first time must surely be. (Dickens 1985, 183)

Capitalism remakes humans for the worse, too. Here is one of Dickens's accounts of Coketown, where human nature is again remade:[64]

---

64. "More than with social and economic problems, Dickens in *Hard Times* is concerned with the psychic effects of the new industrialization. A new personality type is evolving whose ideal is the lobotomized Bitzer." (Fabrizio 1987, 87)

You saw nothing in Coketown but what was severely workful. If the members of a religious persuasion built a chapel there—as the members of eighteen religious persuasions had done—they made it a pious warehouse of red brick, with sometimes (but this only in highly ornamented examples) a bell in a bird-cage on the top of it. . . . All the public inscriptions in the town were painted alike, in severe characters of black and white. The jail might have been the infirmary, the infirmary might have been the jail, the town-hall might have been either, or both, or anything else, for anything that appeared to the contrary in the graces of their construction. Fact, fact, fact, everywhere in the material aspect of the town; fact, fact, fact, everywhere in the immaterial. The M'Choakumchild school was all fact, and the school of design was all fact, and the relations between master and man were all fact. . . .

A town so sacred to fact, and so triumphant in its assertion, of course got on well? Why no, not quite well. No? Dear me! (1972, 65–66; 1995, 29)

And how is human nature remade? We read in Morley and Dickens's discussion of American slavery how slave owners operating on the *supply* side prevent the dissemination of Christianity and so deform the slaves. Somehow British industrial capitalism operating on the *demand* side prevents the dissemination of Christianity and so deforms the workers. Dickens's workers have a choice of eighteen denominations; Adam Smith's vision of religion as a competitive industry is alive outside of America:

No. Coketown did not come out of its own furnaces, in all respects like gold that had stood the fire. First, the perplexing mystery of the place was, Who belonged to the eighteen denominations? Because, whoever did, the labouring people did not. It was very strange to walk through the streets on a Sunday morning, and note how few of *them* the barbarous jangling of bells that was driving the sick and nervous mad, called away from their own quarter, from their own close rooms, from the corners of their own streets, where they lounged listlessly, gazing at all the church and chapel going, as at a thing with which they had no manner of concern. (1972, 66; 1995, 29–30)

Dickens's workers cannot select among the eighteen denominations. Like stories of the reaction of Soviet refugees to American supermarkets, his workers are frozen by choice:

Nor was it merely the stranger who noticed this, because there was a native organization in Coketown itself, whose members were to be heard of in the

House of Commons every session indignantly petitioning, for acts of parliament that should make these people religious by main force. Then, came
the Teetotal Society, who complained that these same people *would* get
drunk, and showed in tabular statements that they did get drunk, and
proved at tea parties that no inducement, human or Divine (except a
medal), would induce them to forgo their custom of getting drunk. Then,
came the chemist and druggist, with other tabular statements, showing
that when they didn't get drunk, they took opium. (1972, 66; 1995, 29–30)

Surely there never was such fragile china-ware as that of which the millers
of Coketown were made. (1972, 145; 1995, 115)

Decades after *Culture and Society*, Williams returned to *Hard Times* and
noticed something interesting about these and other related passages:

For at its deepest, most formative level, *Hard Times* is composed from two
incompatible ideological positions, which are unevenly held both by Dickens and by many of his intended readers. Put broadly, these positions are:
first, that environment influences and in some sense determines character;
second, that some virtues and vices are original and both triumph over and
in some cases can change any environment. (1983, 169)

Perhaps there is a simple solution to Williams's puzzle. The masters of
mankind are outside the chain of cause and effect. The higher orders can—for
good or evil—remake the lower orders. They are like our parents would be if
we never grew up. And if these lower orders object to their remaking? As we
learn from the Eyre Controversy, that only proves that they are not fit to be
human and are outside the rule of law.

In this context, perhaps, we might wish to reread Dickens's famous letter
of June 17, 1854, about his quarrel with Mr. Gradgrind:

I often say to Mr. Gradgrind that there is reason and good intention in
much that he does—in fact, in all that he does—but that he over-does it.
Perhaps by dint of his going his way and my going mine, we shall meet at
last at some halfway house where there are flowers on the carpets, and a little standing-room for Queen Mab's Chariot among the Steam Engines.
(1993, 354)

As I read this, Dickens renounces any deep quarrel with the market economy;
he just wants to have a hand in the mastering.

Conclusion

There are three mistakes that I find scholars making in reading *Hard Times*. The first is to assume that what Dickens said about his opponents is always an accurate statement of their views. The charge of misrepresentation was made while he lived. The second mistake is to read midcentury antimarket British works in isolation from antislavery American works of the same period. The charge of anti-antislavery was made while Dickens lived.

In my view, whatever theorists might argue about a possible socialism, the material world of the 1850s was divided between people who believed in markets and people who believed in slavery. What made one less attractive made its alternative more attractive. The third and final mistake—the one my fellow economists often commit—is to fail to treat Dickens with all due seriousness, to assume that his opinions are the result of some drab combination of ignorance and stupidity. I find it most fitting that I close on a point of full agreement with F. R. Leavis, who first taught the world that *Hard Times* is worthy of the most serious study.

Part 3
The Katallactic Moment

EIGHT

❧❧❧

Exchange between Actor and Spectator

The chapters in this section attempt to explicate from the point of view of economic analysis the theoretical basis for the antislavery coalition between classical economists and biblical literalists. This theoretical basis cannot be just neoclassical economics made old and stupid, if for no other reason than that the early neoclassical economists made peace with the racism with which classical economists warred (Peart and Levy 2000). We risk getting things completely upside down if we read neoclassical back into classical economics.

The foundational difference between classical and neoclassical economics to which I should point is a difference in how many agents we need to populate an economic model. The current thinking among economists is that one suffices. And that one need not be human. The classical economics that descends from Adam Smith requires two. It takes two to exchange and talk.

And with two agents we need to make a foundational commitment: are these people the same or are they different? Reflect upon the texts discussed earlier; it is easy to see the relation between the biblical account of human homogeneity—all the people in the world share common ancestors—and Adam Smith's account of human homogeneity. For a biblical literalist, the account in Genesis is true. The *Wealth of Nations* can be read this way: Let us model humans *as if* the Genesis account were true.

These two claims—one is a truth claim and the other is a claim about the best way to build a model—are not the same. In philosophical jargon, the former is a realist position and the latter is a pragmatic position. Evangelical Christians might well worry about Smith's lack of commitment but gratefully employ his model for their common ends.

Instructively enough, if the modeler begins with two agents at the foundation then the supposition that each actor has a spectator comes for nothing. And if we suppose that the two are language users, then perhaps the actor and the spectator will have something to say to one another. Smith's attitude is not, I shall argue, a simple matter of taste that we are at liberty to accept or reject on a whim. Rather, it flows from his acceptance of George Berkeley's remarkable demonstration that it takes two people to know something as simple as whether the proposition "$\alpha > \beta$" is true or not. In Berkeley's theory of vision, the isolated viewer cannot distinguish between small objects up close and large objects far away. This is the "identification problem"—the realization that there are two unknowns—distance and magnitude—and one sense datum. The problem cannot be solved as stated. The Berkeleyan's solution is for the viewer to obtain additional information. Information is carried in rules or heuristics. These rules or heuristics require at least a second person.

But this is not all that Berkeley accomplished. With what one might call his strict finitism, he demonstrated that one can accept the infinity of Heaven and Hell while denying that any such belief will have much impact on our behavior. As Berkeley writes as an unquestioned Christian, his coreligionists cannot therefore exclude consideration of the models of economists for whom Heaven and Hell have little if any motivational importance. I believe this is of central importance to the workings of the antislavery coalition.[1]

The disagreement between coalition partners on these issues do not come over the issue of how to model choice but rather of how to interpret the model. This offers an explanation of why well-informed opponents of the coalition could see little if any interesting differences between them.

Broad Utilitarianism

What do Christians and Utilitarians have common? In one respect this commonality is trivial. Francis Hutcheson, a Christian philosopher, first put forward the Utilitarian slogan. In the only full-length study of Smith's life published in the twentieth century, Ian Ross puts Smith's teaching in the context of the doctrines of his great teacher:

> Our account stresses the fact, however, that Smith does apply the criterion of utility, formulated by Hutcheson . . . as procuring the "greatest happiness of the greatest numbers" when evaluating practices, institutions, and systems (including economic ones). (1994, xxii)

But it surprises scholars to learn that Utilitarianism has roots in Scottish Christianity, if only because Utilitarianism is read as simple materialism. This is of course the foundational basis for F. R. Leavis's important reading of Dickens, which we encountered in chapter 7. In the following sections, I propose to

---

1. A. M. C. Waterman is turning his vast erudition to the historical oddity that only in Britain were major economists within the Christian tradition. I have stressed the importance of non-Christian economists in coalition with Christians, but these are not unrelated.

describe aspects of utilitarianism in Adam Smith's work that bridge Hutcheson and Bentham.

As a way of focusing attention on this issue, I shall consider the assertion that Utilitarianism—read as supposing society to be an isolated individual writ large—could have served as a substitute for racism as a justification for racial slavery. By this claim is meant something vastly more interesting than the triviality that an anti-Utilitarian argument like Carlyle's can be reexpressed in utilitarian dress. Thomas Holt makes a case that the hierarchy of culture could have been an effective substitute for the hierarchy of race. The scholarship revealed in his admirable study of how the Carlyle-Mill debate in 1849–50 was transformed into the one over Governor Eyre compels our attention:

> Mill was no racist, but variants of his argument for Irish exceptionalism might provide racist thinkers a way of evading the inherent contradictions in liberal democratic thought. *A philosophy that pictured society as an aggregation of innately self-seeking individuals had difficulty accounting for the influence of communal values and the impact of culture and history on human thought and behavior.* To the extent that racial differences could be invoked to explain deviations from expected behavior, no adjustments in basic propositions were required. For racist ideologues the blacks' cultural differences were cause to cast them into outer darkness, as exceptions to humankind. For liberals like Mill, those same differences could be invoked to make them objects of special treatment. In both cases, their "otherness" meant that basic premises about human nature and behavior, as applied to Europeans, need not be reexamined. (1992, 328)[2]

The sentence I emphasize in Holt's passage seems to me to be the heart of the matter. The assertion that utilitarianism in its broadest sense could have been substituted for racism in the justification of racial slavery is of course counterfactual. Could the fact that utilitarians were on the antislavery side of the debate only derive from the fact that they were good people?

Holt's counterfactual assertion is supposed to follow from the fact that

---

2. I have added the emphasis. Edward Said (1994, 14): "[I]t will not take a modern Victorian specialist long to admit that liberal cultural heroes like John Stuart Mill, Arnold, Carlyle, Newman, Macaulay, Ruskin, George Eliot, and even Dickens had definite views on race and imperialism, which are quite easily to be found at work in their writing. So even a specialist must deal with the knowledge that Mill, for example, made it clear in *On Liberty* and *Representative Government* that his views there could not be applied to India (he was an India Office functionary for a good deal of his life, after all) because the Indians were civilizationally, if not racially, inferior." Said's class of "liberal cultural heroes," which includes Carlyle-Mill as one unarticulated whole as well as Dickens-Macaulay as another whole, is worthy of notice.

those theorists who considered society to be the aggregation of self-seeking individuals cut themselves off from a recognition of cultural differences when it came to explaining behavior.[3] The argument, if I understand it well enough to fill in the gaps, works like this. The Utilitarian focus on the atomic individual forces Mill and other economists to think in materialist terms because by starting with the atomic individual they cannot take the fact of human relationships as foundational. Human relationships can at best be instrumental. If individuals in other cultures do not behave the way economic Utilitarianism predicts, then the fault may be attributed to the culture itself.

The failure of such a sparse theory of culture to explain actual behavior could have been used to justify the enslavement of that culture. This argumentative strategy is precisely how I have reconstructed the logic of racial quackery. Holt explains clearly and distinctly that this hypothesis is a counterfactual, and it is this counterfactual that motivates much of this introduction to the technical material to come.

I shall proceed by making the case that all too many "facts" that people "know" about Utilitarianism are simply false. And, since I do not want to drag around so many quotation marks, I need a label to describe these putative "facts" that are not real facts. I propose the word *ffact*. It has the virtue of being as ugly as the reality it describes. The first ffact is that the economists following Smith presumed an isolated atomic individual at the starting point of the analysis. The second ffact, which is intimately related to the first, is that Utilitarians thought mainly in material terms and as a consequence they were opposed by those who thought in higher, more spiritual terms. The third ffact is that a Utilitarian calculus maps unambiguously from individual well-being in material terms to social well-being through the mathematical operation described by "the greatest happiness of the greatest number."

The first ffact will be challenged by the construction in the chapters to follow, which reconstruct the way classical economics of the Smith-Whately variant starts with two exchanging individuals. Because the issue is purely mathematical, the third is the simplest ffact to expose and has been dispatched a hundred years ago.[4] What I propose to do here is to develop some consequences of this construction for the larger purposes of the book and to meet the

---

3. I use the word *aggregate* in a vague sense, which includes mathematical operations other than addition. One of the technical points to be made subsequently is precisely that there are more ways of finding an "average" than by adding and dividing. The unfortunate feasible alternative to explicit technical matter is implicit technical matter.

4. Think about how one would go about generating the "greatest illumination with the greatest number of lamps" (Edgeworth 1881, 117). "Pure mathematics, on the other hand, seems to me a rock on which all idealism founders: 317 is a prime, not because we think so, or because our minds are shaped in one way rather than another, but *because it is so*, because mathematical reality is built that way" (Hardy 1990, 130).

challenge of the sort Holt lays down. Thus, I shall worry here about the second ffact.

Violating conventional pieties, I shall argue that utilitarianism is not so much a philosophy as an agreement about the rules under which philosophical debates will be conducted.[5] The rule is simply this: the well-being of a society is determined by the well-being of the constituents of that society and by nothing else. Agreement that this rule is "right" is only the price one pays to enter into debate; it does not solve any substantive problems *because* utilitarians— now broadly conceived—can differ both on how well-being is counted and on how to map from individual well-beings to a judgment of social well-being. Instead of agreement on positive results, one commonality is the conclusion that a certain type of argument fails. That was a justification of slavery on the claim that it was for the benefit of the slave.

What questions divide utilitarians? Perhaps the most important is: how do we actually determine human well-being? Do we look at what people do or at what they say about their choices? If we equate well-being with happiness, do we observe happiness directly or must we estimate it?[6] Do we think about decisions in "worst-case" or "realistic" terms? Nineteenth-century disagreement cannot come as much of a surprise; utilitarians today do not agree on these issues either!

Anti-utilitarians as a matter of definition must therefore oppose any claim that one maps from individual to social well-being. And the alternative is what? The alternative with which we have been most closely concerned is Thomas Carlyle's supposition that the goodness of a society can be judged on the basis of the order it reveals:

> For *Thou shalt* was from of old the condition of man's being, and his weal and blessedness was in obeying that. Woe for him when, were it on the hest of the clearest necessity, rebellion, disloyal isolation, and mere *I will*, becomes his rule. (1956, 266)

Order by exchange is the antithesis of real order; indeed, it is worse than order by terror:

> Mammon, cries the generous heart out of all ages and countries, is the basest of known Gods, even of known Devils. In him what glory is there, that ye should worship him? No glory discernible; not even terror: at best, detestability, ill-matched with despicability! (611)

---

5. Loren Lomasky helped me see things this way.

6. Happiness is an internal matter; perhaps we ought to focus exclusively on aspects of well-being that might be shared? If we cannot directly observe this internal state, how can we still be utilitarians? Adam Smith's answer will be studied later.

This passage frames the state terror that Carlyle would later defend.

While Carlyle succeeded in passing as the voice of DESTINY ITSELF, this privilege was denied to his disciples. The hegemonic status of utilitarianism required the lesser Carlyleans to give a utilitarian defense for slavery. When anti-utilitarians are required to reexpress their position in utilitarian terms, many things are made clear. Just why is slavery better for the slaves?

Recall James Froude's explication of the "Negro question." Slavery improved the condition of the slaves:

> He did not mean that the "Niggers" should have been kept as cattle, and sold as cattle at their owners' pleasure. He did mean that they ought to have been treated as human beings, for whose souls and bodies the whites were responsible; that they should have been placed in a position suited to their capacity, like that of the English serfs under the Plantagenets. (1885, 2:15)

Froude needs two claims to make his case. First, the white masters might be thought of as farsighted parents, and, second, the black slaves might be thought of as nearsighted children. As Froude is willing to express the most anti-utilitarian claims in the lingua franca of utilitarianism, we ought to see what follows from these ffacts. Were these ffacts facts, would they justify the Carlyle-Froude conclusion that the masters ought to have the slaves' bodies and souls in their charge?

Consider figure 4, which will help explain how the debate played out. The picture is new, but the intuition here is far older, dating from a time before *utilitarianism* was a word heard in the world.[7] There is only one individual to consider, so mapping from individual to social well-being will present no difficulty. Let the vertical axis—Good Stuff—be whatever metric of individual well-being we wish. Let the horizontal axis—Theory—represent the theorized understanding of how the world hangs together. Consider one particular theory—the Carlyle-Froude supposition of farsighted, benevolent masters and childish, nearsighted slaves—and call it τ. Repaying our debt to Froude for his candor, stipulate that at τ slavery would indeed be better than freedom for the slave. At τ slaverity is paternalism.

Does figure 4, which expresses our stipulation of the Carlyle-Froude claim, justify slavery? Although some were persuaded, others were not. And as I reconstruct their argument it works like this: what happens if the theory is not exactly true? What happens if we deviate from τ? This is not to deny that there

---

7. Gib Bassett drew the picture at a memorable Public Choice seminar on Bassett and Persky 1999.

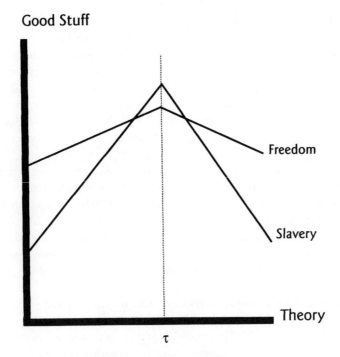

Fig. 4.   A defense of slavery?

is *any* benevolence in the slave owner; the argument will fail if there is any real deviation from *pure* benevolence because the defense of slavery on the basis of the interests of the slave is so fragile.

Two historical objections we have considered in some detail asked what happens when the world deviates from τ. What if there is in fact no real difference between masters and slaves other than experiences? Would not emancipation allow the slaves to become their own masters? What if our supposition of the benevolence of masters is not quite right? Suppose the masters have their own—not just the slaves'—interests to consider. Might not they notice that slaves are valuable assets and that one can obtain valuable assets through the sexual use of one's slaves? The proslavery conclusion vanishes if τ is not exactly true.

Getting market utilitarianism right is nontrivial in the context of disciplinary specialization. The most interesting textual instances to which I pointed earlier occur in the separate reviews by two great British economists, Nassau Senior and Richard Whately, of an American novel, *Uncle Tom's Cabin,* in which the voice of the British Carlyleans is confronted. Even specialists seem not to think to that this is how the debate might play out.[8]

These two objections to slavery do not of course exhaust the list. They do, however, have a basis in the economics of the time, which I can explicate. There is a third objection which I commend to the attention of specialists knowledgeable about the nineteenth-century revival of the Reformation controversy. When slave literacy was outlawed and the slave's knowledge of the Bible was limited to what suited his or her master's interests, is there reason to believe that God's Word could penetrate this veil?[9]

The first objection accepts the benevolence of masters. The second and third deny it. The second objection asks whether sexual usage is conducive to a slave's well-being. The third concerns the state of the slave's soul. I shall argue that these are all utilitarian objections to slavery, with utilitarianism conceived as broadly as I believe necessary. It ought to surprise no one that those who advanced these objections differed among themselves on many issues. But those disagreements would wait until the world was remade and the great evil purged.

The reader might be surprised to learn that the simple point—and the picture drawn above to illustrate the point—is at the center of thinking in what is called "robust statistics."[10] The simple point is not only how a statistical procedure performs under ideal conditions but how it performs when those conditions fail. The intuition is very old;[11] the machinery to make sure that the intuition is sound is rather new.

One of the reasons for the machinery employed below is to allow us to work through just how thinking in robust terms can illuminate the texts of classical economics. Why does Adam Smith worry about the well-being of the majority of society, the well-being of the median? Why does he worry about how people commonly overestimate the importance of the rich? If one perceives the rich to be demigods, raised by their position above human cares, then perhaps the Carlyle-Froude line of argument makes sense. If the rich slave owner is akin to a god, he or she surely must care for the slaves' well-being.

---

8. John Hawley (1986) misses the response of Whately to the voice of Kingsley.

9. The illuminating "proslavery" commentary on *Uncle Tom's Cabin* by "Nicholas Brimblecomb" asserted that those parts of the Bible describing how Moses led the slaves out of Egypt are abolitionist forgeries. "In all these observations, it clearly appears that Moses was not only an imposter and necromancer, but a wholesale enticer and robber" (1853, 156).

10. The greatest single work in this tradition in my estimation is that of D. F. Andrews et al. (1972). Economists of a Bayesian persuasion, I believe, have insufficiently reflected upon the estimator denoted LJS.

11. "Political writers have established it as a maxim, that, in contriving any system of government, and fixing the several checks and controuls of the constitution, every man ought to be supposed a *knave*, and to have no other end, in all his actions, than private interest" (Hume 1987, 42).

The Role of Approbation in Social Norms

I propose to deny that utilitarianism is simply materialism. To this end, I propose to argue that for Smith the desire for approbation is important and that approbation is not some markup of material income. The importance of approbation for the argument to come is that without a desire for approbation Smith's argument cannot explain trade. And, to add some zest to the argument, neither can neoclassical accounts!

This argument of Smith's about the importance of approbation is not confined to such foundational questions as the basis of trade, nor is it something mainly confined to *Moral Sentiments*. On the contrary, the treatment in the *Wealth of Nations* of the effect of the desire for approbation carried by cultural norms on the rational choice of one's occupation begins one of the great set topics in nineteenth-century British classical economics.

This example is worth considering prefatory to the detailed exercises to come. Here we see that the desire for approbation is completely unproblematic in the accounts of later economists of occupational choice. Stipulate with Smith that people are physically the same. Then, with the competitive assumption that any individual can select from any occupation, explain the distribution of money wages.

If all people are the same and they can all pick from any occupation, wouldn't wages be equal? Indeed, Smith claims that this is so when we take *wages* to reflect the net advantages of employment. Money wages comprise one part only of the net advantage. There are five nonpecuniary considerations that Smith lists. Of these, only the first is of importance now.

> First, The wages of labour vary with the ease or hardship, the cleanliness or dirtiness, the honourableness or dishonourableness of the employment. Thus in most places, take the year round, a journeyman tailor earns less than a journeyman weaver. His work is much easier. A journeyman weaver earns less than a journeyman smith. His work is not always easier, but it is much cleanlier. A journeyman blacksmith, though an artificer, seldom earns so much in twelve hours as a collier, who is only a labourer, does in eight. His work is not quite so dirty, is less dangerous, and is carried on in day-light, and above ground. Honour makes a great part of the reward of all honourable professions. In point of pecuniary gain, all things considered, they are generally under-recompensed, as I shall endeavour to show by and by. Disgrace has the contrary effect. The trade of a butcher is a brutal and an odious business; but it is in most places more profitable than the greater part of common trades. The most detestable of all employments, that of public executioner, is in proportion to the quantity of work done, better paid than any common trade whatever. (1976a, 117)

Let us stop right now and walk through the argument. Smith does *not* make the leap from the assertion that an occupation is useful to the assertion that the occupation is approved. This is where the materialism reading fails. There is not the slightest hint that Smith denies the usefulness of either butcher or executioner even though they are both despised professions. Why is it, in Smith's account, that when death is in the picture approbation does not tag along after usefulness? This, I shall argue, is one way to appreciate Smith's emphasis on the importance of life expectancy as a metric of well-being.

There are social judgments that, as far as I can see, Smith makes no claim to understand. He uses the term *prejudice* in this context. Why, for example, are ballet dancers regarded as public prostitutes? Could not this judgment be reversed? Of course it could. Indeed, Smith works out the consequences. What about the social judgment that a man must follow his father's occupation in the social context of a caste system? Even before book 1, chapter 10, Smith works out the consequence of this judgment, which it is enforced by state power. It is possibly worthy of notice that Smith's example is informed by his knowledge about non-European cultures:

> The police must be as violent as that of Indostan or ancient Egypt (where every man was bound by a principle of religion to follow the occupation of his father, and was supposed to commit the most horrid sacrilege if he changed it for another) which can in any particular employment, and for several generations together, sink either the wages of labour or the profits of stock below their natural rate. (1976a, 80)[12]

One of the exercises to come will attempt to determine how Smith's procompetitive stance is explicitly developed to enhance the well-being of the majority of the society in a sense that they can understand.

An account of the formation of judgment is the announced topic of *Theory of Moral Sentiments*, but the economists who followed Smith seemed not to care how approbation came about. For them, as long as the rational choosers desire approbation and wish to avoid disapprobation, their money wages would adjust.

Income from approbation or disapprobation can be modeled no differently than income from money wages. In Smith's account, one trades the one for the other. If people trade material income for the approbation carried by social norms, then a utilitarian might select either as the basis of judgment. Consider figure 4 again. The Good Stuff could be material income or it could be one of

---

12. The reader who "detects" a Eurocentric sneer has not read Smith's polemic against local European policy, which kept the competitive market from functioning (1976a, 135–59). Smith's point is only that the anticompetitive practices near at hand do not have a religious basis.

the systematic cultural norms (e.g., life expectancy) or one of the nonsystematic cultural norms (e.g., nonmarried sexuality).

The obvious objection to my casual recitation of facts from Adam Smith's work here, or in the more detailed consideration to come, is to question my right to adduce arguments from this wide-ranging philosopher to characterize the doctrines of those narrow souls who followed. This objection illustrates the difference between a problem-oriented discipline like economics and humanistic disciplines in which personal opinion remains unconstrained. Let us reflect upon the judgments of later economists on how well Smith did in his attempt to solve this particular problem. And let us not forget that because the account in Smith's chapter on wages within a market supposes homogenous individuals so acceptance of the results is consent to the homogeneity postulate.

We begin with David Ricardo, writing in 1821:

> In speaking, however, of labour, as being the foundation of all value, and the relative quantity of labour as almost exclusively determining the relative value of commodities, I must not be supposed to be inattentive to the different qualities of labour, and the difficulty of comparing an hour's or a day's labour, in one employment, with the same duration of labour in another. The estimation in which different qualities of labour are held, comes soon to be adjusted in the market with sufficient precision for all practical purposes. (1951, 1:20)

The paragraph concludes with a note from the *Wealth of Nations*, book 1 chapter 10, which expresses Ricardo's judgment that Smith said all there was to be said on the topic.

Perhaps not surprisingly, given this endorsement, J. R. McCulloch's 1825 edition of *Wealth of Nations* prefaces the chapter this way:

> This is one of the most important and valuable chapters in the *Wealth of Nations*. With very few exceptions the principles and reasonings are equally sound and conclusive. (Smith 1828, 1:164)

The reservations McCulloch will press in his notes concern what later scholars know as the "alienation argument."

Is this just a Ricardian trope? Consider Mountiford Longfield's sharpening of Smith's argument. This is how Longfield begins:

> This subject has been so well and perspicuously explained and illustrated by Adam Smith, that subsequent writers are in general content to copy from him. (1834, 65)

Here is how Smith's conclusions follow from the assumption of *local* mobility:

> Increased profits of bricklayers, or the diminished gains of barristers, will not induce any person to become a bricklayer who would otherwise become a barrister. Neither will the diminished profits of bricklayers, or the increased gains of barristers, enable a man who would otherwise become a bricklayer to pursue the profession of the bar, and by his competition reduce the gains of the profession to their proper level. This may be the case, and yet the due proportion between the gains of those two professions, so remote from each other, may be preserved by means of the intermediate professions. These act as media of communication. (84)

In what I consider to be the most interesting of all the editions of *Wealth of Nations*, E. G. Wakefield made the following assertion.

> This, one of the most admired and admirable chapters in the Wealth of Nations, is allowed on all hands to be free from error, and to contain, even now, the only complete account of the subject to which it relates. (Smith 1835, 1:328)

Not surprisingly for a topic of this importance, it is easy to find discussion reflected outside the marginalia of successive editions of *Wealth of Nations*. Nassau Senior, as the consulting economist behind the New Poor Law, has perhaps reflected carefully upon the impact of disapprobation on our choices, as he adds texture to Smith's account in his 1836 *Outline:*

> But the fear of popular odium, and, what is always strongest amongst the least educated, the fear of popular ridicule, as they are amongst the most powerful feelings of our nature, are the most effectual means by which the wages of an employment can be increased. To Adam Smith's instance of a public executioner may be added that of a common informer; both of whom are remunerated at a rate quite disproportioned to the quantity of work which they do. They are paid not so much for encountering toil as for being pelted and hissed. The most degrading of all common trades, perhaps, is that of a beggar; but, when pursued as a trade, it is believed to be a very gainful one. (1938, 201)

The final comment we quote on Smith's analysis is from Mill's *Principles of Political Economy* of 1852, the third edition, the one which follows the exchange with Carlyle:

A well-known and very popular chapter of Adam Smith* [*bk. 1, chap. 10] contains the best exposition yet given of this portion of the subject. I cannot indeed think his treatment so complete and exhaustive as it has sometimes been considered; but as far as it goes, his analysis is tolerably successful. (1965, 2:380)

In a paragraph added in the 1852 edition, Mill says this about theory and fact:

These inequalities of remuneration, which are supposed to compensate for the disagreeable circumstances of particular employments, would, under certain conditions, be natural consequences of perfectly free competition: and as between employments of about the same grade, and filled by nearly the same description of people, they are, no doubt, for the most part, realized in practice. But it is altogether a false view of the state of facts, to present this as the relation which generally exists between agreeable and disagreeable employments. The really exhausting and the really repulsive labours, instead of being better paid than others, are almost invariably paid the worst of all, because performed by those who have no choice. (383)

The debate with Carlyle over the Gospel of Labor raised this point with a vengeance. In Mill's statement, Carlyle was proposing to fulfill his labor obligation by writing improving tracts while condemning black people to drain the swamps of the world.

NINE

The Partial Spectator in the *Wealth of Nations:* A Robust Utilitarianism

The theory that unifies Adam Smith's *Wealth of Nations* gives considerable emphasis to the role played by the partial spectator.[1] The partial spectator, I shall argue, plays a role in Smith's theory akin to that played by the theory of rational ignorance in the formative works of public choice (Downs 1957). The belief that common opinion might use correction would come naturally to a college professor of moral philosophy if only because that is part of what moral philosophers are paid to do.[2] Of course, in book five of *Wealth of Nations* Smith has an elaborate discussion in which he endogenizes both moral and natural philosophy within the division of labor. Here and elsewhere in *Wealth of Nations,* spectators do not simply observe the division of labor but function within it.

Given that most of us are partial spectators, what sort of judgments can we make about the world around us? Smith makes an inference that passes from the perceived well-being of the majority to a judgment about the well-being of society. I shall argue that this is an instance of what we might label "robust utilitarianism."[3] I shall ask whether Smith's judgments in *Wealth of Nations* are consistent with his account in *Theory of Moral Sentiments* of how we form judgments. Finally, I shall consider how *Theory of Moral Sentiments*'s account of how we judge conduct was enhanced by his argument in *Wealth of Nations* to reconcile the judgment of the spectator with the common facts of moral intuition.[4]

---

1. For this and the remaining chapters, all citations to Smith's work will be to the Glasgow edition; thus, *WN* refers to Smith 1976a and *TMS* refers to Smith 1976b. *LJ* refers to Smith 1978, *Essays* refers to Smith 1980, and *Rhetoric* refers to Smith 1985.

2. "The over-weening conceit which the greater part of men have of their own abilities, is an antient evil remarked by the philosophers and moralists of all ages. Their absurd presumption in their own good fortune, has been less taken of. It is, however, if possible, still more universal" (*WN*, 124).

3. This offers an alternative to organic society readings of Smith: "Thus, while Bentham found it difficult to pass from utility for individual pleasure to social utility, for the Scottish thinkers there is no such problem, as the ultimate unit is society" (Macfie 1984, 301–2).

4. "Paradoxical as it may seem, the theory of ethics was less directly normative than the scientific work on economics. The moral theory was in the main descriptive; the economic theory neatly wove prescriptive elements into its descriptive-predictive fabric" (Bittermann 1940, 516).

By "facts of moral intuition," I simply mean that judgments of "right" and "wrong" are not promiscuously distributed (Levy 1992).

The theory developed at great length in *Theory of Moral Sentiments* posits that a person, as a spectator, can imagine exchanging *situations* with another subject and in this new situation can impute a kind of as-if well-being. Smith calls the difference between directly perceived well-being and that imputed sympathetically the difference between the substance and the shadow (*Theory of Moral Sentiments*, 219).[5] Spectators preserve their personalities as they make their imagined exchanges of situation; consequently, they have no warrant to judge other minds or other utility functions:[6]

> As we have no immediate experience of what other men feel, we can form no idea of the manner in which they are affected, but by conceiving what we ourselves should feel in the like situation. (9)

Seeing the Partial Spectator

In the first chapter of *Theory of Moral Sentiments,* Smith gives a dramatic example in which the naive spectator's imputed as-if well-being is surely not the subject's actual well-being:

> We sympathize even with the dead, and overlooking what is of real importance in their situation, that awful futurity which awaits them, we are chiefly affected by those circumstances which strike our sense, but can have no influence upon their happiness. It is miserable, we think, to be deprived the light of the sun; to be shut out from life and conversation; to be laid in the cold grave, a prey to the corruption and the reptiles of the earth. . . . The happiness of the dead, however, most assuredly, is affected by none of these circumstances; nor is it the thought of these things which can ever disturb the profound security of their repose. The idea of that dreary and endless melancholy, which the fancy naturally ascribes to their condition, arises altogether from our joining to the change which has been produced upon them, our own consciousness of that change, from our putting ourselves in their situation, and from our lodging, if I may be allowed to say

---

5. Spectators can imagine themselves as species other than human. This topic concerned other spectator theorists, for example, Francis Hutcheson, although Smith touches on this in *TMS* (94–95).

6. It is important to stress this because some students of Smith, perhaps under the influence of "ideal observer" theory, simply assert the contrary. D. D. Raphael (1985, 29): "[H]e uses the word 'sympathy' in a somewhat unusual way to mean not just sharing the feelings of another, but being aware that one shares the feelings of another."

so, our own living souls in their inanimated bodies, and thence conceiving what would be our emotions in this case. (12–13)[7]

In *Theory of Moral Sentiments*, Smith gives a famous account of how partial spectators may learn to become impartial. Too often, I think, readers of *Wealth of Nations* have looked for the impartial spectator and perhaps overlooked the role of the humble partial spectator.[8] Indeed, if we were to interpret some books of commentary on Adam Smith by means of their own indexes, for an index to a book with a living author is surely an authorized interpretation, there is *only* the impartial spectator in Smith's corpus.[9] The consequence of this oversight is our inability to see how Smith grounds *Theory of Moral Sentiments* and *Wealth of Nations* on the same supposition of widespread rational ignorance.

In the first chapter of *Wealth of Nations*, like the first chapter of *Theory of Moral Sentiments*, a naive and partial spectator appears. The first paragraph of the chapter reads:

The greatest improvement in the productive powers of labour, and the greater part of the skill, dexterity, and judgment with which it is any where directed, or applied, seem to have been the effects of the division of labour. (13)

Paragraph two starts this way:

The effects of the division of labour, in the general business of society, will be more easily understood, by considering in what manner it operates in some particular manufactures. (14)

---

7. Smith continues: "It is from this very illusion of the imagination, that the foresight of our own dissolution is so terrible to us, and that the idea of those circumstances, which undoubtedly can give us no pain when we are dead, makes us miserable while we are alive. And from thence arises one of the most important principles in human nature, the dread of death, the great poison to the happiness, but the great restraint upon the injustice of mankind, while it afflicts and mortifies the individual, guards and protects the society" (13). This is an important passage that shows how little Smith's argument needs a belief in the infinite rewards and punishment of the afterlife. The purging of infinities is discussed in chapter 12.

8. "It may seem true that the impartial spectator is not in the premises of that book" (Schneider 1979, 59). "In the *Wealth of Nations* the impartial spectator puts in no appearance, unless perhaps Smith casts himself in that role" (Bittermann 1940, 520).

9. For instance, T. D. Campbell (1971, 243) has the following index entries: "Spectator, impartial . . . , ideal . . . , indifferent . . . , well-informed." Gerald O'Driscoll (1979, 178) has "impartial spectator" but nothing for "spectator." Raphael (1985, 118) has "impartial spectator" but not "spectator." Maurice Brown (1988, 186) has "impartial spectator" with several subheads but nothing for "spectator." The texts of these books discuss actual spectators, although perhaps the most attentive to how actual spectators learn how to make adjustment for distance is Ralph Lindgren (1973, 27–30). It is not therefore surprising that Lindgren (163) has the entries: "Spectator, average . . . ; ideal . . . ; impartial.

The next sentence, I think, is complicated and worthy of considerable reflection.

> It is commonly supposed to be carried furthest in some very trifling ones. (14)

Smith notes the content of common suppositions and then proceeds to explain *why* this common supposition might be made:

> [N]ot perhaps that it really is carried further in them than in others of more importance: but in those trifling manufactures which are destined to supply the small wants of but a small number of people, the whole number of workmen must necessarily be small; and those employed in every differ-ent branch of the work can often be collected into the same workhouse, and placed at once under the view of the spectator. (14)

Although the sixty-two-page index of the Glasgow edition of *Wealth of Nations* does not have an entry for *spectator*, there is one in sentence three. Pre-sumably, this is not an "impartial" or imaginary spectator, simply some ordi-nary person who walks into a shop, physically *looks* around, and is impressed with the elaborate nature of the enterprise. The spectator's ability to *see* how the small shop hangs together is contrasted with his or her ability to *see* how huge enterprises hang together:

> In those great manufacturers, on the contrary, which are destined to sup-ply the great wants of the great body of people, every different branch of the work employs so great a number of workmen, that it is impossible to collect them all into the same workhouse. We can seldom see more, at one time, than those employed in one single branch. (14)

The consequence of the naive spectator's inability to see the division of labor in the great manufacturers biases common opinion toward the belief that the division of labor is more extensive in small shops:

> Though in such manufacturers, therefore, the work may really be divided into a much greater number of parts, than in those of a more trifling nature, the division is not near so obvious, and has accordingly been much less observed. (14)

Paragraph 2 of this most famous chapter in the book thus has three aspects of vision: "spectator," "see," and "observe." With his visual model, Smith gives an account of how partial, unreflective spectating forms the basis of common opinion about the division of labor even though this common opinion is simply incorrect. A naive spectator who sees an extensive division of labor in a small establishment but who cannot see anything like this in a great establishment concludes that the division of labor is more extensive in the small shop. Although Smith will go on to argue that the division of labor is carried out more fully in the great manufactures than in small shops, he has explained the basis for the common opinion to the contrary.[10]

Although *spectator* is only used here and just once more in *Wealth of Nations,* this line of argument is advanced elsewhere with the phrase "at first sight." Here is one of Smith's most memorable contributions to the English language:

> To found a great empire for the sole purpose of raising up a people of customers, may at first sight appear a project fit only for a nation of shopkeepers. (*Wealth of Nations,* 613)

Needless to say, Smith goes on to explain that first sight misleads. He reuses the phrase "at first sight" fifteen pages later and deepens the visual metaphors:

> At first sight, no doubt, the monopoly of the great commerce of America, naturally seems to be an acquisition of the highest value. To the undiscerning eye of giddy ambition, it naturally presents itself amidst the confused scramble of politicks and war, as a very dazzling object to fight for. (628)

One frequent theme in Smith's argument is how much better we perceive things up close than we do things far away. Perception across physical distance is offered as a general model for what we know in more general contexts. We know more about moral philosophy than we do about natural philosophy in the same way that we know more about our own parish than we do about the distant world:

> The vortices of Des Cartes were regarded by a very ingenious nation, for near a century together, as a most satisfactory account of the revolutions of the heavenly bodies. Yet is has been demonstrated, to the conviction of all mankind, that these pretended causes of those wonderful effects, not only do not actually exist, but are utterly impossible, and if they did exist, could produce no such effects as are ascribed to them. But it is otherwise with systems of moral philosophy, and an author who pretends to account for the origin of our moral sentiments, cannot deceive us so grossly, nor depart

---

10. I learned to see this argument in Smith from George Stigler's lectures on the *Wealth of Nations,* which, much to the loss of later scholars, he never published.

so very far from all resemblance to the truth. When a traveller gives an account of some distant country, he may impose upon our credulity the most groundless and absurd fictions as the most certain matters of fact. But when a person pretends to inform us of what passes in our neighbhourhood, and of the affairs of the very parish which we live in, though here too, if we are so careless as not to examine things with our own eyes, he may deceive us in many respects, yet the greatest falsehoods which he imposes upon us must bear some resemblance to the truth, and must even have a considerable mixture of the truth in them. (*Theory of Moral Sentiments*, 313–14)

Perception across physical distance is offered as a general model for what we know.

The hint in *Wealth of Nations* that seems to be most important to follow up occurs when in chapter I Smith stresses the link between observation of *distant objects* and philosophers in inducing innovation.

Many improvements have been made by the ingenuity of the makers of the machines, when to make them became the business of a peculiar trade; and some by that of those who are called philosophers or men of speculation, whose trade it is, not do any thing, but to observe every thing; and who, upon that account, are often capable of combining together the powers of the most distant and dissimilar objects. (21)

If philosophers specialize in analysis at a distance, then we might not be surprised to find that this philosopher offers advice for judging distant events.

Interpretation as Ramsification

At the outset, I wish to make it is as clear as can be that I do *not* propose to "rationally reconstruct" Smith in the sense in which Rudolf Carnap proposed to rationally reconstruct (i.e, to "correct") ordinary thinking about life and science.[11] The point of my exercise is not to say what Smith should have said; rather, it is to say how some aspects of Smith's work fit together.

Modern economists within the neoclassical tradition have been criticized, not perhaps too unfairly, for picturing Adam Smith exclusively within a methodological, individualistic, economic setup. It will turn out that my particular problem can be formulated in terms of classes just as easily as it can be

---

11. "[This theory] is meant not merely as an uncritical representation of customary ways of thinking with all their defects and inconsistencies, but rather as a rational, critically corrected reconstruction" (Carnap 1950, 576).

in terms of individuals; consequently, the old controversy about individualistic versus class readings of Smith can be evaded. What seems to get economists in trouble is the now common belief, pungently expressed by George Stigler, that the market for ideas in economic science is efficient. What is useful in the past is embedded in the current thinking. How could a fruitful theorem be overlooked by generations of technically adept readers?[12] When we take for granted an efficient market in ideas, we suppose that Smith cannot know more than modern economists know. It is, perhaps, this unhappiness with an Adam Smith who can never know more, and in hands less careful than Stigler somehow ends up knowing just what modern economists know, that motivates noneconomists to try their hand. For instance, here is Donald Winch's manifesto about reading Smith:

> For the present I will simply record my belief that one of the primary responsibilities of the historian—as opposed to those who are in the business of constructing decorative or more immediately usable pasts—to be concerned with what it would be conceivable for Smith, or someone fairly like him, to maintain, rather than with what later generations would like him to have maintained. (1978, 5)

"Conceivable" is a strange notion to apply to some "like" Smith.[13]

The approach to the history of economics that I should like to defend starts with the presupposition that the theories of economists in the distant past are per se unobservable. The theoretical apparatus is sufficiently ill-defined and unformalized that we cannot directly observe it in the same sense that we can directly observe the theoretical constructions of, say, Paul Samuelson or Kenneth Arrow. The evidence I have for believing in this claim is simply that in fact we, qua historians of economics, do not agree what to make of the theoretical apparatus of someone even as legendarily rigorous as David Ricardo. We do not seem to have the same difficulty making sense of Arrow's

---

12. Stigler 1982, 108. A strong form of the efficient market theorem holds that there are no lost problems to be found. A weak form of the efficient market theorem predicts that someone with consulting rates as high as George Stigler's will not find "lost problems" but someone with David Levy's might! In terms of the Berkeleyan machinery to come, it might help to see these problems in the past once they are posed in the present (see, e.g., Levy and Peart 2002).

13. W. B. Yeats (1990, 50): "Lord, what would they say / Did their Catullus walk that way?" "All but one of the economists I quote were highly intelligent, disciplined men whose views on subjects related to economics deserves your attention and thoughtful consideration, but no more. One, Adam Smith, is differently placed: if on first hearing a passage of his you are inclined to disagree, you are reacting inefficiently: the correct response is to say to yourself: I wonder where I went amiss?" (Stigler 1982, 4).

impossibility theorems as we have with Ricardian distribution theory.[14] And we have been arguing about the latter for over a hundred years without overwhelming evidence of an unproblematic convergence toward a sensible interpretation.

I suppose that there are different levels of fuzziness about the theory embodied in these objective texts. The most fuzzy is the theoretical apparatus that we believe unifies the text. The least fuzzy is the problems that are posed. Someplace in between these two are the solutions to these problems. As Thomas Kuhn says, "the unit of scientific achievement is the solved problem."[15]

Again, I have to defend this supposition on the basis of the experience of readers. To give a subjective defense of at least fuzzy objectivity, Stigler and I were never able to agree on the content of Ricardian distribution theory, but we never had an argument about whether Ricardo's text concerned wages. After a fashion, we came to a tolerable consensus about what the text said about the impact of taxation on corn wages. Kuhn's argument that science is not cumulative depends upon his claim that problems get lost as science changes.[16] This claim takes for granted, as I think it should, that we observe problems in a sense in which we may not be able to observe theories.[17] If problems are lost, then the question of an efficient market in science is called into question.

This context should suggest how I think we ought to address the problem of interpretation. In 1929, Frank Ramsey posed his famous problem about the content of theory.[18] What if, he asked, we can distinguish between perfectly observable things, like the color red, and perfectly unobservable theoretical concepts, like the electron?[19] Ramsey proved, supposing only a rich bag of

---

14. This is an example of W. V. Quine's thesis about the indeterminacy of translation (1981). We are in a language community that contains Arrow's impossibility theorems, but we have to translate from a community that contains Ricardian distribution theories.

15. Thomas Kuhn (1962, 169) emphasizes the "concrete" nature of solved problems.

16. "In the process the community will sustain losses. Often some old problems must be banished" (ibid., 170).

17. "Because the unit of scientific achievement is the solved problem and because the group knows well which problems have already been solved, few scientists will easily be persuaded to adopt a viewpoint that again opens to question many problems that had previously been solved. Nature itself must first undermine professional security by making prior achievements seem problematic. . . . two all-important conditions [must] be met. First, the new candidate must seem to resolve some outstanding and generally recognized problem that can be met in no other way. Second, the new paradigm most promise to preserve a relatively large part of the concrete problem-solving ability that has accrued to science through is predecessors" (ibid., 169).

18. Ramsey 1990, 112–36. Discussions are found in Carnap 1966, 247–64; and Quine 1981, 1–23.

19. Quine (1981, 1–21) weakens this condition.

mathematical notation, that we can translate from unobservables to observables. The resulting translation has been called ever since a Ramsey sentence. An entire theory so translated is said to be Ramsified. Different theories having the same set of Ramsey sentences will be observationally equivalent.

The ideal interpretation of a text, I believe, is simply a Ramsification in problem space.[20] Thus, a problem-oriented Ramsification of a theory is a series of solutions to the problems we find in the text. Presumably, the solutions must be expressed in our language as an interpretative model of the text. One question ought then to be: do the solutions match what we find in the text? Another question ought to be: is there another interpretation that solves more problems?

The Problem of Illusion

If problems in texts are easier to see than the theories that solve them, then we should not observe much controversy about what the problem is. Here is what John Pocock says about late-seventeenth- and early-eighteenth-century capitalism:

> I have tried to show elsewhere that since capitalism in this form was perceived in terms of speculation rather than calculation, its epistemological foundation appeared as fantasy rather than rationality . . . and that goods had to be reified, and the laws of the market discovered or invented, in order to restore reality and rationality to an otherwise purely speculative universe. The interests succeeded the passions—as is beginning to emerge from the researches of scholars—as a means of disciplining and rendering them manageable and intelligible. (1985, 69)

In particular, the problem of illusion shows up in Stigler (1982, 136–45), Winch criticizes:

> Stigler takes the bolder line of criticising Smith for failing to carry through the project of creating a thorough-going economic theory of political behavior. He notes a number of cases which Smith appears to give "a larger role to emotion, prejudice, and ignorance in political affairs than he ever allowed in economic affairs"; and he regrets Smith's apparent unwillingness to unite *homo economicus* with *homo politicus* by applying "the organon

---

20. I learned this from Stigler, who wrote that if you understand Ricardo's distribution theory you should be able to write his theory of taxation (1982, 110). The classroom version was to propose a student's edition of Ricardo in which the "applied" chapters had only the title. The attentive student could write the rest!

of self-interest to political behavior." . . . Stigler's counter-factual approach—considering why Smith did not do something Stigler feels he ought to have done—rests on two assumptions which are common to most economic theories of politics: first, that economic man and political man are basically the same animal pursuing the same ends by different means. (1978, 165–66)

Here is the problem: what do we make of the account of human illusion in Smith's work? Is this something à la Pocock from speculation? Indeed, Smith thinks poorly of prodigals and projectors? Is this something à la Stigler that is mainly restricted to politics? If we constrain ourselves to Winch's criterion, can we find the contemporary building blocks out of which Smith built a theory that deals with illusion? If so, and the theory has interesting implications, we have found a lost problem, and indeed a lost solution, thus contradicting the strong version of the theory of efficient science.

How could this be? Perhaps the answer is simply that economists, post-Ricardo, have specialized in analyzing choice under a full information assumption. Smith is simply walking in a path that we have not trodden recently. It is, in the space of ideas, far away. Perhaps Smith's theory of partial spectators can teach us about seeing distant objects, even when the distant object is Smith's theory of partial spectators.

Seeing Berkeley

We do not have to search very far to find out where Smith might have obtained his ideas on vision and distance:[21]

> Dr. Berkley, in his New Theory of Vision, one of the finest examples of philosophical analysis that is to be found, either in our own, or in any other language, has explained, so very distinctly, the nature of the objects of Sight. . . . Whatever I shall say upon it, if not directly borrowed from him, has at least been suggested by what he has already said. (*Essays*, 148)

This statement sends us back to look into Berkeley's *New Theory of Vision.*

Berkeley's *Vision* contains the remarkable claim that the perception of distance is learned by experience. This thesis is rooted in Berkeley's doctrine that the physical basis of optical perception is angular. An impression of angle, Θ, has an impact upon the optic nerve; the interpretative problem confronting an individual is that of reconstructing *two* pieces of information, distance, d, and

---

21. Joseph Cropsey (1957, 5–6) emphasizes Smith's avowed dependence on Berkeley's doctrine of vision.

magnitude, m, from one datum, Θ. Let the ratio of m/d form arctan Θ. How do we come to distinguish the pair m^1/d^1 from the pair m^2/d^2 when $m^1/d^1 = m^2/d^2$? How do we distinguish big objects at a distance from small objects up close? The evidence Berkeley provides for this thesis is of a funny sort. He gives examples that show that we do in fact distinguish large distant objects from small near objects. Since the arctan of both pairs is by Berkeley's hypothesis the same, then recognizing distance must be a learned ability.

There has been more than a century of debate on the truth of Berkeley's doctrine, a debate that postdates the Scottish acceptance of this teaching. Let me be curt about learned quarrels with Berkeley's knowledge of optical nerves: the issue is not neurology. The issue is how we obtain two unknowns from one sense datum. To see Berkeley's point, let us find a community where life is lived without the visual perception of great distance. Take any individual from this community and test whether distance from his or her perspective is understood as we understand it. One society that fulfills the test criterion is that of the BaMbuti people, who live in a very dense African forest. Moreover, such a test was reported thirty years ago.

The American anthropologist Colin Turnbull conducted the test when he took his friend from the BaMbuti, Kenge, to the top of a hill. Turnbull's famous report gives these test results:

> Then he saw the buffalo, still grazing lazily several miles away, far down below. He turned to me and said, "What insects are those?"
>
> At first I hardly understood; then I realized that in the forest the range of vision is so limited that there is no great need to make an automatic allowance for distance when judging size. Out here in the plains, however, Kenge was looking for the first time over apparently unending miles of unfamiliar grasslands, with not a tree worth the name to give him any basis for comparison. The same thing happened later on when I pointed out a boat in the middle of the lake. It was a large fishing boat with a number of people in it but Kenge at first refused to believe this. He thought it was a floating piece of wood.
>
> When I told Kenge that the insects were buffalo, he roared with laughter and told me not to tell such stupid lies. When Henri, who was thoroughly puzzled, told him the same thing . . . Kenge still did not believe, but he strained his eyes to see more clearly and asked what kind of buffalo were so small. I told him they were sometimes nearly twice the size of a forest buffalo, and he shrugged his shoulders and said we would not be standing out there in the open if they were. . . .
>
> The road led on down to within about half a mile of where the herd was grazing, and as we got closer, the "insects" must have seemed to get bigger and bigger. Kenge, who was now sitting on the outside, kept his face glued

to the window, which nothing would make him lower. I even had to raise mine to keep him happy. I was never able to discover just what he thought was happening—whether he thought the insects were changing into buffalo, or that they were miniature buffalo growing rapidly as we approached. His only comment was that they were not real buffalo, and he was not going to get out of the car again until we left the park. (1968, 252–53)

So Berkeley is right: people have to learn how to interpret what they see, to distinguish big things far away from small things up close. This is the philosophical problem that arises with vision at a distance. We have to learn to interpret what we physically see. When in *Theory of Moral Sentiments* Smith writes about learning to see our interests in their true perspective, vis-à-vis the interests of others, he makes this discussion *explicitly* analogous to Berkeley's theory of vision:

As to the eye of the body, objects appear great or small, not so much according to their real dimensions, as according to the nearness or distance of their situation; so do they likewise to what may be called the natural eye of the mind: and we remedy the defects of both these organs pretty much in the same manner. In my present situation an immense landscape of lawns, and woods, and distant mountains, seems to do no more than cover the little window which I write by, and to be out of all proportion less than the chamber in which I am sitting. I can form a just comparison between those great objects and little objects around me, in no other way, than by transporting myself, at least in fancy, to a different station, from whence I can survey both at nearly equal distances, and thereby form some judgement of their real proportions. . . .

In the same manner, to the selfish and original passions of human nature, the loss or gain of a very small interest of our own, appears to be of vastly more importance, excites a much more passionate joy or sorrow . . . than the greatest concern of another with whom we have no particular connexion. . . . it requires, in this case too, some degree of reflection, and even of philosophy, to convince us, how little interest we should take in the greatest concerns of our neighbour, how little we should be affected by whatever relates to him, if the sense of propriety and justice did not correct the otherwise natural inequality of our sentiments. (135)[22]

Smith's argument that the outcome of a good moral education is learning how to see oneself as others see us was immortalized in Robert Burns's poetry.

---

22. The passage is quoted by Lindgren (1973, 27) but without the Berkeleyan context.

O wad some Pow'r the giftie gie us
To see oursels as other see us.[23]

I propose, therefore, that a critical mark of a spectator theory in *Wealth of Nations* is how poorly individuals, in cases in which they are unguided by either education or experience, perceive their *own* interests. If everyone perceived their own interests correctly in all possible states of the world, then there would be no interesting spectator *theory* in *Wealth of Nations* in spite of a few casual words at the beginning. Because everyone does not perceive their own interests correctly, we can ask what helps influence this perception.

Learning to See Our Interests

To demonstrate that this sort of spectator theory is prevalent in *Wealth of Nations,* I shall provide evidence that a persistent theme throughout is that people have to learn what their own interests are.[24] In addition to the fact that his spectators have very partial perspectives from which to obtain their beliefs, the people he models usually do not know their own interests when they venture into choice far from their own experience and education. Here is what he says about the laborers and their interests:

> But though the interests of the labourer is strictly connected with that of the society, he is incapable either of comprehending that interest, or of understanding its connection with his own. His condition leaves him no time to receive the necessary information, and his education and habits are commonly such as to render him unfit to judge even though he was fully informed. In the publick deliberations, therefore, his voice is little heard and less regarded, except upon some particular occasions, when his clamour is animated, set on, and supported by his employers, not for his, but their own particular purposes. (266)

If some people in Smith's framework do not necessarily perceive their own interests correctly, then perhaps one group of people might perceive their interests better than others:

> Merchants and master manufacturers are, in this order, the two classes of people who commonly employ the largest capitals, . . . As during their

---

23. Quoted in Raphael 1985, 35.

24. "It goes without saying that Smith did not assume all men to be perfectly wise in their own affairs. The *Wealth of Nations* is replete with instances of individuals misunderstanding their interest" (Cropsey 1957, 10). In this context, one can model why moral rules or consumption constraints might be both useful and dangerous (Levy 1988b; Feigenbaum and Levy 1992).

whole lives they are engaged in plans and projects, they have frequently more acuteness of understanding than the greater part of the country gentlemen. As their thoughts, however, are commonly exercised rather about the interest of their own particular branch of business, than about that of the society, their judgement, even when given the greatest candour (which is has not been upon every occasion) is much more to be depended upon with regard to the former of those two objects, than with regard to the latter. Their superiority over the country gentleman is, not so much in their knowledge of the publick interest, as in their having a better knowledge of their own interests than he has of his. It is by this superior knowledge of their own interest that they have frequently imposed upon his generosity, and persuaded him to give up both his own interest and that of the publick. (266–67)

The central thesis of Berkeley's theory of vision is that people have to learn to perceive distance. In *Theory of Moral Sentiments,* Smith extends Berkeley's theory of vision to explain how people must learn to perceive their own interests. In *Wealth of Nations,* Smith finds that in many interesting cases—cases that encompass the *majority of the population*—people do not perceive their own interests very well. These are instances in which they have not invested in this learning.

To Prove Efficiency?

Let us sharpen the point further by asking how Smith used his spectator to prove that trade in one setting is more efficient than trade in another. Smith uses visual language to make claims for which the modern literature would employ notions of imperfect or asymmetric information.[25] When Smith compares private and public monitoring of investment, he does so in *visual* terms:

> The servants of the most careless private person are, perhaps, more under the eye of their master than those of the most careful prince. (*Wealth of Nations,* 839)

The issue is not simply one of private versus public direction of investment. Smith stresses that it is important to be close to economic activity to see it clearly:

> Thus upon equal or nearly equal profits, every wholesale merchant naturally prefers the home-trade to the foreign trade of consumption, and the

---

25. Mary Ann Dimand helped me here.

> foreign trade of consumption to the carrying trade. In the home-trade his
> capital is never so long out of his sight as it frequently is in the foreign trade
> of consumption. (*Wealth of Nations*, 454)

Smith continues to explain why we see better up close:

> He can know better the character and situation of the persons whom he
> trusts, and if he should happen to be deceived, he knows better the laws of
> the country from which he must seek redress. (454)

This ability to see things near at hand more clearly than those far away motivates Smith's security motive in investment. Trade in local markets costs less
than trade in distant markets. The security motive, the insurance costs foregone, is important in Smith's argument about why the rational investor prefers
domestic to foreign investment.[26] Who should guide investment? Should it be
someone close or someone far away?

> What is the species of domestick industry which his capital can employ,
> and of which the produce is likely to be the greatest value, every individual,
> it is evident, can, in his local situation, judge much better than any states-
> man or lawgiver can do for him. The statesman, who should attempt to
> direct private people in what manner they ought to employ their capitals,
> would not only load himself with a most unnecessary attention, but assume
> an authority which could safely be trusted, not only to no single person, but
> to no council or senate whatever, and which would nowhere be so danger-
> ous as in the hands of a man who had folly and presumption enough to
> fancy himself fit to exercise it. (456)

Not only is this a spectator defense of private investment—close is better than
far away—but it is a moral criticism of public investment since the authority
fails to understand his or her own inability. He or she does not see himself or
herself as others do. To Smith, of course, a moral criticism is a spectator criticism.

The same genius who wrote these passages also defended usury laws (Levy
1987). In Smith's view, I believe, usury laws were like moral constraints, which
are defensible when perception failure is widespread. Usury laws, like morals,
constrain private investment decisions, yet they do not replace them with a distant authority.

---

26. This links up with Smith's argument that the rational investor would employ more productive labor than the purely profit-maximizing investor would (Levy 1987).

Visual metaphors animate the arguments that explain the difficulties the English government has with distant colonies.

> It was a long time before even the parliament of England, though placed immediately under the eye of the sovereign . . . (*Wealth of Nations*, 619)

> But the distance of the colony assemblies from the eye of the sovereign . . . (619)

These passages were taken from *Wealth of Nations*. There is a kindred set of passages in *Theory of Moral Sentiments* in which Smith emphasizes the relation among distance, knowledge, and the responsibility for the employment of resources:

> Every man, as the Stoics used to say, is first and principally recommended to his own care; and every man is certainly, in every respect, fitter and abler to take care of himself than of any other person. Every man feels his own pleasures and his own pains more sensibly than those of other people. The former are the original sensations; the latter the reflected or sympathetic images of those sensations. The former may be said to be the substance; the latter the shadow.
>
>   After himself, the members of his own family, those who usually live in the same house with him, his parents, his children, his brothers and sisters, are naturally the objects of his warmest affections. (219)[27]

Smith uses this principle to argue for home tutoring or day schools for children.[28]

Spectator Norms: Majority Rules

We have seen why Smith thinks that while spectating gives people the ability to calculate as-if well-being it does not give them the ability to calculate actual well-being.[29] This simple-minded point is useful to stress because it implies

---

27. These passages are emphasized by Cropsey (1957, 28).

28. "The education of boys at distant great schools, of young men at distant colleges, of young ladies in distant nunneries and boarding-schools, seems, in the higher ranks of life, to hurt most essentially the domestic morals, and consequently the domestic happiness, both of France and England. . . . From their parent's house they may, with propriety and advantage, go out every day to attend public schools: but let their dwelling be always at home" (*TMS*, 222). This passage is discussed by Campbell (1971, 183).

29. Another example Smith gives is that we feel sorry for the insane even if we have no reason to believe them unhappy (*TMS*, 13).

that if Smith uses his spectator model to judge different economic situations he has neither the need nor the warrant to make interpersonal comparisons of utility. Anyone, Smith or his reader, can look over different societies, for instance, and calculate as-if well-being in any of them.

With this in mind, let us consider why Smith thinks economic growth is a good thing. The answer is not a unanimity criterion because Smith argues that all classes do not benefit from growth. Consider the interest of the employers:

> But the rate of profit does not, like rent and wages, rise with the prosperity, and fall with the declension of the society. On the contrary, it is naturally low in rich, and high in poor countries, and it is always highest in the countries which are going fastest to ruin. The interest of this third order [masters], therefore, has not the same connection with the general interest of the society as that of the other two [laborers and landlords]. (*Wealth of Nations*, 266)

Why do the interests of the masters not influence the general interest?

Smith thinks the general interest in growth is quite easy to ascertain: we look for the interest of the majority.[30] Interestingly enough, the words *at first sight*, which earlier gave misleading results, now give us the correct answer. Smith does give us reason to believe that the spectator gets it right:

> Is this improvement in the circumstances of the lower ranks of the people to be regarded as an advantage or as an inconveniency to the society? The answer seems *at first sight* abundantly plain. Servants, labourers and workmen of different kinds, make up the far greater part of every great political society. But what improves the circumstances of the greater part can never be regarded as an inconveniency to the whole. No society can surely be flourishing and happy, of which the far greater parts of the members are poor and miserable. It is but equity, besides, that they who feed, cloath and lodge the whole body of the people, should have such a share of the produce of their own labour as to be themselves tolerably well fed, cloathed and lodged. (*Wealth of Nations*, 96; emphasis added)

Moreover, Smith thinks that the workers have a claim in equity to some part of the their output (96).

---

30. In the passages I cite, Smith is of course not discussing cases of violent redistribution. This would violate deep moral constraints (*WN*, 84–85): "In order to bring the point to a speedy decision, they [workmen's combinations] have always recourse to the loudest clamour, and sometimes to the most shocking violence and outrage. They are desperate, and act with the folly and extravagance of desperate men, who must either starve, or frighten their masters into an immediate compliance with their demands."

Because a spectator theory gives no insight into the *actual* utility levels of individuals in different societies, Smith's spectator theory does not warrant the Utilitarian calculus in which the utility of the N individuals in two possible societies is added together and then divided by N to find the mean society utility. Smith says, rather, that the majority can be judged to be better off in high growth, so therefore high growth is better.

Why is he so confident that his readers, who presumably included the masters themselves, would share his answer? Judgments of as-if well-being will have person specific elements, so Smith is careful to point out that growth not only has material consequences for workers but has life and death consequences for their children. I think this is important because in *Theory of Moral Sentiments* Smith pointed out how important children are in a spectator model:

> In the eye of nature, it would seem, a child is a more important object than an old man; and excites a much more lively, as well as a much more universal sympathy. It ought to do so. Every thing may be expected, or at least hoped, from the child. In ordinary cases, very little can be either expected or hoped from the old man. The weakness of childhood interests the affections of the most brutal and hard-hearted. It is only to the virtuous and humane, that the infirmities of old age are not the objects of contempt and aversion. In ordinary cases, an old man dies without being much regretted by any body. Scarce a child can die without rending asunder the heart of somebody. (219)

Let us read again what Smith says about the impact of economic growth on the life and death of children. Here is the condition of children in rapidly growing America:

> In the British colonies of North America, it has been found, that they double in twenty or five-and-twenty years. Nor in the present times is this increase principally owing to the continual importation of new inhabitants, but to the great multiplication of the species. Those who live to old age, it is said, frequently see there from fifty to a hundred, and sometimes many more, descendants from their own body. . . . A young widow with four or five young children, who, among the middling or inferior ranks of people in Europe, would have so little chance for a second husband, is there frequently courted as a sort of fortune. (*Wealth of Nations*, 88)

Here is their condition in slowly growing Scotland:

> But poverty, thought it does not prevent the generation, is extremely unfavourable to the rearing of children. The tender plant is produced, but

> in so cold a soil and so severe a climate, soon withers and dies. It is not uncommon, I have been frequently told, in the Highlands of Scotland for a mother who has borne twenty children not to have two alive. (97)

Here is their condition in stagnant China:

> Marriage is encouraged in China, not by the profitableness of children, but by the liberty of destroying them. In all great towns several are every night exposed in the street, or drowned like puppies in the water. The performance of this horrid office is even said to be the avowed business by which some people earn their subsistence. (90)[31]

If we know that the majority is judged better off with high growth than with low growth, then while we know absolutely nothing about the state of the *mean as-if* well-being—the sufferings of the rich might indeed be exquisite and so outweigh the gains of the poor—we know that the *median* individual can be judged better off.

It seems to me that Smith is relying on a belief that modestly informed spectators would reach a common judgment about the level of well-being of the median member of different societies to defend economic growth. Smith has told us three things. First, he tells us that the as-if well-being of children is easy for everyone to impute. Second, he has told us that the children of the median member of society will do best in a rapidly growing society. Third, he has told us that one and two suffice for us to conclude that rapid growth is best. This is evidence that Smith is using the results from his spectator model to reach important and interesting welfare conclusions. It appears that Smith draws upon the *median* of the as-if well-being to judge growth good.

This reading is consistent with Smith's emphasis on the well-being of a greater number:

> [T]hose exertions of the natural liberty of a few individuals, which might endanger the security of the whole society, are, and ought to be, restrained by the laws of all governments; of the most free, as well as of the most despotical. The obligation of building party walls, in order to prevent the communication of fire, is a violation of natural liberty, exactly of the same kind with the regulations of the banking trade which are here proposed. (*Wealth of Nations*, 324)

Quoting this passage and others like it, one of the great commentators on Smith's work called his social policy "roughly utilitarian," perhaps because

---

31. Smith's discussion of infanticide occurs at *TMS*, 209–10.

Smith only attended to the number affected by the policy, not to magnitude of the impact.[32] Let us see whether we can give this "roughness" another name.

Is Smith's Spectator Theory Robust Utilitarianism?

The fact that spectators in *Wealth of Nations* seem to make judgments on the basis of the median as-if well-being should cause us to reflect upon the properties of spectator theories of judgment.[33] For reasons that are mysterious to me, consequentialist moral philosophers in the last hundred years have focused on the mean as a normative measure for comparing states of affairs.[34] The mean well-being requires both the obnoxious interpersonal additivity requirement and is terribly sensitive to "utility monsters," the philosophical counterpart of statistical outliers. On the contrary, the *median* well-being requires only being able to order the well-being of individuals across institutions, and it is maximally insensitive to outliers or computational errors at the extremes.[35] In fact, the median does not even require a complete order of the observations. If the observations are censored at either extreme—a case that Smith will argue for in our ability to impute as-if well-being to the rich—the median will not be influenced.

Thinking about spectator theories as possibly robust versions of classical Utilitarianism might encourage further research into their properties.[36] In liter-

---

32. "Smith's criterion of social policy was only roughly utilitarian. He argued in the *Moral Sentiments* that, in general, the interest of the group was to be preferred to that of the individual, and that of the larger groups to that of the smaller" (Bittermann 1940, 727). Campbell (1971, 209–10): "It would appear, therefore, that Smith elevates the principle of utility into *the* principle of his normative theory of political obligation." Campbell's argument, but not Bittermann's, is disputed by Lindgren (1973, 66).

33. "Though he agreed with the utilitarians in the practical consequences, Smith based this judgment of social policy upon the sentiments of the spectators rather than upon direct considerations of utility" (Bittermann 1940, 520). Campbell (1971, 128–34) has a useful discussion of "Ideal Observer" theory in which, at least in one version, the ideal observer is supposedly omniscient with respect to nonethical facts. Campbell then contrasts this with Smith's modest requirements for impartiality (134–45). Under some circumstances, there is a link between the preferences of a median voter and the outcome of a democratic political process (Plott 1967). Francis Galton's overlooked contribution to the median-voter argument is discussed in Levy and Peart 2002. This being so, then the democratic thrust in Smith's writing that Cropsey (1957, 64) sees is sensible, contra Lindgren (1973, 125).

34. John Harsanyi (1973) has been very important for modern economists in making the link between utilitarianism and the mean utility. The text assumes that those who actually defended "the greatest happiness for the greatest number" were explicitly thinking of a mean type of utilitarianism. I offer evidence in the appendix to this chapter of Bentham's attitude on this as expressed in newly published texts. Alan Ebenstein (1991) also discusses these texts.

35. Andrews et al. 1972; Hampel et al. 1986. Of course, the median is not robust in the case of bimodal distributions.

36. Serious reconsideration of Smith's spectator theory as a living theory of ethics begins with Harman 1986.

ary expositions, it is sometimes not made clear that the average utility is not the same thing as the utility of the average person. For instance, Yeager's defense of what he calls "utilitarianism" states the maximand as the well-being of a person taken at random (1988, 6). The median of a sample has the nice, albeit unusual, property of actually belonging to the sample. Say the sample is {1,2,3,4,100}. The sample median is 3 and is an element of the sample. The sample mean is 22 and is not an element of the sample.[37] There is no reason to believe that there will be a real person to whom the mean utility of a society corresponds.[38]

The median of as-if well-being may be person specific, that is, different spectators will produce different medians, but by Smith's argument, in the dramatic case of the life and death of children, it should give us very robust results.[39] With this possibility in mind, let us return to *Theory of Moral Sentiments*, in which Smith works out the details of his spectator model.

The first order of business is to establish that Smith moves from the well-being of individuals to judgment about social states:

> All constitutions of government, however, are valued only in proportion as they tend to promote the happiness of those who live under them. This is their sole use and end. (*Theory of Moral Sentiments*, 185)

To this weak statement, Smith adds a strong one about judgments of conduct:

> Though the standard by which casuists frequently determine what is right or wrong in human conduct, be its tendency to the welfare or disorder of society, it does not follow that a regard to the welfare of society should be the sole virtuous motive of action, but only that, in any competition, it ought to cast the balance against all other motives. (304–5)

I would read this as saying that as long as common moral constraints are not violated the welfare of society ought to be the metric for judgment. (The caveat

---

37. The text silently assumes that the sample is odd where the median is unique. If it is even, we can randomly select either of the two innermost observations as the median to preserve the property that the median is an element of the sample. Where this property is not a requirement, the convention is to average the two innermost observations.

38. Thus, the mean utility is just as fictional as the social contracts that Yeager (1988) criticizes; they are both computations.

39. Smith's focus on the role of the life expectancy of children for informed normative judgments ought to be seen in conjunction with the recent work by A. K. Sen (1993) on life expectancy and norms. Although Sen does not stress this point, judgments about well-being on the basis of life expectancy should be much more robust than those guided by gross national product per capita numbers produced under monopoly conditions. The recent experience with the fabrication of Soviet economic growth "statistics" ought to call into question the belief in the beneficence of data provision (Levy 1993b).

shall be addressed later when we ask what the conditions are for the spectator's judgment to accord with moral facts.) Earlier in *Theory of Moral Sentiments* Smith has written about how important natural moral constraints are for making certain that ideologically guided political reform actually is an amelioration (232–34).

One possible justification for use of the median or kindred location statistic is the claim that the extremes are likely to be measured with more error than the central observations and these measurement errors affect the median much less than the mean. This is, I think, critical for an appreciation of Smith's spectator theory because he writes about this difficulty with extremes of passion very early in *Theory of Moral Sentiments:*

> The propriety of every passion excited by objects peculiarly related to ourselves, the pitch which the spectator can go along with, must lie, it is evident, in a certain mediocrity. If the passion is too high, or if it is too low, we cannot enter into it. Grief and resentment for private misfortunes and injuries may easily, for example, be too high, and in the greater part of mankind they are so. They may likewise, though this more rarely happens, be too low. We denominate the excess, weakness and fury: and we call the defect stupidity, insensibility, and want of spirit. We can enter into neither of them, but are astonished and confounded to see them.
>
> This mediocrity, however, in which the point of propriety consists, is different in different passions. (27)

By "mediocrity" Smith does not mean the word in its twentieth-century connotation of "unacceptable," but rather he translates the Latin *mediocritas:* "the avoidance of extremes, the keeping of a middle course."[40]

This difficulty that spectators have with extremes shows up when Smith points out how poorly we impute the as-if well-being of the rich. The real differences between the happiness of rich and poor are small:

> What can be added to the happiness of the man who is in health, who is out of debt, and has a clear conscience? To one in this situation, all accessions of fortune may properly be said to be superfluous; and if he is much elevated upon account of them, it must be the effect of the most frivolous levity. This situation, however, may very well be called the natural and ordinary state of mankind. (45)

---

40. The *Oxford Latin Dictionary* goes on to add "the mean." The problem with this translation is that all too often the sample mean does not avoid extremes well enough! Peter Jones contributed the Latin.

> When we consider the condition of the great, in those delusive colours in which the imagination is apt to paint it, it seems to be almost the abstract idea of a perfect and happy state. It is the very state which, in all our waking dreams and idle reveries, we had sketched out to ourselves as the final object of all our desires. We feel, therefore, a peculiar sympathy with the satisfaction of those who are in it. (51–52)

Moral corruption is easy to explain in the presence of the rich:

> Even when the order of society seems to require that we should oppose them, we can hardly bring ourselves to do it. That kings are the servants of the people, to be obeyed, resisted, deposed, or punished, as the public conveniency may require, is the doctrine of reason and philosophy; but it is not the doctrine of Nature. Nature would teach us to submit to them for their own sake. (52–53)

Robust Norms for Class Analysis

The interpretation offered above takes it for granted that we start with a society based on individuals. What if, on the contrary, Smith supposes society is based on groups, e.g., D. A. Reisman (1976)? There is no doubt that much of Smith's analysis is conducted in terms of groups. For instance, Stigler begins a famous article by quoting Smith's self-interest principle, a principle that is expressed in terms of groups:

> [T]hough the principles of common prudence do not always govern the conduct of every individual, they always influence that of the majority of every class or order. (*Wealth of Nations*, 295)[41]

For our purposes, we do not need to debate whether classes are, in Smith's account, in the nature of things or simple analytical conveniences.[42] Rather, we can simply ask what a robust, class-based norm would look like. This question was asked, and answered, by an anonymous reader for the *European Journal of the History of Economic Thought*.

If, for simplicity, society is composed of three classes—landlords, employers, and workers—and more than 50 percent of the population is found in the workers, then we can think about social utility depending upon the group with

---

41. Quoted in Stigler 1982, 136.

42. When Smith (*Essays*, 69) writes about the "uniformity and coherent bestowed" on systems of physics, it is clear that coherence comes from the philosopher, not from the nature of the things themselves.

the most members, the *modal* group. It is worthy of note that this is precisely how Robert Malthus read Smith:

> The professed object of Dr Adam Smith's inquiry is the nature and causes of the wealth of nations. There is another inquiry, however, perhaps still more interesting, which he occasionally mixes with it, I mean an inquiry into the causes which affect the happiness of nations or the happiness and comforts of the lower orders of society, which is the most numerous class in every nation. (1970, 189)

The mode is a very complicated estimator. By the 1980s, it had become the subject of intensive study as a possibly robust estimator. This is perhaps not so much for its own sake as because of its regression generalization, least medians of squares.[43]

Additions to the *Theory of Moral Sentiments* after the *Wealth of Nations*

The normative issues addressed so far are familiar problems in welfare economics. The term *utilitarianism* is used by economists to describe a method by which we can pass from statements about individual well-being to statements about collective well-being. There is more to ethical theory, however, than those concerns with which economists now and again struggle. The question I shall address next is: what, if anything, constrains the judgment from the spectator's vision to conform to the facts of common moral judgment? If there isn't anything, then this failure is cited as a reason to reject spectator theories in favor of a Kantian type of approach (Harman 1971).

Susan Feigenbaum and I (1992) have discussed the argument in *Wealth of Nations* that the poor—the majority in every great society—depend upon what Smith calls a system of austere morality to prosper.[44] This argument seems to have led to an interesting modification Smith made in the sixth edition of

---

43. The classic study of robust estimates of location, Andrews et al. 1972, considers only one mode-type estimator, the "shorth." In the context considered, it had little to offer to compensate for its newly discovered horrific theoretical complications. Least median of squares, maximally robust against influential observations, it is a modal-type estimator (Rousseeuw and Leroy 1987, 178–83).

44. "In every civilized society . . . there have been always two different schemes or systems of morality current at the same time; of which the one may be called the strict or austere; the other the liberal, or, if you will, the loose system. The former is generally admired and revered by the common people. . . . In the austere system, on the contrary, those excesses are regarded with the utmost abhorrence and detestation. The vices of levity are always ruinous to the common people, and a single week's thoughtlessness and dissipation is often sufficient to undo a poor workman for ever" (*WN*, 794).

the *Theory of Moral Sentiments* concerning the judgment of conduct when our information is very imperfect.

In part I, section 3, chapter 3, in the one major addition, post-*Wealth of Nations,* to *Theory of Moral Sentiments,* Smith elaborated on the theme of how we misjudge the rich. In particular, he points to a market failure in the production of approbation and disapprobation. The rich unjustly receive approbation and the poor unjustly receive disapprobation because virtue is confused with wealth and vice confused with poverty:[45]

> This disposition to admire, and almost to worship, the rich and the powerful, and to despise, or, at least, neglect persons of poor and mean condition, though necessary both to establish and to maintain the distinction of ranks and the order of society, is, at the same time, the great and most universal cause of the corruption of our moral sentiments. That wealth and greatness are often regarded with the respect and admiration which are due only to wisdom and virtue; and that the contempt, of which vice and folly are the only proper objects, is often most unjustly bestowed upon poverty and weakness, has been the complaint of moralists in all ages. (61–62)

It should not be surprising that Smith states this case visually; we are blinded by riches.[46]

It is only in the middle of society that Smith finds morality and interest running together because it is in the interest of ordinary people to behave according to an austere morality.[47] Here, and only here, when we judge virtue by the behavior of the prosperous, we do not go too far wrong. Our judgments of the middle of society are solid because it is in the interest of the median individual in society to practice the austere virtues.

---

45. The ancient theme of approbation as a payment for the provision of public goods is sketched in Levy 1992, 155–74.

46. "Two different roads are presented to us, equally leading to the attainment of this so much desired object; the one, by the study of wisdom and the practice of virtue; the other, by the acquisition of wealth and greatness. Two different characters are presented to our emulation; the one, of proud ambition and ostentatious avidity; the other, of humble modesty and equitable just. Two different models, two different pictures, are held out to us, according to which we may fashion our own character and behaviour; the one more gaudy and glittering in its colouring; the other more correct and more exquisitely beautiful in its outline: the one forcing itself upon the notice of every wandering eye; the other, attracting the attention of scarce any body but the most studious and careful observer" (*TMS,* 62). Since the editors do not gloss this passage, it might be worth mentioning that Smith is presenting his reader with the choice the high gods of pagan antiquity offered Hercules, the hard life of virtue for its own sake or the soft life of luxury.

47. Modern economists who believe the mathematical facts about optimizing mean that moral constraints cannot be utility enhancing are technically incorrect (Levy 1988b, 1988c, 1992).

In the middling and inferior stations of life, the road to virtue and that to fortune, to such fortune, at least, as men in such stations can reasonably expect to acquire, are, happily in most cases, very nearly the same. In all the middling and inferior professions, real and solid professional abilities, joined to prudent, just, firm, and temperate conduct, can very seldom fail of success. Ability will even sometimes prevail where the conduct is by no means correct. Either habitual imprudence, however, or injustice, or weakness, or profligacy, will always cloud, and sometimes depress altogether, the most splendid professional abilities. Men in the inferior and middling stations of life, besides, can never be great enough to be above the law . . . The good old proverb, therefore, That honesty is the best policy, holds, in such situations, almost always perfectly true. In such situations, therefore, we may generally expect a considerable degree of virtue; and, fortunately for the good morals of society, these are the situations of by far the greater part of mankind.

In the superior stations of life the case is unhappily not always the same. (63)

When we make judgments from observed conduct, the spectator who focuses on the median will observe austerity in practice. Thus, the spectator's judgment when focused on the median in society will accord with the facts of common morality. Thus, Smith's spectator can judge conduct "rightly" even when there is reason to believe that the spectator's vision is clouded at the extremes of distance. There is good reason why Smith was Immanuel Kant's favorite among the British moralists.

Conclusion: The Impartial Spectator in the *Wealth of Nations*

One answer given in the commentary to the question "Where is the impartial spectator in *Wealth of Nations?*" is "It is Adam Smith." Does this answer make sense in light of what he teaches about spectators? One of the charms of Smith's spectator model is the guidance he gives for checking the computations. Even when we are fully developed moral agents, we need to make certain that our computations are correct:

In solitude, we are apt to feel too strongly whatever relates to ourselves: we are apt to over-rate the good offices we may have done, and the injuries we may have suffered: we are apt to be too much elated by our own good, and too much dejected by our own bad fortune. The conversation of a friend brings us to a better, that of a stranger to a still better temper. The man within the breast, the abstract and ideal spectator of our sentiments and conduct, requires often to be awakened and put in mind of his duty, by the presence of the real spectator: and it is always from that spectator, from whom we can expect the least sympathy and indulgence, that we are likely to learn the most complete lesson of self-command. (*Theory of Moral Sentiments*, 153–54)

Thus, Smith would regard his judgments of various states of affairs to be testable in the common opinion of the moderately informed. It is not Platonic experts alone who are capable of discerning the real in the midst of the shadows of the material world:

To approve of another man's opinion is to adopt those opinions, and to adopt them is to approve of them. If the same arguments which convince you convince me likewise, I necessarily approve of your conviction; and if they do not, I necessarily disapprove of it: neither can I possibly conceive that I should do the one without the other. To approve or disapprove, therefore, of the opinions of others is acknowledged, by every body, to mean no more than to observe their agreement or disagreement with our own. But this is equally the case with regard to our approbation or disapprobation of the sentiments or passions of others. (17)[48]

Perhaps, therefore, it is the reader of *Wealth of Nations* who is a real impartial spectator—or at least the reader who has been taught to see rightly.

Appendix: Bentham on Median Utility

What did Bentham mean by the phrase "greatest happiness for the greatest number"? In fact, in an article written for the *Westminster Review* in 1829, but not published until 1983, Bentham explains why "the greatest number" should be dropped. It wrongly emphasized the importance of the majority. His analysis points both to a weakness in utilitarianism and a case in which a median utilitarianism gives counterintuitive results.

---

48. This aspect of Smith's argument has been widely criticized from a logical empiricist point of view. I show how a pragmatic defense of Smith can be mounted (Levy 1992, 50–61). If this argument is successful, it shows how Smith can be both an ethical absolutist—"right" and "wrong" are like "true" and "false"—as well as a cultural relativist. Under this Ramsification, both those who see in Smith's work a pre-Kantian absolutism and those who see a cultural relativity are seeing part of the whole. These readings of Smith that seem flatly inconsistent (Lindgren 1973, 35–36) are from a pragmatic point of view only incomplete. The pragmatic interpretation I offer is simply that the distinction between fact and logic, or between fact and norm, is a decision inside a language community.

54. Greatest happiness *of the greatest number.* Some years have now elapsed since, upon a closer scrutiny, reason, altogether incontestable, was found for discarding this appendage. On the surface, additional clearness and correctness [was] given to the idea: at the bottom, the opposite qualities. Be the community in question what it may, divide it into two unequal parts, call one of them the majority, the other the minority, lay out of account the feelings of the minority, include in the account no feelings but those of the majority, the result you will find is that to the aggregate stock of the happiness of the community, loss, not profit, is the result of the operation. Of this proposition the truth will be the more palpable the greater the ratio of the number of the minority to that of the majority: in other words, the less the difference between the two unequal parts: and suppose the condivident parts equal, the quantity of the error will then be at its maximum.

55. Number of the majority, suppose, 2001: number of the minority, 2000. Suppose, in the first place, the stock of happiness in such sort divided that by every one of the 4001 an equal portion of happiness shall be possessed. Take now from every one of the 2000 his share of happiness, and divide it anyhow among the 2001: instead of augmentation, vast is the diminution you will find to be the result. The feelings of the minority being by the supposition laid entirely out of the account (for such in the enlarged form is the import of the proposition), the vacuum thus left may, instead of remaining a *vacuum,* be filled with unhappiness, positive suffering—magnitude, intensity and duration taken together, the greatest which it is in the power of human nature of endure.

56. Take from your 2000 and give to your 2001 all the happiness you find your 2000 in possession of: insert, in the room of the happiness you have taken out, unhappiness in as large a quantity as the receptacle will contain. To the aggregate amount of happiness possessed by the 4001 taken together, will the result be net profit? On the contrary, the whole profit will have given place to loss. How so? Because so it is that, such is the nature of the receptacle, the quantity of unhappiness it is capable of containing during any given portion of time is greater than the quantity of happiness. (1983, 309–10)

Need I stress the fact that this is not a real argument, that the gains are outweighed by the losses? Bentham is surely appealing to moral intuition that there is something wrong with this transfer. He is not calculating. This moral intuition shows most clearly in his denunciation of slavery:

58. Were it otherwise, not now the practical application that would be to be made of it in the British Isles. In Great Britain, take the whole body of the Roman Catholics, make slaves of them and divide them in any pro-

portion, them and their progeny, among the whole body of Protestants. In Ireland, take the whole body of the Protestants and divide them in like manner among the whole body of the Roman Catholics. (1983, 310)

Why not, if the gains are greater than the losses?

Bentham's example could be improved by supposing that we take a vast amount from the minority, transfer a small amount to the majority—improving the median member of society—and waste the rest. This is unlikely to satisfy anyone's moral intuition of a "rightful" transfer. Here, we have an instance in which the nonrobustness of the median—there are two large groups at considerable distance from each other—illustrates the danger of using any nonrobust estimate of well-being. This is so even when in other contexts the estimate is robust.

TEN

Katallactic Rationality: Language, Approbation, and Exchange

Introduction

Why is it that when subjects in prisoner-dilemma experiments can talk, they cooperate more than when they cannot (Isaac and Walker 1988)? There is nothing in the logic of neoclassical economic theory suggesting this regularity. In search of an answer to this puzzle, I propose to consider the claims advanced by Adam Smith in the *Wealth of Nations* that linked trade and language.[1] Perhaps in Smith's analysis we can find hints toward a solution to the experimentalist's puzzle of the link between cooperation and language.

In *Wealth of Nations*, Smith begins his analysis of choosing agents by considering two individuals exchanging, not an isolated individual optimizing against an impersonal nature. Indeed, it was in his commentary on Smith's account that Richard Whately in his Oxford lectures coined the term *catallactic* from one of the Greek words for exchange, καταλλάτειν.[2] To emphasize that exchange is a social act, as he proposed this name for political economy, he simultaneously asserted that an isolated individual, Robinson Crusoe in partic-

---

1. "Whether this propensity be one of those original principles in human nature of which no further account can be given; or whether, as seems more probable, it be the necessary consequence of the faculties of reason and speech, it belongs not to our present subject to inquire. It is common to all men, and to be found in no other race of animals, which seem to know neither this nor any other species of contracts. Two greyhounds, in running down the same hare, have sometimes the appearance of acting in some sort of concert. Each turns her towards his companion, or endeavours to intercept her when his companion turns her towards himself. This, however, is not the effect of any contract, but of the accidental concurrence of their passions in the same object at that particular time. Nobody ever saw a dog make a fair and deliberate exchange of one bone for another with another dog. Nobody ever saw one animal by its gestures and natural cries signify to another, this is mine, that yours; I am willing to give this for that" *(WN,* 25). The relationship between modern experimental research and Smith's texts is discussed in Levy 1992. Chapter 11 considers Smith's research in linguistics.

2. I see no good reason to maintain nineteenth-century conventions that transliterate the Greek κ into a *c* instead of a *k*.

ular, was outside the purview of our discipline.[3] So began the katallactic moment in economics, that period, long dead, buried and forgotten, in which economists modeled humans as inevitably social beings. It is completely in this spirit that F. Y. Edgeworth wrote in *Mathematical Psychics* of the "isolated couple, the catallactic *atom*" (1881, 31), but, famously, Edgeworth explained cooperation without reference to language and turned katallactics into economics.[4]

For all good things, there is a cost. That is economics in one lesson. We who teach this notion in the space of commodities ought not to be deeply surprised if the thought is pursued into the space of economic models describing the choice of commodities. If we take an isolated individual as the foundation of economic modeling, we cannot take two individuals trading as the foundation. The cost of a Robinson Crusoe model is a katallactic model foregone. To make the cost clear, we consider katallactics before Edgeworth.

Katallactics or Robinson Crusoe?

With katallactics, the model gains access to the judgment of the spectator. The judgment of the spectator, which is itself a model of conduct, offers approbation for choice in accord with the judgment.[5] As I reconstruct the pre-Edgeworth katallactic approach, approbation is something that people value. If they do not, the katallactic model collapses into a Robinson Crusoe model. We can appreciate the importance of this empirical specification by noticing how Smith in *Theory of Moral Sentiments* emphasizes that the desire for approbation is central to the sociability of humans:[6]

> Nature, when she formed man for society, endowed him with an original desire to please, and an original aversion to offend his brethren. She taught him to feel pleasure in their favourable, and pain in their unfavourable regard. She rendered their approbation most flattering and most agreeable

---

3. "A man, for instance, in a desert island, like Alex. Selkirke, or the personage his adventures are supposed to have suggested, Robinson Crusoe, is in a situation of which Political-Economy takes no cognizance" (Whately 1831, 7). As far as I know, only James Buchanan (1979, 27) in this century has pointed out the relevance of Whately's resistance to Robinson Crusoe models.

4. When Edgeworth pointed out the incoherence of the slogan "the greatest happiness for the greatest number" and formalized utilitarianism as the norm of maximizing the *average* happiness (Edgeworth 1881, 116–17), Smith's concern for the majority, the happiness of the *median*, dropped out of sight (see chapter 9).

5. Some details of the idea that "moral" judgment reflects the economic ideas of ordinary people, that is, those agents who are the subject of formal economic models, are carried out in Levy 1992.

6. Studies of nonhuman primate sociability emphasize the role of approbation carried by grooming (ibid., 25–26, gives references). The approbation carried by language may have more than an arm's reach.

to him for its own sake; and their disapprobation most mortifying and most offensive. (116)

Language comes into the account because approbation is carried by language. Experimental contexts that allow talking between subjects make it easier to exchange approbation.

If we are going to suppose that individuals value approbation, it is surely a good idea to find out how approbation is supposed to be earned. To that task, we turn our attention.

Regularities of Approbation

What did Whately mean by his katallactic proposal? If he had proposed "exchangeology" the meaning would be obvious to us. But he didn't; he used a Greek word. When we, in the waning of the twentieth century, discuss a nineteenth-century proposal to apply a Greek word to the discipline, we might worry if we catch the full meaning of the enterprise by giving one English word as a sufficient translation. Classical Greek, like modern English, has many words for *exchange*. Is there any connotation carried by this one?[7]

Let us therefore consider what an older generation of historians of economics, who grew up with Greek, have said about Whately's proposal. It seems that mainly they ask the sensible question: why it did not catch on?[8] Of particular note is Joseph Schumpeter's discussion. While comparing the broad Continental meaning, "political economy," with the narrow "English" meaning—"economic theory"—he has this to say:

> Realizing the danger that lurked in this terminology, Archbishop Whately made the unsuccessful suggestion: to replace the term Political Economy *in this sense* by the term Catallactics—from καταλλάτειγ, to exchange. In this he showed his usual good sense. But having failed to make his meaning clear, he himself was misunderstood and thus made matters worse. The reader will not have to tax his imagination very heavily in order to visualize how this must have struck critics: What!—Political Economy, the science of the economic fate of humanity, entirely reduced to a miserable theory of bargaining! (1954, 536)

---

7. There is also a problem when, as in the present case, we propose to take a word from a such grammatically rich language as Greek and move it to a vocabulary-rich language such as English. If there are fewer words in Greek than English, then the grammar will be required to convey meaning (see chapter 11).

8. Karl Pribram (1983, 172): "He proposed to apply quite generally to political economy the expression 'Katallactics,' or the science dealing with exchanges. But that proposal was too subtle to find significant approval." Ludwig von Mises seconded Whately's proposal (1949, 3).

Schumpeter's command of the texts hardly ever fails—this was precisely the response of people like John Ruskin to "catallactics," as a quick trip to the *Oxford English Dictionary* will attest.[9] Schumpeter's sympathy fails him, and thus he fails the reader, rather more frequently. He seems not to have caught the importance of Whately's variation on a common theme of Aristotle and Smith in his definition of *human* as "an animal that makes exchanges" (Whately 1831, 6). "Miserable" bargaining is the fate of humanity itself.

Schumpeter's erudition was unique, but there is more to scholarship than a single individual's knowledge and memory. Only F. A. Hayek, in his old age, seems to have had the patience to look up the Greek in that century-spanning cooperative venture of classical scholarship, Liddell-Scott-Jones's *Greek-English Lexicon,* and report some of the family of meanings carried by the grammatical inflections available in Greek.[10] Liddell-Scott-Jones gives the adverbial form, καταλλάγην: *reciprocally.* Then, from classical times—"exchange, esp. of money then change from enmity to friendship, reconciliation"—and, from the Christian Era, Saint Paul's "reconciliation of sinners with God" (2 Corinthians 5:18).

Although in English we can "exchange" with nature, this notion of apersonal exchange seems foreign to the meaning carried by *katallactics* since Robinson Crusoe could "exchange" with nature.[11] These connotations, the emphasis on reciprocity, prepare us for what Smith tells us about the workings of judgments that carry approbation. Prefatory to his section on justice and remorse (*Theory of Moral Sentiments,* 82–91), Smith emphasizes reciprocity:

> As every man doth, so shall it be done to him, and retaliation seems to be the great law which is dictated to us by Nature. (82)

The norm of reciprocity is embodied in rules of justice, so Smith gives the disapprobation one feels from violating these rules great stress. In the next passage we quote, Smith describes how a moral agent—someone who has learned to view his or her past action with the gaze of a disinterested spectator—will view his or her past violations of the norms of justice:

---

9. Schumpeter (1954, 483) warns the reader that he has not seen the first edition, only the 1855 edition. This no doubt explains his trivial confusion of the timing—Whately was not archbishop when he made the proposal. The 1831 edition lists him as principal of St. Alban's Hall and a professor of political economy at the University of Oxford.

10. Hayek 1976, 108, 185. Hayek proposes that a market order be called a "catallaxy" for precisely the reason that the market will reconcile former enemies. Albert Hirschman's dismissal of Jacob Viner's demonstration of the ancient roots of the *doux commerce* thesis is in seeming ignorance of this family of meaning (1997, 60).

11. Thus, when Heraclitus sang Walras' Law—"All things are an equal exchange for fire and fire for all things, as goods are for gold and gold for goods"—he used the word ἀνταμοιβὴ (Kirk and Raven 1981, 199). Liddell-Scott-Jones define this as "exchange one thing with another." There are secondary meanings of *punish.*

> The violator of the more sacred laws of justice can never reflect on the sentiments which mankind must entertain with regard to him, without feeling all the agonies of shame, and horror, and consternation. When his passion is gratified, and he begins coolly to reflect on his past conduct, he can enter into none of the motives which influenced it. They appear now as detestable to him as they did always to other people. (84)

Here Smith breaks apart one agent into intertemporal slices; the past actor is judged by the present spectator, who has inherited his or her skin. But since the present actor knows that his or her choice will be judged by a future spectator, he or she will take the future approbation/disapprobation that follows from the choice into account.

Approbation and disapprobation from the spectator are acquired in many ways. Here is Smith's discussion of approbation from material income itself:

> It is because mankind are disposed to sympathize more entirely with our joy than with our sorrow, that we make parade of our riches, and conceal our poverty. . . . Nay, it is chiefly from this regard to the sentiments of mankind, that we pursue riches and avoid poverty. For to what purpose is all the toil and bustle of the world? what is the end of avarice and ambition, of the pursuit of wealth, of power, and preheminence? Is it to supply the necessities of nature? The wages of the meanest labourer can supply them. . . . It is the vanity, not the ease, or the pleasure which interests us. But vanity is always founded upon the belief of our being the object of attention and approbation. (50)

Increasing wealth increases approbation by moving an individual up social ranks. Smith compares the approbation due the humble with that of the rich:

> The man of rank and distinction, on the contrary, is observed by all the world. Every body is eager to look at him, and to conceive, at least by sympathy, that joy and exultation with which his circumstances naturally inspire him. His actions are the objects of the public care. Scarce a word, scarce a gesture, can fall from him that is altogether neglected. (51)

Modeling the link between income and approbation in terms of a discrete change in social ranks has important technical ramifications.[12]

---

12. One small financial loss, such as a losing lottery ticket, will not change one's social rank, but many such losses will. Thus, we ought to be prepared to do without the assumption of transitivity. The power of Smith's insight can be appreciated by seeing how easy it is to develop a katallactic model of gambling for occupation that blocks the Friedman-Savage, St. Petersburg, and Allais paradoxes (Levy 1999a).

Katallactic Rationality and Competitive Equilibrium

The katallactic moment—katallactics before Edgeworth—could not have had ready and easy access to such devices as utility functions or preference orderings. Indeed, a katallactic model can make no substantial appeal to knowledge of subjective states.[13] We must make do with what we can observe about individuals, choosing physical amounts of income and approbation.[14] Because there is reason to believe that approbation is relative to a language community, we have to be very careful when generalizing across language communities.[15] However, we have learned from Smith two universal claims: first, that approbation flows from acts requiring reciprocity, and, second, that approbation flows from changes in income large enough to change one's rank in society.

We require a modest collection of logical symbols: $\neg$ (not), $\rightarrow$ (if . . . then . . .), $\vee$ (inclusive or), $\wedge$ (and). We shall have need of an exclusive *or*, but this will be made from the standard components. The choices we consider are observed in a society, j, which we denote as S_j. The elements of social world S_j are described in terms of a pair of material income and approbation. We might have need of the particular social context if the approbation is not universal but rather localized to this particular society.[16] These states of the social world we denote by lower case letters in italics, thus, a, b, c . . . . In the case of certainty, we mark the material income at each state of the world, a, b, c . . . , as $x(a)$, $x(b)$, $x(c)$ and similarly, for approbation, $A(a)$, $A(b)$, $A(c)$.

When the choices involve probabilities, we suppose that we can define both expected material income and expected approbation. Economizing on parentheses, these are respectively $Ex(a)$, $Ex(b)$, $Ex(c)$, and $EA(a)$, $EA(b)$, $EA(c)$. To minimize the employment of brackets as statement separators, we employ the convention that the relation $>$ binds more tightly than the logical operators $\vee$ and $\wedge$.

---

13. One of the technical differences between Edgeworth's focus on mean utility and what I reconstruct as Smith's focus on the happiness of the median individual is that the mean requires complete knowledge of subjective states, a claim Smith renounced, (see chapter 9).

14. It is therefore a great historical irony that those subjectivists who have kept the notion of katallactics alive in modern economics—von Mises, Hayek, Buchanan, and Wiseman—have not recognized the potential for conflict.

15. Smith claims that in any great society there are two moral systems: a liberal one and an austere one (Feigenbaum and Levy 1992, 74–91).

16. We could think about approbation carried by language as something that can flow theoremlike from the language community that makes up a society. In this case, notation of the form $S \vDash A(a)$ would be sensible in making the claim that all societies—so there is no subscript on S—make the same judgment of an act a. Smith's position that judgments of "right" and "wrong" share structure with "true" and "false" is defended in Levy 1992. One could then look at Kant's enterprise as defending the position that there are norms of the following form: $\vDash A(a)$. These would be judgments made by all rational beings.

A valuable piece of neoclassical notation, *aPb*, sometimes read as a hypothetical assertion that if a decision maker were given a choice between *a* and *b*, *a* would be chosen. Following distinguished exemplars, I propose to keep the symbol and change the meaning: *aPb* is to be emptied of subjective content.[17] It only means that we observe an individual selecting *a* when *b* is observed to be feasible. We have no access to subject states, so it is our responsibility to specify why this choice was made; consequently, what imputation is it reasonable to make? The necessary condition of katallactic rationality (KR) we require is that one does not turn down a bundle with both more expected material income and more expected approbation. Thus:

$$aPb \rightarrow [\text{Ex}(a) > \text{Ex}(b) \vee \text{EA}(a) > \text{EA}(b)].$$

The left-hand side of $\rightarrow$ is an observed choice; the right-hand side is something that we can go out and measure.[18] KR only requires that if *a* is chosen over *b* there cannot be more of both material income and approbation at *b* than at *a*.

How does this relate to neoclassical assumptions? The relation is very straightforward: a choice is KR if it does not violate the revealed preference axiom that more is preferred to less. A bundle is KR if there isn't any other bundle that dominates it in the space of *both* material income and approbation. The assumption of transitivity would create a trap of our own making because it can be proven false once we take into account that approbation comes from spectators with an ability to make distinctions somewhat less precise than the greater than relation over the real numbers.[19]

Needless to say, many interesting problems will involve cases in which both *a* and *b* satisfy KR. Because we condition the states of affairs to a social world, *S*, we have the possibility of comparing the relative frequency of a type of action across societies. These societies could be separated by time or space. Let a_i, b_i be states of affair in S_i that correspond to a_j, b_j in S_j. Examples might be the occupation of a ballet dancer in two states of society or the policy of

---

17. "And in thus preserving the form while modifying the interpretation I am following the great school of mathematical logicians who, in virtue, of a series of startling definitions, have saved mathematics from the skeptics, and provided a rigid demonstration of its propositions" (Ramsey 1990, 219). The prince of the skeptics was Berkeley (see chapter 12).

18. Approbation is in some contexts straightforward to measure. One of the building blocks of the metrics of science is the citation index. One problem with use of the indices to discuss approbation is that they only count the absolute value, leaving it to the researcher to figure out how to distinguish positive from negative approbation (Feigenbaum and Levy 1997). An approach based on Erdös's coauthorship graphs might avoid this problem: one does not coauthor with people one thinks foolish (Schechter 1998).

19. This is the consequence of Berkeley's strictly finite theory of vision. The failure of transitivity results from the general inability of the modeler to make substitutions of what the model builder knows are identical statements across the beliefs of the actor (Levy 1999a).

honest dealing in two states of society. Then to describe the claim that a_i is more frequently observed than a_j, we employed the notation $f(a_i) > f(a_j)$.

Because we have no insight into subjective states—an issue that we shall confront in due course is that we have no insight into the time preference of the members of society—we shall assume that the distribution of subjective states is the same across societies. This will allow us to make the second defining characteristic of KR: that incentives matter across societies. If the disapprobation of ballet dancing falls and pecuniary wages do not, we shall observe more dancing. If the rewards of honest dealing differ across societies, we shall observe more honest dealing when it pays the most. This will be expressed in partial equilibrium terms:

$$[\text{Ex}(a_i) \geq \text{Ex}(a_j) \wedge \text{EA}(a_i) \geq \text{EA}(a_j)] \rightarrow f(a_i) \geq f(a_j).$$

And we suppose that if one of the weak inequalities to the left of the arrow is replace with a strong inequality the inequality right of the arrow changes to strong, too.

This principle that social characteristics, that is, the relative frequency of observed behavior, can be explained by the incentives facing the individuals comprising the group created an intellectual war that continues to this day. The consequence of this katallactic doctrine is that neither race nor national characteristics matter; only incentives matter. Many intellectuals, then and now, found this a "dismal" doctrine.

These two principles comprise KR as I understand it. Perhaps the most celebrated development of KR occurs in book 1, chapter 10, of the *Wealth of Nations*, the explanation of the process by which the net advantages of employment are brought into equilibrium. The nonpecuniary aspects of employment, honor and shame in particular, are explained as compensating for the pecuniary aspects.[20] We can give this principle a name—katallactic competitive equilibrium (KCE). In such a state of equilibrium, one will not find alternatives for which one option gives more of both income and approbation. The competitive process will not allow such options to persist. Thus, it is necessary in KCE that for any move you make you cannot have both more expected income and more expected approbation:

$$aPb \rightarrow [\text{Ex}(a) > \text{Ex}(b) \vee \text{EA}(a) > \text{EA}(b)] \wedge \neg [\text{Ex}(a) > \text{Ex}(b) \wedge \text{EA}(a) > \text{EA}(b)].$$

---

20. "Honour makes a great part of the reward of all honourable professions. In point of pecuniary gain, all things considered, they are generally under-recompensed, as I shall endeavour to show by and by. Disgrace has the contrary effect. The trade of a butcher is a brutal and an odious business; but it is in most places more profitable than the greater part of common trades. The most detestable of all employments, that of public executioner, is, in proportion to the quantity of work done, better paid than any common trade whatever" (*WN*, 117).

Absent competition, it may be easy to find choices involving more of both good things; state policy or social institutions keep away competitors or restrict one to a particular occupation.[21]

In one of Smith's exquisite analytical set pieces, he asks what would happen to the wages of ballet dancers if public performance lost its stigma. Our solution would be that the increase in approbation, holding constant material income, would draw people into the profession. This influx would reduce material income. Here is Smith's solution:

> There are some very agreeable and beautiful talents of which the possession commands a certain sort of admiration; but of which the exercise for the sake of gain is considered, whether from reason or prejudice, as a sort of publick prostitution. The pecuniary recompense, therefore, of those who exercise them in this manner must be sufficient, not only to pay for the time, labour, and expense of acquiring the talents, but for the discredit which attends the employment of them as the means of subsistence. The exorbitant rewards of players, opera-singers, opera-dancers, & c., are founded upon those two principles; the rarity and beauty of the talents, and the discredit of employing them in this manner. It seems absurd at first sight that we should despise their persons, and yet reward their talents with the most profuse liberality. While we do the one, however, we must of necessity do the other. Should the publick opinion or prejudice ever alter with regard to such occupations, their pecuniary recompense would quickly diminish. More people would apply to them, and the competition would quickly reduce the price of their labour. (*Wealth of Nations*, 124)

The reception in the nineteenth-century economics community of this argument has been described.

Why Language Matters

Smith claims that a reciprocity norm is central to the social order. The traditional prisoner's dilemma logic makes it easy to make operational such a reciprocity norm: if there are two choices confronting each of two individuals, no less approbation is earned when their strategies match—the diagonal elements of the prisoner's dilemma—than when their strategies do not match—the off-diagonal elements. We let A_1 be the approbation from reciprocal strategies and

---

21. Smith recognizes such possibilities: "The police must be as violent as that of Indostan or ancient Egypt (where every man was bound by a principle of religion to follow the occupation of his father, and was supposed to commit the most horrid sacrilege if he changed it for another), which can in any particular employment, and for several generations together, sink either the wages of labour or the profits of stock below their natural rate" (*WN*, 80).

A_0 be the approbation from nonreciprocal strategies and require that $A_1 \geq A_0$. The condition that $A_1 = A_0$—which we allow—corresponds to the case in which approbation is not part of the game. The condition of $A_1 > A_0$ corresponds to the case in which approbation is earned by, and only by, the relation between one's play and that of the other players.

In our first analysis, we shall explicitly assume that the game is played with sufficiently small stakes that no change in material income changes one's social rank. As Smith was quoted earlier, if social rank changes then the approbation one receives will change. Within a small movement of income, the social rank does not change, and so we can restrict changes in approbation to only changes in the play. After we obtain conditions of katallactic rationality, we can then consider the consequences of a change in income large enough to change the player's approbation.

As is commonplace, we consider two individuals with each of two strategies: Trade or Grab. We depart from the convention by adding the approbation from the spectator's judgment produced by a reciprocity norm.

Matrix 1 contains the familiar prisoner's dilemma, in which the usual facts of income from various decisions are supplemented by the approbation one obtains from following a norm of reciprocity. Thus, if both players Trade, then both will receive three units of income and A_1 of approbation. If both players Grab, then, although their incomes fall to two units each, the approbation is unchanged because they have acted in accord with the reciprocity norm. However, in the off-diagonal cells the reciprocity norm is violated and both parties are judged harshly. While the one who Grabs might be judged a ruffian, the one who continues to Trade is judged a sucker.

MATRIX 1. Prisoner's dilemma: material income and approbation		
	Column Trade	Column Grab
Row Trade	$(3, A_1), (3, A_1)$	$(1, A_0), (4, A_0)$
Row Grab	$(4, A_0), (1, A_0)$	$(2, A_1), (2, A_1)$

This argument supposes that the income gain from moving from (in our notation) three to four units is not large enough to move one up the social ranks. If this rank increase were to happen, then the approbation from the gain in income might well cover the loss in approbation from the violation of the reciprocity norm. It is a grim proverb of statecraft that treason never prospers because when it does "none dare call it treason."

Is KR satisfied by the two strategies? The game being symmetric, we need only consider one player. Let us assume that the player believes that the probability of his partner Trading is p and that he is well enough informed to believe that the probability of Grabbing is therefore $1 - p$. We can solve for his expected income and the expected approbation of the two strategies:

$$\text{Ex(Trade)} = p \cdot 3 + (1 - p) \cdot 1; \; \text{EA(Trade)} = p \cdot A_1 + (1 - p) \cdot A_0.$$

$$\text{Ex(Grab)} = p \cdot 4 + (1 - p) \cdot 2; \; \text{EA(Grab)} = p \cdot A_0 + (1 - p) \cdot A_1.$$

There are two interesting cases—$A_1 = A_0$ and $A_1 > A_0$—which we consider in turn.

Case 1. $A_1 = A_0$. For any p, $0 \le p \le 1$, only Grab satisfies KR. Grab always has more expected income and never has any less approbation than Trade, so it satisfies KR. And, importantly, Trade does not. Thus, dogs who cannot provide approbation in their dealings with strange dogs cannot trade. Nor, by this argument, will people who find themselves in a prisoner's dilemma situation in which they cannot exchange approbation. Of course, in an experimental context it might take subjects some time to realize that this is how the game works.

This result is entirely unsurprising. Once we eliminate the possibility that approbation has anything to do with reciprocity, we collapse the game to the neoclassical commonplace, and from the collapse we obtain the canonical result.

Case 2. $A_1 > A_0$. For any p, $0 \le p \le 1$, Grab satisfies KR since Grab always has more expected income than Trade. What about Trade? Consider the case of $p = 1$, in which one actor is sure than the other will Trade. In this situation, Trade is also KR: Trade obtains more expected approbation than Grab because by assumption $A_1 > A_0$. To expand the range of KR for all nonzero p, all that needs to be done is to increase A_1 / A_0 appropriately. Of course, at $p = 0$ Grab will remain uniquely KR.

We saw that when Smith himself solved for KCE his model had the result that it is always possible to get more material income by giving up approbation. Many a lady who could have earned additional pecuniary income by means of public performance lived frugally so as not to be thought of as a whore.

What happens when a Grab moves one up sufficient social ranks to obtain enough approbation to offset the loss of approbation from violating reciprocity? Then we have returned to an augmented version of case 1 since we have $A_1 \le A_0$. This is what Smith writes in that wonderfully important but much neglected part of the *Theory of Moral Sentiments* that was added after *Wealth of Nations*.

> In the middling and inferior stations of life, the road to virtue and that to fortune, to such fortune, at least, as men in such stations can reasonably expect to acquire, are, happily in most cases, very nearly the same. . . . Men

in the inferior and middling stations of life, besides, can never be great enough to be above the law. . . . The good old proverb, therefore, that honesty is the best policy, holds, in such situations, almost always perfectly true. In such situations, therefore, we may generally expect a considerable degree of virtue; and, fortunately, for the good morals of society, these are the situations of by far the greater part of mankind.

In the superior stations of life the case is unhappily not always the same. (*Theory of Moral Sentiments*, 63)

Smith here and elsewhere shows his distrust of the social extremes.

Iterating with Tit-for-Tat

Approbation comes partly from action in accord with a theory of conduct, here the theory of reciprocity carried by the economic ideas of ordinary people. In the game theory literature, the reciprocity norm has a name as a strategy, Tit-for-Tat, and it has been studied extensively by Robert Axelrod (1984) and many others. Let us consider the sequences that are generated when the Other always plays Tit-for-Tat (matrix 2). You can Grab or play Tit-for-Tat:

MATRIX 2. The other plays Tit-for-Tat					
	Iteration 1	Iteration 2	Iteration 3	. . .	Iteration T
Grab	$(4, A_0)$	$(2, A_1)$	$(2, A_1)$	$(2, A_1)$	$(2, A_1)$
Tit-for-Tat	$(3, A_1)$	$(3, A_1)$	$(3, A_1)$	$(3, A_1)$	$(3, A_1)$

The conclusion that Tit-for-Tat is KR is immediate: there is more approbation in the sequence than Grab. Is Grab KR? This depends upon whether the time-discounted sequence of the additional income in iterations 2 . . . T suffices to compensate for the initial loss from not picking Grab. Indeed, this is the very problem Smith worried about: is the Grab that allows an individual to attain a sufficiently high income, which we mark as 4, sufficient to pay for the lifetime of lower income? Since KR makes no claims about subjective states—most emphatically not about time discounting—we cannot rule out Grab satisfying KR.

Nonetheless, if we compare societies in which the number of iterations increases from 1 to T, we observe that income increases for a Tit-for-Tat strategy and, since approbation does not fall, we can make a prediction about the relative frequency of observation. This is the step at which it is vital to assume that the distribution of subjective states of time preference is constant across societies. Here is Smith's memorable claim made to his students:

Whenever commerce is introduced into a country, probity and punctuality always accompany it. These virtues in a rude and barbarous country are almost unknown. Of all the nations in Europe, the Dutch, the most commercial, are the most faithfull to their word. The English are more so than the Scotch, but much inferiour to the Dutch, and in the remote parts of this country they [are] far less so than in the commercial parts of it. This is not all to be imputed to national character, as some pretend. (*Lectures on Jurisprudence* 538)

It could hardly be coincidence that Hume's notorious remark "I am apt to suspect the negroes to be naturally inferior to the whites" occurs in his essay "Of National Characters" (1987, 208). KR is all there is; race is nothing. But this a story in itself, one not unrelated to the death of katallactics.

An Issue of Robustness

You do not know whether the Other will play, but you know that he or she will either always Grab or always play Tit-for-Tat. You do not know how many iterations the game will take; it could be from 1 to T. What do you do? Grab is the strategy naturally suggested by the Robinson Crusoe model of independent individuals. Tit-for-Tat is the strategy recommended by KR for those disposed to value approbation. Matrix 3 expresses the problem in terms of an optimal decision—it is best to Grab if the Other Grabs—but for players with sufficiently low time discounting it is best to play Tit-for-Tat if the Other plays Tit-for-Tat. What if you get it wrong? If you play Tit-for-Tat and the Other Grabs, you take a one-period loss before you catch on. However, as your time discounting falls and the iterations increase, there is no bound to your loss if you Grab but the Other plays Tit-for-Tat.

MATRIX 3. Grab or Tit-for-Tat		
	Other Plays Grab	Other Plays Tit-for-Tat
You Play Grab	Optimal	Unbounded loss
You Play Tit-for-Tat	Small loss	Optimal

We have transformed the choice between a Robinson Crusoe recommendation of Grab and a KR recommendation of Tit-for-Tat to a problem in robust statistical analysis. Matrix 3 is the canonical form of the robust statistical "insurance" problem. Are we willing to "pay" some small loss in efficiency at one idealized point in space to protect against large losses elsewhere? This insurance paradigm was employed first by F. J. Anscombe (1960) to explain why normality is such a dangerous assumption in some statistical contexts. The classical estimators are ideal at normality but can generate enormous losses at a distribution other than this ideal.[22]

Unfortunately, the topic of robust statistical analysis seems to fall in that part of the econometrics text that time does not allow the teacher to cover and then only in such sharp contexts as when one *knows* that the error distribution is not normal.[23] The sample mean and least squares are the paradigm of estimators that are ideal in a narrow range of circumstances; the sample median and least absolute deviations are estimators that are far superior in a wide range of circumstances.

Least absolute deviations and Tit-for-Tat share the property of inefficiency at normality and independent agent rationality respectively. The assumption of normality in a regression context is in general equivalent to the supposition that everything of real importance is included in the hypothesized model; all that is left out is an infinite number of random variables of infinitesimal importance (Levy 1999–2000). Neoclassical rationality obtains its claim to efficiency by omitting consideration of approbation since it is the regularity of approbation that suggests Tit-for-Tat.

Neoclassical rationality and modern econometrics focus on considerations of efficiency at some idealized point. The fact that they break down badly at situations other than that idealized point suggest their fragility. If a theory of conduct is required to explain how a society hangs together, it would be odd for something so fragile to have evolutionary success. Would not robustness be of paramount importance?

Conclusion

Smith's account gives us reason to believe that circumstances in which the supply of approbation is blocked will feature less Trade and more Grab. When approbation is supplied simultaneously with income, we would expect more Tit-for-Tat. By changing their experiments to allow or disallow talk, the experimentalists offer a test bed for Smith's account. One does not get rich, as George Stigler said on occasion, by betting against Smith. There is a robustness in his enterprise that has yet to be fully appreciated.

---

22. Tukey 1960; Andrews et al. 1972; Mosteller and Tukey 1977; Koenker and Bassett 1978.

23. Some texts do not do even this. Thus, it is completely instructive that when Greene attempts to demonstrate why it would be silly to used medians instead of means, his Monte Carlo experiment "apparently" demonstrates just the opposite except, of course, when the error distribution is fairly close to normal (1997, 182–83). Perhaps, the results in Andrews et al. 1972 have not been absorbed.

Appendix: An Interpretative Challenge

Let me call attention to the fact that the entire textual basis of my enterprise was called into question twenty years ago by Albert Hirschman, who in his enormously influential *Passions and Interests* claimed that in Smith's account there is really only one good thing because higher material income and higher approbation are always found together.[24] If the present model has a textual link to Smith and his followers, income and approbation must be able to move independently. Indeed, there must be positions of negative correlation between income and approbation. Indeed, if Hirshman is correct then there will never be a position of katallactic competitive equilibrium, as defined earlier, because states of higher income correspond to states of higher approbation.[25]

An interpretation that turns Smith's katallactic model into a forerunner of Robinson Crusoe models—if material income and approbation are available in roughly fixed proportions, why worry about approbation?—has the entirely useful property of economizing on hard thinking about interrelations among income and approbation.[26] This view of Smith has become rather popular with noneconomists, who in other contexts express a sometimes justified disdain for the economists' propensity to read the analytical limitations of neoclassical economics back into Smith's economics.[27]

To appreciate the importance Smith attaches to the claim that there is a negative correlation between pecuniary income and approbation, note how chapter 10 of book 1 of *Wealth of Nations* begins. Here Smith explains how honor—a nonpecuniary aspect of employment—can compensate for the pecuniary aspects:

> The whole of the advantages and disadvantages of the different employments of labour and stock must, in the same neighbourhood, be either per-

---

24. "In the passage of *The Theory of Moral Sentiments* that was cited above, Adam Smith then takes the final reductionist step of turning two into one: the drive for economic advantage is no longer autonomous but becomes a mere vehicle for the desire for consideration. By the same token, however, the noneconomic drives, powerful as they are, are all made to feed into the economic ones and do nothing but reinforce them, being thus deprived of their erstwhile independent existence" (Hirshman 1997, 109).

25. "By holding that ambition, the lust for power, and the desire for respect can all be satisfied by economic improvement, Smith undercut the idea that passion can be pitted against passion, or the interests against the passions" (ibid., 110). While everyone can get more material income, it is not clear how everyone gets more approbation. In the future—as Andy Warhol famously said— everyone will be famous for fifteen minutes?

26. The question of the role that the desire for fame plays in scientific discovery is of course a variation on how approbation and material income are linked (Levy 1988a; Coleman 1997).

27. For bald declarations that Smith claims that the motivation by honor or glory is unimportant, see Minowitz 1993, 2, 66–67, 183; and Berry 1994, 154.

fectly equal or continually tending to equality. . . . This at least would be the case in a society where things were left to follow their natural course, where there was perfect liberty, and where every man was perfectly free both to chuse what occupation he thought proper, and to change it as often as he through proper. Every man's interest would prompt him to seek the advantageous, and to shun the disadvantageous employment.

Pecuniary wages and profits, indeed, are every-where in Europe extremely different according to the different employments of labour and stock. But this difference arises partly from certain circumstances in the employments themselves, which, either in really, or at least in the imaginations of men, make up for a small pecuniary gain in some, and counterbalance a great one in others; and partly from the policy of Europe, which nowhere leaves things at perfectly liberty. (116)

I consider gambling for income and approbation elsewhere (Levy 1999a).

ELEVEN

Adam Smith's Rational Choice Linguistics

Language and Other Human Actions

Linguistics may be the last of the social sciences to avoid the rational choice paradigm. Many philosophers, Adam Smith especially, argue that being human is the same as using language. Reason and speech are primitives for Smith; we no more choose to use language than we choose to be human. His argument in the *Wealth of Nations* is that trade and language are two aspects of the same process. Humans trade because we have language; nonhumans do not trade because they do not.[1] Merely because language is a background condition for human choices, however, does not obviate for Smith rational choice *aspects* of language.

Smith's argument exploits the simple possibility of substitution of one feature of language for another in such a way as to minimize the time cost of conveying meaning. He distinguishes sharply between what is true for children naturally learning a language and what is true for adults learning a language in which to trade. Perhaps because the rational choice basis of such trade languages (pidgins) is entirely obvious, pidgins have been *defined* out of existence to keep traditional linguistic theory safe from embarrassing contact with rational choice considerations.[2]

The claim that a language is spoken by those of homogeneous competence is regarded as true by definition. This web of belief traps rational choice considerations because now, by definition, we have precluded the possibility that

---

1. Smith's argument is discussed in Levy 1992 in light of modern experimental economics, which finds that (1) rats have preferences but (2) rats don't trade. Steven Pinker (1994, 340–41) discusses continuing attempts to teach chimpanzees sign language. He does not recognize the importance of the experimental result that chimpanzees who can sign will cooperate more.

2. Here is a Chomskian simply defining pidgin out of existence as a "language" spoken by humans: "Thus we cannot say things like *Last night I slept bad dreams a hangover snoring no pajamas sheets were wrinkled,* even though a listener could guess what that would mean. This marks a major difference between human languages [*sic*] and, for example, pidgins and the signing of chimpanzees, where any word can pretty much go anywhere" (Pinker 1994, 117).

one's fluency in a language increases with exposure.[3] Scholars working in pidgin and/or language death are leading the way in questioning the definitional status of such a specification.[4] Why this might be so will be clearer after we look at Smith's account of a language that loses its grammar.

In Smith's Words

In standard histories of linguistics such as Land 1974, Smith is given credit for developing the argument that languages will grow more grammatically complex over time. It is insufficiently noticed that Smith restricts this argument to an isolated language. His example is classical Greek, a language in which he believed all the words were generated internally.[5] The Smithian problem upon which we shall focus is how the grammar of language evolves as the result of trade between people with different languages.

Smith does not see any reason why a language learned in childhood could not have an arbitrarily large number of what modern linguistics calls inflections:

> As long as any language was spoke by those only who learned it in their infancy, the intricacy of its declensions and conjugations could occasion no great embarrassment. The far greater part of those who had occasion to speak it, had acquired it at so very early a period of their lives, so insensibly and by such slow degrees, that they were scarce ever sensible of the difficulty. (*Rhetoric*, 220)

Something very interesting happens when adults need to conduct business across languages. Rational choice considerations enter into the choice of a language's grammatical structure:

---

3. "What we say is that the child or foreigner has a 'partial knowledge of English,' or is 'on his or her way' toward acquiring knowledge of English, and if they reach the goal, they will then know English. Whether or not a coherent account can be given of this aspect of the commonsense terminology, it does not seem to be one that has any role in an eventual science of language" (Chomsky 1986, 16).

4. David DeCamp (1977, 9) tells of the first great student of pidgins and Creoles: "At one time he was warned by a senior colleague that he should abandon this foolish study of funny dialects and work on Old French if he wished to further his academic career. [Note:] History indeed repeats itself. When I myself began studying Jamaican Creole in 1957, I received from a colleague a similar warning that I should avoid such quasi-languages and should work on an American Indian or other 'real' language." "Pidgins and creoles were long the neglected step-children of linguistics because they were thought to be marginal, and not 'real' full-fledged languages" (Romaine 1988, 1).

5. "The Greek seems to be, in a great measure, a simple, uncompounded language, formed from the primitive jargon of those wandering savages, the ancient Hellenians and Pelasgians, from whom the Greek nation is said to have been descended. All the words in the Greek language are derived from about three hundred primitives, a plain evidence that the Greeks formed their language almost entirely among themselves, and that when they had occasion for a new word, they were not accustomed, as we are, to borrow it from some foreign language, but to form it, either by composition, or derivation from some other word or words, in their own. The declensions and conjugations, therefore, of the Greek are much more complex than those of any other European language with which I am acquainted" (*Rhetoric*, 222).

But when two nations came to be mixed with one another, either by conquest or migration, the case would be very different. Each nation, in order to make itself intelligible to those with whom it was under the necessity of conversing, would be obliged to learn the language of the other. The greater part of individuals too, learning the new language, not by art, or by remounting to its rudiments and first principles, but by rote, and by what they commonly heard in conversation, would be extremely perplexed by the intricacy of its declensions and conjugations. They would endeavor, therefore, to supply their ignorance of these, by whatever shift the language could afford them. Their ignorance of the declensions they would naturally supply by the use of prepositions; . . . The same alteration has, I am informed, been produced upon the Greek language, since the taking of Constantinople by the Turks. *The words are, in a great measure, the same as before; but the grammar is entirely lost,* prepositions having come in the place of the old declensions. This change is undoubtedly a simplification of the language, in point of rudiments and principle. It introduces, instead of a great variety of declensions, one universal declension, which is the same in every word, of whatever gender, number, or termination. (*Rhetoric,* 220–21; emphasis added)

The phrase emphasized in this passage—"the grammar is entirely lost"—is a signature of a type of language heavily studied by modern linguists where *degrammaticalization* is a term of choice (Romaine 1989, 379). Continuing with Smith, we read:

A similar expedient enables men, in the situation above mentioned, to get rid of almost the whole intricacy of their conjugations. There is in every language a verb, known by the name of the substantive verb; in Latin, *sum;* in English, *I am.* This verb denotes not the existence of any particular event, but existence in general. It is, upon this account, the most abstract and metaphysical of all verbs; and, consequently, could by no means be a word of early invention. When it came to be invented, however, as it had all the tenses and modes of any other verb, by being joined with the passive participle, it was capable of supplying the place of the whole passive voice, and of rendering this part of their conjugations as simple and uniform, as the use of prepositions had rendered their declensions. (*Rhetoric,* 221)[6]

---

6. Smith writes for an audience with a background in Latin grammar. When Latin teachers today explain the declension of nouns and the agreement of adjectives to English speakers, they appeal to English prepositions. "Consider the Latin roots *port* (gate) and *magna* (large). The genitive case, *portae magnae,* is 'of' the large gate, and so on for cases which cover 'to/for,' 'by/with/from,' etc." (Wheelock 1992, 7–8).

A Model of Inflection and Trade

Our jumping off point is Smith's claim that language is like a machine.[7] This encourages us to think about language in terms of production functions. In particular, let us think about the production of meaning by different properties of language. Inflections can be viewed as a method of economizing on vocabulary. Knowledge of the root and inflectional formula—this is what linguistics call a "paradigm"—allows one to solve for the right word. To the language learner, a grammatical paradigm is really closer in spirit to a regression equation than to a nonstochastic equation because of grammatical irregularity. Irregularity is the paradigm's residual.

Consider the English inflection for number with its two explicit cases: singular and plural. The paradigm is to add an *s* if it is plural and do nothing to the root if it is singular:

cow + *s* (if more than one cow)

cow (if one cow).

There are wonderfully bizarre exceptions, or residuals in regression terminology, to the paradigm. *Child* changes to *children, goose* changes to *geese, mouse* changes to *mice, wharf* changes to *wharves,* and *dwarf* changes either to *dwarves* or *dwarfs* depending upon whom you read. Steven Pinker (1994, 141–43) claims that these irregularities are themselves the vestigial evidence of other rules for inflecting number. If this is so, then the residuals come from something akin to random regime shifts.

Do we need this explicit inflection? English speakers seem not to be terribly disadvantaged by the lack of an explicit marker for the dual case. Surely, we could treat *cow* the way we treat *deer.* There is exactly the same word for one deer as for many deer; we let plurality be indicated with a cardinal number.

---

7. "It is in this manner that language becomes more simple in its rudiments and principles, just in proportion as it grows more complex in its composition, and the same thing has happened in it, which commonly happens with regard to mechanical engines. All machines are generally, when first invented, extremely complex in their principles, and there is often a particular principle of motion for every particular movement which it is intended they should perform. Succeeding improvers observe, that one principle may be so applied as to produce several of those movements; and thus the machine becomes gradually more and more simple, and produces its effects with fewer wheels, and fewer principles of motion. In language, in the same manner, every case of every noun, and every tense of every verb, was originally expressed by a particular distinct word, which served for this purpose and for no other. But succeeding observation discovered, that one set of words was capable of supplying the place of all that infinite number, and that four or five prepositions, and half a dozen auxiliary verbs, were capable of answering the end of all the declensions, and of all the conjugations in the ancient languages" (*Rhetoric,* 223–24).

Alternatively, we could have a special word for a multitude of cows; indeed, we have one, *cattle*.[8]

Let us consider other inflections. Suppose we wish to convey information that a certain subject, Robert, beat a certain object, John. Different languages have different methods for this. Inflected languages may have a nominative inflection that has a marker indicating what part of speech the noun fulfills. Once the markers are in place, the meaning is fixed whether we write the subject, the object, or the verb first. Word order may be selected on poetic grounds.[9] In English, except for pronouns, inflections indicating differences between subject and object do not exist.[10]

The alternative technology for indicating subject and object is fixed word order. Comparing English to inflected classical languages, such as Greek and Latin, Smith advises writers to accept the natural structure of English (*Rhetoric*, 225). It turns out that the advice is efficient (Diamond and Levy 1994).

The consideration that vocabulary and inflections are alternative methods for conveying information encourages us to us write the production of meaning as a function of the size of vocabulary and the complexity of the inflections. The number of inflections in the language could measure the inflectional dimensionality of the language.

Meaning = M(Vocabulary, Inflections).

We suppose that we can extend the visual representations of equal quantities of output—isoquants—to draw isomeaning relationships for any language. Figure 5 gives an equal isomeaning relationship in each of two languages, a vocabulary-rich E and an inflection-rich G. We suppose a time budget for children (*cc* in fig. 5) such that the choice of E or G is a matter of indifference. Given the budget *cc*, an equal amount of information can be conveyed with an equal expenditure of time. This specification is a simple consequence of something agreed upon by serious linguistic scholars: all languages learned from childhood are equally good at conveying any sort of information. As Pinker (1994, 27) observes, there may be people with Stone Age technology; however, there are no Stone Age languages.

---

8. The example points to the complicated interrelations between gender and number in English: *Cow* has feminine gender; *cattle* does not. The lack of an ungendered pronoun of singular number is a source of much discomfort in modern style manuals.

9. "The variety of termination in the Greek and Latin, occasioned by their declensions and conjugations, gives a sweetness to their language altogether unknown to ours, and a variety unknown to any other modern language" (*Rhetoric*, 224).

10. It is interesting that the pair *who* and *whom* are losing their distinction in standard American English (Pinker 1994, 116). In radio American English, other pairs of pronouns are merging.

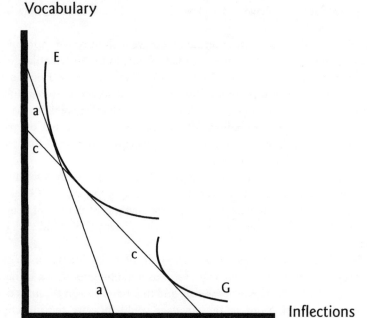

Fig. 5.   The production of meaning

But this is only supposed to be true for languages learned from childhood. Suppose, now, that adults wish to conduct business with this amount of meaning. Which language will they pick? We have agreed that from the point of view of children it would not make any difference. Can we say anything about *adult* budget constraints? Smith asserts that it is relatively more difficult in terms of time for adults to pick up inflection patterns than vocabulary. Without inflections, words are words. The word for *pen* in French is no more problematic than the word for *plume* in English. But knowledge of the inflections of one language might not predict another's inflections.

The reason for this is simply that, while some grammatical distinctions (e.g., number) are simple correlatives of the world outside language, other grammatical distinctions (e.g., gender) are wound up in a cultural web of belief.[11] The inflection of number seems to be linked to the world in a way that

---

11. As Dan Slobin (1993, 247) notes, "I would imagine, for example, that if your language lacked a plural marker, you would not have insurmountable difficulty in learning to mark the category of plurality in a second language, since this concept is evident to the nonlinguistic mind and eye. Or if your language lacked an instrumental marker it should not be difficult to learn to add a grammatical inflexion to nouns that name objects manipulated as instruments. Plurality and manipulation are notions that are obvious to the senses in ways that, for example, definiteness and relative tense are not."

the inflection of gender is not. If "there are two cows out there" is true, then there really are two cows out there. But even if "the *Enterprise* launched an F–18 from her deck" is true, aircraft carriers are not obviously female, even though warships are gendered feminine in demotic English. While standard European languages are gendered on the basis of sex, other languages are gendered on many other principles.[12]

Moreover, there are different ways to slice common experience about movements in time and space. For instance, one language, such as English, has verbs conjugated on the basis of time. Other languages, such as Navajo, have verbs conjugated on the basis of aspect.[13] Linguistics since Smith has discovered other inflections in isolated languages, for example, the ergative inflection, which indicates transitivity and the location markers (Dixon 1989, 99, 162).

The difference in the dimensions of language means that one would have to find the structure of the inflectional equations by a trial and error procedure in which the dimension of the specification search increases with the number of inflections of the language.[14] Thus, the adult language learner confronts the full horror of exploratory data analysis in an unknown number of dimensions (Mosteller and Tukey 1977). Inflections often involve a worldview that children learn simultaneously with the language.[15] The adult language learner has to either replace one worldview with another or switch between them on demand.[16]

If Smith is right, then the adult budget constraint will look something like that of *aa* in figure 5. This suggests that languages that adults learn in which to conduct business will be richer in vocabulary than inflections.[17] Of course, lan-

---

12. R. M. W. Dixon (1989, 77) reports that Dyirbal has four genders: masculine, feminine, neuter, and edible. Pinker (1994, 127) gives other wonderful examples.

13. According to Clyde Kluchkhohn and Martha Leighton (1956, 194): "Aspect defines the geometrical character of an event, stating its definability with regard to line and point rather than its position in an absolute time scale or in time as broken up by the moving present of the speaker. . . . Thus, the momentaneous aspect in Navaho means that action is thought of as beginning and ending within an instant, while the continuative suggests that action lasts. Inceptive, cessative, durative, imperfective, and semelfactive, are some of the other aspects in Navaho—with a different paradigm of every verb stem for each."

14. Dixon (1989, 103) describes the problem: "Just asking from English may reveal similarities and likenesses to English patterns, but it is unlikely to uncover things in a language which *do not occur* in English—for example, the complex set of forms for uphill, downhill, upriver, downriver and across the river."

15. Dixon (ibid., 132–35) reports that gendering in Jirrbal encodes creation beliefs.

16. Kluchkhohn and Leighton (1956, 184) suggest that "Every language is a different system of categorizing and interpreting experience. This system is the more insidious and pervasive because native speakers are so unconscious of it as a system, because to them it is part of the very nature of things, remaining always in the class of background phenomena. . . . They take such ways of thought as much for granted as the air they breathe, and unconsciously assume that all human beings in their right minds think the same way."

17. "The remarkable freedom of English construction is not the least cause of the readiness of foreigners to use it among themselves, in preference to their own less analytical tongues" (Ogden 1935, 108).

guages such as these have been studied by twentieth-century linguists: they are called pidgins.[18] *Pidgin* is supposed to be based on the Chinese pidgin English word for *business*.[19] When children grow up in this language, a regular grammar is generated and the language becomes a Creole (Pinker 1994, 33). Creoles are rich in vocabulary but poor in inflections. We can look at such languages as a way of turning high-dimensionality optimization problems into a sequence of low-dimensionality optimization problems. In a dynamic programming context, Richard Bellman (1957, ix) called such transformations attempts to avoid the "curse of dimensionality."

Language Death

As transportation costs fall, of course, there will be more cross-language trading. In the index to their popular book, *Story of English*, Robert McCrum et al. (1986) have more than two-dozen page references to English pidgin to make their case that people are increasingly trading in English-influenced pidgins. What happens to the native language when economic activity moves elsewhere?

Linguists report that somewhere between 10 and 50 percent of the world's languages are dying. One rational choice element in language choice is obvious; as the costs of moving labor falls, parents discover that their children can obtain higher wages in a world language than in their own. But there is something nonobvious about the grammatical trajectory in language death: dying languages become pidginized.[20]

Can our account of Smith's model explain this? Trivially, it predicts that when time is withdrawn from language learning the amount of language learned decreases. When parents decide to move their children into a world language, they do so by talking to them in the world language even if they do not have native competence in it.[21] The children's competence in their parents' language falls; words drop out, and the grammar shifts. To keep with the definition of a language community populated with homogeneous speakers,

---

18. Lingua franca is a pidgin that Smith might have known about (Whinnom 1977).

19. "Many scholars believe that the word *pidgin* was first used for Chinese pidgin English (in which *pidgin* is the word for "business") and was later generalized to mean any language of this type" (DeCamp 1977, 6). According to Robert Hall (1966, xiv): "[O]nly a few hours' trading is necessary for the establishment of a rudimentary pidgin, and a few months or years suffice for the pidgin to assume settled form."

20. Peter Mühlhäusler (1986, 89) observes that "The grammar of a dying language . . . can in many ways be regarded as the mirror image of the grammatical enrichment processes occurring in creolization or pidgin development in expanded pidgins." Lyle Campbell and Martha Muntzel (1989, 191) agree that "Language death may be accompanied by some degree of morphological reduction. . . . While we have several examples in our data, since this is reasonably well established . . . we present only two examples here."

21. Ekkehart Malotki (1983, 622) reports that "For some reason the parents of these children, although perfectly versed in their vernacular, prefer to communicate with their children in English."

students of language death have coined the terms *semispeakers* and *imperfect speakers* to save the phenomenon from being ruled out of court by definition.[22] There is a regular age-competence profile that characterizes dying languages: the oldest speakers—the ones with the most time in the language—speak the most fluently.[23] For instance, the unique mother-in-law language that Dixon documented in Australian languages was only recovered in the memories of the oldest speakers (1989, 144–45, 168). Everyone else had forgotten it.

Conclusion

Smith's ideas about language choice are consistent with twentieth-century research on pidgin languages. As has been demonstrated, his ideas can be immediately developed to explain the grammatical trajectory of languages as they die, showing the relationship between a pidgin language and that spoken by semispeakers. How naturally and easily these results follow from rational choice considerations argues for taking seriously a wide-ranging rational choice linguistics.

Interesting questions will present themselves in this endeavor. Can we estimate the wage premium elasticity of moving children to a world language? Does the linguistic distance—French is closer to English than Navajo is— matter in the decision to move children from one language to another? Can we make operational the idea that languages are like currency areas?[24] Can one successfully rent seek by impairing movement from one language to another? Can we explain the role of "language mavins"? If every person within a language community is equally fluent, then this activity seems to make no sense (Pinker 1994). If fluency varies with income and education, and income varies with fluency, is there not a possible economic explanation?

---

22. As Nancy Dorian (1981, 115) puts it, "As the language dies, a group of imperfect speakers characteristically appears who have not had sufficiently intensive exposure to the home language, or who have been much more intensively exposed to some other language; and if they continue to use the home language at all, they use it in a form which is markedly different from the fluent-speaker norm."

23. Malotki (1983, 616) found this to be true in his study of the Hopi perception of time: "The present study of Hopi time was accomplished with knowledgeable consultants from an age bracket of approximately forty years and up. Great portions of it could not have been accomplished, however, with informants that are now between twenty and thirty years old. While members from this age group may theoretically still be classified as fluent speakers, they have lost the vital umbilical connection to their linguistic heritage, in particular the traditional knowledge lodged in older Hopi."

24. This analogy was suggested to me by Thomas Borcherding.

Bishop Berkeley Exorcises
the Infinite

It all began simply enough when Molyneux asked the wonderful question whether a person born blind, now able to see, would recognize by sight what he or she knew by touch (Davis 1960). After George Berkeley elaborated an answer, that we learn to perceive by means of heuristics, the foundations of contemporary mathematics were in ruins. Contemporary mathematicians waved their hands and changed the subject.[1] Berkeley's answer received a much more positive response from economists. Adam Smith, in particular, seized upon Berkeley's doctrine that we learn to perceive distance to build an elaborate system in which one learns to perceive one's self-interest.[2] Perhaps because older histories of mathematics are a positive hindrance in helping us understand the importance of Berkeley's argument against infinitesimals,[3] its consequences for *economics* have passed unnoticed. If infinitesimal numbers are ruled

---

1. The mathematically decisive event that changed the situation and let historians appreciate the past was Abraham Robinson's development of nonstandard analysis. "The vigorous attack directed by Berkeley against the foundations of the Calculus in the forms then proposed is, in the first place, a brilliant exposure of their logical inconsistencies. But in criticizing infinitesimals of all kinds, English or continental, Berkeley also quotes with approval a passage in which Locke rejects the actual infinite. . . . It is in fact not surprising that a philosopher in whose system perception plays the central role, should have been unwilling to accept infinitary entities" (Robinson 1974, 280–81). Robinson's appreciation of Berkeley has yet to be fully taken into account by philosophers. For example, Gabriel Moked's discussion of Berkeley's doctrine of strict finitism might have considered Berkeley's claim that mathematics can do without infinitesimals to ask what sort of mathematics results (1988).

2. Smith has been criticized by Salim Rashid—and not without evidence—for insufficient acknowledgment of his intellectual debts (1998). Smith's debt to Berkeley is paid with the customary coin of scholarship (*Essays*, 148): "Dr. Berkeley, in his New Theory of Vision, one of the finest examples of philosophical analysis that is to be found, either in our own, or in any other language, has explained, so very distinctly, the nature of the objects of Sight. . . . Whatever I shall say upon it, if not directly borrowed from him, has at least been suggested by what he has already said."

3. "The last chapter [of *Non-standard Analysis*] contains a review of certain stages in the history of the Differential and Integral Calculus that had to do with the theory of infinitesimals. The fact that the more recent writers in this field were convinced that no such theory can be developed effectively, colored their historical judgment. Thus, a revision has now become necessary" (Robinson 1974, 4).

out, who cares? But we wish to maintain an algebra with division, so we rule out infinite numbers, which were conventionally employed to represent the cost of Hell and the benefit of Heaven. *This* implication of Berkeley's argument has a dramatic implication for our understanding of the basis of the anti-slavery coalition, which included both utilitarians who believed in Heaven and Hell and those who did not.

The social doctrine set forth by John Locke, outside the *Two Treatises,* depends critically upon individual belief about possible states of infinite pain or pleasure. The critical reason for Locke's refusal to tolerate atheism is his claim that without belief in the infinite bliss of Heaven, foregone by a criminal, there is no reason to think a calculating atheist will avoid crime (Levy 1982b, 1992). In Locke's formulation, there can be no basis of agreement between believers and unbelievers.

In the discussion of religion by David Hume and Smith, questions of the substance of belief—the infinite worth of Heaven—have largely vanished. What happened between Locke and Hume-Smith? One answer is Pierre Bayle and Bernard Mandeville (Levy 1992). Berkeley's doctrine that only the finite is perceived is, I think, a better answer. Out of sight, out of mind.

I propose to give a close look at the content and consequences of Bishop Berkeley's once famous *Towards a New Theory of Vision.* While there are other aspects of Berkeley's work that attract attention from historians of economics (Levy 1982a; Rashid 1990), I claimed in chapter 9 that Berkeley's insight into human perception in *Theory of Vision* is central to Adam Smith's attempt to found economic behavior on the self-awareness of systematic illusion. There is no doubt that Smith finds much of human behavior characterized by illusion. The difficulty economists have with these arguments arises, or so it seems to me, from a modern unwillingness to believe that illusion can be systematic.

There are four pieces to my argument. First, we consider Berkeley's statement of what we shall call his doctrine of strict finitism in perception.[4] Berkeley puts forward two postulates: (1) that there exists some minimum perceptible quantity and (2) that distance is not perceived directly but by experience. Second, we define strict finitism and demonstrate that it translates into the claim that perception is fuzzy in a technical sense. If Berkeleyan perception is fuzzy, then some modern criticism of Berkeley's strict finitism is based upon a simple misunderstanding of the properties of fuzzy relations. This is quite easy to set right. Getting right the doctrine of those who implicitly take perception to be fuzzy (Adam Smith is my prime candidate) will be much harder. Third,

---

4. I hope this does not clash with established usage. There are two possibilities of confusion of which I am aware. Wittgenstein's doctrine in *Tractatus* sometimes goes by this name. For example, his number theory is criticized by Russell (1971, xx) on this ground. Finitary methods are employed in mathematics when infinity is accepted only as a potential (Kleene 1971, 62–63).

we reconsider Berkeley's dispute with Mandeville on the role of infinite gain in choice. Here, we find Mandeville putting forward the Berkeleyan position that if infinite amounts mattered people would not behave as they do. Berkeley's position against Mandeville, however, seems to depend upon the supposition that infinite distance is sensible.[5] Earlier, however, the position that Mandeville argued for was defended by Berkeley.

Fourth, we ask why all this is not well known. The debate between Berkeley and Mandeville has been well studied, as has been the link between Berkeley and the Scots. In fact, our work focuses on one aspect of Berkeley's work that leads to his challenge of the contemporary foundations of the calculus. If sense is a matter of perception and infinitesimals cannot be perceived, then they are quite literally nonsense. Armed with this insight, Berkeley refuted contemporary mathematics. Nevertheless, the calculus was too valuable to give up. After, but only after, the infinitesimal calculus had been put on secure foundations, it was costless for mathematicians to acknowledge that Berkeley's criticism was correct. By delaying this acknowledgment, they gave up little except the reputation of those long dead. Before the repairs were made, they would have had to give up calculus to maintain consistency.[6] The unfortunate consequence is that the formal aspects of Berkeley's insight about perception have been buried. There is a wonderful irony in the fact that the mathematical work of a founding father of pragmatism can be pointed to as an exemplar of deflection from falsification allowed in the modern pragmatic tradition that mixes together elements of desire and inference.[7]

I suspect that only after the high seriousness of Berkeley's destructive arguments are appreciated will scholars be willing to make the effort to struggle

---

5. Berkeley's difficulties with maintaining consistency between the strict finitism of his mathematics and the free and easy use of infinities in Christian doctrine has been noted before (Belfrage 1987, 51–55). As far as I know, this difficulty has not been seen in Berkeley's controversy with Mandeville, as an example of such blindness (Levy 1982b).

6. In wonderful confirmation of the fact that after revolutions textbooks acquire new heroes (Kuhn 1962, 137), Berkeley has made his appearance in a calculus text! "All three approaches had serious inconsistencies which were criticized most effectively by Bishop Berkeley in 1734. However, a precise treatment of the calculus was beyond the state of the art at the time, and the intuitive descriptions . . . of the derivative competed with each other for the next two hundred years" (Keisler 1976, 874).

7. C. S. Peirce (1955, 269): "Any philosophical doctrine that should be completely new could hardly fail to prove completely false; but the rivulets at the head of the river of pragmatism are easily traced back to almost any desired antiquity. Socrates bathed in these waters. Aristotle rejoices when he can find them. They run, where least one would suspect them, beneath the dry rubbish-heaps of Spinoza. Those clean definitions that strew the pages of the *Essay concerning Humane Understanding* (I refuse to reform the spelling) had been washed out in the same pure spring. It was this medium, and not tar-water, that gave health and strength to Berkeley's earlier works, his *Theory of Vision* and what remains of his *Principles*."

with the positive consequences of his doctrine. It is a remarkable coincidence that both nonstandard analysis and fuzzy set theory are products of the 1960s.[8] Nonstandard analysis has knocked down the technical barriers to appreciating the destructive force of Berkeley's doctrine; fuzzy set theory may open the technical door to appreciating his positive doctrine.

The Mediation of Mathematical Concepts by Perception

Pragmatism is the philosophical doctrine holding that desire influences the ways we think of and use language.[9] Berkeley's avowed intention is to place the semiotics of vision upon a pragmatic foundation.[10] To this end, he asks how the mathematical language of distance is mediated by perception.

The first of Berkeley's principles is that distance is not perceived directly; we learn to interpret sense data in terms of size and distance. Thus,

> it is plain that distance is in its own nature imperceptible, and yet it is per-
> ceived by sight. It remains, therefore, that it be brought into view by means
> of some other idea that is itself immediately perceived in the act of vision.
> (1975, 10)

Berkeley's account is that the fuzziness of an object—fuzzy in a nontechnical sense—is interpreted as a key to its distance:[11]

> [A]n object placed at a certain distance from the eye, to which the breadth
> of the pupil bears a considerable proportion, being made to approach, is
> seen more confusedly: and the nearer it is brought the more confused

---

8. A useful bibliography of work in fuzzy set theory is found in Klir and Folger 1988.

9. "Let us therefore try to get an idea of a human logic which shall not attempt to be reducible to formal logic. Logic, we may agree, is concerned not with what men actually believe, but what they ought to believe, or what it would be reasonable to believe. . . . [T]he highest ideal would be always to have a true opinion and be certain of it; but this ideal is more suited to God than to man. We have therefore to consider the human mind and what is the most we can ask of it. The human mind works essentially according to general rules or habits; . . . We can therefore state the problem of the ideal as 'What habits in a general sense would it be best for the human mind to have? This is a kind of pragmatism: we judge mental habits by whether they work, i.e. whether the opinions they lead to are for the most part true, or more often true than those which alternative habits would lead to. Induction is such a useful habit, and so to adopt it is reasonable. All that philosophy can do is to analyse it, determine the degree of its utility, and find on what characteristics of nature this depends" (Ramsey 1990, 89–90, 93–94).

10. "Upon the whole, I think we may fairly conclude that the proper objects of vision constitute a universal language of the Author of Nature, whereby we are instructed how to regulate our actions in order to attain those things that are necessary to the preservation and well-being of our bodies, as also to avoid whatever may be hurtful and destructive of them" (Berkeley 1975, 51–52).

11. The implication here is that vision in a world without dust, for example, on the space shuttle, would require retraining since the "further is fuzzier" rule would not hold.

> appearance it makes. And this being found constantly to be so, there
> ariseth in the mind an habitual connexion between the several degrees of
> confusion and distance; the greater confusion still implying the lesser dis-
> tance, and the lesser confusion the greater distance of the object. (12)

Vision gives signals that must be interpreted. Berkeley sketches how the semiotics of morals would work:

> Nor doth it avail to say there is not any necessary connexion between con-
> fused vision and distance, great or small. For I ask any man what necessary
> connexion he sees between the redness of a blush and shame? And yet no
> sooner shall he behold that colour to arise in the face of another, but it
> brings into his mind the idea of that passion which hath been observed to
> accompany it. (12)

Berkeley claims that our perception of magnitude and distance are mixed:

> I have now done with distance, and proceed to shew how it is that we per-
> ceive by sight the magnitude of objects. It is the opinion of some that we
> do it by angles, or by angles in conjunction with distance: but neither
> angles nor distance being perceivable by sight, and the things we see being
> in truth at no distance from us, it follows that as we have shewn lines and
> angles not to be the medium the mind makes use of in appending the
> apparent place, so neither are they the medium whereby it apprehends the
> apparent magnitude of objects.
>
> It is well known that the same extension at a near distance shall subtend
> a greater angle, and at a further distance a lesser angle. And by this princi-
> ple (we are told) the mind estimates the magnitude of an object, compar-
> ing the angle under which it is seen with its distance, and thence inferring
> the magnitude thereof. What inclines men to this mistake . . . is that the
> same perceptions or ideas which suggest distance do also suggest magni-
> tude. But if we examine it we shall find they suggest the latter as immedi-
> ate as the former. (22–23)

To identify an object we must separate distance and magnitude. It is in this
context that Berkeley claims that there is a minimum visible object:

> It hath been shewn there are two sorts of objects apprehended by sight;
> each whereof hath its distinct magnitude, or extension. The one, property
> tangible, i.e. to be perceived and measured by touch, and not immediately
> falling under the sense of seeing: the other, properly and immediately visi-
> ble, by mediation of which the former is brought into view. Each of these

magnitudes are greater or lesser, according as they contain in them more or fewer points, they being made up of points of minimums. For, whatever may be said of extension in abstract, it is certain sensible extension is not infinitely divisible. There is a *Minimum Tangible* and a *Minimum Visible*, beyond which sense cannot perceive. This everyone's experience will inform him. (Berkeley 1975, 23)

Berkeley often refers to this minimum as a "mite," abbreviated in his *Philosophical Commentaries* as "**M**."[12]

The hypothesis that our perception is bounded at some finite **M** is completely innocuous if it is independent of distance. If we perceive the same **M** at a distance of one meter, as we do between here and the moons of Jupiter, we have gutted the assumption of any substance. Berkeley knows this and blocks it with the following claim:

Now for any object to contain several distinct visible parts, and at the same time be a *minimum visible,* is a manifest contradiction.

Of these visible points we see at all times an equal number. It is every whit as great when our view is contracted and bounded by near objects as when it is extended to larger and remoter. For it being impossible that one *minimum visible* should observe or keep out of sight more than one other, it is a plain consequence that when my view is on all sides bounded by the walls of my study, I see just as many visible points as I could, in case that the removal of the study-walls and all other obstructions, I had a full prospect of the circumjacent fields, mountains, sea, and open firmament: for so long as I am shut up within the walls, by their interposition every point of the external objects is covered from my view: but each point that is seen being able to cover to exclude from sight one only other corresponding point, it follows that whilst my sight is confined to those narrow walls I see as many points, or *minima visibilia,* as I should were those walls away, by looking on all the external objects whose prospect is intercepted by them. (Berkeley 1975, 33)

This argument can be expressed geometrically. Suppose that at some unit of distance along the horizontal, Δ, the minimum perceptible magnitude along the vertical is **M**. Berkeley argues that if at some status quo **M** can block some X from view, X must be a minimum visible too. Assuming linearity at $1,000\Delta$

---

12. Berkeley's mathematical conjecture, soon to be considered in more detail, is that **M** could serve to refound calculus (1975, 281 [B333]): "Newton's fluxions needless, any thing below an **M**. might serve for Leibnitz's Differential Calculus." This passage is not considered by Moked (1988) in his list of *Philosophical Commentary* passages that deal with minima.

the minimum visible is 1,000**M**. We can solve for the angle Θ as the minimum angle of perception; Θ is simply arctan **M**/Δ.

If visual sense is based on angles, then the problem for the perceiving subject is to distinguish between distance and size. In the term that econometricians coined, this is the *classical identification problem*. We have one sense datum, Θ, and two unknowns, size and distance. Looking at the problem this way, it is clear why touch is important for Berkeley's argument. Touch gives another piece of information to help with the object's identification. With touch, there are two pieces of sense data and two unknowns. A problem with two observations and two unknowns is a good deal more promising than a problem with one observation and two unknowns.

Outside the range of touch, then what? We learn to infer that the moon is farther away than a cloud because a cloud can cover the moon. Ideas allow us to interpret perception. This is why, in my interpretation, Smith's theory of conduct is intertwined with ideas. Rules, heuristics, guide inferences. This interpretation of Berkeley's argument demonstrates why Samuel Bailey's objections did not sway Berkeley's admirers. J. S. Mill and James Ferrier's defense of Berkeley's doctrine point to the identification problem.[13]

Fuzzy Perception

Berkeley's account concerns vision over physical distance. As we have seen, Smith generalizes this principle in his spectator theory of morality. If we cannot judge distance over material income perfectly, then what reason do we have to believe that we can pursue our material self-interest correctly? A doctrine of imperfect perception makes it easier to appreciate why individuals might prefer constraining rules of conduct to choice guided purely by perception of self-interest. The rules we have encountered above are the Golden Rule of Christianity and the Greatest Happiness Principle of Utilitarianism. When percep-

---

13. "[I]f a child fancies the moon to be no larger than a cheese, it is because he forgets that it is farther off, and draws from the visual appearance an inference which would be well grounded if the moon and the cheese were really at an equal distance from him" (Mill 1842, 321). Ferrier (1988, 839) works through the identification problem, pointing out the problem of distinguishing size and distance. One part of Bailey's objection to Berkeley is strange because it seems to rest on a property of Berkeley's model that Berkeley nowhere defends: "Berkeley's theory takes for granted, that when we see objects at various distances, those distances, or in other words, the intervening tangible spaces between us and the objects, are suggested to the mind" (1988, 84–85).

Mill is also puzzled, observing that "we see bodies and their distances by precisely the same mechanism. We see two stars, if they are imaged on the retina, and not otherwise; we see the interval between those stars if there is an interval on the retina between two images, and if there is no such interval we see it not. . . . Surely this argument does not depend upon an implied assumption that the intervals between objects are physical lines joining them." (1843, 492).

tion fails, rules may serve as substitutes (Levy 1992). To this end, we consider, somewhat seriously, what an individual believes about distance.

Following Smith's lead, we consider not only distance over space but distance over commodities. In the standard (sharp) account of choice, in a one-commodity world, preferences over commodity space flow automatically from commodity space itself since for any bundles a, b, $c \in R^1$ if $a > b$ then $P(a,b)$ holds and conversely.[14] In this context, indifference in choice between a and b, $I(a,b)$, follows from equality of a and b. The standard (sharp) axioms of transitivity of P and I and completeness over R^N with respect to P and I are unnecessary in R^1 since they follow from the familiar facts about the relations "greater than" and "equal." Our modification is to suggest that preferences over b and a, $P(b,a)$, follow from the perception over commodity space rather than from commodity space itself. To this end, we introduce the relation $BB(b,a|sq)$ to signify the belief, at the status quo, that is at sq, b is greater than a.

We write down the details of BB, where as far as possible the argument shall proceed by a reinterpretation of standard assumptions. For instance, we know in the standard account for all $b \in R^1$ there exists a b-roof and b-floor, which we write as $\bar{b}$ and $\underline{b}$ which are respectively the greatest lower bound of all elements of R^1 perceived to be strictly larger than b and the least upper bound of all elements of R^1 perceived to be strictly less than b. These names are imported from computer science where considerations of finite precision of computations are paramount (Iverson 1962, 12). In standard (sharp) consumer theory, we can easily prove that both $\bar{b}$ and $\underline{b}$ exist and are equal to b. Where our account shall diverge from the standard one is the specification that the difference between $\bar{b}$ and $\underline{b}$ is noninfinitesimal.

It will be quite convenient to take the truth value of BB to be a function of a, b, and sq. The way this can be expressed in the standard (sharp) account is $BB(a,b|sq)$ holds (is true or equals 1) if and only if $a > b$, regardless of the state of sq.

$BB(a,b|sq) = 0$ if $a \le b$

$BB(a,b|sq) = 1$ if $a > b$, $\forall \ sq \in R^1$

Using 1 and 0 as marks of truth and falsity is convenient. Binary theory conditions are indicated by allowing the set of truth values to describe BB to be $\{0,1\}$.

What is required of $BB(a,b|sq)$ is the following:

Axiom 1. $BB(a,b|sq) = \Phi \in [0,1] \ \forall \ a, b, sq \in R^1$

---

14. The relational notation employed follows that of Robinson 1974.

This formulation allows for the possibility that truth values are fuzzy, that is, they take on values outside {0,1} (Kaufmann 1975). The case of sharp truth values is consistent with axiom 1 because {0,1} is a special case of [0,1].

These fuzzy truth values can be given an objective probabilistic interpretation. We could interpret the claim that $BB(a,b|sq)$ has a truth value Φ as the claim that standing from sq we would believe a to be bigger than b with relative frequency Φ. Thus, fuzziness is akin to indifference in that if given a choice between a and b sometimes one picks a and sometimes one picks b. Allowing indifference to range between 0 and 1 obviates any requirement that observed relative frequency of choice between a and b be only zero, 100, or 50 percent (fig. 6).

Figure 6 gives a picture of the perception from the status quo sq of b. Any amount at or above $\bar{b}$ is perceived clearly to be bigger than b; any amount at or below $\underline{b}$ is perceived to be smaller than b. Inside the open interval $(\underline{b}, \bar{b})$ perception is fuzzy; thus, Φ can be anywhere on the [0,1] interval. If perceptions were sharp, the judgment BB would jump from a Φ of 0 to one of 1 at b, as indicated by the dotted line.

We assume the existence of these roof and floor bounds:

Axiom 2. $BB(a,b|sq) = 0$ if $a \leq \underline{b}$

$BB(a,b|sq) = 1$ if $a > \bar{b} \; \exists \; \underline{b}, \bar{b} \in R^1 \; \forall \; a, b, sq \in R^1.$

If $\bar{b}$ and $\underline{b}$ are both b, then axiom 2 collapses to the sharp version. In terms of the relation BB, we can then define the principle of strict finitism.

Strict finitism requires the following: (1) there exists some positive finite **M** such that if something less than **M** is added (or subtracted) from any point $a \in R^1$ relative to a fixed b and a status quo sq for any individual, *no one* can perceive the difference; and (2) a BB relation with a truth value of one can be perceived by an outside observer to differ from a relation with a truth value of zero.

Theorem. Strict finitism implies that the relation BB takes on fuzzy truth values.

Proof. Without loss of generality, we take Φ to be a function of a variable a with respect to fixed b and sq. Assume the contrary of what is to be proved, that truth values of BB are restricted to {0,1}. Then, we can find some a where the addition of some amount smaller than **M** would change $\Phi(a)$ from zero to one. The existence of this a is guaranteed by the suppositions (1) that truth values are dichotomous and (2) that at some point more will be perceived to differ from some fixed lesser point. The outside observer can detect a change in $\Phi(a)$ from zero to one. Thus, an imperceptible change in a has a perceptible consequence: the change in Φ from zero to one. This contradicts strict finitism. Thus, the change in $\Phi(a)$ must itself be imperceptible and be smaller than the

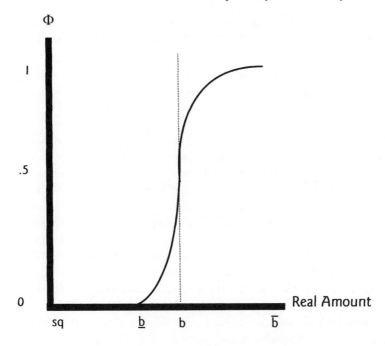

Fig. 6.   Believed bigger than *b* at *sq*

change from zero to one. This establishes that $\Phi(a)$ takes on fuzzy truth values.

Given that *BB* has fuzzy truth values, or is a fuzzy relation, we can immediately free Berkeley's construction from recent charges of inconsistency. One defining feature of fuzzy relations is that they are not transitive. That is to say, consider some heap of coffee composed of a very large number of very small grains. Consider the no discernible difference relation in perception and let us suppose that no one grain makes a difference. Step by step, one removes grains. Obviously, after most of the heap is removed one can distinguish the starting point the case of the almost removed heap *even though* at no point in the procedure could one distinguish a heap with one grain more or less. Thus, the no discernible difference in perception relation is not transitive. It is indeed part of the attraction of fuzzy mathematics to deal with the discomfort first expressed by Henri Poincaré that only in mathematics is equality transitive.

If Berkeley is describing fuzzy perceptions, then it is quite beside the point

---

15. Armstrong (1960, 43) describes "difficulties" with the doctrine of the minimum perceptible: "We may put a dilemma: either these minima have an extension ('the smallest'), or they do not. If they *do* have an extension, it is not difficult to show that they will have parts, that is, they will

to assume a perception relation that is transitive. The mathematical relations that are required to describe Berkeley's minimum of perception will not be transitive.[15]

To make a link between perception and choice, one simply asserts

Axiom 3. $P(a,b|sq) = BB(a,b|sq) \ \forall \ a, \ b, \ sq \in R^1$

This is the fuzzy equivalent of more is preferred to less. It only requires that what is perceived to be more is preferred to what is perceived to be less.

To give the model some structure, we can require that the amount of the perception band, $\bar{b} - \underline{b}$, is a function of the distance between b and the status quo, sq, $d(b,sq)$. Thus, as $d(b,sq)$ increases, $\bar{b} - \underline{b}$ increases. Rule-directed perception will be important for a utilitarian if learning can change the perception band $\bar{b} - \underline{b}$ for a constant sq. The utilitarians we have encountered held the equivalence of the Great Happiness Principle and the Golden Rule.

The utilitarians we have encountered had different views on Heaven and Hell. Suppose that these states have infinite consequences. We consider now how Berkeley's strict finitism purged social analysis of infinites and thus how post-Berkeley Christians would not expect belief in Heaven and Hell to be a decisive explanatory variable in one's behavior.

The vast amount of research on the economics and probability of gambling behavior has been motivated by the observed fact that people do not seem to act to maximize the expected value of a gamble. It is common knowledge that vast numbers of lottery tickets are sold for considerably more than their expected value. Paying a dollar for a one in a million chance to win $200,000 obviously cannot be an instance in which one maximizes the expected value of the action. The expected value of not playing the game ($1.00) is higher than the expected value of playing ($0.20).

To see at a glance how fuzzy perceptions make the assertion that we cannot use expected value considerations to explain gambling less obvious, let us define a *perceived number* $\tilde{b}$ relative to sq as some number selected from the interval $\bar{b} - \underline{b}$. Different people will surely have different perceived numbers. In the case in point, how do we know that for someone with a status quo considerably below $200,000 the vast sum of $1 million is not in fact contained within the perception band of $200,000? If it is, then perhaps the individual gambler is maximizing the *perceived* expected value.[16]

---

not be minima. This is easily seen if we consider three adjoining minima, say three in a straight line. By hypothesis, the boundary of the first and the second is separated from the boundary of the second and the third, that is the second minimum has distinguishable boundaries, which implies that after all it *does* have parts." This argument is accepted by Stack (1970, 40–41).

16. An account of gambling as exchange—the *actor* has sharp perception of income but the *spectators* have fuzzy perception over income (and thus approbation from status)—is given in Levy 1999a.

The gambling problem we encounter—gambles with infinite stakes—is known by humanists as Pascal's wager but by economists as the St. Petersburg paradox, although Savage (1972) links gambles with infinity to Pascal. The traditional approach to resolving the St. Petersburg paradox is to bound the utility function, that is, some finite level of income; our axioms deny that vastly more is preferred to less (Samuelson 1977). Our method of dealing with infinity is rather different in spirit. Instead of denying satiation, we require that distant levels of income are heavily depreciated from every status quo. As the status quo changes, the consumer presumably learns to adjust. Instead of assuming satiation, this fuzzy perception formulation requires only a weak type of algebraic closure of the perceived numbers in our theory in conjunction with the principle that there are no perceived infinitesimals.

Start with any two perceived numbers, $\tilde{b}$ and $\tilde{c}$. Suppose they are perceived to be distinct, for example, $(\underline{b}, \bar{b}) \cap (\underline{c}, \bar{c}) = \varnothing$. Let $\tilde{c} > \tilde{b}$ with $\tilde{b}$ finite. If we wish to allow an algebra in which we can prove that $1 > \tilde{b}/\tilde{c}$, that is, one in which we allow division over the *perceived* numbers, then we know that $\tilde{c}$ cannot be infinite. Assume that it is; thus, the resulting $\tilde{b}/\tilde{c}$ is infinitesimal. But this contradicts the supposition that we cannot perceive infinitesimals. Thus, $\tilde{c}$ cannot be an infinite number.

Algebraic closure might be thought of as an odd requirement. Be that as it may, when we assume that perception is perfect over the real line of commodity space, we automatically assume that perception is closed over algebraic operations over the real numbers.

Of course, Berkeley knew this. Here are some passages from *Philosophical Commentary:*

> An idea cannot exist unperceiv'd. (1975, 285 [B377])

> Axiom. No reasoning about things whereof we have no idea. Therefore no reasoning about Infinitesimals. (283 [B354])

> We cannot imagine a line or space infinitely great therefore absurd to talk or make propositions about it. (289 [A417])

Mandeville as a Follower of Berkeley

Mandeville's teaching can be seen as a response to some version of Pascal's wager. If people believed what they said about Heaven and Hell, Mandeville asserts, they would not behave the way they do. What they say is wrapped up in notions of infinite gain and infinite loss (Levy 1992).

Here is Pascal's memorable statement of the principle at issue:

A game is being played at the extremity of this infinite distance where heads or tails will turn up. What will you wager? According to reason, you can do neither the one thing nor the other; according to reason, you can defend neither of the propositions.

Do not then reprove for error those who have made a choice; for you know nothing about it. "No, but I blame them for having made, not this choice, but a choice; for again both he who chooses heads and he who chooses tails are equally at fault, they are both in the wrong. The true course is not to wager at all."

Yes; but you must wager. It is not optional. . . . Your reason is no more shocked in choosing one rather than the other, since you must of necessity choose. This is one point settled. But your happiness? Let us weigh the gain and the loss in wagering that God is. . . . And thus, when one is forced to play, he must renounce reason to preserve his life, rather than risk it for infinite gain, as likely to happen as the loss of nothingness. (1958, 66–67)

To consider Pascal's wager, we require a 2 × 2 matrix that gives us our choice. If we act in accord with God's will, we have a singularly dull existence now, say, receiving zero in material income, but we receive an infinite H later. If we act in accord with what is reported as God's will, but He does not exist, we get zero. If we act contrary to God's will, and He does not really exist, we have a good time, getting positive, albeit finite, material income x. But if God does exist then we must balance the current x with infinite negative $-H$. Matrix 4 gives our choice. From which column do we wish to choose?

MATRIX 4. Pascal's wager		
	Act as if God Exists	Act as if God does not exist
In Fact, God Exists	H	$-H + x$
In Fact, God Does Not Exist	0	x

Let us call the probability that God actually exists p. As long as we block infinitesimal probabilities, the strategy of acting as if God exists generates a higher expected value than acting as if God does not exist. That is, for any noninfinitesimal probability p, $0 < p < 1$ the expected value of the game with the universe is

$$p H + (1 - p) 0 > [p(-H + x) + (1 - p)x] \tag{1}$$

This is so because the expression to the left of the inequality is a positive infinite number and one to the right of the inequality is a negative infinite. Needless to say, the argument can be weakened by removing either H or $-H$. We would then compare an infinite with a real number that also can be signed directly. The argument goes through as Pascal claims. The size of x is quite irrelevant; the proof goes through for any finite x. Here is Pascal's statement:

> *The end of this discourse.*—Now, what harm will befall you in taking this side? You will be faithful, honest, humble, grateful, generous, a sincere friend, truthful. Certainly you will not have those poisonous pleasures, glory and luxury; but will you not have others? I will tell you that you will thereby gain in this life, and that, at each step you take on this road, you will see so great certainty of gain, so much nothingness in what you risk, that you will at last recognise that you have wagered for something certain and infinite, for which you have given nothing. (1958, 68)

Now, suppose that instead of dealing with Heaven and Hell directly we work with perceptions of Heaven and Hell. We replace H with $\tilde{H}$ and $-H$ with $-\tilde{H}$ and since these perceptions are finite, the game becomes finite and Pascal's argument fails as an a priori principle. An easy way to see how the division operates is to consider equation 1 in the case without Hell. Thus, let $-\tilde{H} = 0$. Thus, the right-hand side (eq. 1) is x and the left-hand side is $p\tilde{H}$. Divide both sides by $p\tilde{H}$. If $p\tilde{H}$ is infinite, then we generate the forbidden infinitesimal.

What the issue will hinge upon is the details of $\tilde{H}$ and $-\tilde{H}$, the details of the utility function, the actual probabilities, and so on.

Computing Correctly?

Berkeley's response to Mandeville is based on the notion that free thinkers do not compute correctly, just as the response to his free thinking in mathematics is precisely that free thinkers cannot compute correctly.

> *EUPH.* But *Socrates*, who was no Country Parson, suspected your Men of pleasure were such through ignorance.
>
> *LYS.* Ignorance of what?
>
> *EUPH.* Of the art of computing. It was his opinion that Rakes cannot reckon. And that for want of this skill they make wrong judgments about pleasure, on the right choice of which their happiness depends. . . . To make a right computation, shou'd you not consider all the faculties and all the kinds of Pleasure, taking into your account the future as well as the present, and rating them all according to their true value?
>
> *CRI.* The *Epicureans* themselves allowed, that Pleasure which procures a greater Pain, or hinders a greater Pleasure, shou'd be regarded as a Pain; and, that Pain which procures a greater Pleasure, or prevents a greater Pain, is to be accounted a Pleasure. In order therefore to make a true estimate of Pleasure, the great spring of action, and that from which whence the conduct of Life takes its bias, we ought to compute

> intellectual Pleasures and future Pleasures, as well as present and sen-
> sible: We ought to make allow in the valuation of each particular Plea-
> sure, for all the Pains and Evils, for all the Disgust, Remorse, and
> Shame that attend to it . . .
>
> EUPH. And all these points duly considered, will not *Socrates* seem to have
> had reason of his side, which he thought ignorance made Rakes, and
> particularly their being of what he calls the Science of more and less,
> greater and smaller, equality and comparison, that is to say of the art of
> Computing?
>
> LYS. All this discourse seems notional. For real abilities of every kind it is
> well known we have the brightest Men of the age among us. But all
> those who know the World do calculate that what you call a good
> Christian, who hath neither a larger Conscience, nor unprejudiced
> Mind, must be unfit for the affairs of it. Thus you see, while you com-
> pute your selves out of pleasure, other compute you out of business.
> What then are you good for with all computations?
>
> EUPH. I have all imaginable respect for the abilities of Free-thinkers. My
> only fear was, their parts might be too lively for such slow talents as
> Forecast and Computation, the gifts of ordinary Men. (1732, 1:
> 119–21)

Mandeville responded to Berkeley with a challenge about infinite gain and
infinite loss. If behavior tracked with what we said about infinite gains from
Heaven, here is what we would see:

> Since this worldly Greatness is not to be attain'd to without the Vices of
> Man, I will have Nothing to do with it; since it is impossible to serve God
> and Mammon, my Choice shall be soon made: No temporal Pleasure can
> be worth running the Risque of being eternally miserable; and, let who will
> labour to aggrandise the Nation, I will aim at higher Ends, and take Care
> of my own Soul.
>
> The Moment such a Thought enters into a Man's Head, all the Poison
> is taken away from the Book, and every Bee has lost his Sting.
>
> Those who should in Reality prefer Spirituals to Temporals, and be
> seen to make more Pains attain an everlasting Felicity, than they did for
> the Enjoyment of the fading Pleasures and transient Glorie of this Life,
> would not grudge to make some Abatements in the Ease, the Conve-
> niences, and the Comfort of it, or even to part with some of their Posses-
> sion upon Earth, to make sure of their Inheritance of the Kingdom of
> Heaven. Whatever Liking they might have to the curious Embellishments
> and elegant Inventions of the Voluptuous, they would refuse to purchase

them at the Hazard of Damnation. . . . No Book would be plainer or more intelligible to them than the Gospel; and without consulting either Fathers or Councils, they would be satisfied, that mortifying the Flesh never could signify to indulge every Appetite, not prohibited by an Earthly Legislator. (1953, 22–23)

Mandeville is appealing to a doctrine of strict finitism. Is this possible? Reading Berkeley and Mandeville on the same side of an issue is unusual. Is there evidence? Let us read what Berkeley wrote in his first sermon, "On Immortality":

Let us but look a little into matter of fact. how far I beseech you do we Xtians surpass ye old Heathen Romans in temperance & fortitude, in honour & integrity? are we less given to pride & avarice, strife & faction than our Pagan Ancestors? With us yt have immortality in view is not ye old doctrine of eat & drink for to morrow we die as much in vogue as ever? We inhabitants of Xtendom enlighten'd with ye light of ye Gospel, instructed by ye Son of God, are we such shining examples of peace and vertue to ye unconverted Gentile world? . . .

I come now to enquire into ye cause of this strange blindness & infatuation of Xtians. whence it is that immortality a happy immortality has so small influence . . . Wherein consists the wondrous mechanism of our passions wch are set a going by the small inconsiderable objects of sense whilst things of infinite weight & moment are altogether ineffectual. (1948–57, 7:10–11)[17]

One explanation is, of course, that the pleasures of Heaven are a great distance away (12–13).

The Pragmatic Response to Berkeley's Mathematical Free Thinking

We have seen how Berkeley offers a pragmatic account of the role of perception across distance. Chief among his premises is his insistence on the irrelevance of the unperceived. Hence, infinitesimals and their algebraic kin are strictly nonsense. Armed with such insight, Berkeley pointed out that at the heart of the calculus wishful thinking was being passed as theorem.

The lynchpin of the pragmatic philosophy of science is the Duhem-Quine thesis, which represents philosophers as rational choosers. All we need to

---

17. Berkeley (1948–57, 7:12–13) has a version of Pascal's wager.

assume is that theories, such as A and B, have some utility, thus $U(A)$ and $U(B)$, which perhaps depend upon the problems they can solve. A might be the machinery we use to prove that income-compensated demand curves fall, and B might be the specification that the demand curve is log-linear. Suppose we apply A and B to data and discover that the sign is wrong. Now what? One thing we surely will not do is to reject the rationality assumption that gives our sign prediction. So we think a bit more about income effects; voilà, how silly, if we have an inferior good, it cannot be globally log-linear.[18]

The question is whether theory acceptance can be put on a machinelike basis. If so, we need not appeal to pragmatic considerations. To avoid defining away the problem, let us take the operator $\therefore$ to denote "rational acceptance." Popperian philosophy of science emphasizes the logical basic of theory development by focusing on a case in which $\therefore$ would satisfy the deducible relation (Kleene 1971, 90–102). Let $\rightarrow$ denote implication, & conjunction and ~ negation. Commas separate statements. Then for some statements A and X the template of the Popperian $\therefore$ is $A \rightarrow X, ~X \therefore ~A$. The attractive feature of the Popperian view of rational acceptance is precisely that there are no subjective elements.

The difficulty is that many interesting theoretical systems are conjunctions. What decision do we make when $(A \& B) \rightarrow X, ~X$? The Popperian $\therefore$ only gives us $~(A \& B)$, but suppose we must pick one A or B to drop. What do we do then?

We can look at the Duhem-Quine thesis as extending $\therefore$ to close the ambiguity of the modus tolens in the case of joint hypotheses. We can introduce desire into the center of inference by allowing the following deduction rule for $\therefore$

$$(A \& B) \rightarrow X, ~X, U(A) > U(B) \therefore ~B.$$

This econometric example is harmless because our bag of functional forms is endless. What Berkeley did, however, was not harmless. He showed that the calculus, as presented by Newton and Leibnitz, was inconsistent at its very foundations.[19]

---

18. Why not? Because a good cannot be globally inferior if (1) the budget constraint allows zero consumption at zero income and (2) negative consumption is ruled out. As income rises from zero, the good must be normal before it becomes inferior.

19. Robinson (1974, 265–66): "Additional interest is lent to the axiom by the fact that is implies, clearly and immediately, a glaring contradiction, i.e., that the (infinitesimal) differences between two quantities may, at the same time, be both equal to, and different from, zero. . . . Berkeley pointed out some forty years later that the same weakness was present in the method of fluxions. This is true although the absence of a clear basis for that method made it harder to argue against. . . . However, there can be little doubt that the inconsistency in question contributed to the eventual eclipse of the method of infinitely small and infinitely large numbers at the beginning of the nineteenth century."

Infinitesimals were sometimes something and sometimes nothing. If infinitesimal is zero, then

$a + 500$ nothings = $a + 50$ nothings, an innocent, silly truth (Berkeley 1975, 281 [B338]).

But for the calculus to go through, there needs to be some $\Delta > 0$ such that $a + 500\Delta = a + 50\Delta$. How could this be?

A naive response would be "We'll get back to you in two hundred years." This would be very costly because what would replace the calculus in the meantime? The traditional Duhem-Quine position is that an important theory can be saved from empirical contradiction by the sacrifice of an auxiliary aspect of the theory. But what could have saved the calculus if a contradiction were admitted? What stood between the real contradiction and an admitted contradiction? Character assassination, flat denial, and hand waving all seem to have been employed. Character assassination is easy to spot. The hand waving takes the form of the claim: "That is easy to fix, you just do . . ." without bothering to do it. This is noticeable when one can prove that the patch does not work.

Here is a famous response to Berkeley from James Jurin, which proposes a remarkable metamathematical doctrine:

> I do assure you, Sir, from my own experience, and that of many others whom I could name, that the doctrine may be clearly conceived and distinctly comprehended. If *your imagination is strained and puzzled with it,* if it appears to you to contain *obscure and inconceivable mysteries,* in short, if you do not understand it, I tell you others do; and you may do so too, if you will read it with due attention, and with a desire of comprehending it, rather than an inclination to censure it. (1989, 31)

Out of kindness to his intellectual inferiors, Jurin sketched the requisite proof:

> I shall here beg leave, for the sake of readers less mathematically qualified, to put a very easy and familiar case. Suppose two Arithmeticians to be disputing whether vulgar fractions are to be preferred to decimal; would it be fair in him who is for expressing the third part of a farthing by the vulgar 1/3, to affirm that his antagonist proceeding blindfold, and without knowing what he did, when he pretended to express it by 0.33333 &c. because this expression did not give the rigorous, exact value of one third of a farthing? Might not the other reply that, if this expression was not rigorously exact, yet it could not be said he *proceeded blindfold, or without clearness and without science* in using it, because adding more figures he could approach as near as he pleased, he could clearly and distinctly find and demonstrate how much he felt short of the rigorous and exact value? (36)

Later writers amused themselves by debating whether Berkeley was honest but simply stupid in bringing these objections or whether he knew all the time that his objections would vanish like infinitesimals (Cajori 1919, 90).

Let us take a closer look at Jurin's argument and the later reaction to it.

[T]he second supposed fallacy . . . gives $2x(2y) \div (2y + dy)$. Both of these expressions are equal to $2x$, "which is the result either of two errors or of none at all." If you claim that $2x(2y + dy) \div (2y) > 2x$, how much greater is it, supposing $2x = 1000$ miles? Not as much as the thousand-millionth part of an inch. (Cajori 1919, 68–69)

Although Cajori (91) is troubled by the fact that Jurin offers the argument for popular consumption, he does not seem to appreciate the difficulties which arise in treating dy as if it were a small positive real number. The equality holds only the case in which $dy = 0$, which is Berkeley's point. Berkeley depends upon the trichotomy property of real numbers, that is, for any x, one and only one of the following hold: $x > 0$, $x < 0$, $x = 0$. Hence, if $dy = 0$ it cannot be positive too.

The hope behind Jurin's "escape" from Berkeley is to use finite approximations to real number numbers. Of course, this substitution will be needed for computation purposes, but will it pass muster as an account of the foundations of real numbers?

One of the elementary facts about real numbers is that multiplication is associative. Consider two nonzero real numbers, a and x. Then the following holds:

$$(aa^{-1})x = a(a^{-1}x) \tag{2}$$

Suppose, however, that these are just finite approximations to real numbers. Does equation 2 continue to hold? No. The precision with which aa^{-1} can be computed for any nonzero a may vastly exceed the precision with which $a^{-1}x$ can be computed for some x. One way to see the nonassociative property is that we can prove within an infinite precision calculus that $aa^{-1} = 1$. This insight can be used to make finite precision mathematics more closely resemble infinite precision mathematics. The left hand-side of equation 2 can be solved with infinite precision; the right-hand side characteristically cannot.[20] Without the infinite precision calculus as normative guidance, the failure of associative multiplication would mean that any number of answers hold. This

---

20. The introduction of infinite precision insight in a finite precision environment makes it possible to produce counterexamples to such intuitively obvious propositions as that constraints upon optimization cannot be likelihood enhancing (Levy 1988c).

fact makes numerical computations using a finite-precision computer very interesting (Knuth 1981, 214–30).

After it became clear that Berkeley was not stupid—and calculus in terms of limits had been well-founded—it became interesting to ask why Berkeley said what he did. Let us return to Cajori in a 1985 reprinted edition:

> The publication of Berkeley's *Analyst* was the most spectacular mathematical event of the eighteenth century in England. Practically all British discussions of fluxional concepts of that time involve issues raised by Berkeley. Berkeley's object in writing the *Analyst* was to show that the principles of fluxions are no clearer than those of Christianity. . . . A friend of Berkeley, when on a bed of sickness, refused spiritual consolation, because the great mathematician Halley had convinced him of the inconceivability of the doctrines of Christianity. This induced Berkeley to write the *Analyst.**
> (1985, 239)

We will consider the footnote indicated by the asterisk—it was supplied by the editor—momentarily.

The most illuminating attempt to explain Berkeley's lack of vision was made by John Wisdom, using methods that leave one breathless. First, Wisdom explains to the reader how the notion of a limit depends upon continuity:

> Despite his superb criticism of Newton's methods of fluxions, Berkeley showed a certain lack of insight into what Newton was trying to do, and this was certainly due to his not being able to grasp the notion, the then current crude notion, of a limit approached by a mathematical function. This notion depends psychologically (though not logically) upon continuity—one thinks of a limit as a goal *towards* which a function *moves* and moves *continuously* . . . Berkeley could not agree that a function could become smaller and smaller indefinitely; any attempt to make it less than a certain minimal size would instantly reduce it to zero; here therefore there was a breach of continuity. In his philosophy also Berkeley denied continuity. (1953, 158–59)

Having established his credentials to criticize Berkeley's mathematics, Wisdom reaches into the Freudian bowl of wisdom:

> *Interpretation XIX: Berkeley's antagonism to the method of fluxions and his attempt to replace it by a method involving discrete quantities were due to his fear that his insides would dissolve into a flux and to his need to have his insides solid, even though this in its turn would prove disturbing.*
>
> This would, of course, imply that there was for Berkeley a faecal element in mathematics itself. (160)

Wisdom gives us his thoughts on infinite divisibility:

> Thus his conception of mathematics banished the notion of flux from very small quantities just as the principles of *Esse percipi* banished Matter. While, however, his conception of mathematics was directly related to repudiation of flux, *Esse percipi* was only indirectly related to it: *Esse percipi* banished the solid poison and, interestingly enough, conveyed the solipsistic picture of a dream-like flux—an example of what Freud has called the "return of the repressed." (161)

We may conclude this chapter by making part of Interpretation XVIII more specific:

> *Interpretation XX: What Berkeley envied in mathematicians was their freedom to regard some faeces as good and to manipulate derivations from these.* (Wisdom 1953, 161)

Is it necessary to remark that Wisdom's book has not been republished? However, Cajori's *History of Mathematics* has been. The asterisk noted earlier was added by the editor of the 1985 edition. The appended note has this to say:

> Berkeley's objections were well taken and could not be dealt with until 1966, with the creation of Non-standard Analysis. Non-standard Analysis has built a new structure of the Calculus within the framework of which infinitesimals are accommodated and in which Berkeley's objections no longer apply. (1985, 490)[21]

So ends the claim of recourse to Christian apologetics, the claim that constipation precludes the understanding of continuity, and Jurin's metamathematical proposal that if three people think the proof is correct it is.

Conclusion

Historians of economics are often reluctant to admit the possibility that our subjects know more than we do. If they knew something that was worth knowing, why has not it been absorbed into modern economics? Perhaps the difficulty is that they did not know how to persuade later economists that they knew something. This is not quite the same as not knowing what they claim to know.

---

21. Modern histories of mathematics (Burton 1985, 498–99) are most careful to point out Berkeley's role.

Bibliography

Ackroyd, Peter. 1990. *Dickens.* New York: HarperCollins.

Adams, F. C. 1853. *Uncle Tom at Home.* Philadelphia: W. P. Hazard.

Aldrich, Mark. [1979] 1995. "Progressive Economists and Scientific Racism." In *Economics and Discrimination,* edited by William Darity Jr. Brookfield, Vt.: Edward Elgar.

Altick, Richard D. 1951. "*Cope's Tobacco Plant:* An Episode in Victorian Journalism." *Papers of the Bibliographic Society of America* 45:333–50.

Altick, Richard. 1973. *Victorian People and Ideas.* New York: Norton.

American Statistical Assocation. 2000. *Ethical Guidelines for Statistical Practice.* Arlington, Va.: American Statistical Association.

Amor Patriae. 1858. *Slavery, Con. and Pro; or, a Sermon and Its Answer.* Washington, D.C.: H. Polkinhorn.

Andrews, D. F., F. R. Hampel, P. J. Huber, W. Rodgers, and J. W. Tukey. 1972. *Robust Estimates of Location.* Princeton: Princeton University Press.

Anscombe, F. J. 1960. "Rejection of Outliers." *Technometrics* 2:123–47.

[Archer, James H. L.]. 1866. "Jamaica, and the Recent Insurrection There." *Fraser's Magazine for Town and Country* 73:161–79.

Armstrong, D. M. 1960. *Berkeley's New Theory of Vision.* Parkville, Vic.: Melbourne University Press.

Arnold, Matthew. 1993. *Culture and Anarchy and Other Writings,* edited by Stefan Collini. Cambridge: Cambridge University Press.

Arrow, Kenneth J. 1963. *Social Choice and Individual Value.* 2d ed. New Haven: Yale University Press.

Arrow, Kenneth J. 1972. "The Theory of Discrimination." In *Discrimination in Labor Markets,* edited by Orley Ashenfelter and Albert Rees. Princeton: Princeton University Press.

Ashton, Jean W. 1977. *Harriet Beecher Stowe: A Reference Guide.* Boston: G. K. Hall.

[Austin, James Trecothick]. 1839. *Review of the Rev. Dr. Channing's Letter to Jonathan Phillips, Esq. on the Slavery Question.* Boston: J. H. Eastburn.

Axelrod, Robert. 1984. *The Evolution of Co-operation.* New York: Basic Books.

[Aytoun, W. E.]. November 1850. "Alton Locke, Tailor and Poet: An Autobiography." *Blackwood's Edinburgh Magazine* 68:592–610.

"Babel." 1849. *Fraser's Magazine for Town and Country* 40 (September): 318–27.

Baker, John R. 1974. *Race.* New York: Oxford University Press.

Bailey, Samuel. 1842 [1988]. *A Review of Berkeley's Theory of Vision. Berkeley on Vision,* edited by George Pitcher. New York and London: Garland.

Banton, Michael. 1977. *The Idea of Race.* London: Tavistock.

Barber, Paul. 1988. *Vampires, Burial, and Death: Folklore and Reality.* New Haven: Yale University Press.

Barzun, Jacques. 1937. *Race: A Study in Modern Superstition.* New York: Harcourt, Brace.

Bassett, Gilbert, Jr., and Robert Persky. 1999. "Robust Voting." *Public Choice* 99:299–310.

Baumgarten, Murray. 1980. "In the Margins: Carlyle's Marking and Annotations in His Gift Copy of Mill's *Principles of Political Economy.*" In *Carlyle: Books and Margins.* University of California at Santa Cruz Bibliographical Series, no. 3. Santa Cruz: University of California Press.

Belfrage, Bertil. 1987. *George Berkeley's Manuscript Introduction.* Oxford: Doxa.

Bellman, Richard. 1957. *Dynamic Programming.* Princeton: Princeton University Press.

Belsey, Catherine. 1980. *Critical Practice.* London: Routledge.

Bennett, William J. E. 1850. *A First Letter to the Right Honourable Lord John Russell, M.P. on the Present Persecution of a Certain Portion of the English Church.* 6th ed. London: W. J. Cleaver.

[Bentham, Jeremy]. 1823. *Not Paul, but Jesus.* Edited by Francis Place [Gamaliel Smith]. London: John Hunt.

Bentham, Jeremy. 1983. *Deontology Together with a Table of the Springs of Action and the Article on Utilitarianism.* Edited by Amnon Goldworth. Oxford: Clarendon.

[Berkeley, George]. 1732. *Alciphron.* London: J. Tonson.

Berkeley, George. 1948–57. *The Works of George Berkeley, Bishop of Cloyne.* Edited by A. A. Luce and T. E. Jessop. London: Thomas Nelson and Sons.

Berkeley, George. 1975. *Philosophical Works.* London: Dent.

Bernal, Martin. 1987. *Black Athena.* New Brunswick, N.J.: Rutgers University Press.

Berry, Christopher J. 1994. *The Idea of Luxury: A Conceptual and Historical Investigation.* Cambridge: Cambridge University Press.

Bittermann, Henry J. 1940. "Adam Smith's Empiricism and the Law of Nature." *Journal of Political Economy* 48:487–520, 703–34.

Blaug, Mark. 1958. *Ricardian Economics.* New Haven: Yale University Press.

Bowley, Marian. 1937. *Nassau Senior and Classical Economics.* London: G. Allen and Unwin.

Bright, John. 1930. *The Diaries of John Bright.* Foreword by Philip Bright. London: Cassell and Company.

Brimblecomb, Nicholas. 1853. *Uncle Tom's Cabin in Ruins! Triumphant Defence of Slavery!* Boston: C. Waite.

"British and American Slavery." 1853. *Southern Quarterly Review* 8 (October): 369–411. Available from the Making of America data base at <http://www.umdl.umich.edu/moa>.

Brown, Maurice. 1988. *Adam Smith's Economics.* London: Croom Helm.

Buchanan, James. 1954. "Individual Choice in Voting and the Market." *Journal of Political Economy* 62:334–43.

Buchanan, James M. 1979. *What Should Economists Do?* Indianapolis: Liberty Press.

Buchanan, James M., and Geoffrey Brennan. 1980. *The Power to Tax: Analytical Foundations of a Fiscal Constitution.* Cambridge: Cambridge University Press.

Buckle, Henry Thomas. 1876. *The History of Civilization in England.* 2d ed. New York: D. Appleton and Company.

Burton, David M. 1985. *The History of Mathematics.* Boston: Allyn and Bacon.

[Burton, Richard F.]. 1926. *The Kasîdah of Hâjî Abdû El-Yezdî.* Translated and Annoted by his Friend and Pupil Sir Richard Burton. New York: Brentanos.

Butterworth, R. D. 1992. "Dickens the Novelist: The Present Strike and *Hard Times.*" *The Dickensian* 88:91–102.

Buxton, Thomas Fowell. 1925. *Memoirs of Sir Thomas Fowell Buxton, Bart.* Edited by Charles Buxton. London: J. M. Dent and Sons.

Cajori, Florian. 1919. *A History of the Conceptions of Limits and Fluxions in Great Britain from Newton to Woodhouse.* Chicago and London: Open Court Publishing.

Cajori, Florian. [1919] 1985. *A History of Mathematics.* 4th ed. New York: Chelsea.

Campbell, Lyle, and Martha C. Muntzel. 1989. "The Structural Consequence of Language Death." In *Investigating Obsolescence,* edited by Nancy C. Dorian. Cambridge: Cambridge University Press.

Campbell, T. D. 1971. *Adam Smith's Science of Morals.* London: Allen and Unwin.

Caplan, Bryan. 2000. "Rational Irrationality." *Eastern Economic Journal* 26:191–211.

Carlyle, Jane. 1883. *Letters and Memorials of Jane Welsh Carlyle Prepared for Publication by Thomas Carlyle.* Edited by James Froude. London: Longmans, Green, and Co.

Carlyle, Thomas. 1840. *Chartism.* London: J. Fraser.

[Carlyle, Thomas]. 1849. "Occasional Discourse on the Negro Question." *Fraser's Magazine for Town and Country* 40:670–79. Available at <http://www.econlib.org>.

Carlyle, Thomas. 1850a. "Carlyle on West India Emancipation." *Commercial Review* 2:527–38. Available from the Making of America data base at <http://www.umdl.umich.edu/moa/>.

Carlyle, Thomas. 1850b. *Latter-Day Pamphlets.* London: Chapman and Hall. Available at <http://www.econlib.org>.

Carlyle, Thomas. 1851. "Mr. Carlyle's Letter." ["Occasional Discourse on the Negro Question."] In *Negro-Mania,* edited by John Campbell. Philadelphia: Campbell and Power.

Carlyle, Thomas. 1867. *Shooting Niagara: And After?* London: Chapman and Hall.

Carlyle, Thomas. 1890. *Table Talk.* Cope's Smoke Room Booklet, no. 5. Liverpool: Cope's.

Carlyle, Thomas. 1904. *Edinburgh Edition: The Works of Thomas Carlyle in Thirty Volumes.* New York: C. Scribner.

Carlyle, Thomas. 1956. *The French Revolution.* New York: Heritage.

Carlyle, Thomas. 1965. *Past and Present.* Edited by Richard D. Altick. Boston: Houghton Mifflin.

Carlyle, Thomas. 1971. *The Nigger Question.* John Stuart Mill. In *The Negro Question,* edited by Eugene R. August. New York: Appleton Century Crofts.

Carlyle, Thomas. 1987. *Sartor Resartus.* Edited by Kerry McSweeney and Peter Sabor. Oxford: Oxford University Press.

Carlyle, Thomas. 1993. *On Heroes, Hero-Worship, and the Heroic in History.* Edited by Michael K. Golberg, Joel J. Brattin, and Mark Engel. Berkeley: University of California Press.

Carnap, Rudolf. 1950. *Logical Foundations of Probability.* Chicago: University of Chicago Press.

Carnap, Rudolf. 1966. *Philosophical Foundations of Physics.* Edited by Martin Gardner. New York: Basic Books.

Casteras, Susan P. 1993. "The Germ of a Museum, Arranged First for 'Workers in Iron.'" In *John Ruskin and the Victorian Eye.* New York: Abrams.

Cate, George Allan. 1982. *The Correspondence of Thomas Carlyle and John Ruskin.* Stanford: Stanford University Press.

Cate, George Allan. 1988. *John Ruskin, a Reference Guide. A Selective Guide of Significant and Representative Works about Him.* Boston: G. K. Hall.

Chang, C. C., and H. J. Keisler. 1973. *Model Theory.* 3d ed. Amsterdam: North-Holland.

"Charles Dickens and David Copperfield." 1850. *Fraser's Magazine for Town Country* 42 (December): 698–710.

Charlesworth, James. H., ed. 1983. *The Old Testament Pseudepigrapha.* Garden City, N.Y.: Doubleday.

Cherry, Robert. [1976] 1995. "Racial Thought and the Early Economics Profession." In *Economics and Discrimination,* edited by William Darity Jr. Brookfield, Vt.: Edward Elgar.

Chomsky, Noam. 1986. *Knowledge of Language.* New York: Praeger.

Church and State. 1850. London: J. and C. Mozley. Reprinted from the last number of the *Christian Remembrancer,* April 1850.

Cobden, John C. 1859. *The White Slaves of England.* New York: C. M. Saxton.

Coleman, Charles. 1997. "A Life Cycle Model of Fame." Paper presented at meetings of the the the Southern Economic Association, Atlanta.

Coleridge, Samuel Taylor. 1990. *Table Talk I.* Edited by Carl Woodring. Vol. 14 of *The Collected Works of Samuel Taylor Coleridge.* Princeton: Princeton University Press.

"The Colonists versus the Anti-Slave Society." 1831. *Fraser's Magazine for Town and Country* 3 (February): 114–25.

Collins, Philip, ed. 1971. *Dickens: The Critical Heritage.* New York: Barnes and Noble.

Conan Doyle, Arthur. 1930. *The Complete Sherlock Holmes.* Garden City, N.Y.: Doubleday.

Cook, E. T., and Alexander Wedderburn. 1912. *Bibliography.* Vol. 38 of *The Works of John Ruskin.* London: G. Allen.

Cope's Tobacco Plant. 1870–71. Liverpool. Various issues.

[*Cope's Key*]. 1878. *The Plenipotent Key to Cope's Correct Card of the Peerless Pilgrimage to Saint Nicotine of the Holy Herb: &c.* Liverpool: Cope's.

Coupland, R. 1923. *Wilberforce: A Narrative.* Oxford: Clarendon Press.

Craft, William. 1860. *Running a Thousand Miles for Freedom; or, the Escape of William and Ellen Craft from Slavery.* London: William Tweedie.

[Craft, William]. 1863. "Anthropology at the British Association." *Anthropological Review* 1:388–89.

Crompton, Louis. 1985. *Byron and Greek Love.* Berkeley: University of California Press.

Cropsey, Joseph. 1957. *Polity and Economy.* The Hague: Martinus Nijhoff.

Cunliffe, Marcus. 1979. *Chattel Slavery and Wage Slavery: The Anglo-American Context, 1830–1860.* Athens: University of Georgia Press.

Curry, Kenneth. 1975. *Southey.* London: Routledge and Kegan Paul.

Curtis, L. P., Jr. 1968. *Anglo-Saxons and Celts.* Bridgeport: Conference on British Studies at the University of Bridgeport.

Daniell, David. 1994. *William Tyndale.* New Haven: Yale University Press.

Darity, William, Jr. 1995. Introduction to *Economics and Discrimination,* edited by William Darity Jr. Brookfield, Vt.: Edward Elgar.

Darwall, Stephen L. 1995. *The British Moralists and the Internal "Ought," 1640–1740.* Cambridge: Cambridge University Press.

Davis, John W. 1960. "The Molyneux Problem." *Journal of the History of Ideas* 21:392–408.

DeCamp, David. 1977. "The Development of Pidgin and Creole Studies." In *Pidgin and Creole Linguistics,* edited by Albert Valdman. Bloomington: Indiana University Press.

Demaus, R. 1871. *William Tyndale: A Biography.* London: Religous Tract Society.

Denman, Lord. 1853. *Uncle Tom's Cabin, Bleak House, Slavery and Slave Trade.* 2d ed. London: Longman, Brown, Green, and Longmans.

Denton, Frank. 1985. "Data Mining as an Industry." *Review of Economics and Statistics.* 57:124–27.

Desmond, Adrian. 1994. *Huxley: The Devil's Disciple.* London: M. Joseph.

Desmond, Adrian, and James Moore. 1991. *Darwin.* New York: Warner Books.

Diamond, Arthur M., and David M. Levy. 1994. "Stylometrics: Adam Smith Teaches Efficient Rhetoric." *Economic Inquiry* 32:138–45.

[Dickens, Charles]. 1853a. "The Noble Savage." *Household Words. A Weekly Journal Conducted by Charles Dickens* (June 11):337–39.

[Dickens, Charles]. 1853b. "Frauds on the Fairies." *Household Words. A Weekly Journal Conducted by Charles Dickens* 8 (October 1):97–100.

Dickens, Charles. [1854] 1972. *Hard Times.* Edited by David Craig. Harmondsworth: Penguin.

Dickens, Charles. [1854] 1990. *Hard Times.* Edited by George Ford and Sylvère Monod. 2d ed. New York: Norton.

Dickens, Charles. [1854] 1995. *Hard Times.* Edited by Kate Flint. Harmondsworth: Penguin.

Dickens, Charles. 1938. *The Letters of Charles Dickens.* Edited by Walter Dexter. *The Nonesuch Dickens.* Bloomsbury: Nonesuch.

Dickens, Charles. 1985. *American Notes for General Circulation.* Edited by John S. Whitley and Arnold Goldman. Harmondsworth: Penguin.

Dickens, Charles. 1993. *The Letters of Charles Dickens.* Vol. 7: *(1853–55).* Edited by Graham Storey, Kathleen Tillotson, and Angus Easson. Oxford: Clarendon.

Dictionary of National Biography. 1997. Version 1.1. Oxford: Oxford University Press. CD-ROM.

Dixon, Robert M. W. 1989. *Searching for Aboriginal Languages.* Chicago: University of Chicago Press.

Donovan, Josephine. 1991. *Uncle Tom's Cabin: Evil, Affliction, and Redemptive Love.* Boston: Twayne.

Dorian, Nancy C. 1981. *Language Death.* Philadelphia: University of Pennsylvania Press.

Downs, Anthony. 1957. *An Economic Theory of Democracy.* New York: Harper and Row.

Eagleton, Terry. 1976. *Criticism and Ideology: A Study in Marxist Literary Theory.* London: NLB.

Easson, Angus. 1973. *Charles Dickens: Hard Times.* London: University of London Press.

Ebenstein, Alan O. 1991. *The Greatest Happiness Principle.* New York: Garland.

Edgeworth, F. Y. 1881. *Mathematical Psychics.* London: C. K. Paul and Co.

Eliot, T. S. 1975. *Selected Prose of T. S. Eliot.* Edited by Frank Kermode. London: Faber and Faber.

Fabrizio, Richard. 1987. "Wonderful No-Meaning: Language and the Psychopathology of the Family in Dickens' *Hard Times.*" *Dickens Studies Annual* 16:61–94.

Fain, John Tyree. 1956. *Ruskin and the Economists.* Nashville: Vanderbilt University Press.

Fain, John Tyree. 1982. "Ruskin and Smart." In *Studies in Ruskin: Essays in Honor of Van Akin Burd,* edited by Robert Rhodes and Del Ivan Janik. Athens: Ohio University Press.

Feigenbaum, Susan, and David M. Levy. 1992. "Who Monitors the Monitors?" In *The Economic Ideas of Ordinary People.* London: Routledge.

Feigenbaum, Susan, and David M. Levy. 1993. "The Market for (Ir)reproducible Econometrics." *Social Epistemology* 7:215–32.

Feigenbaum, Susan, and David M. Levy. 1996. "The Technological Obsolescence of Scientific Fraud." *Rationality and Society* 8:261–76.

Feigenbaum, Susan, and David M. Levy. 1997. "Second Thoughts on First Impressions." Paper presented at the meetings of the Southern Economics Association, Atlanta.

Feinberg, Robert M. 1998. "Ranking Economics Departments." *Journal of Economic Perspectives* 12:231–33.

Felsenstein, Frank. 1995. *Anti-Semitic Stereotypes: A Paradigm of Otherness in English Popular Culture, 1660–1830.* Baltimore: Johns Hopkins University Press.

Ferrier, James F. [1842] 1988. "Berkeley and Idealism." In *Berkeley on Vision,* edited by George Pitcher. New York and London: Garland.

Fielder, Leslie. 1979. *The Inadvertent Epic: From Uncle Tom's Cabin to Roots.* New York: Simon and Schuster.

Fielding, K. J. 1956. "Mill and Gradgrind." *Nineteenth-Century Fiction* 11:148–51.

Fish, Stanley. 1967. *Surprised by Sin: The Reader in Paradise Lost.* Berkeley: University of California Press.

Fitzhugh, George. 1857. *Cannibals All! or Slaves without Masters.* Richmond: A. Morris.

Fletcher, John. 1852. *Studies in Slavery in Easy Lessons.* Natchez: J. Warner.

Forster, John. 1966. *The Life of Charles Dickens.* Edited by A. J. Hoppé. London: Dent.

Foster, Eugene A., et al. 1998. "Jefferson Fathered Slave's Last Child." *Nature* 396 (November 5): 27–28.

[Foxe, John]. 1829. *Fox's Book of Martyrs; or, The Acts and Monuments of the Christian Church.* Revised by John Malham. New York: William Borradaile.

Froeb, Luke M., and Bruce H. Kobayashi. 1996. "Naive, Biased, yet Bayesian: Can Juries Interpret Selectively Produced Evidence?" *Journal of Law, Economics, and Organization* 12 :257–76.

Frost, Robert. 1968. *The Poetry of Robert Frost.* Edited by Edward Connery Lathem. New York: Holt, Rinehart, and Winston.

Froude, James Anthony. 1849. *The Nemesis of Faith.* London: John Chapman.

Froude, James Anthony. 1885. *Thomas Carlyle: A History of His Life in London, 1834–1881.* New York: Harper and Brothers.

George, David. 2000. Discussion held at the meetings of the Eastern Economics Association, Arlington, Virginia, March.

Goldberg, Michael. 1972a. *Carlyle and Dickens.* Athens: University of Georgia Press.

Goldberg, Michael. 1972b. "From Bentham to Carlyle: Dickens' Political Development." *Journal of the History of Ideas* 33:61–76.

Gore, Charles. 1922. *The Deity of Christ.* London: A. R. Mowbray and Co.

Gossett, Thomas F. 1985. *Uncle Tom's Cabin and American Culture.* Dallas: Southern Methodist University Press.

Gould, Stephen Jay. 1981. *The Mismeasure of Man.* New York: Norton.

Grampp, William D. 1960. *The Manchester School of Economics.* Stanford: Stanford University Press.

Gray, Paul Edward. 1969. *Twentieth Century Interpretations of Hard Times.* Englewood Cliffs, N.J.: Prentice-Hall.

Green, Martin. 1964. "A Literary Defense of 'The Two Cultures.'" *Cultures in Conflict: Perspectives on the Snow-Leavis Controversy,* edited by David K. Cornelius and Edwin St. Vincent. Chicago: Scott, Foresman.

Green, William. 1976. *British Slave Emancipation: The Sugar Colonies and the Great Experiment, 1830–1865.* Oxford: Clarendon.

Greene, William. 1997. *Econometric Analysis.* 3d ed. New York: Prentice-Hall.

[Greg, W. R.]. 1866. "The Jamaica Problem." *Fraser's Magazine for Town and Country* 73 (March): 277–305.

[Greg, W. R.]. 1869. "Realities of Irish Life." *Quarterly Review* 126:61–80.

Guppy, Henry F. J. 1864. "Notes on the Capability of the Negro for Civilisation." *Journal of the Anthropological Society* 2:ccix–ccxvi.

Halévy, Elie. 1955. *The Growth of Philosophic Radicalism.* Translated by Mary Morris. Boston: Beacon.

Hall, Catherine. 1992. *White, Male, and Middle-Class: Explorations in Feminism and History.* New York: Routledge.

Hall, Robert A. 1955. *Hands Off Pidgin English!* Sydney: Pacific Publications.

Hall, Robert A. 1966. *Pidgin and Creole Languages.* Ithaca: Cornell University Press.

Haller, John S. [1971] 1995. *Outcasts from Evolution: Scientific Attitudes of Racial Inferiority.* Carbondale and Edwardsville: Southern Illinois University Press.

Hamilton, Earl J. 1952. "Prices as a Factor in Business Growth: Prices and Progress." *Journal of Economic History* 12:325–49.

Hammond, Gerald. 1983. *The Making of the English Bible.* New York: Philosophical Library.

Hammond, James Henry. 1853. "Hammond's Letters on Slavery." In *The Pro-Slavery Argument.* Philadelphia: Lippincott, Grambo, and Co.

Hampel, Frank H., Elvezio M. Ronchetti, Peter J. Rousseeuw, and Werner A. Stahel. 1986. *Robust Statistics.* New York: Wiley.

Hannaford, Ivan. 1996. *Race: The History of an Idea in the West.* Washington, D.C.: Woodrow Wilson Center Press.

Hardy, G. H. 1990. *A Mathematician's Apology.* Cambridge: Cambridge University Press.

Harman, Gilbert. 1971. *The Nature of Morality.* New York: Oxford University Press.

Harman, Gilbert. 1986. *Moral Agent and Impartial Spectator.* Lawrence: University of Kansas Press.

Harris, Jose. 1999. "Ruskin and Social Reform." In *Ruskin and the Dawn of the Modern,* edited by Dinah Birch. Oxford: Oxford University Press.

Harris, Styron. 1981. *Charles Kingsley: A Reference Guide.* Boston: G. K. Hall.

Harrison, Frederic. 1902. *John Ruskin.* New York: Macmillan.

Harper, William. 1853. "Harper on Slavery." In *The Pro-Slavery Argument*. Philadelphia: Lippincott, Grambo, and Co.

Harsanyi, John C. [1955] 1973. "Cardinal Welfare, Individualistic Ethics, and Interpersonal Comparisons of Utility." In *Economic Justice*, edited by Edmund S. Phelps. Baltimore: Penguin.

Hawley, John C. 1986. "Responses to Charles Kingsley's Attack on Political Economy." *Victorian Periodical Review* 19:131–37.

Hayek, F. A. 1949. *Individualism and Economic Order*. Chicago: University of Chicago Press.

Hayek, F. A. 1951. *John Stuart Mill and Harriet Taylor: Their Correspondence and Subsequent Marriage*. Chicago: University of Chicago Press.

Hayek, F. A. 1964. *Road to Serfdom*. Chicago: University of Chicago Press.

Hayek, F. A. 1969. *Studies in Philosophy, Politics, and Economics*. New York: Simon and Schuster.

Hayek, F. A. 1976. *The Mirage of Social Justice*. Vol. 2 of *Law, Legislation, and Liberty*. Chicago: University of Chicago Press.

Hedrick, Joan D. 1994. *Harriet Beecher Stowe: A Life*. New York: Oxford University Press.

Heffer, Simon. 1995. *Moral Desperado*. London: Weidenfeld and Nicolson.

[Helps, Arthur]. 1852a. *A Letter on "Uncle Tom's Cabin."* Cambridge: John Bartlett.

[Helps, Arthur]. 1852b. "Uncle Tom's Cabin." *Fraser's Magazine for Town and Country* 46:237–44.

Henson, Herbert Hensley. 1942–43. *Retrospect of an Unimportant Life*. London: Oxford University Press.

Herrigel, Eugen. 1953. *Zen in the Art of Archery*. Introduction by D. T. Suzuki. Translated by R. F. C. Hull. New York: Pantheon.

Hill, Alicia, Richard Whately, and Samuel Hinds. 1852. "American Slavery and *Uncle Tom's Cabin*." *North British Review* 18:235–58.

Hill, Christopher. 1993. *The English Bible and the Seventeenth-Century Revolution*. London: Penguin.

Hilton, Boyd. 1988. *The Age of Atonement: The Influence of Evangelicalism on Social and Economic Thought, 1795–1865*. Oxford: Clarendon.

Hilton, Tim. 1985. *John Ruskin: The Early Years, 1819–1859*. New Haven: Yale University Press.

Hilton, Tim. 2000. *John Ruskin: The Later Years*. New Haven: Yale University Press.

Hirschman, Albert O. [1977] 1997. *The Passions and the Interests: Political Arguments for Capitalism before Its Triumph*. Twentieth Anniversary Ed. Princeton: Princeton University Press.

Hobbes, Thomas. [1651] 1968. *Leviathan*. Edited by C. B. Macpherson. Harmondsworth: Penguin.

Hobson, J. A. 1898. *John Ruskin: Social Reformer*. Boston: Dana Estes and Company.

Hodgson, William Ballantyne. [1855] 1917. "On the Importance of the Study of Economic Science as a Branch of Education for All Classes." In *Science and Education*, edited by E. Ray Lankester. London: William Heinemann.

Hodgson, William Ballantyne. 1883. *Life and Letters*. Edited by J. M. D. Meiklejohn. Edinburgh: D. Douglas.

Hoecker-Drysdale, Susan. 1992. *Harriet Martineau: First Woman Sociologist*. Oxford: Berg.

Hoffer, Eric. 1951. *True Believer: Thoughts on the Nature of Mass Movement.* New York: Harper.

Holden, Christine. 2000. "Dismal Dragons and Saints." Correspondence, May 23.

Holden, Christine, and David M. Levy. 1993. "Birth Control and the Amelioration Controversy." *History of Political Economy* 25:285–313.

Holden, Christine, and David M. Levy. 2001. "The Career of C. K. Ogden and/as Adelyne More." *Historical Reflections/Réflexions Historique.* 27:79–105.

Hollander, Samuel. 1979. *The Economics of David Ricardo.* Toronto: UToronto Press.

Hollander, Samuel. 1997. *The Economics of Thomas Robert Malthus.* Toronto: University of Toronto Press.

[Hollingshead, John]. 1858. "A New Idea of an Old Slave-Captain." *Household Words. A Weekly Journal Conducted by Charles Dickens* 17 (January 9): 84–87.

Hollington, Michael. 1992. "Physiognomy in *Hard Times." Dickens Quarterly* 9:58–66.

Holt, Thomas C. 1992. *The Problem of Freedom: Race, Labor, and Politics in Jamaica and Britain, 1832–1932.* Baltimore: Johns Hopkins University Press.

Houghton, Walter. E. 1957. *The Victorian Frame of Mind.* New Haven: Yale University Press.

Houghton, Walter E. 1972. *Fraser's Magazine for Town and Country, 1830–1882.* Vol. 2 of *Wellesley Index to Victorian Periodicals.* Edited by Walter E. Houghton. Toronto: University of Toronto Press.

Howse, Ernest Marshall. 1952. *Saints in Politics: The "Clapham Sect" and the Growth of Freedom.* London: Allen and Unwin.

Huber, Peter J. 1981. *Robust Statistics.* New York: Wiley.

Hume, David. 1987. *Essays Moral, Political, and Literary.* Edited by Eugene F. Miller. Rev. ed. Indianapolis: Liberty Classics.

Hunt, James. 1854. *A Treatise on the Curing of Stammering.* London: Longman, Brown, Green, and Longmans.

[Hunt, James]. 1863. "Anthropology at the British Association." *Anthropological Review* 1:390–91.

Hunt, James. 1864. *The Negro's Place in Nature.* New York: VanGurie, Horton, and Company.

[Hunt, James]. 1866a. "On the Negro Revolt in Jamaica." *Popular Magazine of Anthropology* 1:4–20.

[Hunt, James]. 1866b. "Race Antagonism." *Popular Magazine of Anthropology* 1:24–26.

Hunt, James. 1866c . "Race in Legislation and Political Economy." *Anthropological Review* 4:113–35.

Hunt, James. 1867. "President's Address." *Journal of the Anthropological Society* 5:xliv–lxx.

[Hutcheson, Francis]. 1726. *An Inquiry into the Original of Our Ideas of Beauty and Virtue Concerning Moral Good and Evil.* 2d ed. London: J. Darby.

Huxley, Leonard. 1900. *Life and Letters of Thomas Henry Huxley.* New York: D. Appleton and Company.

Isaac, R. Mark, and James M. Walker. 1988. "Communication and Free-Riding Behavior." *Economic Inquiry* 26:585–608.

Iverson, Kenneth E. 1962. *A Programming Language.* New York: Wiley.

James, William. 1987. *Writings, 1902–1910.* New York: Library of America.

Johnson, Edgar. 1952. *Charles Dickens: His Tragedy and Triumph*. New York: Simon and Schuster.

Jones, Iva G. 1967. "Trollope, Carlyle, and Mill on the Negro: An Episode in the History of Ideas." *Journal of Negro History* 52:185–99.

Julius, Anthony. 1995. *T. S. Eliot, Anti-Semitism, and Literary Form*. Cambridge: Cambridge University Press.

Jurin, James. [1734] 1989. *Geometry No Friend to Infidelity. George Berkeley, Eighteenth-Century Responses*. Edited by David Berman. New York: Garland.

Jutzi, Alan. 1971. "Intramuralia." *Huntington Library Quarterly* 34 (May): 289–90.

Kaufmann, Arnold. 1975. *Introduction to the Theory of Fuzzy Subsets*. Translated by D. L. Swanson. New York: Academic Press.

Keisler, H. Jerome. 1976. *Elementary Calculus*. Boston: Prindle, Weber and Schmidt.

Keith, Arthur. 1917. "Presidential Address. How Can the Institute Best Serve the Needs of Anthropology?" *Journal of the Royal Anthropological Institute of Great Britain and Ireland* 47:12–30.

Ker, Leander. 1840. *Slavery Consistent with Christianity*. Baltimore: Sherwood and Co.

Ker, Leander. 1842. *Slavery Consistent with Christianity*. 2d ed. Jefferson City, Mo.: W. Lusk and Son.

Ker, Leander. 1853. *Slavery Consistent with Christianity, with an Introduction, Embracing a Notice of the "Uncle Tom's Cabin" Movement in England*. 3d ed. Weston, Mo.: Finch O'Gorman.

[Kingsley, Charles]. 1850a. *Alton Locke, Tailor and Poet: An Autobiography*. New York: Harper and Brothers.

[Kingsley, Charles]. 1850b. "Sketches of a Life by a Radical." *Harper's New Monthly Magazine* 1:803–7.

[Kingsley, Charles]. 1859. "The Irrationale of Speech." *Fraser's Magazine for Town and Country* 60 (July): 1–14.

Kingsley, Charles. 1864. *The Roman and the Teuton*. Cambridge and London: Macmillan.

Kingsley, Charles. 1866. "Science. A Lecture Delivered at the Royal Institution." *Fraser's Magazine for Town and Country* 74 (July): 15–28.

Kingsley, Charles. 1890. *The Roman and the Teuton*. New ed. Edited by F. Max Müller. London: Macmillan.

Kingsley, Charles. 1983. *Alton Locke, Tailor and Poet. An Autobiography*. Edited by Elizabeth A. Cripps. Oxford: Oxford University Press.

Kingsley, Charles. Charles Kingsley Collection. Letters to James Hunt. Huntington Library, San Marino, Calif.

Kirk, G. S., and J. E. Raven. 1981. *The Presocratic Philosophers*. Cambridge: Cambridge University Press.

Kleene, Stephen C. 1971. *Introduction to Metamathematics*. Amsterdam: North-Holland.

Klir, George J., and Tina A. Folger. 1988. *Fuzzy Sets, Uncertainty, and Information*. Englewood Cliffs, N.J.: Prentice-Hall.

Kluckhohn, Clyde, and Dorothea Leighton. 1956. *The Navaho*. Cambridge: Harvard University Press.

Knight, Frank H. 1982. *Freedom and Reform*. Foreword by James M. Buchanan. Indianapolis: Liberty Classics.

Knox, Robert. 1850. *The Races of Men*. Philadelphia: Lea and Blanchard.

Knuth, Donald E. 1981. *Seminumerical Algorithms.* Vol. 2 of *The Art of Computer Programming.* Reading, Mass.: Addison-Wesley.

Koenker, Roger, and Gilbert Bassett Jr. 1978. "Regression Quantiles." *Econometrica* 46:33–50.

"Kraal." *Encyclopedia Britannica CD-97.* 1997. Chicago: Encyclopedia Britannica. CD-ROM.

Kuhn, Thomas S. 1962. *Structure of Scientific Revolution.* Chicago: University of Chicago Press.

Land, Stephen K. 1974. *From Signs to Propositions.* London: Longman.

Leamer, Edward E. 1983. "Let's Take the Con out of Econometrics." *American Economic Review* 73:31–43.

Leary, Patrick. 1994. "*Fraser's Magazine* and the Literary Life." *Victorian Periodicals Review* 27:105–26.

Leavis, F. R. 1949. *The Great Tradition.* New York: George W. Stewart.

Leavis, F. R. 1969. *English Literature in Our Time and the University.* London: Chatto and Windus.

Leavis, F. R. 1990. "Hard Times: An Analytic Note." In Charles Dickens, *Hard Times,* edited by George Ford and Sylvère Monod. 2d ed. New York: Norton.

Leavis, F. R., and Q. D. Leavis. 1970. *Dickens the Novelist.* London: Chatto and Windus.

Leavis, Q. D. 1989. *Collected Essays.* Edited by G. Singh. Cambridge: Cambridge University Press.

Lebow, Richard Ned. 1976. *White Britain and Black Ireland: The Influence of Stereotypes on Colonial Policy.* Philadelphia: Institute for the Study of Human Issues.

Lehmann, E. L. 1986. *Testing Statistical Hypotheses.* 2d ed. New York: Wiley.

Levine, Lawrence W. 1993. *The Unpredictable Past.* New York: Oxford University Press.

Levine, Lawrence W. 1996. *The Opening of the American Mind.* Boston: Beacon.

Levy, David M. 1982a. "Diamonds, Water, and Z Goods." *History of Political Economy* 14:312–22.

Levy, David M. 1982b. "Rational Choice and Morality." *History of Political Economy* 14:1–36.

Levy, David M. 1987. "Adam Smith's Case for Usury Laws." *History of Political Economy* 19:387–400.

Levy, David M. 1988a. "The Market for Fame and Fortune." *History of Political Economy* 20:615–25.

Levy, David M. 1988b. "Smith and Kant Respond to Mandeville." *Studies in Early Modern Philosophy* 2:25–39.

Levy, David M. 1988c. "Increasing the Likelihood Value by Adding Constraints." *Economics Letters* 28:57–61.

Levy, David M. 1988d. "Utility-Enhancing Consumption Constraints." *Economics and Philosophy* 4:69–88.

Levy, David M. 1990a. "The Bias of Centrally Planned Prices." *Public Choice* 67:213–36.

Levy, David M. 1990b. "Estimating the Impact of Government R&D." *Economics Letters* 32:169–72.

Levy, David M. 1992. *The Economic Ideas of Ordinary People: From Preferences to Trade.* London: Routledge.

Levy, David M. 1993a. "'Magic Buffalo' and Berkeley's *Theory of Vision:* Learning in Society." *Hume Studies* 19:223–26.

Levy, David M. 1993b. "The Public Choice of Data Provision." *Accountability in Research* 3:157–63.

Levy, David M. 1999a. "Adam Smith's Katallatic Model of Gambling: Approbation from the Spectator." *Journal of the History of Economic Thought* 21:81–91.

Levy, David M. 1999b. "Malthusianism and Christianity: The Invisibility of a Successful Radical." *Historical Reflections/Réflexions Historiques* 25:61–93.

Levy, David M. 1999–2000. "Non-normality and Exploratory Data Analysis: Problem and Solution." *Econometric Theory* 15:427–28; 16:296–97.

Levy, David M. 2000a. "The Premature Death of Path Dependence." In *Complexity,* edited by David Collander. London: Routledge.

Levy, David M. 2000b. "Comment." In *Concentrated Ownership,* edited by Randall Morck. Chicago: National Bureau of Economic Research.

Levy, David M., and Sandra Peart. 2002. "Francis Galton's Two Papers on Voting as Robust Estimation." *Public Choice.* Forthcoming.

Lewin, Walter. 1893. John Fraser Collection. Letter. University of Liverpool Library. Liverpool.

Liddell, Henry George, and Robert Scott. 1968. *A Greek-English Lexicon.* Revised by Henry Stuart Jones with the assistance of Roderick McKenzie. Oxford: Clarendon.

Lindgren, J. Ralph. 1973. *The Social Philosophy of Adam Smith.* The Hague: Martinus Nijhoff.

[Littlewood, J. E.]. 1990. *Littlewood's Miscellany.* Edited by Béla Bollobás. Cambridge: Cambridge University Press.

Lively, Jack, and John Rees. 1978. *Utilitarian Logic and Politics.* Oxford: Clarendon.

[Lockhart, J. G.]. 1833. "M. G. Lewis' *West India Journals.*" *Quarterly Review* 50:374–99.

Lodge, David. 1967. Introduction to Charles Kingsley, *Alton Locke, Tailor and Poet: An Autobiography.* London: Cassell.

Lohrli, Anne. 1973. *Household Words: A Weekly Journal, 1850–1859, Conducted by Charles Dickens.* Toronto: University of Toronto Press.

Longfield, Mountiford. 1834. *Lectures on Political Economy.* Dublin: R. Milliken and Sons.

Lorimer, Douglas. 1978. *Colour, Class, and the Victorians.* Leicester: Leicester University Press.

[Lynn, Eliza]. 1857. "Why Is the Negro Black?" *Household Words: A Weekly Journal Conducted by Charles Dickens* 15 (June 20): 587–88.

[Lynn, Eliza, and W. H. Wills]. 1856. "Slaves and Their Masters." *Household Words: A Weekly Journal Conducted by Charles Dickens* 14 (August 23): 133–38.

Macaulay, Thomas Babington. 1961. *Critical and Historical Essays.* Arranged by A. J. Grieve. London: Dent.

MacCarthy, Desmond. 1937. *Leslie Stephen.* Cambridge: Cambridge University Press.

Macfie, A. L. [1961] 1984. "Adam Smith's Theory of Moral Sentiments." In *Adam Smith: Critical Assessments,* edited by John Cunningham Wood. London: Croom Helm.

[Maginn, William]. 1830. "*The Edinburgh Review,* No. C. Art. XI: Southey's Colloquies on Society." *Fraser's Magazine for Town and Country* 1 (June): 584–600.

Malotki, Ekkehart. 1983. *Hopi Time.* Berlin: Mouton.

Malthus, T. R. [1798] 1970. *An Essay on the Principle of Population.* Edited by Anthony Flew. Harmondsworth: Penguin.

Mandeville, Bernard. [1732] 1953. *A Letter to Dion.* Los Angeles: Augustan Reprint Society.

Manning, Sylvia. 1984. *Hard Times: An Annotated Bibliography.* New York: Garland.

Manvell, Roger. 1976. *The Trial of Annie Besant and Charles Bradlaugh.* New York: Horizon Press.

Marks, Patricia. 1986. "Harriet Martineau: *Fraser's* 'Maid of Dishonour.'" *Victorian Periodicals Review* 19:28–33.

Martineau, Harriet. 1837. *Society in America.* London: Saunders and Otley.

Marx, Karl. [1887]. n.d. *Capital.* Edited by Frederick Engels. Translated by Samuel Moore and Edward Aveling. Moscow: Foreign Languages Publishing House.

Marx, Karl, and Frederick Engels. 1959. *Basic Writings on Politics and Philosophy.* Edited by Lewis S. Feuer. Garden City, N.Y.: Doubleday.

Maskell, William. 1850. *A Second Letter on the Present Position of the High Church Party in the Church of England.* London: William Pickering.

McCrum, Robert, William Cran, and Robert MacNeil. 1986. *The Story of English.* New York: Viking.

Mill, John Stuart. [1842] 1988. "Bailey on Berkeley's Theory of Vision." In *Berkeley on Vision,* edited by George Pitcher. New York and London: Garland.

Mill, John Stuart. [1843] 1988. "Rejoinder of Mr. Bailey's Reply." In *Berkeley on Vision,* edited by George Pitcher. New York and London: Garland.

Mill, John Stuart. [1848] 1965. *The Principles of Political Economy with Some of Their Application to Social Philosophy.* Vol. 2 of *Collected Works of John Stuart Mill.* Edited by J. M. Robson. Toronto: University of Toronto Press.

[Mill, John Stuart]. 1850. "The Negro Question." *Fraser's Magazine for Town and Country* 41:25–31. Available at <http:\\www.econlib.org>.

Mill, John Stuart. 1861. "Utilitarianism." *Fraser's Magazine for Town and Country* 64:391–406.

Minowitz, Peter. 1993. *Profits, Priests, and Princes: Adam Smith's Emancipation of Economics from Politics and Religion.* Stanford: Stanford University Press.

Moked, Gabriel. 1988. *Particles and Ideas.* Oxford: Clarendon.

Montagu, Ashley, M. F. 1942. *Man's Most Dangerous Myth: The Fallacy of Race.* New York: Columbia University Press.

Moore, Edmund F. 1852. *The Case of the Rev. G. C. Gorham against the Bishop of Exeter.* London: V. and R. Stevens and G. S. Norton.

[Morley, Henry]. 1851. "Our Phantom Ship: Negro Land." *Household Words. A Weekly Journal Conducted by Charles Dickens* 2 (January 18): 400–407.

[Morley, Henry, and Charles Dickens]. 1852. "North American Slavery." *Household Words. A Weekly Journal Conducted by Charles Dickens* 6 (September 18): 1–6.

Mosteller, Frederick, and J. W. Tukey. 1977. *Data Analysis and Regression: A Second Course in Statistics.* Reading, Mass.: Addison-Welsey.

Motooka, Wendy. 1998. *The Age of Reasons: Quixotism, Sentimentalism, and Political Economy in Eighteenth-Century Britain.* London: Routledge.

"Mr. Buxton and West Indians." 1831. *Fraser's Magazine for Town and Country* 3 (May): 509–11.

Mühlhäusler, Peter. 1986. *Pidgin and Creole Linguistics.* London: Blackwell.

"Negro and White Slavery: Wherein Do They Differ? 1851. *Alton Locke, Tailor and Poet: An Autobiography.*" *Southern Quarterly Review* 4 n.s. (July): 118–32.

Newton, Robert R. 1977. *The Crime of Claudius Ptolemy.* Baltimore: Johns Hopkins University Press.

Noonan, John T., Jr. 1965. *Contraception: A History of Its Treatment by the Catholic Theologians and Canonists.* Cambridge, Mass.: Harvard University Press.

Nussbaum, Martha C. 1991. "Literary Imagination in Public Life." *New Literary History* 22:877–910.

Oddie, William. 1972. *Dickens and Carlyle: The Question of Influence.* London: Centenary Press.

O'Driscoll, Gerald P., Jr., ed. 1979. *Adam Smith and Modern Political Economy.* Ames: Iowa State University Press.

Ogden, C. K. 1935. *Basic English versus the Artificial Languages.* London: K. Paul, Trench, Truber, and Co.

O'Gorman, Francis. 1999. "Ruskin's Science of the 1870s: Science, Education, and the Nation." In *Ruskin and the Dawn of the Modern,* edited by Dinah Birch. Oxford: Oxford University Press.

Olivier, Sydney Haldane. 1933. *The Myth of Governor Eyre.* London: Hogarth Press.

Orwell, George. [1948] 1961. *1984.* New York: New American Library.

Orwell, George. 1968. *The Collected Essays, Journalism, and Letters of George Orwell.* Edited by Sonia Orwell and Ian Angus. New York: Harcourt Brace Jovanovich.

Oxford English Dictionary. 1992. 2d ed. Oxford: Oxford University Press. CD-ROM.

Pascal, Blaise. 1958. *Pascal's Pensées.* Introduction by T. S. Eliot. New York: Dutton.

Paley, William. 1785. *The Principles of Moral and Political Philosophy.* London: R. Faulder.

Papenfuss, Sam. 1998. "Whately's Exchange Theory of Government." Paper presented at the meetings of the Southern Economic Association, Baltimore.

Peart, Sandra, and David M. Levy. 2000. "Denying Homogeneity: Neo-classical Economics and the 'Vanity of the Philosopher.'" Paper presented at the meetings of the History of Economics Society, Vancouver.

Peirce, Charles Sanders. 1955. *Philosophical Writings of Peirce.* Edited by Justus Buchler. New York: Dover.

Persky, Joseph. 1990. "Retrospectives: A Dismal Romantic." *The Journal of Economic Perspectives* 4:165–72.

Phelps, Edwin S. 1972. "The Statistical Theory of Racism and Sexism." *American Economic Review* 62:659–61.

[Phillpotts, Henry (Bishop of Exeter)]. 1850. *A Letter to the Archbishop of Canterbury.* London: J. Murray.

"Philosophers and Negroes." 1866. *Littell's Living Age* [*Saturday Review*], no. 1168 (October 20): 181–82. Available from the Making of America data base at <http://cdl.library.cornell.edu/moa/>.

Pinker, Steven. 1994. *The Language Instinct.* New York: William Morrow.

Plant, Arnold. 1974. *Selected Economic Essays and Addresses.* London: Routledge and Kegan Paul.

Plott, Charles. 1967. "A Notion of Equilibrium and Its Possibility under Majority Rule." *American Economic Review* 57:787–806.

Pocock, J. G. A. 1985. *Virtue, Commerce, and History.* Cambridge: Cambridge University Press.

Poliakov, Léon. 1974. *The Aryan Myth*. Translated by Edmund Howard. New York: Basic Books.

Poovey, Mary. 1998. *A History of the Modern Fact*. Chicago: University of Chicago Press.

Posner, Richard A. 1999. "An Economic Approach to Legal Evidence." *Stanford Law Review* 51:1477–1546.

Prasch, Thomas. 1989. "Which God for Africa: The Islamic-Christian Missionary Debate in Late-Victorian England." *Victorian Studies* 33:51–73.

Pribram, Karl. 1983. *A History of Economic Reasoning*. Baltimore and London: Johns Hopkins University Press.

[Pringle, Edward J.]. 1852a. *Slavery in the Southern States*. 2d ed. Cambridge: J. Bartlett.

[Pringle, Edward J.]. 1852b. "Slavery in the Southern States." *Fraser's Magazine for Town and Country* 46 (October): 476–90.

[*Punch*]. 1878. *The Rt. Hon. John Bright M.P. Cartoons from the Collection of "Mr. Punch."* London: Punch.

Putnam, Hilary. 1975. *Mind, Language, and Reality*. Cambridge, Cambridge University Press.

Quine, W. V. 1961. *From a Logical Point of View*. 2d ed. Cambridge: Harvard University Press.

Quine, W. V. 1981. *Theories and Things*. Cambridge: Belknap Press of Harvard University Press, 1981.

Rainger, Ronald. 1978. "Race, Politics, and Science: The Anthropological Society of London in the 1860s." *Victorian Studies* 22 (Autumn):51–70.

Ramsey, Frank P. 1990. *Philosophical Papers*. Edited by D. H. Mellor. Cambridge: Cambridge University Press.

Raphael, D. D. 1985. *Adam Smith*. Oxford: Oxford University Press.

Rashid, Salim. 1990. "Berkeley's *Querist* and Its Influence." *Journal of the History of Economic Thought* 12:38–60.

Rashid, Salim. 1998. *The Myth of Adam Smith*. Cheltenham: Edward Elgar.

Rather, L. J. 1986. "Disraeli, Freud, and Jewish Conspiracy Theories." *Journal of the History of Ideas* 47:111–31.

Reisman, D. A. 1976. *Adam Smith's Sociological Economics*. London: Croom Helm.

Ricardo, David. 1951. *Works and Correspondence of David Ricardo*. Edited by Piero Sraffa. Cambridge: Cambridge University Press.

Robertson, J. M. 1897. *The Saxon and the Celt*. London: University of London Press.

Robins, T. Valentine. 1867. "A Few Remarks on the Bunu Tribe of Central Africa [and floor discussion]." *Journal of the Anthropological Society* 5:cx–cxiv.

Robinson, Abraham. 1974. *Non-standard Analysis*. 2d ed. Amsterdam: North-Holland.

Romaine, Suzanne. 1988. *Pidgin and Creole Languages*. London: Longman.

Romaine, Suzanne. 1989. "Pidgins, Creoles, Immigrant and Dying Languages." In *Investigating Obsolescence*, edited by Nancy C. Dorian. Cambridge: Cambridge University Press.

Rosenberg, John D. 1961. *The Darkening Glass: A Portrait of Ruskin's Genius*. New York and London: Columbia University Press.

Rosenberg, John D. 1985. *Carlyle and the Burden of History*. Cambridge: Harvard University Press.

Rosenberg, John D. 2000. "*John Ruskin* by Tim Hilton." *New York Review of Books* 47 (June 29): 31–35.

Ross, Ian Simpson. 1994. *Life of Adam Smith.* Oxford: Clarendon.

Rousseeuw, Peter J., and Annick M. Leroy. 1987. *Robust Regression and Outlier Detection.* New York: Wiley.

Ruskin v. Cope Bros. 1893. John Fraser Collection. Transcript. University of Liverpool Library, Liverpool.

[Ruskin, John]. 1878. Ruskin's "Fors Clavigera." *Appleton's Journal* 5 (July): 58–65. Available from the Making of America data base at <http://moa.umdl.umich.edu>.

Ruskin, John. 1880. *Arrows of the Chace.* Edited by an Oxford Pupil. Sunnyside, Kent: George Allen.

Ruskin, John. 1893. *Ruskin on Himself and Things in General.* Edited by William Lewin. Illustration by J[ohn] W[allace]. Cope's Smoke-Room Booklets, no. 13. Liverpool: Cope's.

Ruskin, John. 1903–12. *The Works of John Ruskin.* Edited by E. T. Cook and Alexander Wedderburn. London: George Allen.

Ruskin, John. 1921–27. *The Stones of Venice.* London: J. M. Dent and Sons.

Ruskin, John. 1997. *Unto This Last and Other Writings.* Edited by Clive Wilmer. London: Penguin.

Russell, Bertrand. [1922] 1971. Introduction to Ludwig Wittgenstein, *Tractatus Logico- Philosophical.* London: Routledge and Kegan Paul.

Said, Edward W. 1994. *Orientalism.* New York: Vintage.

Samuels, Allen. 1992. *Hard Times. An Introduction to the Variety of Criticism.* London: Macmillan.

Samuelson, Paul A. 1977. "St. Petersburg Paradoxes." *Journal of Economic Literature* 15:24–55.

Sapir, Edward. 1921 *Language.* New York: Harcourt, Brace, and Company.

Savage, Leonard J. 1972. *Foundations of Statistics.* 2d rev. ed. New York: Dover Publications.

Schacht, Paul. 1990. "Dickens and the Uses of Nature." *Victorian Studies* 34:77–102.

Schechter, Bruce. 1998. *My Brain is Open: The Mathematical Journeys of Paul Erdös.* New York: Simon and Schuster.

Schneider, Louis. 1979. "Adam Smith on Human Nature and Social Circumstance." In *Adam Smith and Modern Political Economy,* edited by Gerald P. O'Driscoll Jr. Ames: Iowa State University Press.

Schumpeter, Joseph A. 1954. *A History of Economic Analysis.* New York: Oxford University Press.

Semmel, Bernard. 1962. *The Governor Eyre Controversy.* London: Macgibbon and Kee.

Sen, Amartya. 1993. "The Economics of Life and Death." *Scientific American* 268 (May): 40–47.

Senior, Nassau W. 1862. *American Slavery.* London: T. Fellowes.

Senior, Nassau W. 1864. *Essays in Fiction.* London: Roberts and Green.

Senior, Nassau W. 1865. *Historical and Philosophical Essays.* London: Longman, Green, Longman, Roberts, and Green.

Senior, Nassau W. 1938. *An Outline of the Science of Political Economy.* London: George Allen and Unwin.

"Shakespeare's Character of Cleopatra." 1849. *Fraser's Magazine for Town and Country* 40 (September): 277–91.

Shaw, Bernard. 1921. *Ruskin's Politics.* London: Ruskin Centenary Council.

[Sigerson, George]. 1870. "History of the Irish Land Tenures." *North British Review* 51 o.s.:435–77.

Simms, William Gilmore. 1853. "The Morals of Slavery." In *The Pro-Slavery Argument.* Philadelphia: Lippincott, Grambo, and Co.

Simpson, Margaret. 1997. *The Companion to* Hard Times. Westport, Conn.: Greenwood.

Slavery: A Treatise, Showing That Slavery is neither a Moral, Political, nor Social Evil. 1844. Penfield, Ga.: R. Brantly.

Slobin, Dan I. 1993. "Adult Language Acquisition: A View from the Child Language Study." In *Adult Language Acquisition: Cross-Linguistic Perspectives,* edited by Clive Perdue. Cambridge: Cambridge University Press.

Smith, Adam. [1776] 1828. *An Inquiry into the Nature and Cause of the Wealth of Nations.* Edited by J. R. McCulloch. London: Adam Black and William Tate.

Smith, Adam. [1776] 1835. *An Inquiry into the Nature and Cause of the Wealth of Nations.* Edited by E. G. Wakefield. London: Charles Knight and Co.

Smith, Adam. [1776] 1976a. *An Inquiry into the Nature and Causes of the Wealth of Nations.* Edited by W. B. Todd. Oxford: Clarendon.

Smith, Adam. [1759] 1976b. *Theory of Moral Sentiments.* Edited by A. L. Macfie and D. D. Raphael. Oxford: Clarendon.

Smith, Adam. 1978. *Lectures on Jurisprudence.* Edited by R. L. Meek, D. D. Raphael, and P. G. Stein. Oxford: Clarendon.

Smith, Adam. 1980. *Essays on Philosophical Subjects.* Edited by W. P. D. Wightman and J. C. Bryce. Oxford: Clarendon.

Smith, Adam. 1985. *Lectures on Rhetoric and Belles Lettres.* Edited by J. C. Bryce. Indianapolis: Liberty Classics.

Smith, James Patterson. 1994. "The Liberals, Race, and Political Reform in the British West Indies, 1866–1874." *Journal of Negro History* 79:131–46.

Snow, C. P. 1959. *The Two Cultures and the Scientific Revolution.* Cambridge: Cambridge University Press.

Snow, C. P. 1975. *Trollope: His Life and Art.* New York: Charles Scribner's Sons.

Snow, C. P. 1993. *The Two Cultures.* Introduction by Stefan Collini. Cambridge: Canto.

"Some Account of Mrs. Beecher Stowe and Her Family." 1852. *Fraser's Magazine for Town and Country* 46:518–25.

Southey, Robert. 1829. *Sir Thomas More: or Colloquies on the Progress and Prospects of Society.* London: J. Murray.

Spear, Jeffrey L. 1984. *Dreams of an English Eden: Ruskin and His Tradition in Social Criticism.* New York: Columbia University Press.

Spencer, Frank. 1986. *Ecce Homo: An Annotated Bibliographic History of Physical Anthropology.* New York: Greenwood.

Stack, George J. 1970. *Berkeley's Analysis of Perception.* The Hague: Mouton.

Stanley, Arthur Penrhyn. 1870. *Essays Chiefly on Questions of Church and State from 1850 to 1870.* London: John Murray.

Stearns, E. J. 1853. *Notes on Uncle Tom's Cabin: Being a Logical Answer to Its Allegations and Inferences against Slavery as an Institution.* Philadelphia: Lippincott, Grambo, and Company.

Stepan, Nancy. 1982. *The Idea of Race in Science.* Hamden, Conn.: Archon.

Stephen, Leslie. 1900. *The English Utilitarians*. London: Duckworth and Co.

Stigler, George J. 1949. *Five Lectures on Economic Problems*. London: London School of Economics and Political Science.

Stigler, George J. 1975. "Adam Smith's Travels on the Ship of State." In *Essays on Adam Smith*, edited by Andrew S. Skinner and Thomas Wilson. Oxford: Clarendon.

Stigler, George J. 1982. *The Economist as Preacher and Other Essays*. Chicago: University of Chicago Press.

Stone, Harry. 1957. "Charles Dickens and Harriet Beecher Stowe." *Nineteenth-Century Fiction* 12:188–202.

Stone, Harry. 1994. *The Night Side of Dickens: Cannibalism, Passion, Necessity*. Columbus: Ohio State University Press.

Stowe, Harriet Beecher. 1982. *Three Novels*. New York: Library of America.

"Stray Notes on the Anti-slavery Monthly Reporter." 1831. *Fraser's Magazine for Town and Country* 3 (March): 205–8.

Strong, Edward W. 1957. "Mathematical Reasoning and Its Objects." In *George Berkeley*. Berkeley and Los Angeles: University of California Press.

The Suppressed Book about Slavery. 1864. New York: Carleton.

Terleckyj, Nestor E. 1975. *Improvements in the Quality of Life: Estimates of Possibilities in the United States, 1974–1983*. Washington, D.C.: National Planning Association.

Theil, Henri. 1971. *Principles of Econometrics*. New York: John Wiley.

Thomas, Deborah A. 1997. *Hard Times: A Fable of Fragmentation and Wholeness*. New York: Twayne.

Thomas, J. J. 1889. *Froudacity*. London: T. Fisher Unwin.

"Thomas Carlyle as a Practical Guide." 1869. *Putnam's Monthly Magazine of American Literature, Science, and Art* 13 (May): 519–31. Available from the Making of America data base at <http://cdl.library.cornell.edu/moa/>.

Thomson, James. 1889. *Selections from Original Contributions by James Thomson to "Cope's Tobacco Plant."* Smoke Room Booklets, no. 3. Liverpool: Cope's.

Thornton, Henry. 1837. *Family Prayers: To Which Is Added, A Family Commentary upon the Sermon on the Mount*. New York: Swords, Stanford, and Co.

Thornton, Henry. 1846. *Female Characters*. London: Hatchard and Son.

Thrall, Miriam M. H. 1934. *Rebellious Fraser's: Nol Yorke's Magazine in the Days of Maginn, Thackeray, and Carlyle*. New York: Columbia University Press.

Tomalin, Claire. 1991. *The Invisible Woman: The Story of Nelly Ternan and Charles Dickens*. New York: Knopf.

Trevelyan, George Otto. 1978. *The Life and Letters of Lord Macaulay*. Oxford: Oxford University Press.

Trevor-Roper, H. R. 1947. *The Last Days of Hitler*. New York: Macmillan.

"A Triad of Novels: *Alton Locke, Tailor and Poet*." 1850. *Fraser's Magazine for Town and Country* 42 (November): 576–85.

Trollope, Anthony. 1860. *West Indies and the Spanish Main*. 2d ed. London: Chapman and Hall.

Trollope, Anthony. 1947. *An Autobiography*. Berkeley: University of California Press.

Trollope, Anthony. 1993. *The Fixed Period*. Edited by David Skilton. Oxford: World's Classics.

Tukey, John W. 1960. "A Survey of Sampling from Contaminated Distributions." In

Contributions to Probabilities and Statistics, edited by Ingram Olkin, Sudhish G. Ghurye, Wassily Hoeffding, William G Madow, and Henry B. Mann. Stanford: Stanford University Press.

Tukey, John W. 1977. *Exploratory Data Analysis.* Reading, Mass.: Addison-Wesley.

Turnbull, Colin M. 1968.*The Forest People.* New York: Simon and Schuster.

"Two English Novelists: Dickens and Thackery." 1871. *Dublin Review* 16 n.s.: 315–50.

Tyndale, William. 1992. *Tyndale's Old Testament.* Edited by David Daniell. New Haven, Yale University Press.

Vanden Bossche, Chris R. 1991. *Carlyle and the Search for Authority.* Columbus: Ohio State University Press.

Van Evrie, J. H. 1868. *White Supremacy and Negro Subordination; or, Negroes, a Subordinate Race, and (So-Called) Slavery, Its Normal Condition.* New York: Van Evrie, Horton, and Co.

Viljoen, Helen Gill. 1956. *Ruskin's Scottish Heritage: A Prelude.* Urbana: University of Illinois Press.

Vogt, Carl. 1864. *Lectures on Man: His Place in Creation and in the History of the Earth.* Translated by James Hunt. London: Longman, Green, Longman, and Roberts.

[Von Goetznitz]. 1858. "A Negro-Hunt." *Household Words. A Weekly Journal Conducted by Charles Dickens* 18 (July 17): 109–13.

Von Mises, Ludwig. 1949. *Human Action.* New Haven: Yale University Press.

Von Mises, Ludwig. 1951. *Socialism.* Translated by J. Kahane. New Haven: Yale University Press,

Wain, John. 1964. "A Certain Judo Demonstration." In *Cultures in Conflict: Perspectives on the Snow-Leavis Controversy,* edited by David K. Cornelius and Edwin St. Vincent. Chicago: Scott, Foresman.

Walker, Amasa. 1866. *The Science of Wealth: A Manual of Political Economy.* Boston: Little, Brown, and Co. Available from the Making of America data base at <http://www.umdl.umich.edu/moa/>.

[Wallace, John]. 1878. *Peerless Pilgrimage to Saint Nicotine of the Holy Herb.* Painting on exhibition at the David M. Levy Center of Cope Studies, Fairfax. Va.

Waller, John O. 1963. "Charles Kingsley and the American Civil War." *Studies in Philology* 60 (July): 554–68.

Walvin, James. 1973. *Black and White: The Negro and English Society, 1555–1945.* London: Allen Lane, the Penguin Press.

Walvin, James. 1996. *Questioning Slavery.* London and New York: Routledge.

Waterman, A. M. C. 1991. *Revolution, Economics, and Religion.* Cambridge: Cambridge University Press.

Watts, Richard J. 1981. *The Pragmalinguistic Analysis of Narrative Texts: Narrative Cooperation in Charles Dickens' 'Hard Times.'* Tübingen: G. Narr Verlag.

Whately, E. Jane. 1868. *Life and Correspondence of Richard Whately, D.D.* New ed. London: Longmans, Green, and Co.

Whately, Richard. 1831. *Introductory Lectures on Political Economy.* London: B. Fellowes.

Whately, Richard. 1832. *Introductory Lectures on Political Economy.* 2d ed. London: B. Fellowes.

Whately, Richard. 1833. *Easy Lessons on Money Matters for the Use of Young People.* London: John W. Parker.

Whately, Richard. 1834. *Remarks on Transportation.* London: B. Fellowes.

Whately, Richard. 1850. *Infant-Baptism Considered in a Charge Delivered at the Triennial Visitation of the Province of Dublin.* 2d ed. London: J. W. Parker.

Wheelock, Frederick. 1992. *Wheelock's Latin Grammar.* New York: Harper Perennial.

Whinnom, Keith. 1977. "Lingua Franca: Historical Problems." In *Pidgin and Creole Linguistics,* edited by Albert Valdman. Bloomington: Indiana University Press.

White, Andrew Dickson. 1993. *A History of the Warfare of Science with Theology in Christendom* . New York: Prometheus Books.

Wilberforce, William. 1823. *An Appeal to the Religion, Justice, and Humanity of the Inhabitants of the British Empire in Behalf of the Negro Slaves in the West Indies.* New ed. London: J. Hatchard.

Wilberforce, William. 1982. *Real Christianity Contrasted with the Prevailing Religious System.* Abridged and edited by James M. Houston. Portland, Ore.: Multnomah.

Willey, Basil. 1949. *Nineteenth Century Studies.* New York: Columbia University Press.

Willey, Basil. 1956. *More Nineteenth Century Studies.* New York: Columbia University Press.

Williams, Raymond. 1958. *Culture and Society, 1780–1950.* New York: Columbia University Press.

Williams, Raymond. 1983. *Writing in Society.* London: Verso.

Wilson, David Alec. 1927. *Carlyle at His Zenith.* London: K. Paul, Trench, Trubner, and Co.

Winch, Donald. 1978. *Adam Smith's Politics.* Cambridge: Cambridge University Press.

Winch, Donald. 1996. *Riches and Poverty: An Intellectual History of Political Economy in Britain, 1750–1834.* Cambridge: Cambridge University Press.

Wisdom, John O. 1953. *The Unconscious Origin of Berkeley's Philosophy.* London: Hogarth.

Woodward, A. 1853. *A Review of Uncle Tom's Cabin; or, An Essay on Slavery.* Cincinnati: Applegate and Co.

Yeager, Leland. 1988. *Ethics in the History and Doctrine of the Virginia School.* Fairfax, Virginia: Center for the Study of Public Choice.

Yeats, W. B. 1990. *The Poems of W. B. Yeats.* Edited by Helen Vendler. San Francisco: Arion.

Young, Robert J. C. 1995. *Colonial Desire: Hybridity in Theory, Culture, and Race.* London: Routledge.

Index

309